184 PLA
Plato.
Five great dialogues /

FRA

D1034194

PLATO

A DRIVER IN A FOUR-HORSE RACING CHARIOT, FROM A JAR ORIGI-
NALLY PAINTED AND FILLED WITH OLIVE OIL AS A PRIZE FOR VICTORY
IN THE GAMES AT ATHENS. BY COURTESY OF THE YALE UNIVERSITY
ART GALLERY

PLATO

FIVE GREAT DIALOGUES

Apology • Crito • Phaedo
Symposium • Republic

Edited with an Introduction by
Louise Ropes Loomis

ST. MARY PARISH LIBRARY
FRANKLIN, LOUISIANA
70538

GRAMERCY BOOKS
New York • Avenel

Copyright © 1942 by Walter J. Black, Inc. Copyright © renewed 1969. Copyrighted under the Universal Copyright Convention. All rights reserved.

This edition is published by Gramercy Books,
distributed by Random House Value Publishing, Inc.,
40 Engelhard Avenue, Avenel, New Jersey 07001.

Random House
New York • Toronto • London • Sydney • Auckland

Printed and bound in the United States of America

A CIP catalog record for this book is available from the Library of Congress.

Plato: Five Great Dialogues: ISBN 0-517-14680-0

8 7 6 5 4 3 2 1

PLATO

CONTENTS

PLATO

INTRODUCTION

S OME twenty-four hundred years ago that part of the world which then represented Western civilization was divided into two opposing leagues of states. One league was headed by a seagoing, trading democracy, mistress of a marine empire of colonies and more or less subject states, scattered through the neighboring seas. The other was led by an inland, military aristocracy, conqueror of considerable territory close around herself and ally of whatever states feared the spread of democratic imperialism. The democracy was Athens, then at the height of her expanding pride and glory. The aristocracy was Sparta, conservative and tenacious, holding on to all that had ever been hers. Athens had a matchless fleet; Sparta an army without equal on shore.

The citizens of democratic Athens were proud of their liberty, their government by popular assemblies and officials chosen yearly by a combination of ballot and lot. Women, foreigners, and slaves were, of course, excluded from politics but the vote of every freeborn Athenian man counted for as much as every other's. They were proud too in Athens of their unparalleled culture, their literature, drama, music, and art. The beautiful new Parthenon, temple of their patron goddess Athene, shone down on them from the Acropolis. In their theaters were produced the tragedies and comedies that are still the marvels of the world. Among writers and intellectuals there was much free thought and speculation on questions of science, philosophy, and religion. The city, however, was strict in performing its duties to the gods of the fathers, celebrating in special state the festivals of Athene, of the nature god Dionysus and the earth mother Demeter. Athenians revered and consulted the mysterious oracle of Apollo in its rocky ravine at Delphi and competed in

3

the pan-Hellenic games at Olympia in honor of the great Zeus. In soldierly Sparta, life was far more austere, more like that of an armed garrison in a country of aliens. As hardened warriors, Spartans scorned the things that made men soft: wealth, trade, luxury, and refinements. They were proud of their physical strength, bravery, and discipline.

In 431 B.C. the long smoldering rivalry between the two leagues broke out in open war over the problem of who was to control the sea routes to the West, that is, to Sicily and South Italy. Until then Sparta's ally Corinth had had almost a monopoly of relations with the flourishing Greek settlements in that region. But now Athens wanted the trade in Western grain and metals for her empire. For twenty-seven years the so-called Peloponnesian War dragged on with the advantage swinging first to one side and then to the other. By 404, Athens was exhausted, drained of men and resources, her harbor empty of ships, her empire shattered. For a few months she was compelled to submit to government by a pro-Spartan, aristocratic clique of her own citizens, the infamous Thirty. In their short term of office they did their best to liquidate all the leading democrats of the city. But that was more than even defeated Athens could endure. At the end of the year the people rose, drove out the Thirty, and set up the forms of democracy once more. But Athens had lost faith in her own powers and the treacherous and cold-blooded behavior of her citizens had shaken her people's confidence in one another. Who was to be trusted when enemies ringed her around and her own turned and stabbed her? The city was split into factions, each hating the other more than they did the Spartans.

For some time there had existed in Greece a class of professional teachers of citizenship, to train young men in the arts of politics, public speaking, and debate, that they might know how to acquit themselves in the assemblies and courts and on the commissions to which they might be appointed. These teachers were called Sophists. Among themselves they differed a good deal both as to method of teaching and as to the kind of moral and intellectual standards they gave their pupils to follow. The more old-fashioned still kept their faith in the gods of Homer and the poets, and in the codes of patriotism and fair dealing that had been accepted before the war. Others were advocates of the new materialistic science that saw the universe as a product of whirling atoms and chance. They doubted whether there were gods who took any interest in men. Others still more skeptical denied that men could ever know anything certain about world, or gods, or anything at all. Many of these went on to assert that right and wrong, justice and injustice, truth and falsehood were merely artificial conventions, agreed on and upheld by human societies for their own convenience or forced upon them by superior might. Everyone could see that they differed from time to time and nation to nation. There were therefore no divine and unchangeable laws of right and wrong, that remained right and wrong always and everywhere. "The truth is that which is agreed on, at the time of agreement and as long as the agreement lasts." The one thing certain was that men by nature were greedy for pleasure, money, and fame and would always get what they could by fair means or foul.

To the mass of plain Athenians teachings like these were horrifying and blasphemous. No wonder, they thought, the gods had ceased to defend a city that sheltered such wickedness and atheism in its walls! On one man in particular, who had long been a conspicuous figure in city life, their suspicion and anger suddenly fell. This man was Socrates (469-399), a stonecutter by trade, frequently called a Sophist, though he protested he was not. He had no classroom, gave no formal instruction and took no pay. He only walked about the places where Athenians congregated, the streets, the market place and the gymnasium, or sat in the houses of acquaintances, talking cheerily to whoever stopped to listen. On the much discussed scientific problems of the nature and origin of the universe he had nothing to say. In that connection the only question, he said, that interested him was *why* the universe was made as it was, and that question he had never found anyone able to answer. Why then waste time arguing over things that all wise men disagreed about, in search for a knowledge that would do one no good if one had it? What men needed to know was how to make the best out of living. Socrates was one of those who, as Cicero said afterward, brought philosophy down from heaven to earth.

To the Sophists and materialists, who denied the existence of any absolute goodness and truth and ridiculed the old moralities and the old faith, he was utterly opposed. Yet neither would he return blindly and uncritically to the old ways simply because they were old. To believe a thing because one's grandfather believed it was no more right than to believe it because a Sophist preached it. The only way now to cure the disillusionment, cynicism and doubt to which Athenian disasters and sophistic reasoning had brought too many of the youth of the day was to push reasoning further. The method he used to persuade people to do this has been a model for imitation ever since. Start with a simple question suggested by something someone else has said. Ask him innocently to explain what he thinks is the meaning of some familiar word, the name of something immaterial but regarded commonly as important—friendship, courage, justice, truth. Show him by more probing questions how stupid his conventional definition is and kindle his interest to try for something better, something that will pierce down to the very heart of the problem of human values. Even if he reaches no positive conclusion, both he and the listening circle will have realized for a moment, at least, how foolishly they have taken for granted habits, opinions, and attitudes that were prejudiced, harmful, and false, and how thrilling and inspiring may be the hunt for honesty and truth. "We shall be better, braver, and less helpless if we think that we ought to inquire [about such things] than we should have been if we indulged in the idle fancy that there was no knowing and no use in trying to know."

To Socrates, as he said at his trial, what the Athenians seemed to need most in these years of bitter discomfiture was not a siren to flatter and soothe them with sham promises of a speedy return of prosperity and grandeur, but a gadfly to sting them to unflinching self-examination, to see where in the past they had been wrong-headed and mistaken and how with patience and hard thinking they might yet build better lives for themselves and for their city. If only men could be brought to see the good, he was sure they would always choose it and understand, as he did, that to do evil was worse even than to suffer it. Men were bad because they were thoughtless and ignorant. Straight thinking must lead to right living.

Socrates was no philosophical innovator with disturbing new theories about the gods. He believed that they were good and that they watched over and protected good men and women. He himself heard often a divine voice forbidding him to do things he should not do. He paid the usual offerings in the temples. But his manner of speaking of divine as well as other matters was unusual. His way of questioning popular ideas, old as well as new, seemed really just one more way of teaching the young to have no respect for their elders and to speculate about what their ancestors had accepted in reverence and trust. If he had only been willing to keep silence and stop his perpetual discussions, that unsettled everybody's mind in this time of danger to the state, the jury would undoubtedly have let him go. But "I shall not change my ways," he said, "though I die a thousand deaths." The jury thereupon condemned him to die.

Like Jesus, Socrates left no written word behind him. But like him, he left devoted followers who wrote their recollections of what he had said and done. Most of this early Socratic literature, like the primitive Christian documents, has disappeared. But one of Socrates' disciples was the author of a series of dialogues that began as a monument to a beloved master, but went on to become the starting point of much that was to be fruitful and profound in European thought to this day. As one of our modern thinkers has remarked, philosophy ever since then has consisted largely of footnotes on Plato.

Plato (427-347) came of a distinguished Athenian family. In his youth, as he tells us in a letter, he had looked forward eagerly to entering public life. He was twenty-three when the war ended with the overthrow of the discredited democratic government. Among the aristocratic Thirty were his mother's brother and cousin and they invited Plato to join them. "I thought," he says, "these men were going to put a stop to the evils that had been happening and govern the city with justice, so I watched their conduct closely to see what they would do. But . . . they very soon showed me that the preceding regime had been a golden age by comparison." The worst weaknesses of the democracy seemed nothing beside the savagery of the Thirty. When, however, the Thirty were expelled, Plato hoped once more to take a part in city politics. The restored democracy was at first surprisingly moderate and even generous in its treatment of those who had tried to destroy it. But ere long the young man's sensitive conscience was shocked again. His teacher Socrates, "whom I would not hesitate to call the most righteous man of that time," was accused by influential democrats of impiety and put to death. "The more I reflected on what was going on and what kind of men were active in politics and what kind of laws and customs we had, and the older I grew, the more I realized how hard it is to reform public life."

Grieving for Socrates and baffled in his hope of doing something with the democrats to improve the state of things at Athens, he went abroad and stayed for over ten years. In Sicily, he spent some time at the court of Dionysius I of Syracuse observing the working of a dictatorship. "At last," he says, "I came to the conclusion that all existing states are badly governed and the condition of their laws practically incurable without the application of drastic remedies and help of fortune . . . and that the ills of the human race will never disappear until by God's gift those who are sincere and true lovers of wisdom attain political power, or the rulers of our cities learn true philosophy."

Some time after reaching this conclusion, Plato returned to Athens and founded his Academy, since called the first European university, on a private estate outside the city walls. Not if he could, would he start another violent revolution in government. He had seen enough of blood, slaughter, and exile. But after the manner of Socrates he would serve his city by teaching young men the love of wisdom, truth, and justice, until reform came peacefully by education and persuasion. Like Socrates, he believed virtue to be a form of knowledge that could be taught. But his program of teaching was more far-reaching and systematic than Socrates' had been. It included preparatory studies in mathematics, astronomy, music, and logic as well as in politics and ethics. Only by strict discipline, did he think, could

a young mind be made keen enough to penetrate beyond the disordered welter of our present world and perceive the unchangeable
principles of truth. Before long the Academy was drawing students
from all over the Greek world. It continued to do so for some nine
hundred years, until the Christian emperor Justinian at last closed
its doors in 529 A.D.

The latter half of his life Plato spent teaching, lecturing, and
writing at his school, except for two trips he made back to Syracuse.
In 367, the second Dionysius succeeded his father. He had ambitions
to be a great ruler, showed a hopeful interest in learning, and was
susceptible to influence. There seemed a chance that under wise
guidance he might become the beneficent statesman that Plato was
longing to see come into power somewhere. Plato paid him two
visits, anxious now that an opportunity seemed at hand, to test his
ideals in practice. But Dionysius was not, after all, the stuff of which
philosopher rulers are made. He tired quickly of study, was easily
excited to jealousy and suspicion. His word could not be relied on.
Deeply disappointed, Plato came home to Athens. He died there at
the age of eighty. The wars between Greek cities and parties were
still going on, breaking down the strength and morale of all of them,
regardless of the menace of a rising new power in the North. Nine
years after Plato's death Greece found herself lying helpless before
the armies of Philip of Macedonia, father of Alexander the Great.
The day of the free Greek city state was over.

Plato left behind him a mass of writings, of which we possess several letters and at least twenty-five authentic dialogues. His own
views as well as his master's he presented in the form, not of imposing
treatises or heavy textbooks, but of dramatic conversations between
friends, fresh, spontaneous, humorous, and informal, held as chance
might have it, in some house or public building or open space of
Athens, where Socrates had been known to talk. In all but the latest
dialogues Socrates figures as the presiding genius and chief speaker,
even when, as time goes on, the ideas he is expressing are no longer
his but his disciple's. Plato in his own person says never a word.
Taken together, however, these dialogues contain his answers to the

three fundamental questions that had been raised by his predecessors and contemporaries. First, where can man find anything which he can know is truth? Second, what are the origin and constitution of the natural world in which man is set? Third, for what purpose was man created and what should he choose as his aim in life?

Put into simple, modern words, Plato's solution of the problem of how we can discover knowledge that is true may be summarized as follows. Our senses, sight, touch, and hearing, often deceive us. Our sense impressions, taken alone, are misleading and superficial and tell us nothing about the real nature of the things around us. Common opinion, grounded as it is on sensation, hearsay, and habit, cannot be trusted as a guide to truth. But through our reason we may arrive at what may be rightfully called true knowledge and understanding. Through reason we may use our sense experiences and memories of past experiences as material for a process of analysis, classification, and synthesis that bit by bit builds up for us a pattern of permanent, invisible order behind the perplexing panorama which is all that our senses alone perceive.

The first steps in this reasoning process we take unconsciously in childhood. We play, for example, with the household cat, noticing the looks and behavior of the little beast as an entirely strange and unique individual. But soon afterward we make the acquaintance of the neighbor's cat, of a stray kitten in the street, and eventually we sift out of our experience with cats and kittens certain traits that we see are common to all cats as distinguished from other animals, such as dogs. Thus we form a conception of cats as a class or species with its own place in nature, sure henceforth that every cat we meet will possess those qualities of cattishness which it shares with every other of its class, however it may differ in accidental details of size, color, or playfulness. The same is true of every object and creature with which we come in contact—stones, trees, rivers, beetles, birds, cows. We learn to see them all not as disconnected, separate individuals but as members of some one permanent class or species, which itself is part of one vast, related universe. Even the belief in our own personal uniqueness we finally lose and accept the fact that we are but one of the great family of mankind.

So with motion and change in our world. From day to day, uncomprehendingly at first, we watch the rising and setting of the sun and moon, the changes in the weather, the wandering of the stars through the night sky. At length we discern behind the show of ceaseless, haphazard variation the fixed and stately march of the planets and the seasons of the year. Certain qualities, that themselves are always the same, appear and reappear in innumerable changing and perishing objects. Many different objects are white—a house, a woman's dress, a cloud. Many different objects are square—a mathematician's diagram, a tile, a rug. Many different objects have beauty—a flower, a sunset, a human face. Many different words and thoughts contain truth—a proposition in geometry, a report of a game, a rule of morals. There are then, we come to see, certain qualities or essences or, as Plato called them, Ideas, such as whiteness, squareness, beauty, truth, which our minds may learn to recognize as permanent realities, continually imparting their unchanging form and character to the transient flux of mortality on our earth. The more persistently we examine with our reason the shifting kaleidoscope which is all our senses perceive, the plainer we find traces of deep and essential connection between objects and movements that previously seemed to us unconnected, the more, as Plato said, we collect "into a unity by means of reason the many particulars of sense." Therewith we arrive at a knowledge that is sure and superior to mere opinion, a knowledge of things not in their superficial aspects, but in their inner nature and purpose, which is their reality.

The problem of the constitution of the universe was then to Plato a double one. From what we have already said it is clear that he saw it as a combination of two contradictory elements or principles. There was, first, the well-knit, harmonious, and changeless pattern running through it for whoever had a mind to understand. There was also the more or less misshapen, conflicting, and short-lived mass of concrete objects, which we daily see, touch, and handle. Our world is made up of these objects, is never at rest, is always in process of dying or being born, of becoming something else. No single object in it, however near it may come to perfection, is ever absolutely perfect or lasting. The pattern running through it is marred by countless flaws of ugliness and decay, storms, earthquakes, deformities of man and beast. "What is that which always is," Plato asks in his dialogue of *Timaeus*, "and is never becoming? What is that which is always becoming and never is?" There are two worlds, was his answer. One is an invisible, spiritual world of perfect order and design, containing in itself the eternal models or Ideas of all that appears temporarily and imperfectly in this—the perfect cat, the perfect color, the perfect square, perfect beauty and truth. That is the heavenly world of true Being, presided over by the greatest of all Ideas, the Idea of the Good, the Supreme One, the Father, God. Our material world by contrast is a world of Non-being, of becoming but never remaining the same, of evil polluting good, of beauty forever fading and passing away, a faulty copy of a peerless pattern. "Life, like a dome of many-colored glass, stains the white radiance of eternity."

The creation and ordering of our world Plato describes in the *Timaeus*. God, the all-perfect ruler of the spiritual world, though himself lacking nothing, beheld the sphere of Non-being, or, as it was to be later called, matter, and found it lifeless, dark, and chaotic. Himself all goodness, he desired all things to be like himself, good and not evil. So he looked to the spiritual world of Ideas about him and framed a material world after its model, bringing down spirit to unite with matter, making it rich and diversified and endowing it with life, soul, and intelligence. The sky he created as a vast globe, placing within it the stars, sun, and moon in their orbits and setting them to revolve as in a great dance. The earth he fastened in the center. Time began as the celestial bodies rolled on, marking the days and nights, months and years.

Next, God made creatures of every sort and capacity to inhabit the universe, following still the patterns already existing in the ideal world. He created first the lesser gods, the Olympian deities, Zeus, Apollo, Athene, and the rest, and after them the beasts, birds, fishes, and land animals, bestowing on each an appropriate soul. Last of all,

he poured what was left of matter into the cup in which he had mixed the world's soul and from this diluted mixture created the throng of human souls, which he distributed among the stars. For a while the souls were content to live there in purity and bliss, but eventually they were drawn by their kinship to the material earth beneath to desire bodies. Thereupon the Creator assigned to the lesser gods the duty of preparing mortal bodies out of material earth, air, fire, and water. Thenceforth each soul, as its turn comes, is joined for a lifetime to a body and joined thereby to the lower appetites and passions that cling to it throughout its earthly career. It finds itself, as Plato says in the *Phaedrus,* driving a chariot with two horses, one a white horse, gallant and gentle, straining continually to mount, keeping his eyes ever on the divine world to which he aspires to return, the other a dark horse, unruly and vicious, obstinately plunging downward and dragging the chariot behind him.

But even after its descent to earth, the soul has its reminders of the world of true Being of which it was once a part. It has its glimpses, as we have said, of the sublime order governing the tangled maze of earthly phenomena. It has also its own memories, faint and blurred though they be, of a wisdom and perfection surpassing anything this world has ever shown it. Our learning is often remembering what we once knew in another life. But few men understand the meaning of these reminders. In the *Phaedo* and again in the *Republic* Plato describes the sight-loving, art-loving folk who are "fond of fine tones and colors and forms and all the artificial products of them but whose minds are not capable of seeing or loving absolute beauty," even when forced to admit that none of the beautiful things they prize is wholly free of ugliness. They can love the many beautiful but not beauty itself, which is one, nor can they follow a guide who points the way thither. True lovers of wisdom, on the contrary, are never content with what their bodily eyes can see but are ever searching with their reasons for the invisible, pure and immutable essence of things. They "distinguish the Idea from the objects that participate in the Idea."

In the course of the inspired speech on love which Socrates delivers in the dialogue called the *Symposium,* he tells how a man may rise, as on a ladder, from love of one fair, earthly face or form to a love that reaches upward to the divine. First, "he will himself perceive that the beauty of one form is akin to the beauty of another; and then . . . how foolish he will be not to recognize that beauty in every form is one and the same." At this point "he will abate his violent love of one object," which now seems a small thing, and become a lover of all beautiful forms. Next, he will realize that beauty of mind is more precious than beauty of body and so mount to a love of beauty of spirit, justice, and truth, as revealed in noble institutions and laws, "from fair forms to fair practices and from fair practices to fair thoughts, until from fair thoughts he arrives at the idea of absolute beauty and at last knows what absolute beauty is." For "he who has learned to see the beautiful in due order and succession, when he comes toward the end, will suddenly perceive a nature of wondrous beauty, . . . not growing and decaying, not waxing and waning, nor fair from one point of view and foul from another, but Beauty only, absolute, separate, simple, everlasting, which without diminution and increase or any change is imparted to the ever growing and perishing beauties of all other things."

But does a man find beauty merely to lose it in death? No, for the soul of man is immortal, as Socrates proves at length in the *Phaedo* and more briefly in the last book of the *Republic.* He who in this life hungers for wisdom and goodness, and trains himself by unwearying exercise to behold and commune with the world of true Being, after death will either be reincarnated in the person of another wise and upright man or, having finished his term of earthly imprisonment, soar back to the life of heaven. Whereas the soul that has lived engrossed in material things, a slave to its lusts and passions, is sent by the powers that rule the afterlife to suffer punishment and be born again in the body of a more brutish man or of an animal. Only after years of pain and struggle in the lowest depths of existence will it emerge purified to reascend the path to the sky. "Wherefore my counsel is that we hold fast ever to the heavenly way and follow after justice and virtue always. . . . Thus we shall live dear to one

another and to the gods, both while we sojourn here and when, like
victors in the games, . . . we receive our reward." And herein lies
the answer to the third of the questions Plato had set before him.
What should a man do with his life?

But for Plato it was not enough to have uncovered the principles
of order, reason, and right in the inner world of man's thought and
conscience and in the outer world of nature. Logic, metaphysics, and
ethics were not complete without politics, the attempt to put these
same principles into operation in the life of humanity in the mass, as
a whole so turbulent and miserable. Could society be reorganized in
such a way as to give all kinds of men, the ignorant and simple as
well as the cultivated and intellectual, both the requisite material
security and the chance to live the best lives of which they were
capable? Could the earthly state be rebuilt to accord with the heavenly ideal of justice? And would such a state, by the mere fact of
being built upon justice, be more peaceful and more happy than
other states?

To answer these questions, not long after he founded the Academy, Plato wrote the *Republic*. It is the earliest and in many respects
the noblest of all works on sociology and political theory. He begins
by describing the rise of a community of the type he knows best, a
Greek city state. It starts in a river valley opening into the sea. It is
small; its boundaries can be traced from any high peak. In one of his
later books, the *Laws*, Plato sets the ideal number of citizen families
at 5040. But small as it is, the community contains in itself enough to
supply its elementary wants. The tops of the encircling hills are
dark with forest, in which woodsmen cut timber and fuel. The slopes
below are pastures for herdsmen and their goats and cattle. Along
the river lie the farmers' fields and orchards. From the river's mouth
fishermen put out with their nets and traders sail with cargoes to
other ports. The population grows and its members feel the need of
closer cooperation. The men from the hills and fields meet the fishermen and traders from the harbor in a market for the exchange of
wares. Modes of life become more diversified and specialized. Walls
are built to protect the wealth of craftsmen and merchants. Money

takes the place of barter. Trade widens and the community estab-
lishes relations, friendly or unfriendly, with its neighbors. As an
independent political and economic unit it holds its own with other
states in its world. For years, in fact, hundreds of such little states
had been growing up and flourishing along the Mediterranean coasts.

The state then has arrived. A society is organized. A simple government is set up by general agreement. The settlers are separated
into classes, the natural outcome of the community needs. The great
majority are workers and producers of all kinds on the soil and the
sea and in the city shops. They have their homes and families, own
their lands, houses, and tools, lead active, healthful lives, sturdy
and temperate. They are not rich but have sufficient for comfort.
But they need assurance of security, that they and their children may
enjoy the fruits of their labors. To give them this security a second
class of citizens is created. A body of men is set apart to have arms
and war for its profession. Its members are chosen as boys for bravery
and enterprise and trained and disciplined in barracks and on athletic
fields. They live apart from the rest of the community and devote
themselves entirely to their calling. They are taught to combine
courage with gentleness, the duties of a police force with those of an
army. To enemies they must be formidable, but to their fellow coun-
trymen protective and helpful, trusty watchdogs of the state and not
wolves. From this class of public-spirited soldiers and guardians rises
in due time the third and smallest class, the rulers and magistrates of
the state.

At this point in the dialogue we realize that Plato has passed
from describing an ordinary Greek community to planning an ideal
state. His bold, courteous, and responsible soldier class is an ideal
aristocracy, like nothing then existing in any Greek commonwealth,
resembling most, of course, the Spartan nobility but without the
harsh Spartan characteristics. For the benefit of democratic Athenians he now explains that not every citizen is fitted for a public
office. Some men are made of gold, some of iron, and some of earth.
All are better and happier when doing just the things for which they
are individually qualified. Not, however—and here he becomes, as

he admits, audacious—that mere differences of physique or sex should be taken as denoting necessarily inferiority in mental endowment. "Women," for instance, "are the same in kind as men." Though in general tending to be inferior, yet "many women are in many things superior to many men." They may be musical, philosophical, skillful in healing disease, able executives. Girls, therefore, should receive the same education and training, intellectual and physical, as boys and be granted the same opportunity to rise to high position in the state. In Plato's time the well-bred, respectable Athenian woman spent her life in almost Oriental seclusion in the women's quarters of her father's or her husband's house. The tragedy writer, Euripides, had put into the mouth of his barbarian heroine, Medea, a fierce complaint of the injustices of a woman's lot. The comedian Aristophanes had produced two half burlesque appeals for women's participation in politics. But as far as we know, Plato was the first to argue seriously that women should share as equals with men in the public life of the state.

Having dared this much, Plato piles one audacity on another, eugenics on women's rights. No considerations of ingrained habit or traditional morality deter him now from building his ideal state logically and scientifically to the last detail. If the life of the community is to be maintained at the highest possible level, every effort must be made to provide the best possible leaders. In other words, leaders must be bred systematically from the best available human stock. Yet how can the best men and women of each generation at the height of their vigor be used for the production of children and yet be protected from the petty distractions and cares of a family, that will inevitably interfere with their services to the state? How can the partiality and favoritism that invariably accompany the family hereditary system be eliminated from the choice and training of rulers, and character and talent be made the only qualifications that count?

And here we arrive at Plato's famous proposal for community of wives and children in the guardian and ruling classes. The men and women whose lives are spent in public duty live all, like the soldiers, in public dormitories, eat in common dining-halls and own no private property whatever. From time to time a committee of elders arrange a set of matings between those whom they judge best matched and suited to become parents. Each mating is a matter of religious ceremony but temporary, for the purpose of child production only. The children born of these unions are taken at once from their mothers, who then are free to return to their work. Their offspring are brought up in state nurseries with the greatest skill and attention. They are the children of the state, no child knowing his mother or father or known to them, no distinction of birth setting one above another. As they grow up, they are solicitously watched, trained and tested to ensure that each receives exactly the education for which he is naturally adapted. If among these offspring of the choicest and best one proves mean-spirited, timid, or dull, he is removed from the nursery and placed in the family of a farmer, shopkeeper, or sailor, to learn a less rigorous profession. If, on the other hand, a golden child is found in a worker's family, he is taken from home and brought up with the best. It is understood that the well-being of the entire state depends on the scrupulousness with which the sifting and rearing of these children is carried out; for a state is what its rulers make it.

At great length Plato discusses the education to be given the gifted girls and boys of his select group. He does not aim to fill their minds with a mass of miscellaneous factual information, such as that which the children in our modern schools are expected to acquire. Instead he would teach them first physical poise and grace of manner, standards of brave and sincere conduct, and reverence for the gods. His curriculum begins with grammar and music, in which are included literature and history. From these the child gathers a knowledge of the illustrious men and deeds of the past and a conception of life and duty. Poets, however, like the mighty Homer, who tell of unworthy acts of the gods, are banned. The child's thoughts are not to be sullied by the immoralities of the old myths. The music is all to be of the heroic, inspiriting sort. From it the child learns rhythm and harmony of movement and gentleness of soul. Voluptuous or riotous music, that lulls the listener to dreams of indolence or intoxicates him with sensual delight, is strictly forbidden. As the child grows tall and strong, he passes intʋ the hands of gymnastic and athletic trainers, who develop in him physical vigor and endurance, temperate habits of food and drink, and a spirit of fearlessness and self-control.

Thus far Plato's ideal education is not very unlike that which was actually given to wellborn Athenian boys in his time, except that they were fed from infancy on stories from Homer and exposed to whatever might be the harmful effects of love ditties and drinking songs. But for the best of his children who give promise of true talent for leadership this kind of education is barely the beginning. They have next to take all the mathematics available in that day, arithmetic and geometry, plane and solid, studied not only from the applied, practical point of view but also from the purely theoretical. Here starts their training in reasoning power and in perception of invisible, abstract law. After mathematics comes astronomy, which means the principles of number and form in motion, as exemplified in the visible orbits of the stars and in the ideal constitution of the heavens. At the age of twenty, the youths and maidens who have so far acquitted themselves most satisfactorily pass on to a still more advanced type of education. For study they take up what Plato calls dialectic, what we might call philosophical logic. Their minds, that have hitherto been occupied with separate sciences, now attempt by a method of questioning and criticism, analysis and synthesis, to rise to a grasp of general principles and to see the relations of each branch of knowledge to the rest. However, they start this process gradually, for young people are easily thrown off their balance by too sudden introduction to the excitements of free thought and speculation, and are apt to end by believing nothing at all. The intervals between study they spend at military camps and on campaign duty in the field, learning the soldier's trade and performing feats of daring and skill.

Ten years go by in this apprenticeship and then the best are ready for the highest reaches of philosophy and responsible posts in the state. For five years more they pursue their inquiries and researches

to "the end of the intellectual world," until at length they arrive at
a conception of the Idea of the Good, the supreme One, that like the
sun in the sky is the cause and the light of all things below, both the
world of Ideas and the world of sense. With its light to enlighten
them, they serve for the next fifteen years in all the departments of
state, leading armies, going on embassies, judging in courts, amass-
ing the widest possible experience of men and affairs. Finally, at the
age of fifty, those who have distinguished themselves throughout
and given evidence of the ripest wisdom come to the end of their long
preparation. In turn they undertake the chief command of the state,
alternating, however, their periods of active ruling with other periods
of retirement, to refresh themselves with lifting up their thoughts
again to the universal Light, that by its radiant guidance they may
order the state and the lives of the people in it. Never have these
rulers handled silver or gold, owned houses or land, lest they should
be tempted to become landlords and tyrants instead of guardians and
saviors. "And when they have brought up in each generation others
like themselves and left them to govern the state in their place, then
they will depart to the islands of the Blest and dwell there and the
city will honor them with public memorials and sacrifices."

In the seventh book of the *Republic,* Plato describes in one of his
best known parables the life, as it must be, of the multitude of mankind. They sit as it were in the depths of a huge cave, their backs to
the entrance, their faces toward the dark. Behind their backs within
the cave a fire is burning that casts a fitful light around the den. Between the fire and the backs of the crowd artificial objects of all
kinds, images of living things in wood and stone, are being passed
continually to and fro. Their shadows are thrown by the fire on the
wall toward which the eyes of the multitude are turned. Thus they
stay, gazing at shadows all their lives, shadows distorted by the
flickering flame. But to the multitude these shadows are realities,
for they know no other. A few cavemen, however, have the curiosity and courage to turn their eyes from the phantoms that rivet the
attention of the rest and make their way, blinking and dazzled at
first, toward the glimmer of daylight at the cave's mouth, and so out

into the world of living nature and the splendor of the sun. There they learn quickly to disdain the images and their shadows, and bask in the light of truth. But having learned this, they must not remain in the upper world, for they were "created not to please themselves." "Each of you, when his turn comes, must descend again into the general underground abode and get the habit of seeing in the dark. When you have acquired it, you will see ten thousand times better than the inhabitants of the den and you will know what the various images are and what they represent, because you have seen the beautiful and just and good in their truth. Then our state . . . will be a reality and not a dream only and be administered in spirit unlike that of other states, where men fight with one another over shadows and go mad in struggles for power."

To Plato then, as when he wrote the letter from which we quoted earlier, the crucial problem of all society was the problem of leadership. "Until philosophers are kings," he declares, "or the kings and princes of this world have the spirit and power of philosophy, and political authority and wisdom are united in one . . . cities will never have rest from their troubles—no, nor the human race, I believe." Poor, human race, to this day it still has more of the rulers who fight over shadows and go mad for power than of those who have the spirit of philosophy! But in the ideal state all rulers will be philosophers. They with their wisdom, the soldiers with their courage, the mass of workers with their thrift and temperance, each class contentedly engaged in the work for which it is best fitted, will compose a community rich in the crowning virtue of all, which is justice or the securing to every man and woman of what is his to have and do. Such a state will manifestly be happy above all others; for it will be at peace within itself and its laws will be laws in the true sense of the word, based on the natural and unvarying principles of reason and right. Similarly, the individual may obey the same principles and cultivate the same four virtues of wisdom, courage, temperance, and justice. He may set his own inner life in order, master his animal passions, and, at peace with himself, be happy and blessed as no disordered soul can be, however pampered by wealth or high estate.

But having enjoyed the perfection of his own creation, Plato turns from it to the actual world with a sigh. What good is there in existing states and systems of governments? What kinds of men now are making or marring their own and other men's lives? One by one he characterizes the current forms of political organization, pointing out their virtues and failings, and along with each the type of individual whose disposition and behavior correspond to the form of state under discussion. A monarchy, or rule of a noble king, and an aristocracy, or rule of the noblest class, are forms assumed by the ideal state and therefore likely to be happiest and best, just as a man is happiest when ruled by the noblest elements in himself.

Unfortunately, in this world of change and becoming, it is all too easy for even ideal states to deteriorate. The magistrates in charge grow careless and no longer enforce the laws for the breeding and training of children. The quality of the ruling stock declines. Its members gradually yield to the temptations of power and possession. They set up private families, acquire houses and lands, accumulate riches, and through their wealth dominate the state. It is then no longer an aristocracy but an oligarchy, ruled by a few in their own instead of the general interest. The men who control it, though outwardly respectable and dignified, are inwardly greedy misers. For a time the people endure their growing oppressiveness, the widening gap that separates the poor workers from their bloated masters, the increasing crowds of unemployed drones that prey on the state. But at last they rise in the name of liberty, eject the oligarchs, and establish a democracy or rule of the multitude for themselves.

On this democracy, however, Plato pours a flood of irony and derision, revealing plainly what a mockery the Athenian democracy in its decadence had seemed to him. It is "a charming form of government, full of variety and disorder, dispensing a sort of equality to equals and unequals alike." The young feel themselves on a level with the old. Teachers fear and flatter their scholars, scholars despise their teachers. Even "horses and asses have a way of marching along with all the rights and dignities of freemen. . . . Everything is just ready to burst with liberty." Citizens "chafe impatiently at the least touch of authority and at length, as you know, cease to pay any regard to laws, written or unwritten." The individual produced by such an environment drifts rudderless, at the mercy of every whim blowing him hither and yon, always looking for some new amusement and never satisfied long with any. But in time men grow disgusted with a freedom that spells mainly lawlessness and insecurity. They rush to enroll under a leader who presently appears, proclaiming himself their champion and deliverer, "kind and good to everyone." As soon, however, as he has made sure of his strength, he turns into a tyrant, ruling by bloodshed and terror. Such a man, who subjects both his people and his own spirit to his brutal lust for power at any price, is at once the most terrible and the most wretched of human beings and his government the lowest form of political degradation. There is left only a hope that some day a true statesman will rise and overthrow him and lead the harassed and suffering people back to a juster order.

But what, asks Plato, is a man to do who has tasted how sweet is philosophy and has known the folly of the multitude? He may try his utmost to make them see the better ways of wisdom but the more faithfully he does this, the more likely he is to arouse their fear and hatred. In their ignorance they will misunderstand him, turn on him, persecute him, even put him to death. (The reader recalls the fate of Socrates.) "No politician is honest, nor is there any champion of justice at whose side he may fight and be saved. Such a man may indeed be compared to one fallen among wild beasts. He will not join in the wickedness of his fellows, but single-handed he is unable to oppose all their fierce natures. So, seeing he can be of no help to the state or his friends, . . . he holds his peace and goes his own way. He is like one who in a storm of dust and sleet, which the driving wind hurries along, retires under the shelter of the wall . . . satisfied if only he can live his own life pure from wrong or unrighteousness and depart in peace and good will with bright hopes." The dark multitude in the cave may refuse to be helped.

What, in that case, of the ideal state? Was it futile even to imagine it? No, for "in heaven . . . there is laid up a pattern of it, which whoever desires may behold and beholding may take up his abode there. . . . He will live after the manner of that city and have naught to do with any other." It is the shining city that every man may build for humanity in idea and in which he may dream that a wiser and braver race will some day, somewhere, come to dwell.

There have been criticisms of the *Republic* ever since it was written. Plato's pupil Aristotle, who also wrote a book on politics, said that it made the life of the rulers too hard, depriving them of all normal sources of happiness, families, private possessions, freedom to choose their own surroundings and occupations, pomps and decorations of office. Human nature, he thought, was bound to resent such restrictions, and if the rulers were unhappy, how could they make a happy state? Plato himself put the same objection into the lips of one of the speakers in the *Republic*. The rulers are like poor soldiers, kept forever at stern garrison duty. How can they be happy? The reply came at once. The aim of this state is "not the disproportionate happiness of one favored class but the greatest happiness of the whole." The rulers are not "peasants at a festival, rollicking through a season of revelry." Even so, to men and women of their high temperament and training their life will not be the hardship it seems to an ordinary, worldly-minded spectator. It has its rare compensations in the scope it offers for the exercise of their gifts in making life good for their fellowmen. In all probability they will prove to be the happiest of human beings.

In his old age Plato compiled a book of *Laws* for the government of what he called a second-best state, which, he admitted, would probably seem more practical to men at large than his ideal commonwealth. In this he omitted the most radical and visionary features of the ideal state, the community of wives, children, and property in the ruling class, the equal education and privileges of women. He restored the family as an institution for all citizens and put merely such limitation on property holdings as would prevent the development of extremes of wealth and poverty. He laid considerably more emphasis on the importance of law in the state and left less room for the exercise of the rulers' personal authority. His rulers, of course, were no longer ideal men. Possibly his experiences with Dionysius II had also made him wary of trusting too much to individuals in power. Aristotle's recommendation, when it came, was for a modified democracy, a constitutional government of the middle class.

Perhaps the nearest approach that has yet been made to a realization of Plato's scheme for the choice and training of rulers was the so-called Ottoman system, which for two hundred years furnished the founders of the Turkish Empire with soldiers and ministers that were the wonder and despair of Christian Europe. In any history of the Near East one may read how it was started by the Moslem conquerors of the Balkan peninsula and Asia Minor in the fourteenth century and how successfully it worked until, during the late sixteenth and seventeenth centuries, a slacker administration relaxed the rules forbidding marriage and hereditary offices. A Viennese ambassador to Constantinople, writing home, comments on the painful contrast between the Turkish practice of searching out and educating as the priceless treasures of the state their most promising boys, regardless of birth or race, and the Western concern for a fine horse, or hawk, or dog and neglect of all human youth save such as happened to be born to money or rank. That Plato might not have been altogether wrong in thinking that men and women of sufficiently generous disposition might be content to live cut off from the common run of experience and dedicated to some absorbing service we may guess from what we have ourselves seen of scientists, explorers, revolutionaries, and devotees of religion, to whom nothing matters in comparison with their ideal or their cause.

The dialogues of Plato, as we have said and as anyone may tell from even this brief and incomplete sketch, are the starting point of many of the important sciences and philosophies of our own day. To begin with, he was the first to lay down certain fundamental rules of logical reasoning. In the dialogues Socrates is represented as insisting on definition of terms, analysis of individual instances as a basis for generalization, the distinction between opinion or wishful thinking and knowledge, and between words and things. Plato's pupil Aristotle formulated logic into a definite science. Political theory, economics, sociology and esthetics all go back to Plato as to their founder. His *Laws* contain numerous detailed provisions for city planning, health regulation, business and administration in his "second-best state." Some of these were taken as models for legislation during the Alexandrian period that came after the Macedonian conquests in Greece, Asia, and Egypt. From the laws of that period the Romans borrowed certain features of their imperial codes. Accordingly, Plato has been called the father of European jurisprudence. The Romans also took over, with a few modifications, his program of youthful education and passed it on to the Middle Ages and beyond to the Renaissance. Literature, history, mathematics, and philosophy are still the traditional backbone of a Liberal Arts course. Women are now claiming the share in education and public life that Plato would have given them.

Finally, Plato was the father of all philosophers who explain our visible, restless world of mixed beauty and perversity by picturing behind it an invisible, creative spirit of intelligence, order, and comeliness, striving to impress itself upon reluctant clay. Man, being a compound of spirit and matter, can be trained from childhood to master the earthly passions that darken his vision and hold him down. He can learn to love goodness and develop his reason to see the law that has been working in our universe from the beginning. So having lived, at death he will fly away from the bodily prison house and return at last to the heaven whence he came. As for the individual, so for the community: there is an ideal life to be created here below, patterned on the principles of justice that are as immutable as those that govern the stars. According to these, no man, woman, or child shall be hindered from having what is his own to have and all shall live willingly together in peace. To Plato the ideal state was a city, a city walled and set in a green valley, like the Greek states he knew. So for centuries after him, when men turned from the tumults and disappointments of this world to hopes of a fairer world above the sky, they imagined it as a city, the city of God. In time the Christian church claimed a part in Plato, believing, though wrongly, that he had been taught these doctrines by the prophet Jeremiah in Egypt. He had, they said, a soul "naturally Christian."

For our book we have chosen five of the dialogues that have special interest for the general reader, using the translation made by Professor Jowett of Oxford. The *Apology* and *Crito* are the earliest of these dialogues. They are a part of Plato's first memorial to his master, his account of Socrates' words and bearing during his trial and imprisonment. The *Phaedo* and *Symposium* were written probably some years later. The dramatic interest still centers around the personality of Socrates but the ideas expressed include much that we are sure was Plato's own maturer thinking on the themes of death and the invisible world, human aspiration and love. In the *Republic* the chief speaker is still Socrates but the thought is wholly Platonic. It is the most comprehensive of the dialogues, in its views of the world above and below and its survey of human life in all its aspects, the life of the individual and of society. Because of their length, we have had to cut the *Phaedo* and the *Republic*, the former slightly and the latter to a larger extent. But the reader will nonetheless, we believe, find the line of the argument clear to follow. Plato in the body he will never discover among the friends who meet and talk so happily or so earnestly around the dinner table or in the prison cell. But Plato's mind he will learn to know a little as the creator of these immortal scenes at a time when the lights of his civilization seemed to be growing dim.

Louise R. Loomis

APOLOGY

It is the year 399 B.C. Four years ago Athens drove out the bloody terror of the Thirty, which the Spartans had set up to govern her after their victory in the Peloponnesian War. She has restored her democratic constitution, but hardly yet begun to recover from the shock of her terrible defeat and humiliation. Her citizens are embittered, suspicious, eager to blame anyone and everyone for the mistakes and failures of the past. In this year Socrates, now seventy years of age, is accused by three men, Meletus, Anytus, and Lycon, of the formidable crimes of corrupting the youth of the city and professing to disbelieve in the ancestral gods. Of the accusers themselves we know almost nothing. Meletus and Lycon, we hear, resent especially Socrates' attitude toward the current fashions in poetry and other literature. Anytus is angered by Socrates' outspoken criticism of the narrow commercial training he is giving his only son. But the charge they bring is such as to stir up superstitious fears of sacrilege and moral uneasiness in the popular mind. Several of Socrates' old pupils have indeed been involved in the disgraceful events of recent years. His case comes before a citizen court of five hundred and one jurors, a majority vote being sufficient to convict.

The *Apology* is Plato's version of his master's speech in his own defense, written down possibly within two or three years after its delivery. That Plato was present and heard it we know from Socrates' allusions to him on pages 52 and 57. How nearly he has reproduced Socrates' very words we cannot, of course, judge. As it comes to us, the *Apology* is actually three speeches. In the first Socrates, fearlessly and with much play of ironical humor, refutes not only the formal charges contained in the plaintiffs' immediate indictment but also the slanderous stories circulated about him by his enemies in

years past. He explains and justifies his way of life and religious be-
liefs, and in a sharp bit of cross-examination exposes the insincerity
of the quickly befuddled Meletus. At the close the court votes him
guilty by the comparatively small majority of sixty. The penalty for
his offense has next to be determined, since it comes under no existing law. The accusers demand a verdict of death. By rule of court,
however, the culprit may propose a counterpenalty, the jurors then
to choose between the two. In a short second speech Socrates, less
conciliatory and more hotly defiant than before, proposes that instead of punishment he receive the reward of a distinguished citizen,
honorable maintenance at the public expense. If he must pay something, he may with his friends' help scrape together enough for a
moderate fine. The court, annoyed, we may suppose, by what seems
his obstinate frivolity, votes to approve the death sentence. In his
final words, Socrates, now calm again, accepts the decision and bids
his judges and fellow-citizens farewell.

APOLOGY

PERSONS OF THE DIALOGUE:
Socrates, Meletus

SCENE: *In the Court*

Socrates speaks:

HOW you, O Athenians, have been affected by my accusers, I cannot tell; but I know that they almost made me forget who I was—so persuasively did they speak; and yet they have hardly uttered a word of truth. But of the many falsehoods told by them, there was one which quite amazed me—I mean when they said that you should be upon your guard and not allow yourselves to be deceived by the force of my eloquence. To say this, when they were certain to be detected as soon as I opened my lips and proved myself to be anything but a great speaker, did indeed appear to me most shameless—unless by the force of eloquence they mean the force of truth; for if such is their meaning, I admit that I am eloquent. But in how different a way from theirs! Well, as I was saying, they have scarcely spoken the truth at all; but from me you shall hear the whole truth: not, however, delivered after their manner in a set oration duly ornamented with words and phrases. No, by heaven! but I shall use the words and arguments which occur to me at the moment; for I am confident in the justice of my cause.[1] At my time of life I ought not to be appearing before you, O men of Athens, in the character of a juvenile orator—let no one expect it of me. And I must beg of you to

1 Or "I trust that what I say is right."

grant me a favor: If I defend myself in my accustomed manner, and you hear me using the words which I have been in the habit of using in the agora,[2] at the tables of the money-changers, or anywhere else, I would ask you not to be surprised, and not to interrupt me on this account. For I am more than seventy years of age, and appearing now for the first time in a court of law, I am quite a stranger to the language of the place; and therefore I would have you regard me as if I were really a stranger, whom you would excuse if he spoke in his native tongue, and after the fashion of his country. Am I making an unfair request of you? Never mind the manner, which may or may not be good; but think only of the truth of my words, and give heed to that: let the speaker speak truly and the judge decide justly.

And first, I have to reply to the older charges and to my first accusers, and then I will go on to the later ones. For of old I have had many accusers, who have accused me falsely to you during many years; and I am more afraid of them than of Anytus and his associates, who are dangerous, too, in their own way. But far more dangerous are the others, who began when you were children, and took possession of your minds with their falsehoods, telling of one Socrates, a wise man, who speculated about the heaven above, and searched into the earth beneath, and made the worse appear the better cause. The disseminators of this tale are the accusers whom I dread; for their hearers are apt to fancy that such inquirers do not believe in the existence of the gods. And they are many, and their charges against me are of ancient date, and they were made by them in the days when you were more impressible than you are now—in childhood, or it may have been in youth—and the cause when heard went by default, for there was none to answer. And hardest of all, I do not know and cannot tell the names of my accusers; unless in the chance case of a Comic poet. All who from envy and malice have persuaded you—some of them having first convinced themselves—all this class of men are most difficult to deal with; for I cannot have them up here, and cross-examine them, and therefore I must simply fight with shadows in my own

2 The market place, where citizens met on all kinds of business. It corresponded to what in a Roman city was called the forum.

defense, and argue when there is no one who answers. I will ask you
then to assume with me, as I was saying, that my opponents are of
two kinds; one recent, the other ancient: and I hope that you will see
the propriety of my answering the latter first, for these accusations
you heard long before the others, and much oftener.

Well, then, I must make my defense, and endeavor to clear away
in a short time a slander which has lasted a long time. May I succeed,
if to succeed be for my good and yours, or likely to avail me in my
cause! The task is not an easy one; I quite understand the nature of it.
And so leaving the event with God, in obedience to the law I will now
make my defense.

I will begin at the beginning, and ask what is the accusation which
has given rise to the slander of me, and in fact has encouraged Meletus
to prefer this charge against me. Well, what do the slanderers say?
They shall be my prosecutors, and I will sum up their words in an
affidavit: "Socrates is an evil-doer, and a curious person, who searches
into things under the earth and in heaven, and he makes the worse
appear the better cause; and he teaches the aforesaid doctrines to
others." Such is the nature of the accusation: it is just what you have
yourselves seen in the comedy of Aristophanes,[3] who has introduced
a man whom he calls Socrates, going about and saying that he walks
in air, and talking a deal of nonsense concerning matters of which I
do not pretend to know either much or little—not that I mean to speak
disparagingly of anyone who is a student of natural philosophy. I
should be very sorry if Meletus could bring so grave a charge against
me. But the simple truth is, O Athenians, that I have nothing to do
with physical speculations. Very many of those here present are witnesses to the truth of this, and to them I appeal. Speak then, you who
have heard me, and tell your neighbors whether any of you have ever
known me hold forth in few words or in many upon such matters.
. . . You hear their answer. And from what they say of this part of
the charge you will be able to judge of the truth of the rest.

As little foundation is there for the report that I am a teacher, and

3 The satiric poet, who in his comedy, *The Clouds,* had introduced an absurd
and bombastic figure of Socrates.

take money; this accusation has no more truth in it than the other. Although, if a man were really able to instruct mankind, to receive money for giving instruction would, in my opinion, be an honor to him. There is Gorgias of Leontium, and Prodicus of Ceos, and Hippias of Elis,[4] who go the round of the cities, and are able to persuade the young men to leave their own citizens by whom they might be taught for nothing, and come to them whom they not only pay, but are thankful if they may be allowed to pay them. There is at this time a Parian philosopher residing in Athens, of whom I have heard; and I came to hear of him in this way: I came across a man who has spent a world of money on the Sophists, Callias, the son of Hipponicus, and knowing that he had sons, I asked him: "Callias," I said, "if your two sons were foals or calves, there would be no difficulty in finding someone to put over them; we should hire a trainer of horses, or a farmer probably, who would improve and perfect them in their own proper virtue and excellence; but as they are human beings, whom are you thinking of placing over them? Is there anyone who understands human and political virtue? You must have thought about the matter, for you have sons; is there anyone?" "There is," he said. "Who is he?" said I; "and of what country? and what does he charge?" "Evenus [5] the Parian," he replied; "he is the man, and his charge is five minae." [6] —Happy is Evenus, I said to myself, if he really has this wisdom, and teaches at such a moderate charge. Had I the same, I should have been very proud and conceited; but the truth is that I have no knowledge of the kind.

I dare say, Athenians, that someone among you will reply, "Yes, Socrates, but what is the origin of these accusations which are brought against you; there must have been something strange which you have been doing? All these rumors and this talk about you would never have arisen if you had been like other men: tell us, then, what is the cause of them, for we should be sorry to judge hastily of you." Now I

4 Gorgias, Prodicus, and Hippias were well-known Sophists and professional teachers of the day. See page 4.

5 A poet and teacher from the island of Paros, then at Athens. None of his poems have come down to us.

6 The mina of this period was worth in our money roughly $20.

regard this as a fair challenge, and I will endeavor to explain to you the reason why I am called wise and have such an evil fame. Please to attend then. And although some of you may think that I am joking, I declare that I will tell you the entire truth. Men of Athens, this reputation of mine has come of a certain sort of wisdom which I possess. If you ask me what kind of wisdom, I reply, wisdom such as may perhaps be attained by man, for to that extent I am inclined to believe that I am wise; whereas the persons of whom I was speaking have a superhuman wisdom, which I may fail to describe, because I have it not myself; and he who says that I have, speaks falsely, and is taking away my character. And here, O men of Athens, I must beg you not to interrupt me, even if I seem to say something extravagant. For the word which I will speak is not mine. I will refer you to a witness who is worthy of credit; that witness shall be the God of Delphi [7] —he will tell you about my wisdom, if I have any, and of what sort it is. You must have known Chaerephon; he was early a friend of mine, and also a friend of yours, for he shared in the recent exile of the people, and returned with you. Well, Chaerephon, as you know, was very impetuous in all his doings, and he went to Delphi and boldly asked the oracle to tell him whether—as I was saying, I must beg you not to interrupt—he asked the oracle to tell him whether anyone was wiser than I was, and the Pythian prophetess answered, that there was no man wiser. Chaerephon is dead himself; but his brother, who is in court, will confirm the truth of what I am saying.

Why do I mention this? Because I am going to explain to you why I have such an evil name. When I heard the answer, I said to myself, What can the god mean? and what is the interpretation of his riddle? for I know that I have no wisdom, small or great. What then can he mean when he says that I am the wisest of men? And yet he is a god, and cannot lie; that would be against his nature. After long consideration, I thought of a method of trying the question. I reflected that if I could only find a man wiser than myself, then I might go to the god with a refutation in my hand. I should say to him, "Here is a man

7 Apollo, the sun god, was also god of Delphi, and the Pythian prophetess was his priestess, through whom his oracle spoke.

who is wiser than I am; but you said that I was the wisest." Accordingly I went to one who had the reputation of wisdom, and observed him—his name I need not mention; he was a politician whom I selected for examination—and the result was as follows: When I began to talk with him, I could not help thinking that he was not really wise, although he was thought wise by many, and still wiser by himself; and thereupon I tried to explain to him that he thought himself wise, but was not really wise; and the consequence was that he hated me, and his enmity was shared by several who were present and heard me. So I left him, saying to myself, as I went away: Well, although I do not suppose that either of us knows anything really beautiful and good, I am better off than he is—for he knows nothing, and thinks that he knows; I neither know nor think that I know. In this latter particular, then, I seem to have slightly the advantage of him. Then I went to another who had still higher pretensions to wisdom, and my conclusion was exactly the same. Whereupon I made another enemy of him, and of many others besides him.

Then I went to one man after another, being not unconscious of the enmity which I provoked, and I lamented and feared this: but necessity was laid upon me—the word of God, I thought, ought to be considered first. And I said to myself, Go I must to all who appear to know, and find out the meaning of the oracle. And I swear to you, Athenians, by the dog I swear!—for I must tell you the truth—the result of my mission was just this: I found that the men most in repute were all but the most foolish; and that others less esteemed were really wiser and better. I will tell you the tale of my wanderings and of the Herculean labors, as I may call them, which I endured only to find at last the oracle irrefutable. After the politicians, I went to the poets; tragic, dithyrambic, and all sorts. And there, I said to myself, you will be instantly detected; now you will find out that you are more ignorant than they are. Accordingly, I took them some of the most elaborate passages in their own writings, and asked what was the meaning of them—thinking that they would teach me something. Will you believe me? I am almost ashamed to confess the truth, but I must say that there is hardly a person present who would not have talked better about their poetry than they did themselves. Then I knew that not by wisdom do poets write poetry, but by a sort of genius and inspiration; they are like diviners or soothsayers who also say many fine things, but do not understand the meaning of them. The poets appeared to me to be much in the same case; and I further observed that upon the strength of their poetry they believed themselves to be the wisest of men in other things in which they were not wise. So I departed, conceiving myself to be superior to them for the same reason that I was superior to the politicians.

At last I went to the artisans, for I was conscious that I knew nothing at all, as I may say, and I was sure that they knew many fine things; and here I was not mistaken, for they did know many things of which I was ignorant, and in this they certainly were wiser than I was. But I observed that even the good artisans fell into the same error as the poets; because they were good workmen they thought that they also knew all sorts of high matters, and this defect in them overshadowed their wisdom; and therefore I asked myself on behalf of the oracle, whether I would like to be as I was, neither having their knowledge nor their ignorance, or like them in both; and I made answer to myself and to the oracle that I was better off as I was.

This inquisition has led to my having many enemies of the worst and most dangerous kind, and has given occasion also to many calumnies. And I am called wise, for my hearers always imagine that I myself possess the wisdom which I find wanting in others: but the truth is, O men of Athens, that God only is wise; and by his answer he intends to show that the wisdom of men is worth little or nothing; he is not speaking of Socrates, he is only using my name by way of illustration, as if he said, "He, O men, is the wisest, who, like Socrates, knows that his wisdom is in truth worth nothing." And so I go about the world, obedient to the god, and search and make inquiry into the wisdom of anyone, whether citizen or stranger, who appears to be wise; and if he is not wise, then in vindication of the oracle I show him that he is not wise; and my occupation quite absorbs me, and I have no time to give either to any public matter of interest or to any concern of my own, but I am in utter poverty by reason of my devotion to the god.

There is another thing: young men of the richer classes, who have not much to do, come about me of their own accord; they like to hear the pretenders examined, and they often imitate me, and proceed to examine others; there are plenty of persons, as they quickly discover, who think that they know something, but really know little or nothing; and then those who are examined by them instead of being angry with themselves are angry with me: "This confounded Socrates," they say; "this villainous misleader of youth!"—and then if somebody asks them, "Why, what evil does he practice or teach?" they do not know, and cannot tell; but in order that they may not appear to be at a loss, they repeat the ready-made charges which are used against all philosophers about teaching things up in the clouds and under the earth, and having no gods, and making the worse appear the better cause; for they do not like to confess that their pretense of knowledge has been detected—which is the truth; and as they are numerous and ambitious and energetic, and are drawn up in battle array and have persuasive tongues, they have filled your ears with their loud and inveterate calumnies. And this is the reason why my three accusers, Meletus and Anytus and Lycon, have set upon me; Meletus, who has a quarrel with me on behalf of the poets; Anytus, on behalf of the craftsmen and politicians; Lycon, on behalf of the rhetoricians: and as I said at the beginning, I cannot expect to get rid of such a mass of calumny all in a moment. And this, O men of Athens, is the truth and the whole truth; I have concealed nothing, I have dissembled nothing. And yet, I know that my plainness of speech makes them hate me, and what is their hatred but a proof that I am speaking the truth? Hence has arisen the prejudice against me; and this is the reason of it, as you will find out either in this or in any future inquiry.

I have said enough in my defense against the first class of my accusers; I turn to the second class. They are headed by Meletus, that good man and true lover of his country, as he calls himself. Against these, too, I must try to make a defense. Let their affidavit be read; it contains something of this kind: It says that Socrates is a doer of evil, who corrupts the youth; and who does not believe in the gods of the state, but has other new divinities of his own. Such is the charge; and now let us examine the particular counts. He says that I am a doer of evil, and corrupt the youth; but I say, O men of Athens, that Meletus is a doer of evil, in that he pretends to be in earnest when he is only in jest, and is so eager to bring men to trial from a pretended zeal and interest about matters in which he really never had the smallest interest. And the truth of this I will endeavor to prove to you.

Come hither, Meletus, and let me ask a question of you. You think a great deal about the improvement of youth?

MELETUS: Yes, I do.

SOCRATES: Tell the judges, then, who is their improver; for you must know, as you have taken the pains to discover their corrupter, and are citing and accusing me before them. Speak, then, and tell the judges who their improver is.—Observe, Meletus, that you are silent, and have nothing to say. But is not this rather disgraceful, and a very considerable proof of what I was saying, that you have no interest in the matter? Speak up, friend, and tell us who their improver is.

MELETUS: The laws.

SOCRATES: But that, my good sir, is not my meaning. I want to know who the person is, who, in the first place, knows the laws.

MELETUS: The judges, Socrates, who are present in court.

SOCRATES: What, do you mean to say, Meletus, that they are able to instruct and improve youth?

MELETUS: Certainly they are.

SOCRATES: What, all of them, or some only and not others?

MELETUS: All of them.

SOCRATES: By the goddess Hera,[8] that is good news! There are plenty of improvers, then. And what do you say of the audience—do they improve them?

MELETUS: Yes, they do.

8 The queen of the Olympian gods, wife of Zeus, the Thunderer, king of the gods.

SOCRATES: And the senators?

MELETUS: Yes, the senators improve them.

SOCRATES: But perhaps the members of the assembly corrupt them?—or do they too improve them?

MELETUS: They improve them.

SOCRATES: Then every Athenian improves and elevates them; all with the exception of myself; and I alone am their corrupter? Is that what you affirm?

MELETUS: That is what I stoutly affirm.

SOCRATES: I am very unfortunate if you are right. But suppose I ask you a question: How about horses? Does one man do them harm and all the world good? Is not the exact opposite the truth? One man is able to do them good, or at least not many; the trainer of horses, that is to say, does them good, and others who have to do with them rather injure them. Is not that true, Meletus, of horses, or of any other animals? Most assuredly it is; whether you and Anytus say yes or no. Happy indeed would be the condition of youth if they had one corrupter only, and all the rest of the world were their improvers. But you, Meletus, have sufficiently shown that you never had a thought about the young: your carelessness is seen in your not caring about the very things which you bring against me.

And now, Meletus, I will ask you another question—by Zeus I will: Which is better, to live among bad citizens, or among good ones? Answer, friend, I say; the question is one which may be easily answered. Do not the good do their neighbors good, and the bad do them evil?

MELETUS: Certainly.

SOCRATES: And is there anyone who would rather be injured than benefited by those who live with him? Answer, my good friend, the law requires you to answer—does anyone like to be injured?

MELETUS: Certainly not.

SOCRATES: And when you accuse me of corrupting and deteriorating the youth, do you allege that I corrupt them intentionally or unintentionally?

MELETUS: Intentionally, I say.

SOCRATES: But you have just admitted that the good do their neighbors good, and the evil do them evil. Now, is that a truth which your superior wisdom has recognized thus early in life, and am I, at my age, in such darkness and ignorance as not to know that if a man with whom I have to live is corrupted by me, I am very likely to be harmed by him; and yet I corrupt him, and intentionally, too—so you say, although neither I nor any other human being is ever likely to be convinced by you. But either I do not corrupt them, or I corrupt them unintentionally; and on either view of the case you lie. If my offense is unintentional, the law has no cognizance of unintentional offenses: you ought to have taken me privately, and warned and admonished me; for if I had been better advised, I should have left off doing what I only did unintentionally—no doubt I should; but you would have nothing to say to me and refused to teach me. And now you bring me up in this court, which is a place not of instruction, but of punishment.

It will be very clear to you, Athenians, as I was saying, that Meletus has no care at all, great or small, about the matter. But still I should like to know, Meletus, in what I am affirmed to corrupt the young. I suppose you mean, as I infer from your indictment, that I teach them not to acknowledge the gods which the state acknowledges, but some other new divinities or spiritual agencies in their stead. These are the lessons by which I corrupt the youth, as you say.

MELETUS: Yes, that I say emphatically.

SOCRATES: Then, by the gods, Meletus, of whom we are speaking, tell me and the court, in somewhat plainer terms, what you mean! for I do not as yet understand whether you affirm that I teach other men to acknowledge some gods, and therefore that I do believe in gods, and am not an entire atheist—this you do not lay to my charge—but only you say that they are not the same gods which the city recognizes: the charge is that they are different gods. Or, do you mean that I am an atheist simply, and a teacher of atheism?

MELETUS: I mean the latter—that you are a complete atheist.

SOCRATES: What an extraordinary statement! Why do you think so, Meletus? Do you mean that I do not believe in the godhead of the sun or moon, like other men?

MELETUS: I assure you, judges, that he does not: for he says that the sun is stone, and the moon earth.

SOCRATES: Friend Meletus, you think that you are accusing Anaxagoras [9] and you have but a bad opinion of the judges, if you fancy them illiterate to such a degree as not to know that these doctrines are found in the books of Anaxagoras the Clazomenian, which are full of them. And so, forsooth, the youth are said to be taught them by Socrates, when there are not unfrequently exhibitions of them at the theater [10] (price of admission one drachma [11] at the most); and they might pay their money, and laugh at Socrates if he pretends to father these extraordinary views. And so, Meletus, you really think that I do not believe in any god?

MELETUS: I swear by Zeus that you believe absolutely in none at all.

SOCRATES: Nobody will believe you, Meletus, and I am pretty sure that you do not believe yourself. I cannot help thinking, men of Athens, that Meletus is reckless and impudent, and that he has written this indictment in a spirit of mere wantonness and youthful bravado. Has he not compounded a riddle, thinking to try me? He said to himself: I shall see whether the wise Socrates will discover my facetious contradiction, or whether I shall be able to deceive him and the rest of them. For he certainly does appear to me to contradict himself in the indictment as much as if he said that Socrates is guilty of not believing in the gods, and yet of believing in them—but this is not like a person who is in earnest.

I should like you, O men of Athens, to join me in examining what I conceive to be his inconsistency; and do you, Meletus, answer. And

9 A philosopher and astronomer, who had taught at Athens, some thirty years before, that the sun and moon were made of rocks and soil, like our earth. His books have all been lost.

10 Aristophanes caricatured the theories of Anaxagoras. Other playwrights, as Euripides, treated them seriously.

11 A drachma was a hundredth part of a mina, that is, worth about twenty cents.

I must remind the audience of my request that they would not make a disturbance if I speak in my accustomed manner.

Did ever a man, Meletus, believe in the existence of human things, and not of human beings? . . . I wish, men of Athens, that he would answer, and not be always trying to get up an interruption. Did ever any man believe in horsemanship, and not in horses? or in flute-playing, and not in flute-players? No, my friend; I will answer to you and to the court, as you refuse to answer for yourself. There is no man who ever did. But now please to answer the next question: Can a man believe in spiritual and divine agencies, and not in spirits or demigods?

MELETUS: He cannot.

SOCRATES: How lucky I am to have extracted that answer, by the assistance of the court! But then you swear in the indictment that I teach and believe in divine or spiritual agencies (new or old, no matter for that); at any rate, I believe in spiritual agencies—so you say and swear in the affidavit; and yet if I believe in divine beings, how can I help believing in spirits or demigods;—must I not? To be sure I must; and therefore I may assume that your silence gives consent. Now what are spirits or demigods? are they not either gods or the sons of gods?

MELETUS: Certainly they are.

SOCRATES: But this is what I call the facetious riddle invented by you: the demigods or spirits are gods, and you say first that I do not believe in gods, and then again that I do believe in gods; that is, if I believe in demigods. For if the demigods are the illegitimate sons of gods, whether by the nymphs or by any other mothers, of whom they are said to be the sons—what human being will ever believe that there are no gods if they are the sons of gods? You might as well affirm the existence of mules, and deny that of horses and asses. Such nonsense, Meletus, could only have been intended by you to make trial of me. You have put this into the indictment because you had nothing real of which to accuse me. But no one who has a particle of understanding will ever be convinced by you that the same men can believe in divine and superhuman things, and yet not believe that there are gods and demigods and heroes.

I have said enough in answer to the charge of Meletus: any elaborate defense is unnecessary; but I know only too well how many are the enmities which I have incurred, and this is what will be my destruction if I am destroyed—not Meletus, nor yet Anytus, but the envy and detraction of the world, which has been the death of many good men, and will probably be the death of many more; there is no danger of my being the last of them.

Someone will say: And are you not ashamed, Socrates, of a course of life which is likely to bring you to an untimely end? To him I may fairly answer: There you are mistaken: a man who is good for anything ought not to calculate the chance of living or dying; he ought only to consider whether in doing anything he is doing right or wrong—acting the part of a good man or of a bad. Whereas, upon your view, the heroes who fell at Troy were not good for much, and the son of Thetis [12] above all, who altogether despised danger in comparison with disgrace; and when he was so eager to slay Hector, his goddess mother said to him, that if he avenged his companion Patroclus, and slew Hector, he would die himself—"Fate," she said, in these or the like words, "waits for you next after Hector"; he, receiving this warning, utterly despised danger and death, and instead of fearing them, feared rather to live in dishonor, and not to avenge his friend. "Let me die forthwith," he replies, "and be avenged of my enemy, rather than abide here by the beaked ships, a laughingstock and a burden of the earth." Had Achilles any thought of death and danger? For wherever a man's place is, whether the place which he has chosen or that in which he has been placed by a commander, there he ought to remain in the hour of danger; he should not think of death or of anything but of disgrace. And this, O men of Athens, is a true saying.

Strange, indeed, would be my conduct, O men of Athens, if I,

12 The Greek Achilles, son of the goddess Thetis, in spite of his mother's warning, fought and slew the Trojan Hector to avenge the death of his comrade Patroclus. See Homer, *Iliad*, XVIII, 94-126.

who, when I was ordered by the generals whom you chose to command me at Potidaea [13] and Amphipolis and Delium, remained where they placed me, like any other man, facing death—if now, when, as I conceive and imagine, God orders me to fulfill the philosopher's mission of searching into myself and other men, I were to desert my post through fear of death, or any other fear; that would indeed be strange, and I might justly be arraigned in court for denying the existence of the gods, if I disobeyed the oracle because I was afraid of death, fancying that I was wise when I was not wise. For the fear of death is indeed the pretense of wisdom, and not real wisdom, being a pretense of knowing the unknown; and no one knows whether death, which men in their fear apprehend to be the greatest evil, may not be the greatest good. Is not this ignorance of a disgraceful sort, the ignorance which is the conceit that a man knows what he does not know? And in this respect only I believe myself to differ from men in general, and may perhaps claim to be wiser than they are: that whereas I know but little of the world below, I do not suppose that I know: but I do know that injustice and disobedience to a better, whether God or man, is evil and dishonorable, and I will never fear or avoid a possible good rather than a certain evil. And therefore if you let me go now, and are not convinced by Anytus, who said that since I had been prosecuted I must be put to death (or if not, that I ought never to have been prosecuted at all); and that if I escape now, your sons will all be utterly ruined by listening to my words—if you say to me, Socrates, this time we will not mind Anytus, and you shall be let off, but upon one condition, that you are not to inquire and speculate in this way any more, and that if you are caught doing so again you shall die; if this was the condition on which you let me go, I should reply: Men of Athens, I honor and love you; but I shall obey God rather than you, and while I have life and strength I shall never cease from the practice and teaching of philosophy, exhorting anyone whom I meet and saying to him after my manner: "You, my friend—a citizen of the great and mighty and wise city of Athens—

[13] Socrates had served in the Athenian infantry during some of the northern .ampaigns of the Peloponnesian War.

are you not ashamed of heaping up the greatest amount of money and honor and reputation, and caring so little about wisdom and truth and the greatest improvement of the soul, which you never regard or heed at all?" And if the person with whom I am arguing, says: "Yes, but I do care;" then I do not leave him or let him go at once; but I proceed to interrogate and examine and cross-examine him, and if I think that he has no virtue in him, but only says that he has, I reproach him with undervaluing the greater and overvaluing the less. And I shall repeat the same words to everyone whom I meet, young and old, citizen and alien, but especially to the citizens, inasmuch as they are my brethren. For know that this is the command of God; and I believe that no greater good has ever happened in the state than my service to the God. For I do nothing but go about persuading you all, old and young alike, not to take thought for your persons or your properties, but first and chiefly to care about the greatest improvement of the soul. I tell you that virtue is not given by money, but that from virtue comes money and every other good of man, public as well as private. This is my teaching, and if this is the doctrine which corrupts the youth, I am a mischievous person. But if anyone says that this is not my teaching, he is speaking an untruth. Wherefore, O men of Athens, I say to you, do as Anytus bids or not as Anytus bids, and either acquit me or not; but whichever you do, understand that I shall never alter my ways, not even if I have to die many times.

Men of Athens, do not interrupt, but hear me; there was an understanding between us that you should hear me to the end; I have something more to say, at which you may be inclined to cry out; but I believe that to hear me will be good for you, and therefore I beg that you will not cry out. I would have you know that if you kill such an one as I am, you will injure yourselves more than you will injure me. Nothing will injure me, not Meletus nor yet Anytus—they cannot, for a bad man is not permitted to injure a better than himself. I do not deny that Anytus may, perhaps, kill him, or drive him into exile, or deprive him of civil rights; and he may imagine, and others may imagine, that he is inflicting a great injury upon him: but there I do not agree. For the evil of doing as he is doing—the evil of unjustly taking away the life of another—is greater far.

And now, Athenians, I am not going to argue for my own sake, as you may think, but for yours, that you may not sin against the God by condemning me, who am his gift to you. For if you kill me you will not easily find a successor to me, who, if I may use such a ludicrous figure of speech, am a sort of gadfly, given to the state by God; and the state is a great and noble steed who is tardy in his motions owing to his very size, and requires to be stirred into life. I am that gadfly which God has attached to the state, and all day long and in all places am always fastening upon you, arousing and persuading and reproaching you. You will not easily find another like me, and therefore I would advise you to spare me. I dare say that you may feel out of temper (like a person who is suddenly awakened from sleep), and you think that you might easily strike me dead as Anytus advises, and then you would sleep on for the remainder of your lives, unless God in his care of you sent you another gadfly. When I say that I am given to you by God, the proof of my mission is this: if I had been like other men, I should not have neglected all my own concerns or patiently seen the neglect of them during all these years, and have been doing yours, coming to you individually like a father or elder brother, exhorting you to regard virtue; such conduct, I say, would be unlike human nature. If I had gained anything, or if my exhortations had been paid, there would have been some sense in my doing so; but now, as you will perceive, not even the impudence of my accusers dares to say that I have ever exacted or sought pay of anyone; of that they have no witness. And I have a sufficient witness to the truth of what I say—my poverty.

Someone may wonder why I go about in private giving advice and busying myself with the concerns of others, but do not venture to come forward in public and advise the state. I will tell you why. You have heard me speak at sundry times and in divers places of an oracle or sign which comes to me, and is the divinity which Meletus ridicules in the indictment. This sign, which is a kind of voice, first began to come to me when I was a child; it always forbids but never commands me to do anything which I am going to do. This is what deters me from being a politician. And rightly, as I think. For I am certain, O men of Athens, that if I had engaged in politics, I should have perished long ago, and done no good either to you or to myself. And do not be offended at my telling you the truth: for the truth is, that no man who goes to war with you or any other multitude, honestly striving against the many lawless and unrighteous deeds which are done in a state, will save his life; he who will fight for the right, if he would live even for a brief space, must have a private station and not a public one.

I can give you convincing evidence of what I say, not words only, but what you value far more—actions. Let me relate to you a passage of my own life which will prove to you that I should never have yielded to injustice from any fear of death, and that as I should have refused to yield, I must have died at once. I will tell you a tale of the courts, not very interesting perhaps, but nevertheless true. The only office of state which I ever held, O men of Athens, was that of senator: [14] the tribe Antiochis, which is my tribe, had the presidency at the trial of the generals who had not taken up the bodies of the slain after the battle of Arginusae; and you proposed to try them in a body, contrary to law, as you all thought afterwards; but at the time I was the only one of the Prytanes who was opposed to the illegality, and I gave my vote against you; and when the orators threatened to impeach and arrest me, and you called and shouted, I made up my mind that I would run the risk, having law and justice with me, rather than take part in your injustice because I feared imprisonment and death. This happened in the days of the democracy. But when the oligarchy

14 As senator, Socrates had been once a member of the government Council of Five Hundred, composed of fifty men elected yearly from each of the ten Attic tribes. Each group of fifty, called a Prytany, held the presidency in turn, acting as an executive committee of the Council for one tenth of the year. In the year 406 B.C. many Athenian sailors were drowned during a naval battle with the Spartans off Arginusae on the Asiatic coast. The battle ended in a victory for Athens, but the generals of the fleet were bitterly blamed for not rescuing the drowned men. Those who returned to Athens were refused the right of individual hearing, tried and executed in a body.

of the Thirty [15] was in power, they sent for me and four others into
the rotunda, and bade us bring Leon the Salaminian from Salamis,
as they wanted to put him to death. This was a specimen of the sort
of commands which they were always giving with the view of im-
plicating as many as possible in their crimes; and then I showed, not
in word only but in deed, that, if I may be allowed to use such an
expression, I cared not a straw for death, and that my great and only
care was lest I should do an unrighteous or unholy thing. For the
strong arm of that oppressive power did not frighten me into doing
wrong; and when we came out of the rotunda the other four went to
Salamis and fetched Leon, but I went quietly home. For which I
might have lost my life, had not the power of the Thirty shortly afterwards come to an end. And many will witness to my words.

Now do you really imagine that I could have survived all these
years, if I had led a public life, supposing that like a good man I had
always maintained the right and had made justice, as I ought, the first
thing? No indeed, men of Athens, neither I nor any other man. But
I have been always the same in all my actions, public as well as private, and never have I yielded any base compliance to those who are
slanderously termed my disciples, or to any other. Not that I have any
regular disciples. But if anyone likes to come and hear me while I am
pursuing my mission, whether he be young or old, he is not excluded.
Nor do I converse only with those who pay; but anyone, whether he
be rich or poor, may ask and answer me and listen to my words; and
whether he turns out to be a bad man or a good one, neither result
can be justly imputed to me; for I never taught or professed to teach
him anything. And if anyone says that he has ever learned or heard
anything from me in private which all the world has not heard, let
me tell you that he is lying.

But I shall be asked, Why do people delight in continually conversing with you? I have told you already, Athenians, the whole

15 The Thirty Tyrants set up by the Spartan commanders to govern Athens after
her final defeat in 404 B.C. They practiced a policy of terror, killing or exiling the
leaders of the democracy and anyone else they disliked. Leon of Salamis seems to
have been an innocent victim. See Plato, *Letters*, VII, 324.

truth about this matter: they like to hear the cross-examination of the pretenders to wisdom; there is amusement in it. Now this duty of cross-examining other men has been imposed upon me by God; and has been signified to me by oracles, visions, and in every way in which the will of divine power was ever intimated to anyone. This is true, O Athenians; or, if not true, would be soon refuted. If I am or have been corrupting the youth, those of them who are now grown up and have become sensible that I gave them bad advice in the days of their youth should come forward as accusers, and take their revenge; or if they do not like to come themselves, some of their relatives, fathers, brothers, or other kinsmen, should say what evil their families have suffered at my hands. Now is their time. Many of them I see in the court. There is Crito, who is of the same age and of the same deme with myself, and there is Critobulus his son, whom I also see. Then again there is Lysanias of Sphettus, who is the father of Aeschines—he is present; and also there is Antiphon of Cephisus, who is the father of Epigenes; and there are the brothers of several who have associated with me. There is Nicostratus the son of Theosdotides, and the brother of Theodotus (now Theodotus himself is dead, and therefore he, at any rate, will not seek to stop him); and there is Paralus the son of Demodocus, who had a brother Theages; and Adeimantus the son of Ariston, whose brother Plato is present; and Aeantodorus, who is the brother of Apollodorus, whom I also see. I might mention a great many others, some of whom Meletus should have produced as witnesses in the course of his speech; and let him still produce them, if he has forgotten—I will make way for him. And let him say, if he has any testimony of the sort which he can produce. Nay, Athenians, the very opposite is the truth. For all these are ready to witness on behalf of the corrupter, of the injurer of their kindred, as Meletus and Anytus call me; not the corrupted youth only—there might have been a motive for that—but their uncorrupted elder relatives. Why should they too support me with their testimony? Why, indeed, except for the sake of truth and justice, and because they know that I am speaking the truth, and that Meletus is a liar.

Well, Athenians, this and the like of this is all the defense which

I have to offer. Yet a word more. Perhaps there may be someone who is offended at me, when he calls to mind how he himself on a similar, or even a less serious occasion, prayed and entreated the judges with many tears, and how he produced his children in court, which was a moving spectacle, together with a host of relations and friends; whereas I, who am probably in danger of my life, will do none of these things. The contrast may occur to his mind, and he may be set against me, and vote in anger because he is displeased at me on this account. Now if there be such a person among you—mind, I do not say that there is—to him I may fairly reply: My friend, I am a man, and like other men, a creature of flesh and blood, and not "of wood or stone," as Homer says; [16] and I have a family, yes, and sons, O Athenians, three in number, one almost a man, and two others who are still young; and yet I will not bring any of them hither in order to petition you for an acquittal. And why not? Not from any self-assertion or want of respect for you. Whether I am or am not afraid of death is another question, of which I will not now speak. But, having regard to public opinion, I feel that such conduct would be discreditable to myself, and to you, and to the whole state. One who has reached my years, and who has a name for wisdom, ought not to demean himself. Whether this opinion of me be deserved or not, at any rate the world has decided that Socrates is in some way superior to other men. And if those among you who are said to be superior in wisdom and courage, and any other virtue, demean themselves in this way, how shameful is their conduct! I have seen men of reputation, when they have been condemned, behaving in the strangest manner: they seemed to fancy that they were going to suffer something dreadful if they died, and that they could be immortal if you only allowed them to live; and I think that such are a dishonor to the state, and that any stranger coming in would have said of them that the most eminent men of Athens, to whom the Athenians themselves give honor and command, are no better than women. And I say that these things ought not to be done by those of us who have a reputation; and if they are done, you

16 Homer, *Odyssey*, XIX, 163.

ought not to permit them; you ought rather to show that you are far more disposed to condemn the man who gets up a doleful scene and makes the city ridiculous than him who holds his peace.

But, setting aside the question of public opinion, there seems to be something wrong in asking a favor of a judge, and thus procuring an acquittal, instead of informing and convincing him. For his duty is, not to make a present of justice, but to give judgment; and he has sworn that he will judge according to the laws, and not according to his own good pleasure; and we ought not to encourage you, nor should you allow yourselves to be encouraged, in this habit of perjury—there can be no piety in that. Do not then require me to do what I consider dishonorable and impious and wrong, especially now, when I am being tried for impiety on the indictment of Meletus. For if, O men of Athens, by force of persuasion and entreaty I could overpower your oaths, then I should be teaching you to believe that there are no gods, and in defending should simply convict myself of the charge of not believing in them. But that is not so—far otherwise. For I do believe that there are gods, and in a sense higher than that in which any of my accusers believe in them. And to you and to God I commit my cause, to be determined by you as is best for you and me.

He is convicted by the judges

There are many reasons why I am not grieved, O men of Athens, at the vote of condemnation. I expected it, and am only surprised that the votes are so nearly equal; for I had thought that the majority against me would have been far larger; but now, had thirty votes gone over to the other side, I should have been acquitted. And I may say, I think, that I have escaped Meletus. I may say more; for without the assistance of Anytus and Lycon, anyone may see that he would not have had a fifth part of the votes, as the law requires, [17] in which case he would have incurred a fine of a thousand drachmas.

And so he proposes death as the penalty. And what shall I propose

[17] If an accuser fell so far short of proving his case that less than one fifth of the jurors voted in his favor, he was liable by law to a fine of a thousand drachmas, about $200.

on my part, O men of Athens? Clearly that which is my due. And what is my due? What return shall be made to the man who has never had the wit to be idle during his whole life; but has been care-less of what the many care for—wealth, and family interests, and military offices, and speaking in the assembly, and magistracies, and plots, and parties. Reflecting that I was really too honest a man to be a politician and live, I did not go where I could do no good to you or to myself; but where I could do the greatest good privately to every one of you, thither I went, and sought to persuade every man among you that he must look to himself, and seek virtue and wisdom before he looks to his private interests, and look to the state before he looks to the interests of the state; and that this should be the order which he observes in all his actions. What shall be done to such an one? Doubtless some good thing, O men of Athens, if he has his reward; and the good should be of a kind suitable to him. What would be a reward suitable to a poor man who is your benefactor, and who desires leisure that he may instruct you? There can be no reward so fitting as maintenance in the Prytaneum,[18] O men of Athens, a reward which he deserves far more than the citizen who has won the prize at Olym-pia in the horse or chariot race, whether the chariots were drawn by two horses or by many. For I am in want, and he has enough; and he only gives you the appearance of happiness, and I give you the reality. And if I am to estimate the penalty fairly, I should say that maintenance in the Prytaneum is the just return.

Perhaps you think that I am braving you in what I am saying now, as in what I said before about the tears and prayers. But this is not so. I speak rather because I am convinced that I never intentionally wronged anyone, although I cannot convince you—the time has been too short; if there were a law at Athens, as there is in other cities, that a capital cause should not be decided in one day, then I believe that I should have convinced you. But I cannot in a moment refute great slanders; and, as I am convinced that I never wronged another, I will assuredly not wrong myself. I will not say of myself that I deserve any

18 The public hall in which were entertained ambassadors, victorious generals, winners at the Olympic games, and other illustrious citizens.

evil, or propose any penalty. Why should I? Because I am afraid of the penalty of death which Meletus proposes? When I do not know whether death is a good or an evil, why should I propose a penalty which would certainly be an evil? Shall I say imprisonment? And why should I live in prison, and be the slave of the magistrates of the year—of the Eleven? [19] Or shall the penalty be a fine, and imprison· ment until the fine is paid? There is the same objection. I should have to lie in prison, for money I have none, and cannot pay. And if I say exile (and this may possibly be the penalty which you will affix), I must indeed be blinded by the love of life, if I am so irrational as to expect that when you, who are my own citizens, cannot endure my discourses and words and have found them so grievous and odious that you will have no more of them, others are likely to endure me. No indeed, men of Athens, that is not very likely. And what a life should I lead, at my age, wandering from city to city, ever changing my place of exile, and always being driven out! For I am quite sure that wherever I go, there, as here, the young men will flock to me; and if I drive them away, their elders will drive me out at their re· quest; and if I let them come, their fathers and friends will drive me out for their sakes.

Someone will say: Yes, Socrates, but cannot you hold your tongue. and then you may go into a foreign city, and no one will interfere with you? Now I have great difficulty in making you understand my answer to this. For if I tell you that to do as you say would be a dis· obedience to the God, and therefore that I cannot hold my tongue, you will not believe that I am serious; and if I say again that daily to discourse about virtue, and of those other things about which you hear me examining myself and others, is the greatest good of man, and that the unexamined life is not worth living, you are still less likely to believe me. Yet I say what is true, although a thing of which it is hard for me to persuade you. Also, I have never been accustomed to think that I deserve to suffer any harm. Had I money I might have estimated the offense at what I was able to pay, and not have been

19 The Eleven were the city police board, one of whose duties was to see to the execution of court sentences.

much the worse. But I have none, and therefore I must ask you to proportion the fine to my means. Well, perhaps I could afford a mina, and therefore I propose that penalty: Plato, Crito, Critobulus, and Apollodorus, my friends here, bid me say thirty minae, and they will be the sureties. Let thirty minae be the penalty; for which sum they will be ample security to you.

He is sentenced to death

Not much time will be gained, O Athenians, in return for the evil name which you will get from the detractors of the city, who will say that you killed Socrates, a wise man; for they will call me wise, even although I am not wise, when they want to reproach you. If you had waited a little while, your desire would have been fulfilled in the course of nature. For I am far advanced in years, as you may perceive, and not far from death. I am speaking now not to all of you, but only to those who have condemned me to death. And I have another thing to say to them: You think that I was convicted because I had no words of the sort which would have procured my acquittal— I mean, if I had thought fit to leave nothing undone or unsaid. Not so; the deficiency which led to my conviction was not of words— certainly not. But I had not the boldness or impudence or inclination to address you as you would have liked me to do, weeping and wailing and lamenting, and saying and doing many things which you have been accustomed to hear from others, and which, as I maintain, are unworthy of me. I thought at the time that I ought not to do anything common or mean when in danger: nor do I now repent of the style of my defense; I would rather die having spoken after my manner, than speak in your manner and live. For neither in war nor yet at law ought I or any man to use every way of escaping death. Often in battle there can be no doubt that if a man will throw away his arms, and fall on his knees before his pursuers, he may escape death; and in other dangers there are other ways of escaping death, if a man is willing to say and do anything. The difficulty, my friends, is not to avoid death, but to avoid unrighteousness; for that runs faster than death. I am old and move slowly, and the slower runner has overtaken me, and my accusers are keen and quick, and the faster runner, who is unrighteousness, has overtaken them. And now I depart hence condemned by you to suffer the penalty of death—they too go their ways condemned by the truth to suffer the penalty of villainy and wrong; and I must abide by my award—let them abide by theirs. I suppose that these things may be regarded as fated—and I think that they are well.

And now, O men who have condemned me, I would fain prophesy to you; for I am about to die, and in the hour of death men are gifted with prophetic power. And I prophesy to you who are my murderers, that immediately after my departure punishment far heavier than you have inflicted on me will surely await you. Me you have killed because you wanted to escape the accuser, and not to give an account of your lives. But that will not be as you suppose: far otherwise. For I say that there will be more accusers of you than there are now; accusers whom hitherto I have restrained: and as they are younger they will be more inconsiderate with you, and you will be more offended at them. If you think that by killing men you can prevent someone from censuring your evil lives, you are mistaken; that is not a way of escape which is either possible or honorable; the easiest and the noblest way is not to be disabling others, but to be improving yourselves. This is the prophecy which I utter before my departure to the judges who have condemned me.

Friends, who would have acquitted me, I would like also to talk with you about the thing which has come to pass, while the magistrates are busy, and before I go to the place at which I must die. Stay then a little, for we may as well talk with one another while there is time. You are my friends, and I should like to show you the meaning of this event which has happened to me. O my judges—for you I may truly call judges—I should like to tell you of a wonderful circumstance. Hitherto the divine faculty of which the internal oracle is the source has constantly been in the habit of opposing me even about trifles, if I was going to make a slip or error in any matter; and now as you see there has come upon me that which may be thought, and is generally believed to be, the last and worst evil.

But the oracle made no sign of opposition, either when I was leaving my house in the morning, or when I was on my way to the court, or while I was speaking, at anything which I was going to say; and yet I have often been stopped in the middle of a speech, but now in nothing I either said or did touching the matter in hand has the oracle opposed me. What do I take to be the explanation of this silence? I will tell you. It is an intimation that what has happened to me is a good, and that those of us who think that death is an evil are in error. For the customary sign would surely have opposed me had I been going to evil and not to good.

Let us reflect in another way, and we shall see that there is great reason to hope that death is a good; for one of two things—either death is a state of nothingness and utter unconsciousness, or, as men say, there is a change and migration of the soul from this world to another. Now if you suppose that there is no consciousness, but a sleep like the sleep of him who is undisturbed even by dreams, death will be an unspeakable gain. For if a person were to select the night in which his sleep was undisturbed even by dreams, and were to compare with this the other days and nights of his life, and then were to tell us how many days and nights he had passed in the course of his life better and more pleasantly than this one, I think that any man, I will not say a private man, but even the great king will not find many such days or nights, when compared with the others. Now if death be of such a nature, I say that to die is gain; for eternity is then only a single night. But if death is the journey to another place, and there, as men say, all the dead abide, what good, O my friends and judges, can be greater than this? If indeed when the pilgrim arrives in the world below, he is delivered from the professors of justice in this world, and finds the true judges who are said to give judgment there, Minos and Rhadamanthus and Aeacus and Triptolemus, and other sons of God who were righteous in their own life, that pilgrimage will be worth making. What would not a man give if he might converse with Orpheus and Musaeus and Hesiod and Homer? Nay, if this be true, let me die again and again. I myself, too, shall have a wonderful interest in there meeting and conversing with

Palamedes, and Ajax the son of Telamon, and any other ancient hero who has suffered death through an unjust judgment; and there will be no small pleasure, as I think, in comparing my own sufferings with theirs. Above all, I shall then be able to continue my search into true and false knowledge; as in this world, so also in the next; and I shall find out who is wise, and who pretends to be wise, and is not. What would not a man give, O judges, to be able to examine the leader of the great Trojan expedition; or Odysseus or Sisyphus, or numberless others, men and women too! What infinite delight would there be in conversing with them and asking them questions! In another world they do not put a man to death for asking questions: assuredly not. For besides being happier than we are, they will be immortal, if what is said is true.

Wherefore, O judges, be of good cheer about death, and know of a certainty, that no evil can happen to a good man, either in life or after death. He and his are not neglected by the gods; nor has my own approaching end happened by mere chance. But I see clearly that the time had arrived when it was better for me to die and be released from trouble; wherefore the oracle gave no sign. For which reason, also, I am not angry with my condemners, or with my accusers; they have done me no harm, although they did not mean to do me any good; and for this I may gently blame them.

Still I have a favor to ask of them. When my sons are grown up, I would ask you, O my friends, to punish them; and I would have you trouble them, as I have troubled you, if they seem to care about riches, or anything, more than about virtue; or if they pretend to be something when they are really nothing—then reprove them, as I have reproved you, for not caring about that for which they ought to care, and thinking that they are something when they are really nothing. And if you do this, both I and my sons will have received justice at your hands.

The hour of departure has arrived, and we go our ways—I to die, and you to live. Which is better God only knows.

CRITO

A MONTH has passed since Socrates was condemned to die and still he waits chained in his cell in prison. For his trial took place just as the sacred ship, bearing the yearly thank offering of Athens to the ancient shrine of Apollo on the island of Delos, was being prepared for her sailing, as Socrates' young friend Phaedo explains in the next dialogue, pages 85-86. The offering commemorates a famous event in the city's legendary history, its delivery by the hero Theseus with the god's aid from the savage tyranny of the king of Crete, who required an annual tribute of the best Athenian youth to satisfy his man-devouring Minotaur. The period from the time when the priest at Athens crowns the ship before its departure until it returns to harbor is, Phaedo says, a "holy season," during which the city must not be polluted by the taking of human life. So Socrates, like any other convicted criminal, must wait to die until the vessel is back at anchor.

But now the weeks of respite are nearly over. The ship has been sighted off Sunium, the southernmost promontory of Attica, less than thirty-five miles by sea from the Peiraeus, the port of Athens. In another day it should arrive. Crito, an old and tried friend of Socrates, one of those who at his trial had volunteered to make up the sum of any fine that might be imposed on him (page 57), visits him in a last desperate effort to persuade him to allow his friends to buy off the jailers and whatever spy informers may be about and arrange for his escape that night to Thessaly or to some other place, where he can live in safety.

CRITO

PERSONS OF THE DIALOGUE:
Socrates, Crito

SCENE: *The Prison of Socrates*

Socrates speaks:

WHY have you come at this hour, Crito? it must be quite early?

CRITO: Yes, certainly.

SOCRATES: What is the exact time?

CRITO: The dawn is breaking.

SOCRATES: I wonder that the keeper of the prison would let you in.

CRITO: He knows me, because I often come, Socrates; moreover, I have done him a kindness.

SOCRATES: And are you only just arrived?

CRITO: No, I came some time ago.

SOCRATES: Then why did you sit and say nothing, instead of at once awakening me?

CRITO: I should not have liked myself, Socrates, to be in such great trouble and unrest as you are—indeed I should not: I have been watching with amazement your peaceful slumbers; and for that reason I did not awake you, because I wished to minimize the pain. I have always thought you to be of a happy disposition; but never did I see anything like the easy, tranquil manner in which you bear this calamity.

SOCRATES: Why, Crito, when a man has reached my age he ought not to be repining at the approach of death.

CRITO: And yet other old men find themselves in similar misfortunes, and age does not prevent them from repining.

SOCRATES: That is true. But you have not told me why you come at this early hour.

CRITO: I come to bring you a message which is sad and painful; not, as I believe, to yourself, but to all of us who are your friends, and saddest of all to me.

SOCRATES: What? Has the ship come from Delos, on the arrival of which I am to die?

CRITO: No, the ship has not actually arrived, but she will probably be here today, as persons who have come from Sunium tell me that they left her there; and therefore tomorrow, Socrates, will be the last day of your life.

SOCRATES: Very well, Crito; if such is the will of God, I am willing; but my belief is that there will be a delay of a day.

CRITO: Why do you think so?

SOCRATES: I will tell you. I am to die on the day after the arrival of the ship.

CRITO: Yes; that is what the authorities say.

SOCRATES: But I do not think that the ship will be here until tomorrow; this I infer from a vision which I had last night, or rather only just now, when you fortunately allowed me to sleep.

CRITO: And what was the nature of the vision?

SOCRATES: There appeared to me the likeness of a woman, fair and comely, clothed in bright raiment, who called to me and said: O Socrates,

The third day hence to fertile Phthia shalt thou go.[1]

CRITO: What a singular dream, Socrates!

SOCRATES: There can be no doubt about the meaning, Crito, I think.

[1] *Iliad*, IX, 363.

CRITO: Yes; the meaning is only too clear. But, oh! my beloved Socrates, let me entreat you once more to take my advice and escape. For if you die I shall not only lose a friend who can never be replaced, but there is another evil: people who do not know you and me will believe that I might have saved you if I had been willing to give money, but that I did not care. Now, can there be a worse disgrace than this—that I should be thought to value money more than the life of a friend? For the many will not be persuaded that I wanted you to escape, and that you refused.

SOCRATES: But why, my dear Crito, should we care about the opinion of the many? Good men, and they are the only persons who are worth considering, will think of these things truly as they occurred.

CRITO: But you see, Socrates, that the opinion of the many must be regarded, for what is now happening shows that they can do the greatest evil to anyone who has lost their good opinion.

SOCRATES: I only wish it were so, Crito; and that the many could do the greatest evil; for then they would also be able to do the greatest good—and what a fine thing this would be! But in reality they can do neither; for they cannot make a man either wise or foolish; and whatever they do is the result of chance.

CRITO: Well, I will not dispute with you; but please to tell me, Socrates, whether you are not acting out of regard to me and your other friends: are you not afraid that if you escape from prison we may get into trouble with the informers for having stolen you away, and lose either the whole or a great part of our property; or that even a worse evil may happen to us? Now, if you fear on our account, be at ease; for in order to save you, we ought surely to run this, or even a greater risk; be persuaded, then, and do as I say.

SOCRATES: Yes, Crito, that is one fear which you mention, but by no means the only one.

CRITO: Fear not—there are persons who are willing to get you out of prison at no great cost; and as for the informers, they are far from being exorbitant in their demands—a little money will satisfy them. My means, which are certainly ample, are at your service, and if you have a scruple about spending all mine, here are strangers who will give you the use of theirs; and one of them, Simmias the Theban,[2] has brought a large sum of money for this very purpose; and Cebes and many others are prepared to spend their money in helping you to escape. I say, therefore, do not hesitate on our account, and do not say, as you did in the court, that you will have a difficulty in knowing what to do with yourself anywhere else. For men will love you in other places to which you may go, and not in Athens only; there are friends of mine in Thessaly,[3] if you like to go to them, who will value and protect you, and no Thessalian will give you any trouble. Nor can I think that you are at all justified, Socrates, in betraying your own life when you might be saved; in acting thus you are playing into the hands of your enemies, who are hurrying on your destruction. And further I should say that you are deserting your own children; for you might bring them up and educate them; instead of which you go away and leave them, and they will have to take their chance; and if they do not meet with the usual fate of orphans, there will be small thanks to you. No man should bring children into the world who is unwilling to persevere to the end in their nurture and education. But you appear to be choosing the easier part, not the better and manlier, which would have been more becoming in one who professes to care for virtue in all his actions, like yourself. And indeed, I am ashamed not only of you, but of us who are your friends, when I reflect that the whole business will be attributed entirely to our want of courage. The trial need never have come on, or might have been managed differently; and this last act, or crowning folly, will seem to have occurred through our negligence and cowardice, who might have saved you, if we had been good for anything; and you might have saved yourself, for there was no difficulty at all. See now, Socrates, how sad and discreditable are the consequences, both to us and you. Make up your mind then, or rather have your mind already made up, for the time of deliberation

2 Simmias and his friend Cebes, pupils of Socrates from the nearby city of Thebes, figure largely in the next dialogue, the *Phaedo*.
3 A province of northern Greece.

is over, and there is only one thing to be done, which must be done this very night, and, if we delay at all, will be no longer practicable or possible; I beseech you therefore, Socrates, be persuaded by me, and do as I say.

SOCRATES: Dear Crito, your zeal is invaluable, if a right one; but if wrong, the greater the zeal the greater the danger; and therefore we ought to consider whether I shall or shall not do as you say. For I am and always have been one of those natures who must be guided by reason, whatever the reason may be which upon reflection appears to me to be the best; and now that this chance has befallen me, I cannot repudiate my own words: the principles which I have hitherto honored and revered I still honor, and unless we can at once find other and better principles, I am certain not to agree with you; no, not even if the power of the multitude could inflict many more imprisonments, confiscations, deaths, frightening us like children with hobgoblin terrors. What will be the fairest way of considering the question? Shall I return to your old argument about the opinions of men?—we were saying that some of them are to be regarded, and others not. Now were we right in maintaining this before I was condemned? And has the argument which was once good now proved to be talk for the sake of talking—mere childish nonsense? That is what I want to consider with your help, Crito: whether, under my present circumstances, the argument appears to be in any way different or not; and is to be allowed by me or disallowed. That argument, which, as I believe, is maintained by many persons of authority, was to the effect, as I was saying, that the opinions of some men are to be regarded, and of other men not to be regarded. Now you, Crito, are not going to die tomorrow—at least, there is no human probability of this—and therefore you are disinterested and not liable to be deceived by the circumstances in which you are placed. Tell me then, whether I am right in saying that some opinions, and the opinions of some men only, are to be valued, and that other opinions, and the opinions of other men, are not to be valued. I ask you whether I was right in maintaining this?

CRITO: Certainly.

SOCRATES: The good are to be regarded, and not the bad?

CRITO: Yes.

SOCRATES: And the opinions of the wise are good, and the opinions of the unwise are evil?

CRITO: Certainly.

SOCRATES: And what was said about another matter? Is the pupil who devotes himself to the practice of gymnastics supposed to attend to the praise and blame and opinion of every man, or of one man only—his physician or trainer, whoever he may be?

CRITO: Of one man only.

SOCRATES: And he ought to fear the censure and welcome the praise of that one only, and not of the many?

CRITO: Clearly so.

SOCRATES: And he ought to act and train, and eat and drink in the way which seems good to his single master who has understanding, rather than according to the opinion of all other men put together?

CRITO: True.

SOCRATES: And if he disobeys and disregards the opinion and approval of the one, and regards the opinion of the many who have no understanding, will he not suffer evil?

CRITO: Certainly he will.

SOCRATES: And what will the evil be, whither tending and what affecting, in the disobedient person?

CRITO: Clearly, affecting the body; that is what is destroyed by the evil.

SOCRATES: Very good; and is not this true, Crito, of other things which we need not separately enumerate? In questions of just and unjust, fair and foul, good and evil, which are the subjects of our present consultation, ought we to follow the opinion of the many and to fear them; or the opinion of the one man who has understanding? ought we not to fear and reverence him more than all the rest of the world: and if we desert him shall we not destroy and injure that principle in us which may be assumed to be improved by justice and deteriorated by injustice—there is such a principle?

CRITO: Certainly there is, Socrates.

SOCRATES: Take a parallel instance: if, acting under the advice of those who have no understanding, we destroy that which is improved by health and is deteriorated by disease, would life be worth having? And that which has been destroyed is—the body?

CRITO: Yes.

SOCRATES: Could we live, having an evil and corrupted body?

CRITO: Certainly not.

SOCRATES: And will life be worth having, if that higher part of man be destroyed, which is improved by justice and depraved by injustice? Do we suppose that principle, whatever it may be in man, which has to do with justice and injustice, to be inferior to the body?

CRITO: Certainly not.

SOCRATES: More honorable than the body?

CRITO: Far more.

SOCRATES: Then, my friend, we must not regard what the many say of us; but what he, the one man who has understanding of just and unjust, will say, and what the truth will say. And therefore you begin in error when you advise that we should regard the opinion of the many about just and unjust, good and evil, honorable and dishonorable.— "Well," someone will say, "but the many can kill us."

CRITO: Yes, Socrates; that will clearly be the answer.

SOCRATES: And it is true: but still I find with surprise that the old argument is unshaken as ever. And I should like to know whether I may say the same of another proposition—that not life, but a good life, is to be chiefly valued?

CRITO: Yes, that also remains unshaken.

SOCRATES: And a good life is equivalent to a just and honorable one—that holds also?

CRITO: Yes, it does.

SOCRATES: From these premises I proceed to argue the question whether I ought or ought not to try and escape without the consent of the Athenians: and if I am clearly right in escaping, then I will make the attempt; but if not, I will abstain. The other considerations which you mention, of money and loss of character and the duty of educating one's children, are, I fear, only the doctrines of the multi-tude, who would be as ready to restore people to life, if they were able, as they are to put them to death—and with as little reason. But now, since the argument has thus far prevailed, the only question which remains to be considered is whether we shall do rightly either in escaping or in suffering others to aid in our escape and paying them in money and thanks, or whether in reality we shall not do rightly; and if the latter, then death or any other calamity which may ensue on my remaining here must not be allowed to enter into the calculation.

CRITO: I think that you are right, Socrates; how then shall we proceed?

SOCRATES: Let us consider the matter together, and do you either refute me if you can, and I will be convinced; or else cease, my dear friend, from repeating to me that I ought to escape against the wishes of the Athenians: for I highly value your attempts to persuade me to do so, but I may not be persuaded against my own better judgment. And now please to consider my first position, and try how you can best answer me.

CRITO: I will.

SOCRATES: Are we to say that we are never intentionally to do wrong, or that in one way we ought and in another way we ought not to do wrong, or is doing wrong always evil and dishonorable, as I was just now saying, and as has been already acknowledged by us? Are all our former admissions which were made within a few days to be thrown away? And have we, at our age, been earnestly discoursing with one another all our life long only to discover that we are no better than children? Or, in spite of the opinion of the many, and in spite of consequences whether better or worse, shall we insist on the truth of what was then said, that injustice is always an evil and dishonor to him who acts unjustly? Shall we say so or not?

CRITO: Yes.

SOCRATES: Then we must do no wrong?

CRITO: Certainly not.

SOCRATES: Nor, when injured, injure in return, as the many imagine; for we must injure no one at all?

CRITO: Clearly not.

SOCRATES: Again, Crito, may we do evil?

CRITO: Surely not, Socrates.

SOCRATES: And what of doing evil in return for evil, which is the morality of the many—is that just or not?

CRITO: Not just.

SOCRATES: For doing evil to another is the same as injuring him?

CRITO: Very true.

SOCRATES: Then we ought not to retaliate or render evil for evil to anyone, whatever evil we may have suffered from him. But I would have you consider, Crito, whether you really mean what you are saying. For this opinion has never been held, and never will be held, by any considerable number of persons; and those who are agreed and those who are not agreed upon this point have no common ground, and can only despise one another when they see how widely they differ. Tell me, then, whether you agree with and assent to my first principle, that neither injury nor retaliation nor warding off evil by evil is ever right. And shall that be the premise of our argument? Or do you decline and dissent from this? For so I have ever thought, and continue to think; but, if you are of another opinion, let me hear what you have to say. If, however, you remain of the same mind as formerly, I will proceed to the next step.

CRITO: You may proceed, for I have not changed my mind.

SOCRATES: Then I will go on to the next point, which may be put in the form of a question: Ought a man to do what he admits to be right, or ought he to betray the right?

CRITO: He ought to do what he thinks right.

SOCRATES: But if this is true, what is the application? In leaving the prison against the will of the Athenians, do I wrong any? or rather do I not wrong those whom I ought least to wrong? Do I not desert the principles which were acknowledged by us to be just—what do you say?

CRITO: I cannot tell, Socrates; for I do not know.

SOCRATES: Then consider the matter in this way: Imagine that I am about to play truant (you may call the proceeding by any name which you like), and the laws and the government come and interrogate me: "Tell us, Socrates," they say; "what are you about? are you not going by an act of yours to overturn us—the laws, and the whole state, as far as in you lies? Do you imagine that a state can subsist and not be overthrown, in which the decisions of law have no power, but are set aside and trampled upon by individuals?"— What will be our answer, Crito, to these and the like words? Anyone, and especially a rhetorician, will have a good deal to say on behalf of the law which requires a sentence to be carried out. He will argue that this law should not be set aside; and shall we reply, "Yes; but the state has injured us and given an unjust sentence." Suppose I say that?

CRITO: Very good, Socrates.

SOCRATES: "And was that our agreement with you?" the law would answer; "or were you to abide by the sentence of the state?" And if I were to express my astonishment at their words, the law would probably add: "Answer, Socrates, instead of opening your eyes: you are in the habit of asking and answering questions. Tell us: What complaint have you to make against us which justifies you in attempting to destroy us and the state? In the first place did we not bring you into existence? Your father married your mother by our aid and begat you. Say whether you have any objection to urge against those of us who regulate marriage?" None, I should reply. "Or against those of us who after birth regulate the nurture and education of children, in which you also were trained? Were not the laws, which have the charge of education, right in commanding your father to train you in music and gymnastic?" Right, I should reply. "Well then, since you were brought into the world and nurtured and educated by us, can you deny in the first place that you are our child and slave, as your fathers were before you? And if this is true you are not on equal terms with us; nor can you think that you have a right to do to us what we are doing to you. Would you have any right to strike or revile or do any other evil to your father or your master, if you had one, because you have been struck or reviled by him, or received some other evil at his hands? You would not say this. And because we think right to destroy you, do you think that you have any right to destroy us in return, and your country as far as in you lies? Will you, O professor of true virtue, pretend that you are justified in this? Has a philosopher like you failed to discover that our country is more to be valued and higher and holier far than mother or father or any ancestor, and more to be regarded in the eyes of the gods and of men of understanding? also to be soothed, and gently and reverently entreated when angry, even more than a father, and either to be persuaded, or if not persuaded, to be obeyed? And when we are punished by her, whether with imprisonment or stripes, the punishment is to be endured in silence; and if she lead us to wounds or death in battle, thither we follow as is right; neither may anyone yield or retreat or leave his rank, but whether in battle or in a court of law, or in any other place, he must do what his city and his country order him; or he must change their view of what is just: and if he may do no violence to his father or mother, much less may he do violence to his country." What answer shall we make to this, Crito? Do the laws speak truly, or do they not?

CRITO: I think that they do.

SOCRATES: Then the laws will say: "Consider, Socrates, if we are speaking truly that in your present attempt you are going to do us an injury. For, having brought you into the world, and nurtured and educated you, and given you and every other citizen a share in every good which we had to give, we further proclaim to any Athenian by the liberty which we allow him, that if he does not like us when he has become of age and has seen the ways of the city, and made our acquaintance, he may go where he pleases and take his goods with him. None of us laws will forbid him or interfere with him. Anyone who does not like us and the city, and who wants to emigrate to a colony or to any other city, may go where he likes, retaining his property. But he who has experience of the manner in which we order justice and administer the state, and still remains, has entered into an implied contract that he will do as we command him. And he who disobeys us is, as we maintain, thrice wrong; first, because in disobeying us he is disobeying his parents; secondly, because we are the authors of his education; thirdly, because he has made an agreement with us that he will duly obey our commands; and he neither obeys them nor convinces us that our commands are unjust; and we do not rudely impose them, but give him the alternative of obeying or convincing us; that is what we offer, and he does neither. These are the sort of accusations to which, as we were saying, you, Socrates, will be exposed if you accomplish your intentions; you, above all other Athenians."

Suppose now I ask, why I rather than anybody else? They will justly retort upon me that I above all other men have acknowledged the agreement. "There is clear proof," they will say, "Socrates, that we and the city were not displeasing to you. Of all Athenians you have been the most constant resident in the city, which, as you never leave, you may be supposed to love. For you never went out of the city either to see the games, except once when you went to the Isthmus,[4] or to any other place unless when you were on military service; nor did you travel as other men do. Nor had you any curiosity to know other states or their laws: your affections did not go beyond us and our state; we were your special favorites, and you acquiesced in our government of you; and here in this city you begat your children, which is a proof of your satisfaction. Moreover, you might in the course of the trial, if you had liked, have fixed the penalty at banishment; the state which refuses to let you go now would have let you go then. But you pretended that you preferred death to exile,[5] and that you were not unwilling to die. And now you have forgotten these fine sentiments, and pay no respect to us, the laws, of whom you are the destroyer; and are doing what only a miserable slave would do, running away and turning your back upon the compacts and agreements which you made as a citizen. And, first of all, answer this very question: Are we right in saying that you agreed to be

4 The Isthmian games, held on the Isthmus of Corinth in honor of the sea god Poseidon, were almost as famous as the Olympian games in honor of Zeus.
5 See *Apology*, page 56.

governed according to us in deed, and not in word only? Is that true or not?" How shall we answer, Crito? Must we not assent?

CRITO: We cannot help it, Socrates.

SOCRATES: Then will they not say: "You, Socrates, are breaking the covenants and agreements which you made with us at your leisure, not in any haste or under any compulsion or deception, but after you have had seventy years to think of them, during which time you were at liberty to leave the city, if we were not to your mind, or if our covenants appeared to you to be unfair. You had your choice, and might have gone either to Lacedaemon [6] or Crete, both which states are often praised by you for their good government, or to some other Hellenic or foreign state. Whereas you, above all other Athenians, seemed to be so fond of the state, or, in other words, of us, her laws (and who would care about a state which has no laws?), that you never stirred out of her; the halt, the blind, the maimed were not more stationary in her than you were. And now you run away and forsake your agreements. Not so, Socrates, if you will take our advice; do not make yourself ridiculous by escaping out of the city.

"For just consider, if you transgress and err in this sort of way, what good will you do either to yourself or to your friends? That your friends will be driven into exile and deprived of citizenship, or will lose their property, is tolerably certain; and you yourself, if you fly to one of the neighboring cities, as, for example, Thebes or Megara, both of which are well governed, will come to them as an enemy, Socrates, and their government will be against you, and all patriotic citizens will cast an evil eye upon you as a subverter of the laws, and you will confirm in the minds of the judges the justice of their own condemnation of you. For he who is a corrupter of the laws is more than likely to be a corrupter of the young and foolish portion of mankind. Will you then flee from well-ordered cities and virtuous men? and is existence worth having on these terms? Or will you go to them without shame, and talk to them, Socrates? And what will you say to them? What you say here about virtue and justice and

6 Another name for Sparta.

institutions and laws being the best things among men? Would that be decent of you? Surely not. But if you go away from well-governed states to Crito's friends in Thessaly, where there is great disorder and license, they will be charmed to hear the tale of your escape from prison, set off with ludicrous particulars of the manner in which you were wrapped in a goatskin or some other disguise, and metamorphosed as the manner is of runaways; but will there be no one to remind you that in your old age you were not ashamed to violate the most sacred laws from a miserable desire of a little more life? Perhaps not, if you keep them in a good temper; but if they are out of temper you will hear many degrading things; you will live, but how?—as the flatterer of all men, and the servant of all men; and doing what?—eating and drinking in Thessaly, having gone abroad in order that you may get a dinner. And where will be your fine sentiments about justice and virtue? Say that you wish to live for the sake of your children—you want to bring them up and educate them—will you take them into Thessaly and deprive them of Athenian citizenship? Is this the benefit which you will confer upon them? Or are you under the impression that they will be better cared for and educated here if you are still alive, although absent from them; for your friends will take care of them? Do you fancy that if you are an inhabitant of Thessaly they will take care of them, and if you are an inhabitant of the other world that they will not take care of them? Nay; but if they who call themselves friends are good for anything, they will—to be sure they will.

"Listen, then, Socrates, to us who have brought you up. Think not of life and children first, and of justice afterwards, but of justice first, that you may be justified before the princes of the world below. For neither will you nor any that belong to you be happier or holier or juster in this life, or happier in another, if you do as Crito bids. Now you depart in innocence, a sufferer and not a doer of evil; a victim, not of the laws, but of men. But if you go forth, returning evil for evil, and injury for injury, breaking the covenants and agreements which you have made with us, and wronging those whom you ought least of all to wrong, that is to say, yourself, your friends, your country, and us, we shall be angry with you while you live, and our brethren, the laws in the world below, will receive you as an enemy; for they will know that you have done your best to destroy us. Listen, then, to us and not to Crito."

This, dear Crito, is the voice which I seem to hear murmuring in my ears, like the sound of the flute in the ears of the mystic; that voice, I say, is humming in my ears, and prevents me from hearing any other. And I know that anything more which you may say will be vain. Yet speak, if you have anything to say.

CRITO: I have nothing to say, Socrates.

SOCRATES: Leave me then, Crito, to fulfill the will of God, and to follow whither he leads.

PHAEDO

SOME time after Socrates' execution, we learn from the dialogue that follows, his disciple Phaedo comes to the town of Phlius in northern Peloponnesus, on his way back, perhaps, to his native city of Elis in the west. At Phlius he meets Echecrates and a group of other friends of Socrates, all anxious to hear how it went with him at the end. Accordingly Phaedo, who had sat on a stool beside Socrates that last afternoon, while Socrates' hand stroked his hair, tells them in full the story of what was done and said.

The fateful ship from Delos had arrived the day before. The little circle of Socrates' intimates therefore had gathered early to spend with him the time until evening, when the poison hemlock would be given him to drink. Crito, the old, close friend of the family, who had previously tried in vain to induce Socrates to escape, was there to take his parting instructions and close his eyes when all was finished. Other Athenians present included Phaedo and the irrepressible Apollodorus, who cried aloud when Socrates drank the cup and made the rest break down. Plato, however, was kept away by illness. Socrates' wife and children came and went. A few friends from other cities were there, among them Simmias and Cebes of Thebes, who had offered through Crito to share in the expense and risks of Socrates' escape (page 68). These last led in the talk with Socrates while the hours passed. The subject of the talk arose naturally out of what was uppermost in all their minds—the reasons why a philosopher should welcome release from the chain of the body and be certain that his soul was immortal.

The dialogue may well represent truly the grandeur, composure, and reasonableness of Socrates in the face of death and his compassionate concern for his friends whom he wished to fortify with some thing of his own strength. The general drift of the conversation too may actually have been as here described. The philosophical proofs, however, which Socrates brings forward to convince his friends that his soul will not vanish like smoke when his body dies imply at points a more developed theory of the universe as matter and spirit than seems ever to have been really his. Opposites spring from opposites in a never-ending rhythm; hence life must infallibly follow death. The soul knows and remembers ideas, he says later. Ideas are the immortal and unchangeable causes of the world. Hence the soul, that has a vision of immortal things and is a bringer always of life to the body, and that departs when death appears, must itself share in the essence of immortality. These are Platonic arguments, beyond what we know as the reach of Socrates' own thinking. The tale of the judgment of souls in the afterlife is set in a background of physical science, in which, Socrates says earlier, he is no longer interested. Our dialogue then is made up partly, perhaps, of genuine memories of Socrates' last words, as reported to Plato afterward, and partly of Plato's own mature reasons for believing his master right in his confidence that soon he would be meeting the great dead in another and a juster world. The personality of Socrates and the thought of Plato together make the *Phaedo* what it is, an unforgettable picture of one of the noblest scenes in European literature.

PHAEDO

PERSONS OF THE DIALOGUE: *Phaedo (the narrator of the Dialogue), Echecrates of Phlius, Socrates, Apollodorus, Simmias, Cebes, Crito, Attendant of the Prison, Xanthippe*

SCENE: *The Prison of Socrates*

Echecrates speaks:

WERE you yourself, Phaedo, in the prison with Socrates on the day when he drank the poison?

PHAEDO: Yes, Echecrates, I was.

ECHECRATES: I should so like to hear about his death. What did he say in his last hours? We were informed that he died by taking poison, but no one knew anything more; for no Phliasian ever goes to Athens now, and it is a long time since any stranger from Athens has found his way hither; so that we had no clear account.

PHAEDO: Did you not hear of the proceedings at the trial?

ECHECRATES: Yes; someone told us about the trial, and we could not understand why, having been condemned, he should have been put to death, not at the time, but long afterwards. What was the reason of this?

PHAEDO: An accident, Echecrates: the stern of the ship which the Athenians send to Delos happened to have been crowned on the day before he was tried.

ECHECRATES: What is this ship?

PHAEDO: It is the ship in which, according to Athenian tradition, Theseus went to Crete when he took with him the fourteen youths, and was the savior of them and of himself. And they are said to have vowed to Apollo at the time, that if they were saved they would send a yearly mission to Delos. Now this custom still continues, and the whole period of the voyage to and from Delos, beginning when the priest of Apollo crowns the stern of the ship, is a holy season, during which the city is not allowed to be polluted by public executions; and when the vessel is detained by contrary winds, the time spent in going and returning is very considerable. As I was saying, the ship was crowned on the day before the trial, and this was the reason why Socrates lay in prison and was not put to death until long after he was condemned.

ECHECRATES: What was the manner of his death, Phaedo? What was said or done? And which of his friends were with him? Or did the authorities forbid them to be present—so that he had no friends near him when he died?

PHAEDO: No; there were several of them with him.

ECHECRATES: If you have nothing to do, I wish that you would tell me what passed, as exactly as you can.

PHAEDO: I have nothing at all to do, and will try to gratify your wish. To be reminded of Socrates is always the greatest delight to me, whether I speak myself or hear another speak of him.

ECHECRATES: You will have listeners who are of the same mind with you, and I hope that you will be as exact as you can.

PHAEDO: I had a singular feeling at being in his company. For I could hardly believe that I was present at the death of a friend, and therefore I did not pity him, Echecrates; he died so fearlessly, and his words and bearing were so noble and gracious, that to me he appeared blessed. I thought that in going to the other world he could not be without a divine call, and that he would be happy, if any man ever was, when he arrived there; and therefore I did not pity him as might have seemed natural at such an hour. But I had not the pleasure which I usually feel in philosophical discourse (for philosophy was the theme of which we spoke). I was pleased, but in the pleasure there was also a strange admixture of pain; for I reflected that he was soon to die, and this double feeling was shared by us all; we were laughing and weeping by turns, especially the excitable Apollodorus—you know the sort of man?

ECHECRATES: Yes.

PHAEDO: He was quite beside himself; and I and all of us were greatly moved.

ECHECRATES: Who were present?

PHAEDO: Of native Athenians there were, besides Apollodorus, Critobulus and his father Crito, Hermogenes, Epigenes, Aeschines, Antisthenes; likewise Ctesippus of the deme of Paeania, Menexenus, and some others; Plato, if I am not mistaken, was ill.

ECHECRATES: Were there any strangers?

PHAEDO: Yes, there were; Simmias the Theban, and Cebes, and Phaedonides; Euclid and Terpsion, who came from Megara.

ECHECRATES: And was Aristippus there, and Cleombrotus?

PHAEDO: No, they were said to be in Aegina.

ECHECRATES: Any one else?

PHAEDO: I think that these were nearly all.

ECHECRATES: Well, and what did you talk about?

PHAEDO: I will begin at the beginning, and endeavor to repeat the entire conversation. On the previous days we had been in the habit of assembling early in the morning at the court in which the trial took place, and which is not far from the prison. There we used to wait talking with one another until the opening of the doors (for they were not opened very early); then we went in and generally passed the day with Socrates. On the last morning we assembled sooner than usual, having heard on the day before when we quitted the prison in the evening that the sacred ship had come from Delos; and so we arranged to meet very early at the accustomed place. On our arrival the jailer who answered the door, instead of admitting us, came out and told us to stay until he called us. "For the Eleven," [1] he said, "are

1 On the Eleven see *Apology*, note 19.

now with Socrates; they are taking off his chains, and giving orders
that he is to die today." He soon returned and said that we might
come in. On entering we found Socrates just released from chains,
and Xanthippe,[2] whom you know, sitting by him and holding his
child in her arms. When she saw us she uttered a cry and said, as
women will: "O Socrates, this is the last time that either you will
converse with your friends, or they with you." Socrates turned to
Crito and said: "Crito, let someone take her home." Some of Crito's
people accordingly led her away, crying out and beating herself.

And when she was gone, Socrates, sitting up on the couch, bent
and rubbed his leg, saying, as he was rubbing: "How singular is the
thing called pleasure, and how curiously related to pain, which might
be thought to be the opposite of it; for they are never present to a man
at the same instant, and yet he who pursues either is generally compelled to take the other; their bodies are two, but they are joined by a
single head. And I cannot help thinking that if Aesop had remembered them, he would have made a fable about God trying to reconcile their strife, and how, when he could not, he fastened their heads
together; and this is the reason why when one comes the other follows: as I know by my own experience now, when after the pain in
my leg which was caused by the chain pleasure appears to succeed."

Upon this Cebes said: "I am glad, Socrates, that you have mentioned the name of Aesop. For it reminds me of a question which has
been asked by many, and was asked of me only the day before yesterday by Evenus [3] the poet—he will be sure to ask it again, and therefore if you would like me to have an answer ready for him, you may
as well tell me what I should say to him: he wanted to know why
you, who never before wrote a line of poetry, now that you are in
prison are turning Aesop's fables into verse, and also composing that
hymn in honor of Apollo."

"Tell him, Cebes," he replied, "what is the truth—that I had no
idea of rivaling him or his poems; to do so, as I knew, would be no
easy task. But I wanted to see whether I could purge away a scruple

2 The wife of Socrates.
3 See *Apology*, page 36.

which I felt about the meaning of certain dreams. In the course of my life I have often had intimations in dreams that I should compose music. The same dream came to me sometimes in one form, and sometimes in another, but always saying the same or nearly the same words: 'Cultivate and make music,' said the dream. And hitherto I had imagined that this was only intended to exhort and encourage me in the study of philosophy, which has been the pursuit of my life, and is the noblest and best of music. The dream was bidding me do what I was already doing, in the same way that the competitor in a race is bidden by the spectators to run when he is already running. But I was not certain of this; for the dream might have meant music in the popular sense of the word, and being under sentence of death, and the festival giving me a respite, I thought that it would be safer for me to satisfy the scruple, and, in obedience to the dream, to compose a few verses before I departed. And first I made a hymn in honor of the god of the festival, and then considering that a poet, if he is really to be a poet, should not only put together words, but should invent stories, and that I have no invention, I took some fables of Aesop, which I had ready at hand and which I knew—they were the first I came upon—and turned them into verse. Tell this to Evenus, Cebes, and bid him be of good cheer; say that I would have him come after me if he be a wise man, and not tarry; and that today I am likely to be going, for the Athenians say that I must."

Simmias said: "What a message for such a man! Having been a frequent companion of his I should say that, as far as I know him, he will never take your advice unless he is obliged."

"Why," said Socrates, "is not Evenus a philosopher?"

"I think that he is," said Simmias.

"Then he, or any man who has the spirit of philosophy, will be willing to die; but he will not take his own life, for that is held to be unlawful."

Here he changed his position, and put his legs off the couch on to the ground, and during the rest of the conversation he remained sitting.

"Why do you say," inquired Cebes, "that a man ought not to take his own life, but that the philosopher will be ready to follow the dying?"

Socrates replied: "And have you, Cebes and Simmias, who are the disciples of Philolaus,[4] never heard him speak of this?"

"Yes, but his language was obscure, Socrates."

"My words, too, are only an echo; but there is no reason why I should not repeat what I have heard: and indeed, as I am going to another place, it is very meet for me to be thinking and talking of the nature of the pilgrimage which I am about to make. What can I do better in the interval between this and the setting of the sun?"

"Then tell me, Socrates, why is suicide held to be unlawful? as I have certainly heard Philolaus, about whom you were just now asking, affirm when he was staying with us at Thebes; and there are others who say the same, although I have never understood what was meant by any of them."

"Do not lose heart," replied Socrates, "and the day may come when you will understand. I suppose that you wonder why, when other things which are evil may be good at certain times and to certain persons, death is to be the only exception, and why, when a man is better dead, he is not permitted to be his own benefactor, but must wait for the hand of another."

"Very true," said Cebes, laughing gently and speaking in his native Boeotian.[5]

"I admit the appearance of inconsistency in what I am saying; but there may not be any real inconsistency after all. There is a doctrine whispered in secret that man is a prisoner who has no right to open the door and run away; this is a great mystery which I do not quite understand. Yet I too believe that the gods are our guardians, and that we men are a possession of theirs. Do you not agree?"

"Yes, I quite agree," said Cebes.

"And if one of your own possessions, an ox or an ass, for example, took the liberty of putting himself out of the way when you had

---

4 A Pythagorean philosopher of Thebes.

5 Boeotia was the province northwest of Attica, of which Thebes was the chief city. Athenians considered the Boeotian dialect countrified and inelegant.

given no intimation of your wish that he should die, would you not be angry with him, and would you not punish him if you could?"

"Certainly," replied Cebes.

"Then, if we look at the matter thus, there may be reason in saying that a man should wait, and not take his own life until God summons him, as he is now summoning me."

"Yes, Socrates," said Cebes, "there seems to be truth in what you say. And yet how can you reconcile this seemingly true belief that God is our guardian and we his possessions, with the willingness to die which you were just now attributing to the philosopher? That the wisest of men should be willing to leave a service in which they are ruled by the gods, who are the best of rulers, is not reasonable; for surely no wise man thinks that when set at liberty he can take better care of himself than the gods take of him. A fool may perhaps think so—he may argue that he had better run away from his master, not considering that his duty is to remain to the end, and not to run away from the good, and that there would be no sense in his running away. The wise man will want to be ever with him who is better than himself. Now this, Socrates, is the reverse of what was just now said; for upon this view the wise man should sorrow and the fool rejoice at passing out of life."

The earnestness of Cebes seemed to please Socrates. "Here," said he, turning to us, "is a man who is always inquiring, and is not so easily convinced by the first thing which he hears."

"And certainly," added Simmias, "the objection which he is now making does appear to me to have some force. For what can be the meaning of a truly wise man wanting to fly away and lightly leave a master who is better than himself? And I rather imagine that Cebes is referring to you; he thinks that you are too ready to leave us, and too ready to leave the gods whom you acknowledge to be our good masters."

"Yes," replied Socrates; "there is reason in what you say. And so you think that I ought to answer your indictment as if I were in a court?"

"We should like you to do so," said Simmias.

"Then I must try to make a more successful defense before you than I did before the judges. For I am quite ready to admit, Simmias and Cebes, that I ought to be grieved at death, if I were not persuaded in the first place that I am going to other gods who are wise and good (of which I am as certain as I can be of any such matters), and secondly (though I am not so sure of this last) to men departed, better than those whom I leave behind; and therefore I do not grieve as I might have done, for I have good hope that there is yet something remaining for the dead, and as has been said of old, some far better thing for the good than for the evil."

"But do you mean to take away your thoughts with you, Socrates?" said Simmias. "Will you not impart them to us?—for they are a benefit in which we too are entitled to share. Moreover, if you succeed in convincing us, that will be an answer to the charge against yourself."

"I will do my best," replied Socrates. "But you must first let me hear what Crito wants; he has long been wishing to say something to me."

"Only this, Socrates," replied Crito: "the attendant who is to give you the poison has been telling me, and he wants me to tell you, that you are not to talk much; talking, he says, increases heat, and this is apt to interfere with the action of the poison; persons who excite themselves are sometimes obliged to take a second or even a third dose."

"Then," said Socrates, "let him mind his business and be prepared to give the poison twice or even thrice if necessary; that is all."

"I knew quite well what you would say," replied Crito; "but I was obliged to satisfy him."

"Never mind him," he said.

"And now, O my judges, I desire to prove to you that the real philosopher has reason to be of good cheer when he is about to die, and that after death he may hope to obtain the greatest good in the other world. And how this may be, Simmias and Cebes, I will endeavor to explain. For I deem that the true votary of philosophy is likely to be misunderstood by other men; they do not perceive that he is always pursuing death and dying; and if this be so, and he has had the desire of death all his life long, why when his time comes should he repine at that which he has been always pursuing and desiring?"

Simmias said laughingly: "Though not in a laughing humor, you have made me laugh, Socrates; for I cannot help thinking that the many when they hear your words will say how truly you have described philosophers, and our people at home will likewise say that the life which philosophers desire is in reality death, and that they have found them out to be deserving of the death which they desire."

"And they are right, Simmias, in thinking so, with the exception of the words 'they have found them out'; for they have not found out either what is the nature of that death which the true philosopher deserves, or how he deserves or desires death. But enough of them— let us discuss the matter among ourselves. Do we believe that there is such a thing as death?"

"To be sure," replied Simmias.

"Is it not the separation of soul and body? And to be dead is the completion of this; when the soul exists in herself, and is released from the body and the body is released from the soul, what is this but death?"

"Just so," he replied.

"There is another question, which will probably throw light on our present inquiry if you and I can agree about it: Ought the philosopher to care about the pleasures—if they are to be called pleasures —of eating and drinking?"

"Certainly not," answered Simmias.

"And what about the pleasures of love—should he care for them?"

"By no means."

"And will he think much of the other ways of indulging the body, for example, the acquisition of costly raiment, or sandals, or other adornments of the body? Instead of caring about them, does he not rather despise anything more than nature needs? What do you say?"

"I should say that the true philosopher would despise them."

"Would you not say that he is entirely concerned with the soul and not with the body? He would like, as far as he can, to get away from the body and to turn to the soul."

"Quite true."

"In matters of this sort philosophers, above all other men, may be observed in every sort of way to dissever the soul from the communion of the body."

"Very true."

"Whereas, Simmias, the rest of the world are of opinion that to him who has no sense of pleasure and no part in bodily pleasure, life is not worth having; and that he who is indifferent about them is as good as dead."

"That is also true."

"What again shall we say of the actual acquirement of knowledge? Is the body, if invited to share in the inquiry, a hinderer or a helper? I mean to say, have sight and hearing any truth in them? Are they not, as the poets are always telling us, inaccurate witnesses? and yet, if even they are inaccurate and indistinct, what is to be said of the other senses?—for you will allow that they are the best of them?"

"Certainly," he replied.

"Then when does the soul attain truth?—for in attempting to consider anything in company with the body she is obviously deceived."

"True."

"Then must not true existence be revealed to her in thought, if at all?"

"Yes."

"And thought is best when the mind is gathered into herself and none of these things trouble her—neither sounds nor sights nor pain nor any pleasure—when she takes leave of the body, and has as little as possible to do with it, when she has no bodily sense or desire, but is aspiring after true being?"

"Certainly."

"And in this the philosopher dishonors the body; his soul runs away from his body and desires to be alone and by herself?"

"That is true."

"Well, but there is another thing, Simmias: Is there or is there not an absolute justice?"

"Assuredly there is."

"And an absolute beauty and absolute good?"

"Of course."

"But did you ever behold any of them with your eyes?"

"Certainly not."

"Or did you ever reach them with any other bodily sense?—and I speak not of these alone, but of absolute greatness, and health, and strength, and of the essence or true nature of everything. Has the reality of them ever been perceived by you through the bodily organs? or rather, is not the nearest approach to the knowledge of their several natures made by him who so orders his intellectual vision as to have the most exact conception of the essence of each thing which he considers?"

"Certainly."

"And he attains to the purest knowledge of them who goes to each with the mind alone, not introducing or intruding in the act of thought sight or any other sense together with reason, but with the very light of the mind in her own clearness searches into the very truth of each; he who has got rid, as far as he can, of eyes and ears and, so to speak, of the whole body, these being in his opinion distracting elements which when they infect the soul hinder her from acquiring truth and knowledge—who, if not he, is likely to attain to the knowledge of true being?"

"What you say has a wonderful truth in it, Socrates," replied Simmias.

"And when real philosophers consider all these things, will they not be led to make a reflection which they will express in words something like the following? 'Have we not found,' they will say, 'a path of thought which seems to bring us and our argument to the conclusion, that while we are in the body, and while the soul is infected with the evils of the body, our desire will not be satisfied? and our desire is of the truth. For the body is a source of endless trouble to us by reason of the mere requirement of food; and is liable also to diseases which overtake and impede us in the search after true being: it fills us full of loves, and lusts, and fears, and fancies of all kinds, and endless foolery, and in fact, as men say, takes away from us the power of thinking at all. Whence come wars, and fightings, and factions? whence but from the body and the lusts of the body? Wars are occasioned by the love of money, and money has to be acquired for the sake and in the service of the body; and by reason of all these impediments we have no time to give to philosophy; and, last and worst of all, even if we are at leisure and betake ourselves to some speculation, the body is always breaking in upon us, causing turmoil and confusion in our inquiries, and so amazing us that we are prevented from seeing the truth. It has been proved to us by experience that if we would have pure knowledge of anything we must be quit of the body —the soul in herself must behold things in themselves: and then we shall attain the wisdom which we desire, and of which we say that we are lovers; not while we live, but after death; for if while in company with the body, the soul cannot have pure knowledge, one of two things follows—either knowledge is not to be attained at all, or, if at all, after death. For then, and not till then, the soul will be parted from the body and exist in herself alone. In this present life, I reckon that we make the nearest approach to knowledge when we have the least possible intercourse or communion with the body, and are not surfeited with the bodily nature, but keep ourselves pure until the hour when God himself is pleased to release us. And thus having got rid of the foolishness of the body we shall be pure and hold converse with the pure, and know of ourselves the clear light everywhere, which is no other than the light of truth. For the impure are not permitted to approach the pure.' These are the sort of words, Simmias, which the true lovers of knowledge cannot help saying to one another, and thinking. You would agree; would you not?"

"Undoubtedly, Socrates."

"But, O my friend, if this be true, there is great reason to hope that, going whither I go, when I have come to the end of my journey, I shall attain that which has been the pursuit of my life. And therefore I go on my way rejoicing, and not I only, but every other man who believes that his mind has been made ready and that he is in a manner purified."

"Certainly," replied Simmias.

"And what is purification but the separation of the soul from the body, as I was saying before; the habit of the soul gathering and collecting herself into herself from all sides out of the body; the dwelling in her own place alone, as in another life, so also in this, as far as she can; the release of the soul from the chains of the body?"

"Very true," he said.

"And this separation and release of the soul from the body is termed death?"

"To be sure," he said.

"And the true philosophers, and they only, are ever seeking to release the soul. Is not the separation and release of the soul from the body their especial study?"

"That is true."

"And, as I was saying at first, there would be a ridiculous contradiction in men studying to live as nearly as they can in a state of death, and yet repining when it comes upon them."

"Clearly."

"And the true philosophers, Simmias, are always occupied in the practice of dying, wherefore also to them least of all men is death terrible. Look at the matter thus: if they have been in every way the enemies of the body, and are wanting to be alone with the soul, when this desire of theirs is granted, how inconsistent would they be if they trembled and repined, instead of rejoicing at their departure to that place where, when they arrive, they hope to gain that which in life they desired—and this was wisdom—and at the same time to be rid of the company of their enemy. Many a man has been willing to go to the world below animated by the hope of seeing there an earthly love, or wife, or son, and conversing with them. And will he who is a true lover of wisdom, and is strongly persuaded in like manner that only in the world below he can worthily enjoy her, still repine at death? Will he not depart with joy? Surely he will, O my friend, if he be a true philosopher. For he will have a firm conviction that there, and there only, he can find wisdom in her purity. And if this be true, he would be very absurd, as I was saying, if he were afraid of death."

"He would indeed," replied Simmias.

"And when you see a man who is repining at the approach of death, is not his reluctance a sufficient proof that he is not a lover of wisdom, but a lover of the body, and probably at the same time a lover of either money or power, or both?"

"Quite so," he replied.

"And is not courage, Simmias, a quality which is specially characteristic of the philosopher?"

"Certainly."

"There is temperance again, which even by the vulgar is supposed to consist in the control and regulation of the passions, and in the sense of superiority to them—is not temperance a virtue belonging to those only who despise the body, and who pass their lives in philosophy?"

"Most assuredly."

"For the courage and temperance of other men, if you will consider them, are really a contradiction."

"How so?"

"Well," he said, "you are aware that death is regarded by men in general as a great evil."

"Very true," he said.

"And do not courageous men face death because they are afraid of yet greater evils?"

"That is quite true."

"Then all but the philosophers are courageous only from fear, and because they are afraid; and yet that a man should be courageous from fear, and because he is a coward, is surely a strange thing."

"Very true."

"And are not the temperate exactly in the same case? They are temperate because they are intemperate—which might seem to be a contradiction, but is nevertheless the sort of thing which happens with this foolish temperance. For there are pleasures which they are afraid of losing; and in their desire to keep them, they abstain from some pleasures, because they are overcome by others; and although to be conquered by pleasure is called by men intemperance, to them the conquest of pleasure consists in being conquered by pleasure. And that is what I mean by saying that, in a sense, they are made temperate through intemperance."

"Such appears to be the case."

"Yet the exchange of one fear or pleasure or pain for another fear or pleasure or pain, and of the greater for the less, as if they were coins, is not the exchange of virtue. O my blessed Simmias, is there not one true coin for which all things ought to be exchanged?—and that is wisdom; and only in exchange for this, and in company with this, is anything truly bought or sold, whether courage or temperance or justice. And is not all true virtue the companion of wisdom, no matter what fears or pleasures or other similar goods or evils may or may not attend her? But the virtue which is made up of these goods, when they are severed from wisdom and exchanged with one another, is a shadow of virtue only, nor is there any freedom or health or truth in her; but in the true exchange there is a purging away of all these things, and temperance, and justice, and courage, and wisdom herself are the purgation of them. The founders of the mysteries [6] would appear to have had a real meaning, and were not talking nonsense when they intimated in a figure long ago that he who passes unsanctified and uninitiated into the world below will lie in a slough, but that he who arrives there after initiation and purification will dwell with the gods. For 'many,' as they say in the mysteries, 'are the thyrsus-bearers,[7] but few are the mystics'—meaning, as I interpret the words, 'the true philosophers.' In the number of whom, during my whole life, I have been seeking, according to my ability, to find a place; whether I have sought in a right way or not, and whether I have succeeded or not, I shall truly know in a little while, if God will, when I myself arrive in the other world—such is my belief. And therefore I maintain

6 Secret rites connected with the worship of several Greek divinities, to which only the purified and initiated were admitted.

7 The thyrsus was a wand, often wreathed with leaf garlands, carried in religious processions.

that I am right, Simmias and Cebes, in not grieving or repining at parting from you and my masters in this world, for I believe that I shall equally find good masters and friends in another world. But most men do not believe this saying; if then I succeed in convincing you by my defense better than I did the Athenian judges, it will be well."

Cebes answered: "I agree, Socrates, in the greater part of what you say. But in what concerns the soul, men are apt to be incredulous; they fear that when she has left the body her place may be nowhere, and that on the very day of death she may perish and come to an end —immediately on her release from the body, issuing forth dispersed like smoke or air and in her flight vanishing away into nothingness. If she could only be collected into herself after she has obtained release from the evils of which you were speaking, there would be good reason to hope, Socrates, that what you say is true. But surely it requires a great deal of argument and many proofs to show that when the man is dead his soul yet exists, and has any force or intelligence."

"True, Cebes," said Socrates; "and shall I suggest that we converse a little of the probabilities of these things?"

"I am sure," said Cebes, "that I should greatly like to know your opinion about them."

"I reckon," said Socrates, "that no one who heard me now, not even if he were one of my old enemies, the Comic poets,[8] could accuse me of idle talking about matters in which I have no concern. If you please, then, we will proceed with the inquiry.

"Suppose we consider the question whether the souls of men after death are or are not in the world below. There comes into my mind an ancient doctrine which affirms that they go from hence into the other world, and returning hither, are born again from the dead. Now if it be true that the living come from the dead, then our souls must exist in the other world, for if not, how could they have been born again? And this would be conclusive, if there were any real evidence

---

8 In the *Apology* Socrates referred to Aristophanes' caricature of him. Page 35, note 3.

that the living are only born from the dead; but if this is not so, then other arguments will have to be adduced."

"Very true," replied Cebes.

"Then let us consider the whole question, not in relation to man only, but in relation to animals generally, and to plants, and to everything of which there is generation, and the proof will be easier. Are not all things which have opposites generated out of their opposites? I mean such things as good and evil, just and unjust—and there are innumerable other opposites which are generated out of opposites. And I want to show that in all opposites there is of necessity a similar alternation; I mean to say, for example, that anything which becomes greater must become greater after being less."

"True."

"And that which becomes less must have been once greater and then have become less."

"Yes."

"And the weaker is generated from the stronger, and the swifter from the slower."

"Very true."

"And the worse is from the better, and the more just is from the more unjust."

"Of course."

"And is this true of all opposites? and are we convinced that all of them are generated out of opposites?"

"Yes."

"And in this universal opposition of all things, are there not also two intermediate processes which are ever going on, from one to the other opposite, and back again; where there is a greater and a less there is also an intermediate process of increase and diminution, and that which grows is said to wax, and that which decays to wane?"

"Yes," he said.

"And there are many other processes, such as division and composition, cooling and heating, which equally involve a passage into and out of one another. And this necessarily holds of all opposites, even though not always expressed in words—they are really generated out of one another, and there is a passing or process from one to the other of them?"

"Very true," he replied.

"Well, and is there not an opposite of life, as sleep is the opposite of waking?"

"True," he said.

"And what is it?"

"Death," he answered.

"And these, if they are opposites, are generated the one from the other, and have their two intermediate processes also?"

"Of course."

"Now," said Socrates, "I will analyze one of the two pairs of opposites which I have mentioned to you, and also its intermediate processes, and you shall analyze the other to me. One of them I term sleep, the other waking. The state of sleep is opposed to the state of waking, and out of sleeping waking is generated, and out of waking, sleeping; and the process of generation is in the one case falling asleep, and in the other waking up. Do you agree?"

"I entirely agree."

"Then, suppose that you analyze life and death to me in the same manner. Is not death opposed to life?"

"Yes."

"And they are generated one from the other?"

"Yes."

"What is generated from the living?"

"The dead."

"And what from the dead?"

"I can only say in answer—the living."

"Then the living, whether things or persons, Cebes, are generated from the dead?"

"That is clear," he replied.

"Then the inference is that our souls exist in the world below?"

"That is true."

"And one of the two processes or generations is visible—for surely the act of dying is visible?"

"Surely," he said.

"What then is to be the result? Shall we exclude the opposite process? and shall we suppose nature to walk on one leg only? Must we not rather assign to death some corresponding process of generation?"

"Certainly," he replied.

"And what is that process?"

"Return to life."

"And return to life, if there be such a thing, is the birth of the dead into the world of the living?"

"Quite true."

"Then here is a new way by which we arrive at the conclusion that the living come from the dead, just as the dead come from the living; and this, if true, affords a most certain proof that the souls of the dead exist in some place out of which they come again."

"Yes, Socrates," he said; "the conclusion seems to flow necessarily out of our previous admissions."

"And that these admissions were not unfair, Cebes," he said, "may be shown, I think, as follows: If generation were in a straight line only, and there were no compensation or circle in nature, no turn or return of elements into their opposites, then you know that all things would at last have the same form and pass into the same state, and there would be no more generation of them."

"What do you mean?" he said.

"A simple thing enough, which I will illustrate by the case of sleep," he replied. "You know that if there were no alternation of sleeping and waking, the tale of the sleeping Endymion [9] would in the end have no meaning, because all other things would be asleep too, and he would not be distinguishable from the rest. Or if there were composition only, and no division of substances, then the chaos of Anaxagoras [10] would come again. And in like manner, my dear

9 A beautiful youth, who in the myth sleeps forever in a mountain cave, where he is visited at night by the adoring moon.

10 The philosopher Anaxagoras had taught that in the beginning Mind or Intelligence by separating substances had brought form and order into the chaotic universe.

Cebes, if all things which partook of life were to die, and after they were dead remained in the form of death, and did not come to life again, all would at last die, and nothing would be alive—what other result could there be? For if the living spring from any other things, and they too die, must not all things at last be swallowed up in death?"

"There is no escape, Socrates," said Cebes; "and to me your argument seems to be absolutely true."

"Yes," he said, "Cebes, it is and must be so, in my opinion; and we have not been deluded in making these admissions; but I am confident that there truly is such a thing as living again, and that the living spring from the dead, and that the souls of the dead are in existence, and that the good souls have a better portion than the evil."

Cebes added: "Your favorite doctrine, Socrates, that knowledge is simply recollection, if true, also necessarily implies a previous time in which we have learned that which we now recollect. But this would be impossible unless our soul had been in some place before existing in the form of man; here then is another proof of the soul's immortality."

"But tell me, Cebes," said Simmias, interposing, "what arguments are urged in favor of this doctrine of recollection. I am not very sure at the moment that I remember them."

"One excellent proof," said Cebes, "is afforded by questions. If you put a question to a person in a right way, he will give a true answer of himself, but how could he do this unless there were knowledge and right reason already in him? And this is most clearly shown when he is taken to a diagram [11] or to anything of that sort."

"But if," said Socrates, "you are still incredulous, Simmias, I would ask you whether you may not agree with me when you look at the matter in another way—I mean, if you are still incredulous as to whether knowledge is recollection?"

"Incredulous I am not," said Simmias; "but I want to have this

11 In the *Meno,* an earlier dialogue, Plato had represented Socrates as drawing from an untaught slave boy the right answer to a geometrical problem, thus proving, he said, that knowledge is often recollection of things known in a past existence.

doctrine of recollection brought to my own recollection, and, from what Cebes has said, I am beginning to recollect and be convinced: but I should still like to hear what you were going to say."

"This is what I would say," he replied. "We should agree, if I am not mistaken, that what a man recollects he must have known at some previous time."

"Very true."

"And what is the nature of this knowledge or recollection? I mean to ask whether a person who, having seen, or heard, or in any way perceived anything, knows not only that, but has a conception of something else which is the subject, not of the same but of some other kind of knowledge, may not be fairly said to recollect that of which he has the conception?"

"What do you mean?"

"I mean what I may illustrate by the following instance: The knowledge of a lyre is not the same as the knowledge of a man?"

"True."

"And yet what is the feeling of lovers when they recognize a lyre, or a garment, or anything else which the beloved has been in the habit of using? Do not they, from knowing the lyre, form in the mind's eye an image of the youth to whom the lyre belongs? And this is recollection. In like manner anyone who sees Simmias may remember Cebes; and there are endless examples of the same thing."

"Endless, indeed," replied Simmias.

"And recollection is most commonly a process of recovering that which has been already forgotten through time and inattention."

"Very true," he said.

"Well; and may you not also from seeing the picture of a horse or a lyre remember a man? and from the picture of Simmias, you may be led to remember Cebes?"

"True."

"Or you may also be led to the recollection of Simmias himself?"

"Quite so."

"And in all these cases, the recollection may be derived from things either like or unlike?"

"It may be."

"And when the recollection is derived from like things, then another consideration is sure to arise, which is whether the likeness in any degree falls short or not of that which is recollected?"

"Very true," he said.

"And shall we proceed a step further, and affirm that there is such a thing as equality, not of one piece of wood or stone with another, but that, over and above this, there is absolute equality? Shall we say so?"

"Say so, yes," replied Simmias, "and swear to it, with all the confidence in life."

"And do we know the nature of this absolute essence?"

"To be sure," he said.

"And whence did we obtain our knowledge? Did we not see equalities of material things, such as pieces of wood and stones, and gather from them the idea of an equality which is different from them? For you will acknowledge that there is a difference. Or look at the matter in another way: Do not the same pieces of wood or stone appear at one time equal, and at another time unequal?"

"That is certain."

"But are real equals ever unequal? or is the idea of equality the same as of inequality?"

"Impossible, Socrates."

"Then these (so-called) equals are not the same with the idea of equality?"

"I should say, clearly not, Socrates."

"And yet from these equals, although differing from the idea of equality, you conceived and attained that idea?"

"Very true," he said.

"Which might be like, or might be unlike them?"

"Yes."

"But that makes no difference: whenever from seeing one thing you conceived another, whether like or unlike, there must surely have been an act of recollection?"

"Very true."

"But what would you say of equal portions of wood and stone, or other material equals? and what is the impression produced by them? Are they equals in the same sense in which absolute equality is equal? or do they fall short of this perfect equality in a measure?"

"Yes," he said, "in a very great measure too."

"And must we not allow, that when I or anyone, looking at any object, observes that the thing which he sees aims at being some other thing, but falls short of, and cannot be, that other thing, but is inferior, he who makes this observation must have had a previous knowledge of that to which the other, although similar, was inferior?"

"Certainly."

"And has not this been our own case in the matter of equals and of absolute equality?"

"Precisely."

"Then we must have known equality previously to the time when we first saw the material equals, and reflected that all these apparent equals strive to attain absolute equality, but fall short of it?"

"Very true."

"And we recognize also that this absolute equality has only been known, and can only be known, through the medium of sight or touch, or of some other of the senses, which are all alike in this respect?"

"Yes, Socrates, as far as the argument is concerned, one of them is the same as the other."

"From the senses then is derived the knowledge that all sensible things aim at an absolute equality of which they fall short?"

"Yes."

"Then before we began to see or hear or perceive in any way, we must have had a knowledge of absolute equality, or we could not have referred to that standard the equals which are derived from the senses?—for to that they all aspire, and of that they fall short."

"No other inference can be drawn from the previous statements."

"And did we not see and hear and have the use of our other senses as soon as we were born?"

"Certainly."

"Then we must have acquired the knowledge of equality at some previous time?"

"Yes."

"That is to say, before we were born, I suppose?"

"True."

"And if we acquired this knowledge before we were born, and were born having the use of it, then we also knew before we were born and at the instant of birth not only the equal or the greater or the less, but all other ideas; for we are not speaking only of equality, but of beauty, goodness, justice, holiness, and of all which we stamp with the name of essence in the dialectical process, both when we ask and when we answer questions. Of all this we may certainly affirm that we acquired the knowledge before birth?"

"We may."

"But if, after having acquired, we have not forgotten what in each case we acquired, then we must always have come into life having knowledge, and shall always continue to know as long as life lasts—for knowing is the acquiring and retaining knowledge and not forgetting. Is not forgetting, Simmias, just the losing of knowledge?"

"Quite true, Socrates."

"But if the knowledge which we acquired before birth was lost by us at birth, and if afterwards by the use of the senses we recovered what we previously knew, will not the process which we call learning be a recovering of the knowledge which is natural to us, and may not this be rightly termed recollection?"

"Very true."

"So much is clear—that when we perceive something, either by the help of sight, or hearing, or some other sense, from that perception we are able to obtain a notion of some other thing like or unlike which is associated with it but has been forgotten. Whence, as I was saying, one of two alternatives follows: either we had this knowledge at birth, and continued to know through life; or, after birth, those who are said to learn only remember, and learning is simply recollection."

"Yes, that is quite true, Socrates."

"And which alternative, Simmias, do you prefer? Had we the knowledge at our birth, or did we recollect the things which we knew previously to our birth?"

"I cannot decide at the moment."

"At any rate, you can decide whether he who has knowledge will or will not be able to render an account of his knowledge? What do you say?"

"Certainly, he will."

"But do you think that every man is able to give an account of these very matters about which we are speaking?"

"Would that they could, Socrates, but I rather fear that tomorrow, at this time, there will no longer be anyone alive who is able to give an account of them such as ought to be given."

"Then you are not of opinion, Simmias, that all men know these things?"

"Certainly not."

"They are in process of recollecting that which they learned before?"

"Certainly."

"But when did our souls acquire this knowledge? Not since we were born as men?"

"Certainly not."

"And therefore, previously?"

"Yes."

"Then, Simmias, our souls must also have existed without bodies before they were in the form of man, and must have had intelligence."

"Unless indeed you suppose, Socrates, that these notions are given us at the very moment of birth; for this is the only time which remains."

"Yes, my friend, but if so, when do we lose them? for they are not in us when we are born—that is admitted. Do we lose them at the moment of receiving them, or if not at what other time?"

"No, Socrates, I perceive that I was unconsciously talking nonsense."

"Then may we not say, Simmias, that if, as we are always repeating, there is an absolute beauty, and goodness, and an absolute essence of all things; and if to this, which is now discovered to have existed in our former state, we refer all our sensations, and with this compare them, finding these ideas to be pre-existent and our inborn possession—then our souls must have had a prior existence, but if not, there would be no force in the argument? There is the same proof that these ideas must have existed before we were born, as that our souls existed before we were born; and if not the ideas, then not the souls."

"Yes, Socrates; I am convinced that there is precisely the same necessity for the one as for the other; and the argument retreats successfully to the position that the existence of the soul before birth cannot be separated from the existence of the essence of which you speak. For there is nothing which to my mind is so patent as that beauty, goodness, and the other notions of which you were just now speaking have a most real and absolute existence; and I am satisfied with the proof."

"Well, but is Cebes equally satisfied? for I must convince him too."

"I think," said Simmias, "that Cebes is satisfied: although he is the most incredulous of mortals, yet I believe that he is sufficiently convinced of the existence of the soul before birth. But that after death the soul will continue to exist is not yet proven even to my own satisfaction. I cannot get rid of the feeling of the many to which Cebes was referring—the feeling that when the man dies the soul will be dispersed, and that this may be the extinction of her. For admitting that she may have been born elsewhere, and framed out of other elements, and was in existence before entering the human body, why after having entered in and gone out again may she not herself be destroyed and come to an end?"

"Very true, Simmias," said Cebes; "about half of what was required has been proven; to wit, that our souls existed before we were born. That the soul will exist after death as well as before birth is the other half of which the proof is still wanting, and has to be supplied; when that is given the demonstration will be complete."

"But that proof, Simmias and Cebes, has been already given," said Socrates, "if you put the two arguments together—I mean this and the former one, in which we admitted that everything living is born of the dead. For if the soul exists before birth, and in coming to life and being born can be born only from death and dying, must she not after death continue to exist, since she has to be born again? Surely the proof which you desire has been already furnished. Still I suspect that you and Simmias would be glad to probe the argument further. Like children, you are haunted with a fear that when the soul leaves the body, the wind may really blow her away and scatter her; especially if a man should happen to die in a great storm and not when the sky is calm."

Cebes answered with a smile: "Then, Socrates, you must argue us out of our fears—and yet, strictly speaking, they are not our fears, but there is a child within us to whom death is a sort of hobgoblin: him too we must persuade not to be afraid when he is alone in the dark."

Socrates said: "Let the voice of the charmer be applied daily until you have charmed away the fear."

"And where shall we find a good charmer of our fears, Socrates, when you are gone?"

"Hellas," he replied, "is a large place, Cebes, and has many good men, and there are barbarous races not a few: seek for him among them all, far and wide, sparing neither pains nor money; for there is no better way of spending your money. And you must seek among yourselves too; for you will not find others better able to make the search."

"The search," replied Cebes, "shall certainly be made. And now, if you please, let us return to the point of the argument at which we digressed."

"By all means," replied Socrates; "what else should I please?"

"Very good."

"Must we not," said Socrates, "ask ourselves what that is which, as we imagine, is liable to be scattered, and about which we fear? and what again is that about which we have no fear? And then we may proceed further to inquire whether that which suffers dispersion is or is not of the nature of soul—our hopes and fears as to our own souls will turn upon the answers to these questions."

"Very true," he said.

"Now the compound or composite may be supposed to be naturally capable, as of being compounded, so also of being dissolved; but that which is uncompounded, and that only, must be, if anything is, indissoluble."

"Yes; I should imagine so," said Cebes.

"And the uncompounded may be assumed to be the same and unchanging, whereas the compound is always changing and never the same."

"I agree," he said.

"Then now let us return to the previous discussion. Is that idea or essence, which in the dialectical process we define as essence or true existence—whether essence of equality, beauty, or anything else—are these essences, I say, liable at times to some degree of change? or are they each of them always what they are, having the same simple self-existent and unchanging forms, not admitting of variation at all, or in any way, or at any time?"

"They must be always the same, Socrates," replied Cebes.

"And what would you say of the many beautiful—whether men or horses or garments or any other things which are named by the same names and may be called equal or beautiful—are they all unchanging and the same always, or quite the reverse? May they not rather be described as almost always changing and hardly ever the same, either with themselves or with one another?"

"The latter," replied Cebes; "they are always in a state of change."

"And these you can touch and see and perceive with the senses, but the unchanging things you can only perceive with the mind—they are invisible and are not seen?"

"That is very true," he said.

"Well then," added Socrates, "let us suppose that there are two sorts of existences—one seen, the other unseen."

"Let us suppose them."

"The seen is the changing, and the unseen is the unchanging?"

"That may be also supposed."

"And, further, is not one part of us body, another part soul?"

"To be sure."

"And to which class is the body more alike and akin?"

"Clearly to the seen—no one can doubt that."

"And is the soul seen or not seen?"

"Not by man, Socrates."

"And what we mean by 'seen' and 'not seen' is that which is or is not visible to the eye of man?"

"Yes, to the eye of man."

"And is the soul seen or not seen?"

"Not seen."

"Unseen then?"

"Yes."

"Then the soul is more like to the unseen, and the body to the seen?"

"That follows necessarily, Socrates."

"And were we not saying long ago that the soul, when using the body as an instrument of perception, that is to say, when using the sense of sight or hearing or some other sense (for the meaning of perceiving through the body is perceiving through the senses)—were we not saying that the soul too is then dragged by the body into the region of the changeable, and wanders and is confused; the world spins round her, and she is like a drunkard, when she touches change?"

"Very true."

"But when returning into herself she reflects, then she passes into the other world, the region of purity, and eternity, and immortality, and unchangeableness, which are her kindred, and with them she ever lives, when she is by herself and is not let or hindered; then she ceases from her erring ways, and being in communion with the unchanging is unchanging. And this state of the soul is called wisdom?"

"That is well and truly said, Socrates," he replied.

"And to which class is the soul more nearly alike and akin, as far as may be inferred from this argument, as well as from the preceding one?"

"I think, Socrates, that, in the opinion of everyone who follows the argument, the soul will be infinitely more like the unchangeable —even the most stupid person will not deny that."

"And the body is more like the changing?"

"Yes."

"Yet once more consider the matter in another light. When the soul and the body are united, then nature orders the soul to rule and govern, and the body to obey and serve. Now which of these two functions is akin to the divine? and which to the mortal? Does not the divine appear to you to be that which naturally orders and rules, and the mortal to be that which is subject and servant?"

"True."

"And which does the soul resemble?"

"The soul resembles the divine, and the body the mortal—there can be no doubt of that, Socrates."

"Then reflect, Cebes: of all which has been said is not this the conclusion?—that the soul is in the very likeness of the divine, and immortal, and intellectual, and uniform, and indissoluble, and unchangeable; and that the body is in the very likeness of the human, and mortal, and unintellectual, and multiform, and dissoluble, and changeable. Can this, my dear Cebes, be denied?"

"It cannot."

"But if it be true, then is not the body liable to speedy dissolution? and is not the soul almost or altogether indissoluble?"

"Certainly."

"And do you further observe, that after a man is dead, the body, or visible part of him, which is lying in the visible world, and is called a corpse, and would naturally be dissolved and decomposed and dissipated, is not dissolved or decomposed at once, but may remain for some time, nay even for a long time, if the constitution be sound at the time of death, and the season of the year favorable? For the body, when shrunk and embalmed, as the manner is in Egypt, may remain almost entire through infinite ages; and even in decay, there are still some portions, such as the bones and ligaments, which are practically indestructible. Do you agree?"

"Yes."

"And is it likely that the soul, which is invisible, in passing to the place of the true Hades, which like her is invisible, and pure, and noble, and on her way to the good and wise God, whither, if God will, my soul is also soon to go—that the soul, I repeat, if this be her nature and origin, will be blown away and destroyed immediately on quitting the body, as the many say? That can never be, my dear Simmias and Cebes. The truth rather is, that the soul which is pure at departing and draws after her no bodily taint, having never voluntarily during life had connection with the body, which she is ever avoiding, herself gathered into herself; and making such abstraction her perpetual study—which means that she has been a true disciple of philosophy; and therefore has in fact been always engaged in the practice of dying—for is not philosophy the study of death?"

"Certainly."

"That soul, I say, herself invisible, departs to the invisible world —to the divine and immortal and rational: thither arriving, she is secure of bliss and is released from the error and folly of men, their fears and wild passions and all other human ills, and forever dwells, as they say of the initiated, in company with the gods. Is not this true, Cebes?"

"Yes," said Cebes, "beyond a doubt."

"But the soul which has been polluted, and is impure at the time of her departure, and is the companion and servant of the body always, and is in love with and fascinated by the body and by the desires and pleasures of the body, until she is led to believe that the truth only exists in a bodily form, which a man may touch and see and taste, and use for the purposes of his lusts—the soul, I mean, accustomed to hate and fear and avoid the intellectual principle, which to the bodily eye is dark and invisible, and can be attained only by philosophy— do you suppose that such a soul will depart pure and unalloyed?"

"Impossible," he replied.

"She is held fast by the corporeal, which the continual association and constant care of the body have wrought into her nature."

"Very true."

"And this corporeal element, my friend, is heavy and weighty and earthy, and is that element of sight by which a soul is depressed and dragged down again into the visible world, because she is afraid of the invisible and of the world below—prowling about tombs and sepulchers, near which, as they tell us, are seen certain ghostly apparitions of souls which have not departed pure, but are cloyed with sight and therefore visible."

"That is very likely, Socrates."

"Yes, that is very likely, Cebes; and these must be the souls, not of the good, but of the evil, which are compelled to wander about such places in payment of the penalty of their former evil way of life; and they continue to wander until, through the craving after the corporeal which never leaves them, they are imprisoned finally in another body. And they may be supposed to find their prisons in the same natures which they have had in their former lives."

"What natures do you mean, Socrates?"

"What I mean is that men who have followed after gluttony, and wantonness, and drunkenness, and have had no thought of avoiding them, would pass into asses and animals of that sort. What do you think?"

"I think such an opinion to be exceedingly probable."

"And those who have chosen the portion of injustice, and tyranny, and violence, will pass into wolves, or into hawks and kites—whither else can we suppose them to go?"

"Yes," said Cebes; "with such natures, beyond question."

"And there is no difficulty," he said, "in assigning to all of them places answering to their several natures and propensities?"

"There is not," he said.

"Some are happier than others; and the happiest both in themselves and in the place to which they go are those who have practiced the civil and social virtues which are called temperance and justice, and are acquired by habit and attention without philosophy and mind."

"Why are they the happiest?"

"Because they may be expected to pass into some gentle and social kind which is like their own, such as bees or wasps or ants, or back again into the form of man, and just and moderate men may be supposed to spring from them."

"Very likely."

"No one who has not studied philosophy and who is not entirely pure at the time of his departure is allowed to enter the company of the gods, but the lover of knowledge only. And this is the reason, Simmias and Cebes, why the true votaries of philosophy abstain from all fleshly lusts, and hold out against them and refuse to give themselves up to them—not because they fear poverty or the ruin of their families, like the lovers of money, and the world in general; nor like the lovers of power and honor, because they dread the dishonor or disgrace of evil deeds."

"No, Socrates, that would not become them," said Cebes.

"No, indeed," he replied; "and therefore they who have any care of their own souls, and do not merely live molding and fashioning the body, say farewell to all this; they will not walk in the ways of the blind: and when philosophy offers them purification and release from evil, they feel that they ought not to resist her influence, and whither she leads they turn and follow."

"What do you mean, Socrates?"

"I will tell you," he said. "The lovers of knowledge are conscious that the soul was simply fastened and glued to the body—until philosophy received her, she could only view real existence through the bars of a prison, not in and through herself; she was wallowing in the mire of every sort of ignorance, and by reason of lust had become the principal accomplice in her own captivity. This was her original state; and then, as I was saying, and as the lovers of knowledge are well aware, philosophy, seeing how terrible was her confinement, of which she was to herself the cause, received and gently comforted her and sought to release her, pointing out that the eye and the ear and the other senses are full of deception, and persuading her to retire from them, and abstain from all but the necessary use of them, and be gathered up and collected into herself, bidding her trust in herself and her own pure apprehension of pure existence, and to mistrust whatever comes to her through other channels and is subject to variation; for such things are visible and tangible, but what she sees in her own nature is intelligible and invisible. And the soul of the true philosopher thinks that she ought not to resist this deliverance, and therefore abstains from pleasures and desires and pains and fears, as far as she is able; reflecting that when a man has great joys or sorrows or fears or desires, he suffers from them, not merely the sort of evil which might be anticipated—as for example, the loss of his health or property which he has sacrificed to his lusts—but an evil greater far, which is the greatest and worst of all evils, and one of which he never thinks."

"What is it, Socrates?" said Cebes.

"The evil is that when the feeling of pleasure or pain is most intense, every soul of man imagines the objects of this intense feeling to be then plainest and truest: but this is not so, they are really the things of sight."

"Very true."

"And is not this the state in which the soul is most enthralled by the body?"

"How so?"

"Why, because each pleasure and pain is a sort of nail which nails and rivets the soul to the body, until she becomes like the body, and believes that to be true which the body affirms to be true; and from agreeing with the body and having the same delights she is obliged to have the same habits and haunts, and is not likely ever to be pure at her departure to the world below, but is always infected by the body; and so she sinks into another body and there germinates and grows, and has therefore no part in the communion of the divine and pure and simple."

"Most true, Socrates," answered Cebes.

"And this, Cebes, is the reason why the true lovers of knowledge are temperate and brave; and not for the reason which the world gives."

"Certainly not."

"Certainy not! The soul of a philosopher will reason in quite another way; she will not ask philosophy to release her in order that
when released she may deliver herself up again to the thralldom of
pleasures and pains, doing a work only to be undone again, weaving
instead of unweaving her Penelope's web.12 But she will calm passion, and follow reason, and dwell in the contemplation of her, beholding the true and divine (which is not matter of opinion), and
thence deriving nourishment. Thus she seeks to live while she lives,
and after death she hopes to go to her own kindred and to that which
is like her, and to be freed from human ills. Never fear, Simmias and
Cebes, that a soul which has been thus nurtured and has had these
pursuits, will at her departure from the body he scattered and blown
away by the winds and be nowhere and nothing."

When Socrates had done speaking, for a considerable time there
was silence; he himself appeared to be meditating, as most of us were,
on what had been said; only Cebes and Simmias spoke a few words
to one another. And Socrates observing them asked what they thought
of the argument, and whether there was anything wanting? "For,"
said he, "there are many points still open to suspicion and attack, if
anyone were disposed to sift the matter thoroughly. Should you be
considering some other matter I say no more, but if you are still in
doubt do not hesitate to say exactly what you think, and let us have
anything better which you can suggest; and if you think that I can be
of any use, allow me to help you."

Simmias said: "I must confess, Socrates, that doubts did arise in
our minds, and each of us was urging and inciting the other to put the
question which we wanted to have answered but which neither of us
liked to ask, fearing that our importunity might be troublesome at
such a time."

Socrates replied with a smile: "O Simmias, what are you saying? I
am not very likely to persuade other men that I do not regard my

<hr/>

12 In the *Odyssey*, Homer tells how Penelope, the wife of Odysseus, as a device
to keep her suitors at bay, pulled out every night on her loom what she had woven
by day. XIX, 130-150.

present situation as a misfortune, if I cannot even persuade you that I am no worse off now than at any other time in my life. Will you not allow that I have as much of the spirit of prophecy in me as the swans? For they, when they perceive that they must die, having sung all their life long, do then sing more lustily than ever, rejoicing in the thought that they are about to go away to the god whose ministers they are. But men, because they are themselves afraid of death, slanderously affirm of the swans that they sing a lament at the last, not considering that no bird sings when cold, or hungry, or in pain, not even the nightingale, nor the swallow, nor yet the hoopoe; which are said indeed to tune a lay of sorrow, although I do not believe this to be true of them any more than of the swans. But because they are sacred to Apollo, they have the gift of prophecy, and anticipate the good things of another world; wherefore they sing and rejoice in that day more than ever they did before. And I too, believing myself to be the consecrated servant of the same God, and the fellow servant of the swans, and thinking that I have received from my master gifts of prophecy which are not inferior to theirs, would not go out of life less merrily than the swans. Never mind then, if this be your only objection, but speak and ask anything which you like, while the eleven magistrates of Athens allow it."

"Very good, Socrates," said Simmias; "then I will tell you my difficulty, and Cebes will tell you his. I feel myself (and I daresay that you have the same feeling), how hard or rather impossible is the attainment of any certainty about questions such as these in the present life. And yet I should deem him a coward who did not prove what is said about them to the uttermost, or whose heart failed him before he had examined them on every side. For he should persevere until he has achieved one of two things: either he should discover, or be taught the truth about them; or, if this be impossible, I would have him take the best and most irrefragable of human theories and let this be the raft upon which he sails through life—not without risk, as I admit, if he cannot find some word of God which will more surely and safely carry him. And now, as you bid me, I will venture to question you, and then I shall not have to reproach myself here-

after with not having said at the time what I think. For when I consider the matter, either alone or with Cebes, the argument does certainly appear to me, Socrates, to be not sufficient."

Socrates answered: "I dare say, my friend, that you may be right,
but I should like to know in what respect the argument is insuffi-
cient."

"In this respect," replied Simmias. "Suppose a person to use the
same argument about harmony and the lyre—might he not say that
harmony is a thing invisible, incorporeal, perfect, divine, existing in
the lyre which is harmonized, but that the lyre and the strings are
matter and material, composite, earthy, and akin to mortality? And
when someone breaks the lyre, or cuts and rends the strings, then he
who takes this view would argue as you do, and on the same analogy,
that the harmony survives and has not perished—you cannot imagine,
he would say, that the lyre without the strings, and the broken strings
themselves which are mortal remain, and yet that the harmony,
which is of heavenly and immortal nature and kindred, has perished
—perished before the mortal. The harmony must still be somewhere,
and the wood and strings will decay before anything can happen to
that. The thought, Socrates, must have occurred to your own mind
that such is our conception of the soul; and that when the body is in
a manner strung and held together by the elements of hot and cold,
wet and dry, then the soul is the harmony or due proportionate admixture of them. But if so, whenever the strings of the body are un-
duly loosened or overstrained through disease or other injury, then
the soul, though most divine, like other harmonies of music or of
works of art, of course perishes at once; although the material remains
of the body may last for a considerable time, until they are either
decayed or burnt. And if anyone maintains that the soul, being the
harmony of the elements of the body, is first to perish in that which
is called death, how shall we answer him?"

Socrates looked fixedly at us as his manner was, and said with a
smile: "Simmias has reason on his side; and why does not some one
of you who is better able than myself answer him? for there is force
in his attack upon me. But perhaps, before we answer him, we had

better also hear what Cebes has to say, that we may gain time for reflection, and when they have both spoken, we may either assent to them, if there is truth in what they say, or if not, we will maintain our position. Please to tell me then, Cebes," he said, "what was the difficulty which troubled you?"

Cebes said: "I will tell you. My feeling is that the argument is where it was, and open to the same objections which were urged before; for I am ready to admit that the existence of the soul before entering into the bodily form has been very ingeniously, and, if I may say so, quite sufficiently proven; but the existence of the soul after death is still, in my judgment, unproven. Now my objection is not the same as that of Simmias; for I am not disposed to deny that the soul is stronger and more lasting than the body, being of opinion that in all such respects the soul very far excels the body. Well then, says the argument to me, why do you remain unconvinced? When you see that the weaker continues in existence after the man is dead, will you not admit that the more lasting must also survive during the same period of time? Now I will ask you to consider whether the objection, which, like Simmias, I will express in a figure, is of any weight. The analogy which I will adduce is that of an old weaver, who dies, and after his death somebody says: 'He is not dead, he must be alive—see, there is the coat which he himself wove and wore, and which remains whole and undecayed.' And then he proceeds to ask of some one who is incredulous, whether a man lasts longer, or the coat which is in use and wear; and when he is answered that a man lasts far longer, thinks that he has thus certainly demonstrated the survival of the man, who is the more lasting, because the less lasting remains. But that, Simmias, as I would beg you to remark, is a mistake; anyone can see that he who talks thus is talking nonsense. For the truth is, that the weaver aforesaid, having woven and worn many such coats, outlived several of them; and was outlived by the last; but a man is not therefore proved to be slighter and weaker than a coat. Now the relation of the body to the soul may be expressed in a similar figure; and anyone may very fairly say in like manner that the soul is lasting, and the body weak and shortlived in comparison.

He may argue in like manner that every soul wears out many bodies, especially if a man live many years. While he is alive the body deliquesces and decays, and the soul always weaves another garment and repairs the waste. But of course, whenever the soul perishes, she must have on her last garment, and this will survive her; and then at length, when the soul is dead, the body will show its native weakness, and quickly decompose and pass away. I would therefore rather not rely on the argument from superior strength to prove the continued existence of the soul after death. For granting even more than you affirm to be possible, and acknowledging not only that the soul existed before birth, but also that the souls of some exist, and will continue to exist after death, and will be born and die again and again, and that there is a natural strength in the soul which will hold out and be born many times—nevertheless, we may be still inclined to think that she will weary in the labors of successive births, and may at last succumb in one of her deaths and utterly perish; and this death and dissolution of the body which brings destruction to the soul may be unknown to any of us, for no one of us can have had any experience of it: and if so, then I maintain that he who is confident about death has but a foolish confidence, unless he is able to prove that the soul is altogether immortal and imperishable. But if he cannot prove the soul's immortality, he who is about to die will always have reason to fear that when the body is disunited, the soul also may utterly perish."

All of us, as we afterwards remarked to one another, had an unpleasant feeling at hearing what they said. When we had been so firmly convinced before, now to have our faith shaken seemed to introduce a confusion and uncertainty, not only into the previous argument, but into any future one; either we were incapable of forming a judgment, or there were no grounds of belief.

ECHECRATES: There I feel with you—by heaven I do, Phaedo, and when you were speaking, I was beginning to ask myself the same question: What argument can I ever trust again? For what could be more convincing than the argument of Socrates, which has now fallen into discredit? That the soul is a harmony is a doctrine which has always had a wonderful attraction for me, and, when mentioned, came back to me at once, as my own original conviction. And now I must begin again and find another argument which will assure me that when the man is dead the soul survives. Tell me, I implore you, how did Socrates proceed? Did he appear to share the unpleasant feeling which you mention? Or did he calmly meet the attack? And did he answer forcibly or feebly? Narrate what passed as exactly as you can.

PHAEDO: Often, Echecrates, I have wondered at Socrates, but never more than on that occasion. That he should be able to answer was nothing, but what astonished me was, first, the gentle and pleasant and approving manner in which he received the words of the young men, and then his quick sense of the wound which had been inflicted by the argument, and the readiness with which he healed it. He might be compared to a general rallying his defeated and broken army, urging them to accompany him and return to the field of argument.

ECHECRATES: What followed?

PHAEDO: You shall hear, for I was close to him on his right hand, seated on a sort of stool, and he on a couch which was a good deal higher. He stroked my head, and pressed the hair upon my neck—he had a way of playing with my hair—and then he said: "Tomorrow, Phaedo, I suppose that these fair locks of yours will be severed." [13]

"Yes, Socrates, I suppose that they will," I replied.

"Not so, if you will take my advice."

"What shall I do with them?" I said.

"Today," he replied, "and not tomorrow, if this argument dies and we cannot bring it to life again, you and I will both shave our locks: and if I were you, and the argument got away from me, and I could not hold my ground against Simmias and Cebes, I would myself take an oath, like the Argives, not to wear hair any more until I had renewed the conflict and defeated them."

[13] A custom of many ancient peoples, to cut off the hair in sign of mourning.

"Yes," I said; "but Heracles himself is said not to be a match for two."

"Summon me then," he said, "and I will be your Iolaus [14] until the sun goes down."

"I summon you rather," I rejoined, "not as Heracles summoning Iolaus, but as Iolaus might summon Heracles."

"That will do as well," he said. "But first let us take care that we avoid a danger."

"Of what nature?" I said.

"Lest we become misologists," [15] he replied; "no worse thing can happen to a man than this. For as there are misanthropists or haters of men, there are also misologists or haters of ideas, and both spring from the same cause, which is ignorance of the world. Misanthropy arises out of the too great confidence of inexperience; you trust a man and think him altogether true and sound and faithful, and then in a little while he turns out to be false and knavish; and then another and another, and when this has happened several times to a man, especially when it happens among those whom he deems to be his own most trusted and familiar friends, and he has often quarreled with them, he at last hates all men, and believes that no one has any good in him at all. You must have observed this trait of character?"

"I have."

"And is not the feeling discreditable? Is it not obvious that such a one, having to deal with other men, was clearly without any experience of human nature; for experience would have taught him the true state of the case, that few are the good and few the evil, and that the great majority are in the interval between them."

"What do you mean?" I said.

"I mean," he replied, "as you might say of the very large and very small—that nothing is more uncommon than a very large or very small man; and this applies generally to all extremes, whether of great and small, or swift and slow, or fair and foul, or black and white: and whether the instances you select be men or dogs or anything else, few are the extremes, but many are in the mean between them. Did you never observe this?"

"Yes," I said, "I have."

"And do you not imagine," he said, "that if there were a competition in evil, the worst would be found to be very few?"

"Yes, that is very likely," I said.

"Yes, that is very likely," he replied; "although in this respect arguments are unlike men—there I was led on by you to say more than I had intended; but the point of comparison was that when a simple man who has no skill in dialectics believes an argument to be true which he afterwards imagines to be false, whether really false or not, and then another and another, he has no longer any faith left, and great disputers, as you know, come to think at last that they have grown to be the wisest of mankind; for they alone perceive the utter unsoundness and instability of all arguments, or indeed, of all things, which, like the currents in the Euripus,[16] are going up and down in never-ceasing ebb and flow."

"That is quite true," I said.

"Yes, Phaedo," he replied, "and how melancholy, if there be such a thing as truth or certainty or possibility of knowledge, that a man should have lighted upon some argument or other which at first seemed true and then turned out to be false, and instead of blaming himself and his own want of wit, because he is annoyed, should at last be too glad to transfer the blame from himself to arguments in general: and forever afterwards should hate and revile them, and lose truth and the knowledge of realities."

"Yes, indeed," I said; "that is very melancholy."

"Let us then, in the first place," he said, "be careful of allowing or of admitting into our souls the notion that there is no health or soundness in any arguments at all. Rather say that we have not yet attained to soundness in ourselves, and that we must struggle manfully and do our best to gain health of mind—you and all other men

16 A narrow strait between the island of Euboea and the Greek mainland, through which the tides swirl constantly in and out.

having regard to the whole of your future life, and I myself in the prospect of death. For at this moment I am sensible that I have not the temper of a philosopher; like the vulgar, I am only a partisan. Now the partisan, when he is engaged in a dispute, cares nothing about the rights of the question, but is anxious only to convince his hearers of his own assertions. And the difference between him and me at the present moment is merely this—that whereas he seeks to convince his hearers that what he says is true, I am rather seeking to convince myself; to convince my hearers is a secondary matter with me. And do but see how much I gain by the argument. For if what I say is true, then I do well to be persuaded of the truth; but if there be nothing after death, still, during the short time that remains, I shall not distress my friends with lamentations, and my ignorance will not last, but will die with me, and therefore no harm will be done. This is the state of mind, Simmias and Cebes, in which I approach the argument. And I would ask you to be thinking of the truth and not of Socrates: agree with me, if I seem to you to be speaking the truth; or if not, withstand me might and main, that I may not deceive you as well as myself in my enthusiasm, and like the bee, leave my sting in you before I die.

"And now let us proceed," he said. "And first of all let me be sure that I have in my mind what you were saying. Simmias, if I remember rightly, has fears and misgivings whether the soul, although a fairer and diviner thing than the body, being as she is in the form of harmony, may not perish first. On the other hand, Cebes appeared to grant that the soul was more lasting than the body, but he said that no one could know whether the soul, after having worn out many bodies, might not perish herself and leave her last body behind her; and that this is death, which is the destruction not of the body but of the soul, for in the body the work of destruction is ever going on. Are not these, Simmias and Cebes, the points which we have to consider?"

They both agreed to this statement of them.

He proceeded: "And did you deny the force of the whole preceding argument, or of a part only?"

"Of a part only," they replied.

"And what did you think," he said, "of that part of the argument in which we said that knowledge was recollection, and hence inferred that the soul must have previously existed somewhere else before she was enclosed in the body?"

Cebes said that he had been wonderfully impressed by that part of the argument, and that his conviction remained absolutely unshaken. Simmias agreed, and added that he himself could hardly imagine the possibility of his ever thinking differently.

"But," rejoined Socrates, "you will have to think differently, my Theban friend, if you still maintain that harmony is a compound, and that the soul is a harmony which is made out of strings set in the frame of the body; for you will surely never allow yourself to say that a harmony is prior to the elements which compose it."

"Never, Socrates."

"But do you not see that this is what you imply when you say that the soul existed before she took the form and body of man, and was made up of elements which as yet had no existence? For harmony is not like the soul, as you suppose; but first the lyre, and the strings, and the sounds exist in a state of discord, and then harmony is made last of all, and perishes first. And how can such a notion of the soul as this agree with the other?"

"Not at all," replied Simmias.

"And yet," he said, "there surely ought to be harmony in a discourse of which harmony is the theme?"

"There ought," replied Simmias.

"But there is no harmony," he said, "in the two propositions that knowledge is recollection, and that the soul is a harmony. Which of them will you retain?"

"I think," he replied, "that I have a much stronger faith, Socrates, in the first of the two, which has been fully demonstrated to me, than in the latter, which has not been demonstrated at all, but rests only on probable and plausible grounds; and is therefore believed by the many. I know too well that these arguments from probabilities are impostors, and unless great caution is observed in the use of them, they are apt to be deceptive—in geometry, and in other things too. But the doctrine of knowledge and recollection has been proven to me on trustworthy grounds: and the proof was that the soul must have existed before she came into the body, because to her belongs the essence of which the very name implies existence. Having, as I am convinced, rightly accepted this conclusion, and on sufficient grounds, I must, as I suppose, cease to argue or allow others to argue that the soul is a harmony."

"Let me put the matter, Simmias," he said, "in another point of view: Do you imagine that a harmony or any other composition can be in a state other than that of the elements, out of which it is compounded?"

"Certainly not."

"Or do or suffer anything other than they do or suffer?"

He agreed.

"Then a harmony does not, properly speaking, lead the parts or elements which make up the harmony, but only follows them."

He assented.

"For harmony cannot possibly have any motion, or sound, or other quality which is opposed to its parts."

"That would be impossible," he replied.

"And does not the nature of every harmony depend upon the manner in which the elements are harmonized?"

"I do not understand you," he said.

"I mean to say that a harmony admits of degrees, and is more of a harmony, and more completely a harmony, when more truly and fully harmonized, to any extent which is possible; and less of a harmony, and less completely a harmony, when less truly and fully harmonized."

"True."

"But does the soul admit of degrees? Or is one soul in the very least degree more or less, or more or less completely a soul than another?"

"Not in the least."

"Yet surely of two souls, one is said to have intelligence and virtue, and to be good, and the other to have folly and vice, and to be an evil soul: and this is said truly?"

"Yes, truly."

"But what will those who maintain the soul to be a harmony say of this presence of virtue and vice in the soul? Will they say that here is another harmony, and another discord, and that the virtuous soul is harmonized, and herself being a harmony has another harmony within her, and that the vicious soul is inharmonical and has no harmony within her?"

"I cannot tell," replied Simmias; "but I suppose that something of the sort would be asserted by those who say that the soul is a harmony."

"And we have already admitted that no soul is more a soul than another; which is equivalent to admitting that harmony is not more or less harmony, or more or less completely a harmony?"

"Quite true."

"And that which is not more or less a harmony is not more or less harmonized?"

"True."

"And that which is not more or less harmonized cannot have more or less of harmony, but only an equal harmony?"

"Yes, an equal harmony."

"Then one soul, not being more or less absolutely a soul than another, is not more or less harmonized?"

"Exactly."

"And therefore has neither more nor less of discord, nor yet of harmony?"

"She has not."

"And having neither more nor less of harmony or of discord, one soul has no more vice or virtue than another, if vice be discord and virtue harmony?"

"Not at all more."

"Or speaking more correctly, Simmias, the soul, if she is a harmony, will never have any vice; because a harmony, being absolutely a harmony, has no part in the inharmonical."

"No."

"And therefore a soul which is absolutely a soul has no vice?"

"How can she have, if the previous argument holds?"

"Then, if all souls are equally by their nature souls, all souls of all living creatures will be equally good?"

"I agree with you, Socrates," he said.

"And can all this be true, think you?" he said; "for these are the consequences which seem to follow from the assumption that the soul is a harmony?"

"It cannot be true."

"Once more," he said, "what ruler is there of the elements of human nature other than the soul, and especially the wise soul? Do you know of any?"

"Indeed, I do not."

"And is the soul in agreement with the affections of the body, or is she at variance with them? For example, when the body is hot and thirsty, does not the soul incline us against drinking? And when the body is hungry, against eating? And this is only one instance out of ten thousand of the opposition of the soul to the things of the body."

"Very true."

"But we have already acknowledged that the soul, being a harmony, can never utter a note at variance with the tensions and relaxations and vibrations and other affections of the strings out of which she is composed; she can only follow, she cannot lead them?"

"It must be so," he replied.

"And yet do we not now discover the soul to be doing the exact opposite—leading the elements of which she is believed to be composed; almost always opposing and coercing them in all sorts of ways throughout life, sometimes more violently with the pains of medicine and gymnastic; then again more gently; now threatening, now admonishing the desires, passions, fears, as if talking to a thing which is not herself, as Homer in the Odyssey represents Odysseus doing in the words—

He beat his breast, and thus reproached his heart:
Endure, my heart; far worse hast thou endured! [17]

Do you think that Homer wrote this under the idea that the soul is a harmony capable of being led by the affections of the body, and not rather of a nature which should lead and master them—herself a far diviner thing than any harmony?"

"Yes, Socrates, I quite think so."

"Then, my friend, we can never be right in saying that the soul is a harmony, for we should contradict the divine Homer, and contradict ourselves."

"True," he said.

"Thus much," said Socrates, "of Harmonia, your Theban goddess, who has graciously yielded to us; but what shall I say, Cebes, to her husband Cadmus,[18] and how shall I make peace with him?"

"I think that you will discover a way of propitiating him," said Cebes; "I am sure that you have put the argument with Harmonia in a manner that I could never have expected. For when Simmias was mentioning his difficulty, I quite imagined that no answer could be given to him, and therefore I was surprised at finding that his argument could not sustain the first onset of yours, and not impossibly the other, whom you call Cadmus, may share a similar fate."

"Nay, my good friend," said Socrates, "let us not boast, lest some evil eye should put to flight the word which I am about to speak. That, however, may be left in the hands of those above; while I draw near in Homeric fashion, and try the mettle of your words. Here lies the point: You want to have it proven to you that the soul is imperishable and immortal, and the philosopher who is confident in death appears to you to have but a vain and foolish confidence, if he believes that he will fare better in the world below than one who has led another sort of life, unless he can prove this: and you say that the demonstration of the strength and divinity of the soul, and

17 *Odyssey*, XX, 17, 18.
18 The fabulous first king of Thebes and inventor of the Greek alphabet. Socrates is playfully speaking of Simmias and Cebes, the Thebans, as mouthpieces respectively of the Theban goddess of music and the Theban king of letters.

of her existence prior to our becoming men, does not necessarily imply her immortality. Admitting the soul to be long-lived, and to have known and done much in a former state, still she is not on that account immortal; and her entrance into the human form may be a sort of disease which is the beginning of dissolution, and may at last, after the toils of life are over, end in that which is called death. And whether the soul enters into the body once only or many times, does not, as you say, make any difference in the fears of individuals. For any man, who is not devoid of sense, must fear, if he has no knowledge and can give no account of the soul's immortality. This, or something like this, I suspect to be your notion, Cebes; and I designedly recur to it in order that nothing may escape us, and that you may, if you wish, add or subtract anything."

"But," said Cebes, "as far as I see at present, I have nothing to add or subtract: I mean what you say that I mean."

Socrates paused awhile, and seemed to be absorbed in reflection. At length he said: "You are raising a tremendous question, Cebes, involving the whole nature of generation and corruption, about which, if you like, I will give you my own experience; and if anything which I say is likely to avail towards the solution of your difficulty you may make use of it."

"I should very much like," said Cebes, "to hear what you have to say."

"Then I will tell you," said Socrates. "When I was young, Cebes, I had a prodigious desire to know that department of philosophy which is called the investigation of nature; to know the causes of things, and why a thing is and is created or destroyed appeared to me to be a lofty profession; and I was always agitating myself with the consideration of questions such as these: Is the growth of animals the result of some decay which the hot and cold principle contracts, as some have said? [19] Is the blood the element with which we think, or the air, or the fire? or perhaps nothing of the kind—but the brain may be the originating power of the perceptions of hearing and sight

[19] This sentence might be better translated: "Do heat and cold by a sort of fermentation bring about the growth of living things, as some people say?"

and smell, and memory and opinion may come from them, and science may be based on memory and opinion when they have attained fixity. And then I went on to examine the corruption of them, and then to the things of heaven and earth, and at last I concluded myself to be utterly and absolutely incapable of these inquiries, as I will satisfactorily prove to you. For I was fascinated by them to such a degree that my eyes grew blind to things which I had seemed to myself, and also to others, to know quite well; I forgot what I had before thought self-evident truths; e.g. such a fact as that the growth of man is the result of eating and drinking; for when by the digestion of food flesh is added to flesh and bone to bone, and whenever there is an aggregation of congenial elements, the lesser bulk becomes larger and the small man great. Was not that a reasonable notion?"

"Yes," said Cebes, "I think so."

"Well; but let me tell you something more. There was a time when I thought that I understood the meaning of greater and less pretty well; and when I saw a great man standing by a little one, I fancied that one was taller than the other by a head; or one horse would appear to be greater than another horse: and still more clearly did I seem to perceive that ten is two more than eight, and that two cubits are more than one, because two is the double of one."

"And what is now your notion of such matters?" said Cebes.

"I should be far enough from imagining," he replied, "that I knew the cause of any of them, by heaven I should; for I cannot satisfy myself that, when one is added to one, the one to which the addition is made becomes two, or that the two units added together make two by reason of the addition. I cannot understand how, when separated from the other, each of them was one and not two, and now, when they are brought together, the mere juxtaposition or meeting of them should be the cause of their becoming two: neither can I understand how the division of one is the way to make two; for then a different cause would produce the same effect—as in the former instance the addition and juxtaposition of one to one was the cause of two, in this the separation and subtraction of one from the other would be the cause. Nor am I any longer satisfied that I understand the reason why one or anything else is either generated or destroyed or is at all, but I have in my mind some confused notion of a new method, and can never admit the other.

"Then I heard someone reading, as he said, from a book of Anaxagoras,[20] that mind was the disposer and cause of all, and I was delighted at this notion, which appeared quite admirable, and I said to myself: If mind is the disposer, mind will dispose all for the best, and put each particular in the best place; and I argued that if anyone desired to find out the cause of the generation or destruction or existence of anything, he must find out what state of being or doing or suffering was best for that thing, and therefore a man had only to consider the best for himself and others, and then he would also know the worse, since the same science comprehended both. And I rejoiced to think that I had found in Anaxagoras a teacher of the causes of existence such as I desired, and I imagined that he would tell me first whether the earth is flat or round; and whichever was true, he would proceed to explain the cause and the necessity of this being so, and then he would teach me the nature of the best and show that this was best; and if he said that the earth was in the center, he would further explain that this position was the best, and I should be satisfied with the explanation given, and not want any other sort of cause.

"And I thought that I would then go on and ask him about the sun and moon and stars, and that he would explain to me their comparative swiftness, and their returnings and various states, active and passive, and how all of them were for the best. For I could not imagine that when he spoke of mind as the disposer of them, he would give any other account of their being as they are, except that this was best; and I thought that when he had explained to me in detail the cause of each and the cause of all, he would go on to explain to me what was best for each and what was good for all. These

20 Anaxagoras laid down the general principle that Mind was the cause of the universe (See *Phaedo*, note 10) but never went on to show either how Mind acted on matter to produce its results or why it saw fit to produce these results and no others. In specific instances he spoke of physical substances as if they, taken alone, were sufficient explanation.

hopes I would not have sold for a large sum of money, and I seized the books and read them as fast as I could in my eagerness to know the better and the worse.

"What expectations I had formed, and how grievously was I disappointed! As I proceeded, I found my philosopher altogether forsaking mind or any other principle of order, but having recourse to air, and ether, and water, and other eccentricities. I might compare him to a person who began by maintaining generally that mind is the cause of the actions of Socrates, but who, when he endeavored to explain the causes of my several actions in detail, went on to show that I sit here because my body is made up of bones and muscles; and the bones, as he would say, are hard and have joints which divide them, and the muscles are elastic, and they cover the bones, which have also a covering or environment of flesh and skin which contains them; and as the bones are lifted at their joints by the contraction or relaxation of the muscles, I am able to bend my limbs, and this is why I am sitting here in a curved posture—that is what he would say; and he would have a similar explanation of my talking to you, which he would attribute to sound, and air, and hearing, and he would assign ten thousand other causes of the same sort, forgetting to mention the true cause, which is, that the Athenians have thought fit to condemn me, and accordingly I have thought it better and more right to remain here and undergo my sentence; for I am inclined to think that these muscles and bones of mine would have gone off long ago to Megara or Boeotia—by the dog they would, if they had been moved only by their own idea of what was best, and if I had not chosen the better and nobler part, instead of playing truant and running away, of enduring any punishment which the state inflicts.

"There is surely a strange confusion of causes and conditions in all this. It may be said, indeed, that without bones and muscles and the other parts of the body I cannot execute my purposes. But to say that I do as I do because of them, and that this is the way in which mind acts, and not from the choice of the best, is a very careless and idle mode of speaking. I wonder that they cannot distinguish the cause from the condition, which the many, feeling about in the dark, are always mistaking and misnaming. And thus one man makes a vortex all round and steadies the earth by the heaven; another gives the air as a support to the earth, which is a sort of broad trough. Any power which in arranging them as they are arranges them for the best never enters into their minds; and instead of finding any superior strength in it, they rather expect to discover another Atlas [21] of the world who is stronger and more everlasting and more containing than the good; of the obligatory and containing power of the good they think nothing; and yet this is the principle which I would fain learn if anyone would teach me. But as I have failed either to discover myself, or to learn of anyone else, the nature of the best, I will exhibit to you, if you like, what I have found to be the second best mode of inquiring into the cause."

"I should very much like to hear," he replied.

Socrates proceeded: "I thought that as I had failed in the contemplation of true existence, I ought to be careful that I did not lose the eye of my soul; as people may injure their bodily eye by observing and gazing on the sun during an eclipse, unless they take the precaution of only looking at the image reflected in the water, or in some similar medium. So in my own case, I was afraid that my soul might be blinded altogether if I looked at things with my eyes or tried to apprehend them by the help of the senses. And I thought that I had better have recourse to the world of mind and seek there the truth of existence. I daresay that the simile is not perfect—for I am very far from admitting that he who contemplates existences through the medium of thought, sees them only 'through a glass darkly,' any more than he who considers them in action and operation. However, this was the method which I adopted: I first assumed some principle which I judged to be the strongest, and then I affirmed as true whatever seemed to agree with this, whether relating to the cause or to anything else; and that which disagreed I regarded as untrue.

21 The mountain in Libya that was popularly supposed to support heaven on its crest.

But I should like to explain my meaning more clearly, as I do not think that you as yet understand me."

"No, indeed," replied Cebes, "not very well."

"There is nothing new," he said, "in what I am about to tell you; but only what I have been always and everywhere repeating in the previous discussion and on other occasions: I want to show you the nature of that cause which has occupied my thoughts. I shall have to go back to those familiar words which are in the mouth of everyone, and first of all assume that there is an absolute beauty and goodness and greatness, and the like; grant me this, and I hope to be able to show you the nature of the cause, and to prove the immortality of the soul."

Cebes said: "You may proceed at once with the proof, for I grant you this."

"Well," he said, "then I should like to know whether you agree with me in the next step; for I cannot help thinking, if there be anything beautiful other than absolute beauty, should there be such, that it can be beautiful only in so far as it partakes of absolute beauty —and I should say the same of everything. Do you agree in this notion of the cause?"

"Yes," he said, "I agree."

He proceeded: "I know nothing and can understand nothing of any other of those wise causes which are alleged; and if a person says to me that the bloom of color, or form, or any such thing is a source of beauty, I leave all that, which is only confusing to me, and simply and singly, and perhaps foolishly, hold and am assured in my own mind that nothing makes a thing beautiful but the presence and participation of beauty in whatever way or manner obtained; for as to the manner I am uncertain, but I stoutly contend that by beauty all beautiful things become beautiful. This appears to me to be the safest answer which I can give, either to myself or to another, and to this I cling, in the persuasion that this principle will never be overthrown, and that to myself or to anyone who asks the question, I may safely reply, that by beauty beautiful things become beautiful. Do you not agree with me?"

"I do."

"And that by greatness only great things become great and greater greater, and by smallness the less become less?"

"True."

"Then if a person were to remark that A is taller by a head than B, and B less by a head than A, you would refuse to admit his statement, and would stoutly contend that what you mean is only that the greater is greater by, and by reason of, greatness, and the less is less only by, and by reason of, smallness; and thus you would avoid the danger of saying that the greater is greater and the less less by the measure of the head, which is the same in both, and would also avoid the monstrous absurdity of supposing that the greater man is greater by reason of a head, which is small. You would be afraid to draw such an inference, would you not?"

"Indeed, I should," said Cebes, laughing.

"In like manner you would be afraid to say that ten exceeded eight by, and by reason of, two; but would say by, and by reason of, number; or you would say that two cubits exceed one cubit not by a half, but by magnitude?—for there is the same liability to error in all these cases."

"Very true," he said.

"Again, would you not be cautious of affirming that the addition of one to one, or the division of one, is the cause of two? And you would loudly asseverate that you know of no way in which anything comes into existence except by participation in its own proper essence, and consequently, as far as you know, the only cause of two is the participation in duality—this is the way to make two, and the participation in one is the way to make one. You would say: I will let alone puzzles of division and addition—wiser heads than mine may answer them; inexperienced as I am, and ready to start, as the proverb says, at my own shadow, I cannot afford to give up the sure ground of a principle. And if anyone assails you there, you would not mind him, or answer him, until you had seen whether the consequences which follow agree with one another or not, and when you are further required to give an explanation of this principle, you would go on to assume a higher principle, and a higher, until you found a resting-place in the best of the higher; but you would not confuse the principle and the consequences in your reasoning, like the Eristics [22]— at least if you wanted to discover real existence. Not that this confusion signifies to them, who never care or think about the matter at all, for they have the wit to be well pleased with themselves however great may be the turmoil of their ideas. But you, if you are a philosopher, will certainly do as I say."

"What you say is most true," said Simmias and Cebes, both speaking at once.

ECHECRATES: Yes, Phaedo; and I do not wonder at their assenting. Anyone who has the least sense will acknowledge the wonderful clearness of Socrates' reasoning.

PHAEDO: Certainly, Echecrates; and such was the feeling of the whole company at the time.

ECHECRATES: Yes, and equally of ourselves, who were not of the company, and are now listening to your recital. But what followed?

PHAEDO: After all this had been admitted, and they had agreed that ideas exist, and that other things participate in them and derive their names from them, Socrates, if I remember rightly, said:

"This is your way of speaking; and yet when you say that Simmias is greater than Socrates and less than Phaedo, do you not predicate of Simmias both greatness and smallness?"

"Yes, I do."

"But still you allow that Simmias does not really exceed Socrates, as the words may seem to imply, because he is Simmias, but by reason of the size which he has; just as Simmias does not exceed Socrates because he is Simmias, any more than because Socrates is Socrates, but because he has smallness when compared with the greatness of Simmias?"

"True."

"And if Phaedo exceeds him in size, this is not because Phaedo is

22 The name given to a philosophic school in Megara, where much attention was paid to the art of disputation.

Phaedo, but because Phaedo has greatness relatively to Simmias, who
is comparatively smaller?"

"That is true."

"And therefore Simmias is said to be great, and is also said to be
small, because he is in a mean between them, exceeding the smallness
of the one by his greatness, and allowing the greatness of the other
to exceed his smallness." He added, laughing, "I am speaking like a
book, but I believe that what I am saying is true."

Simmias assented.

"I speak as I do because I want you to agree with me in thinking,
not only that absolute greatness will never be great and also small,
but that greatness in us or in the concrete will never admit the small
or admit of being exceeded: instead of this, one of two things will
happen, either the greater will fly or retire before the opposite, which
is the less, or at the approach of the less has already ceased to exist;
but will not, if allowing or admitting of smallness, be changed by
that; even as I, having received and admitted smallness when compared with Simmias, remain just as I was, and am the same small
person. And as the idea of greatness cannot condescend ever to be or
become small, in like manner the smallness in us cannot be or become
great; nor can any other opposite which remains the same ever be or
become its own opposite, but either passes away or perishes in the
change."

"That," replied Cebes, "is quite my notion."

Hereupon one of the company, though I do not exactly remember
which of them, said: "In heaven's name, is not this the direct contrary of what was admitted before—that out of the greater came the
less and out of the less the greater, and that opposites were simply
generated from opposites; but now this principle seems to be utterly
denied."

Socrates inclined his head to the speaker and listened. "I like your
courage," he said, "in reminding us of this. But you do not observe
that there is a difference in the two cases. For then we were speaking
of opposites in the concrete, and now of the essential opposite which,
as is affirmed, neither in us nor in nature can ever be at variance

with itself: then, my friend, we were speaking of things in which opposites are inherent and which are called after them, but now about the opposites which are inherent in them and which give their name to them; and these essential opposites will never, as we maintain, admit of generation into or out of one another." At the same time, turning to Cebes, he said: "Are you at all disconcerted, Cebes, at our friend's objection?"

"No, I do not feel so," said Cebes; "and yet I cannot deny that I am often disturbed by objections."

"Then we are agreed, after all," said Socrates, "that the opposite will never in any case be opposed to itself?"

"To that we are quite agreed," he replied.

"Yet once more let me ask you to consider the question from another point of view, and see whether you agree with me: There is a thing which you term heat, and another thing which you term cold?"

"Certainly."

"But are they the same as fire and snow?"

"Most assuredly not."

"Heat is a thing different from fire, and cold is not the same with snow?"

"Yes."

"And yet you will surely admit, that when snow, as was before said, is under the influence of heat, they will not remain snow and heat; but at the advance of the heat, the snow will either retire or perish?"

"Very true," he replied.

"And the fire too at the advance of the cold will either retire or perish; and when the fire is under the influence of the cold, they will not remain as before, fire and cold."

"That is true," he said.

"And in some cases the name of the idea is not only attached to the idea in an eternal connection, but anything else which, not being the idea, exists only in the form of the idea, may also lay claim to it. I will try to make this clearer by an example: The odd number is always called by the name of odd?"

"Very true."

"But is this the only thing which is called odd? Are there not other things which have their own name, and yet are called odd, because, although not the same as oddness, they are never without oddness?—that is what I mean to ask—whether numbers such as the number three are not of the class of odd. And there are many other examples: would you not say, for example, that three may be called by its proper name, and also be called odd, which is not the same with three? and this may be said not only of three but also of five, and of every alternate number—each of them without being oddness is odd; and in the same way two and four, and the other series of alternate numbers, have every number even, without being evenness. Do you agree?"

"Of course."

"Then now mark the point at which I am aiming: not only do essential opposites exclude one another, but also concrete things, which, although not in themselves opposed, contain opposites; these, I say, likewise reject the idea which is opposed to that which is contained in them, and when it approaches them they either perish or withdraw. For example: Will not the number three endure annihilation or anything sooner than be converted into an even number, while remaining three?"

"Very true," said Cebes.

"And yet," he said, "the number two is certainly not opposed to the number three?"

"It is not."

"Then not only do opposite ideas repel the advance of one another, but also there are other natures which repel the approach of opposites."

"Very true," he said.

*　　*　　*　　*　　*

"Tell me, then, what is that of which the inherence will render the body alive?" [23]

23 Or, "what is that which by its presence in the body makes it alive?"

"The soul," he replied.

"And is this always the case?"

"Yes," he said, "of course."

"Then whatever the soul possesses, to that she comes bearing life?"

"Yes, certainly."

"And is there any opposite to life?"

"There is," he said.

"And what is that?"

"Death."

"Then the soul, as has been acknowledged, will never receive the opposite of what she brings."

"Impossible," replied Cebes.

"And now," he said, "what did we just now call that principle which repels the even?"

"The odd."

"And that principle which repels the musical or the just?"

"The unmusical," he said, "and the unjust."

"And what do we call that principle which does not admit of death?"

"The immortal," he said.

"And does the soul admit of death?"

"No."

"Then the soul is immortal?"

"Yes," he said.

"And may we say that this has been proven?"

"Yes, abundantly proven, Socrates," he replied.

"Supposing that the odd were imperishable, must not three be imperishable?"

"Of course."

"And if that which is cold were imperishable, when the warm principle came attacking the snow, must not the snow have retired whole and unmelted—for it could never have perished, nor could it have remained and admitted the heat?"

"True," he said.

"Again, if the uncooling or warm principle were imperishable, the fire when assailed by cold would not have perished or have been extinguished, but would have gone away unaffected?"

"Certainly," he said.

"And the same may be said of the immortal: if the immortal is also imperishable, the soul when attacked by death cannot perish; for the preceding argument shows that the soul will not admit of death, or ever be dead, any more than three or the odd number will admit of the even, or fire, or the heat in the fire, of the cold. Yet a person may say: But although the odd will not become even at the approach of the even, why may not the odd perish and the even take the place of the odd? Now to him who makes this objection, we cannot answer that the odd principle is imperishable; for this has not been acknowledged, but if this had been acknowledged, there would have been no difficulty in contending that at the approach of the even the odd principle and the number three took their departure; and the same argument would have held good of fire and heat and any other thing."

"Very true."

"And the same may be said of the immortal: if the immortal is also imperishable, then the soul will be imperishable as well as immortal; but if not, some other proof of her imperishableness will have to be given."

"No other proof is needed," he said; "for if the immortal, being eternal, is liable to perish, then nothing is imperishable."

"Yes," replied Socrates, "and yet all men will agree that God, and the essential form of life, and the immortal in general, will never perish."

"Yes, all men," he said; "that is true; and what is more, gods, if I am not mistaken, as well as men."

"Seeing then that the immortal is indestructible, must not the soul, if she is immortal, be also imperishable?"

"Most certainly."

"Then when death attacks a man, the mortal portion of him may be supposed to die, but the immortal retires at the approach of death and is preserved safe and sound?"

"True."

"Then, Cebes, beyond question, the soul is immortal and imperishable, and our souls will truly exist in another world!"

"I am convinced, Socrates," said Cebes, "and have nothing more to object; but if my friend Simmias, or anyone else, has any further objection to make, he had better speak out, and not keep silence, since I do not know to what other season he can defer the discussion, if there is anything which he wants to say or to have said."

"But I have nothing more to say," replied Simmias; "nor can I see any reason for doubt after what has been said. But I still feel and cannot help feeling uncertain in my own mind, when I think of the greatness of the subject and the feebleness of man."

"Yes, Simmias," replied Socrates, "that is well said: and I may add that first principles, even if they appear certain, should be carefully considered; and when they are satisfactorily ascertained, then, with a sort of hesitating confidence in human reason, you may, I think, follow the course of the argument; and if that be plain and clear, there will be no need for any further inquiry."

"Very true."

"But then, O my friends," he said, "if the soul is really immortal, what care should be taken of her, not only in respect of the portion of time which is called life, but of eternity! And the danger of neglecting her from this point of view does indeed appear to be awful. If death had only been the end of all, the wicked would have had a good bargain in dying, for they would have been happily quit not only of their body, but of their own evil together with their souls. But now, inasmuch as the soul is manifestly immortal, there is no release or salvation from evil except the attainment of the highest virtue and wisdom. For the soul, when on her progress to the world below, takes nothing with her but nurture and education; and these are said greatly to benefit or greatly to injure the departed, at the **very** beginning of his journey thither.

"For after death, as they say, the genius of each individual, to whom he belonged in life, leads him to a certain place in which the dead are gathered together, whence after judgment has been given they pass into the world below, following the guide, who is appointed to conduct them from this world to the other: and when they have there received their due and remained their time, another guide brings them back again after many revolutions of ages. Now this way to the other world is not, as Aeschylus says in the *Telephus,* a single and straight path—if that were so no guide would be needed, for no one could miss it; but there are many partings of the road, and windings, as I infer from the rites and sacrifices which are offered to the gods below in places where three ways meet on earth. The wise and orderly soul follows in the straight path and is conscious of her surroundings; but the soul which desires the body, and which, as I was relating before, has long been fluttering about the lifeless frame and the world of sight, is, after many struggles and many sufferings, hardly and with violence carried away by her attendant genius; and when she arrives at the place where the other souls are gathered, if she be impure and have done impure deeds, whether foul murders or other crimes which are the brothers of these, and the works of brothers in crime—from that soul everyone flees and turns away; no one will be her companion, no one her guide, but alone she wanders in extremity of evil until certain times are fulfilled, and when they are fulfilled, she is borne irresistibly to her own fitting habitation; as every pure and just soul which has passed through life in the company and under the guidance of the gods has also her own proper home.

Socrates next describes the earth at length, "a round body in the center of the heavens," kept in place by the fact that it is in the center and therefore "in equipoise." Men live in a hollow of it, engulfed in mists and the lower air, like creatures on the bottom of the sea, too feeble to climb to the true surface and see the true heaven, the true light, and the true earth. This upper earth is filled with pure and uncorrupted beauty of rock, tree, and flower. Animals and men may live there free from disease, in constant communion with the gods.

The body of earth is pierced with chasms and channels, through which flow huge subterranean streams of water, fire and mud. The vast and quaking central chasm, out of which all streams rise and into which they ultimately fall again, is Tartarus. Of the streams the greatest are, first, Ocean, that flows in a circle around the earth, then Acheron, that empties into the Acherusian lake, to which the souls of the dead are sent for purification. The third is the boiling river Pyriphlegethon, "that throws up jets of fire in different parts of the earth." The fourth is the dark Cocytus of strange powers, that drops into Lake Styx.

"Such is the nature of the other world; and when the dead arrive at the place to which the genius of each severally guides them, first of all, they have sentence passed upon them, as they have lived well and piously or not. And those who appear to have lived neither well nor ill go to the river Acheron, and embarking in any vessels which they may find, are carried in them to the lake, and there they dwell and are purified of their evil deeds, and having suffered the penalty of the wrongs which they have done to others, they are absolved, and receive the rewards of their good deeds, each of them according to his deserts. But those who appear to be incurable by reason of the greatness of their crimes—who have committed many and terrible deeds of sacrilege, murders foul and violent, or the like—such are hurled into Tartarus which is their suitable destiny, and they never come out. Those again who have committed crimes, which, although great, are not irremediable—who in a moment of anger, for example, have done some violence to a father or a mother, and have repented for the remainder of their lives, or, who have taken the life of another under the like extenuating circumstances—these are plunged into Tartarus, the pains of which they are compelled to undergo for a year, but at the end of the year the wave casts them forth—mere homicides by way of Cocytus, parricides and matricides by Pyriphlegethon—and they are borne to the Acherusian lake, and there they

lift up their voices and call upon the victims whom they have slain or wronged, to have pity on them, and to be kind to them, and let them come out into the lake. And if they prevail, then they come forth and cease from their troubles; but if not, they are carried back again into Tartarus and from thence into the rivers unceasingly, until they obtain mercy from those whom they have wronged: for that is the sentence inflicted upon them by their judges. Those too who have been pre-eminent for holiness of life are released from this earthly prison, and go to their pure home which is above, and dwell in the purer earth; and of these, such as have duly purified themselves with philosophy live henceforth altogether without the body, in mansions fairer still, which may not be described, and of which the time would fail me to tell.

"Wherefore, Simmias, seeing all these things, what ought not we to do that we may obtain virtue and wisdom in this life? Fair is the prize, and the hope great!

"A man of sense ought not to say, nor will I be very confident, that the description which I have given of the soul and her mansions is exactly true. But I do say that, inasmuch as the soul is shown to be immortal, he may venture to think, not improperly or unworthily, that something of the kind is true. The venture is a glorious one, and he ought to comfort himself with words like these, which is the reason why I lengthen out the tale. Wherefore, I say, let a man be of good cheer about his soul, who having cast away the pleasures and ornaments of the body as alien to him and working harm rather than good, has sought after the pleasures of knowledge; and has arrayed the soul, not in some foreign attire, but in her own proper jewels, temperance, and justice, and courage, and nobility, and truth—in these adorned she is ready to go on her journey to the world below, when her hour comes. You, Simmias and Cebes, and all other men will depart at some time or other. Me already, as a tragic poet would say, the voice of fate calls. Soon I must drink the poison; and I think that I had better repair to the bath first, in order that the women may not have the trouble of washing my body after I am dead."

When he had done speaking, Crito said: "And have you any

commands for us, Socrates—anything to say about your children, or any other matter in which we can serve you?"

"Nothing particular, Crito," he replied; "only, as I have always told you, take care of yourselves; that is a service which you may be ever rendering to me and mine and to all of us, whether you promise to do so or not. But if you have no thought for yourselves, and care not to walk according to the rule which I have prescribed for you, not now for the first time, however much you may profess or promise at the moment, it will be of no avail."

"We will do our best," said Crito: "And in what way shall we bury you?"

"In any way that you like; but you must get hold of me, and take care that I do not run away from you."

Then he turned to us, and added with a smile: "I cannot make Crito believe that I am the same Socrates who has been talking and conducting the argument; he fancies that I am the other Socrates whom he will soon see, a dead body—and he asks, How shall he bury me? And though I have spoken many words in the endeavor to show that when I have drunk the poison I shall leave you and go to the joys of the blessed—these words of mine, with which I was comforting you and myself, have had, as I perceive, no effect upon Crito. And therefore I want you to be surety for me to him now, as at the trial he was surety to the judges for me: but let the promise be of another sort; for he was surety for me to the judges that I would remain, and you must be my surety to him that I shall not remain, but go away and depart; and then he will suffer less at my death, and not be grieved when he sees my body being burned or buried. I would not have him sorrow at my hard lot, or say at the burial, Thus we lay out Socrates, or, Thus we follow him to the grave or bury him; for false words are not only evil in themselves, but they infect the soul with evil. Be of good cheer then, my dear Crito, and say that you are burying my body only, and do with that whatever is usual, and what you think best."

When he had spoken these words, he arose and went into a chamber to bathe; Crito followed him and told us to wait. So we remained behind, talking and thinking of the subject of discourse, and also of the greatness of our sorrow; he was like a father of whom we were being bereaved, and we were about to pass the rest of our lives as orphans. When he had taken the bath his children were brought to him (he had two young sons and an elder one); and the women of his family also came, and he talked to them and gave them a few directions in the presence of Crito; then he dismissed them and returned to us.

Now the hour of sunset was near, for a good deal of time had passed while he was within. When he came out, he sat down with us again after his bath, but not much was said. Soon the jailer, who was the servant of the Eleven, entered and stood by him, saying: "To you, Socrates, whom I know to be the noblest and gentlest and best of all who ever came to this place, I will not impute the angry feelings of other men, who rage and swear at me, when, in obedience to the authorities, I bid them drink the poison—indeed, I am sure that you will not be angry with me; for others, as you are aware, and not I, are to blame. And so fare you well, and try to bear lightly what must needs be—you know my errand." Then bursting into tears he turned away and went out.

Socrates looked at him and said: "I return your good wishes, and will do as you bid." Then turning to us, he said, "How charming the man is: since I have been in prison he has always been coming to see me, and at times he would talk to me, and was as good to me as could be, and now see how generously he sorrows on my account. We must do as he says, Crito; and therefore let the cup be brought, if the poison is prepared: if not, let the attendant prepare some."

"Yet," said Crito, "the sun is still upon the hilltops, and I know that many a one has taken the draught late, and after the announcement has been made to him, he has eaten and drunk, and enjoyed the society of his beloved; do not hurry—there is time enough."

Socrates said: "Yes, Crito, and they of whom you speak are right in so acting, for they think that they will be gainers by the delay; but I am right in not following their example, for I do not think that I should gain anything by drinking the poison a little later: I should only be ridiculous in my own eyes for sparing and saving a life which is already forfeit. Please then to do as I say, and not to refuse me."

Crito made a sign to the servant, who was standing by; and he went out, and having been absent for some time, returned with the jailer carrying the cup of poison. Socrates said: "You, my good friend, who are experienced in these matters, shall give me directions how I am to proceed."

The man answered: "You have only to walk about until your legs are heavy, and then to lie down, and the poison will act."

At the same time he handed the cup to Socrates, who in the easiest and gentlest manner, without the least fear or change of color or feature, looking at the man with all his eyes, Echecrates, as his manner was, took the cup and said: "What do you say about making a libation out of this cup to any god? May I, or not?"

The man answered: "We only prepare, Socrates, just so much as we deem enough."

"I understand," he said; "but I may and must ask the gods to prosper my journey from this to the other world—even so—and so be it according to my prayer."

Then raising the cup to his lips, quite readily and cheerfully he drank off the poison. And hitherto most of us had been able to control our sorrow; but now when we saw him drinking, and saw too that he had finished the draught, we could no longer forbear, and in spite of myself my own tears were flowing fast; so that I covered my face and wept, not for him, but at the thought of my own calamity in having to part from such a friend. Nor was I the first; for Crito, when he found himself unable to restrain his tears, had got up, and I followed; and at that moment, Apollodorus, who had been weeping all the time, broke out in a loud and passionate cry which made cowards of us all.

Socrates alone retained his calmness: "What is this strange outcry?" he said. "I sent away the women mainly in order that they might not misbehave in this way, for I have been told that a man should die in peace. Be quiet then, and have patience."

When we heard his words we were ashamed, and refrained our

tears; and he walked about until, as he said, his legs began to fail, and then he lay on his back, according to the directions, and the man who gave him the poison now and then looked at his feet and legs; and after a while he pressed his foot hard, and asked him if he could feel; and he said, "No"; and then his leg, and so upwards and upwards, and showed us that he was cold and stiff. And he felt them himself, and said: "When the poison reaches the heart, that will be the end."

He was beginning to grow cold about the groin, when he uncovered his face, for he had covered himself up, and said—they were his last words—he said: "Crito, I owe a cock to Asclepius; [24] will you remember to pay the debt?"

"The debt shall be paid," said Crito; "is there anything else?

There was no answer to this question; but in a minute or two a movement was heard, and the attendants uncovered him; his eyes were set, and Crito closed his eyes and mouth.

Such was the end, Echecrates, of our friend; concerning whom I may truly say, that of all the men of his time whom I have known, he was the wisest and justest and best.

24 The god of health and medicine. Physicians were called his sons.

SYMPOSIUM

Not LONG probably after he wrote the *Phaedo,* some twelve or fifteen years after Socrates' death, Plato composed the lovely dialogue known as the *Symposium.* In it he harked back to an incident of Socrates' earlier life, a banquet held at Athens in the year 416 B.C. The atmosphere of this dialogue, in contrast to that of the three that precede it here, is lighthearted and happy. The war with Sparta is going on but no one yet foresees its disastrous close nor the tragic parts that some of the evening's guests will play in the events to come. No shadow of doom hangs over Socrates. Everyone is carefree and unsuspecting and the talk is not of death and the chances of immortality but of life and love. Because of this particular talk the banquet is long remembered. The same excitable Apollodorus whom we met in the *Phaedo* tells the story of it years afterward to a friend. He himself was not of the company, for in 416 he was still a boy who had not yet made Socrates' acquaintance, but he has his account from Aristodemus, who was there at Socrates' own invitation.

The occasion is the celebration by a youthful poet, Agathon, of the prize won by his tragedy in a dramatic contest just over. Among the guests reclining around his table, besides Socrates and Aristodemus, are two other young literary men, Phaedrus and Pausanias, also Eryximachus, a physician, and Aristophanes, the renowned comedian and satirist. At Eryximachus' suggestion the party agrees to drink sparingly, send away the hired flute-girl, and for its entertainment listen to speeches, made in turn by each man at table in praise of Love. Love, we must understand, in any noble sense of the word, means to Athenian gentlemen of this period the love of men for other men, the protective love of a full-grown man for some gallant and promising youth or the love of two comrades for one another. These were the loves that mattered in a man's life and exalted his character. Women were kept secluded at home and their relationship to men was on a lower plane altogether.

After some chaffing, first Phaedrus makes a pretty speech, sprinkled thick with literary allusions and extolling Love as the mightiest of the deities. Next Pausanias, more cautiously, discriminates between what he calls the heavenly and the vulgar Aphrodite, or goddess of love. Eryximachus draws a physicist's picture of the forces of love and appetite for both good and evil, health and disease, in human affairs and in nature. Aristophanes spins a weird fable of the origin of the persistent craving that human creatures feel for each other's society. Agathon follows with a flowery rhapsody on Love as the source of everything beautiful in life. Socrates, the last to speak, raises the level of the whole discussion by a sublime description of the Love that is itself poor and needy but that lifts man from the passions of earth to a vision of the absolute beauty of God. To avoid, however, any accusation of over-solemnity, he attributes his ideas to a mysterious wise woman, who taught him all he knows on the subject. But the momentary seriousness is broken by the entrance of the laughing, brilliant Alcibiades, drunk from his revels, crowned with ribbons and violets, the spoiled, popular idol of the day, of whose destiny to become the hated betrayer of his city no one dreams. He is haled to a seat at table and called upon for his speech. He starts out, recklessly, impertinently. He will praise Socrates, nothing but Socrates, the fascinating spellbinder, the intrepid soldier, the Socrates who has taught him even against his will the difference between love of the senses and love of the mind, the only man who has ever made him ashamed. He is ribald one moment, serious the next. But again the discourse is interrupted. A mob of hilarious merrymakers pours in. Drinking becomes general. Most of the original guests depart. Aristodemus falls asleep in his place. When he wakes at cock crow, only three are left, Agathon and Aristophanes, the tragic and the comic poets, and Socrates, still serene and talking.

SYMPOSIUM

PERSONS OF THE DIALOGUE: *Apollodorus,
Glaucon, Aristodemus, Phaedrus, Pausan-
ias, Eryximachus, Aristophanes, Agathon,
Socrates, Alcibiades*

SCENE: *The House of Agathon*

Apollodorus speaks:

CONCERNING the things about which you ask to be informed I believe that I am not ill-prepared with an answer.
For the day before yesterday I was coming from my own
home at Phalerum to the city, and one of my acquaintance, who had
caught a sight of me from behind, calling out playfully in the distance, said: "Apollodorus, O thou Phalerian [1] man, halt!" So I did as
I was bid; and then he said, "I was looking for you, Apollodorus,
only just now, that I might ask you about the speeches in praise of
love, which were delivered by Socrates, Alcibiades, and others, at
Agathon's supper. Phoenix, the son of Philip, told another person
who told me of them; his narrative was very indistinct, but he said
that you knew, and I wish that you would give me an account of
them. Who, if not you, should be the reporter of the words of your
friend? And first tell me," he said, "were you present at this meeting?"

"Your informant, Glaucon," I said, "must have been very indis-

---

1 Probably a play of words on φαλαρὸς, "bald-headed."

tinct indeed, if you imagine that the occasion was recent; or that I could have been of the party."

"Why, yes," he replied, "I thought so."

"Impossible," I said. "Are you ignorant that for many years Agathon has not resided at Athens; and not three have elapsed since I became acquainted with Socrates, and have made it my daily business to know all that he says and does. There was a time when I was running about the world, fancying myself to be well employed, but I was really a most wretched being, no better than you are now. I thought that I ought to do anything rather than be a philosopher."

"Well," he said, "jesting apart, tell me when the meeting occurred."

"In our boyhood," I replied, "when Agathon won the prize with his first tragedy, on the day after that on which he and his chorus offered the sacrifice of victory."

"Then it must have been a long while ago," he said; "and who told you—did Socrates?"

"No, indeed," I replied, "but the same person who told Phoenix—he was a little fellow, who never wore any shoes, Aristodemus, of the deme of Cydathenaeum. He had been at Agathon's feast; and I think that in those days there was no one who was a more devoted admirer of Socrates. Moreover, I have asked Socrates about the truth of some parts of his narrative, and he confirmed them."

"Then," said Glaucon, "let us have the tale over again; is not the road to Athens just made for conversation?"

And so we walked, and talked of the discourses on love; and therefore, as I said at first, I am not ill-prepared to comply with your request, and will have another rehearsal of them if you like. For to speak or to hear others speak of philosophy always gives me the greatest pleasure, to say nothing of the profit. But when I hear another strain, especially that of you rich men and traders, such conversation displeases me; and I pity you who are my companions, because you think that you are doing something when in reality you are doing nothing. And I dare say that you pity me in return, whom you regard as an unhappy creature, and very probably you are right.

But I certainly know of you what you only think of me—there is the difference.

COMPANION: I see, Apollodorus, that you are just the same—always speaking evil of yourself, and of others; and I do believe that you pity all mankind, with the exception of Socrates, yourself first of all, true in this to your old name, which, however deserved, I know not how you acquired, of Apollodorus the madman; for you are always raging against yourself and everybody but Socrates.

APOLLODORUS: Yes, friend, and the reason why I am said to be mad, and out of my wits, is just because I have these notions of myself and you; no other evidence is required.

COMPANION: No more of that, Apollodorus; but let me renew my request that you would repeat the conversation.

APOLLODORUS: Well, the tale of love was on this wise—but perhaps I had better begin at the beginning, and endeavor to give you the exact words of Aristodemus:

He said that he met Socrates fresh from the bath and sandaled; and as the sight of the sandals was unusual, he asked him whither he was going that he had been converted into such a beau.

"To a banquet at Agathon's," he replied, "whose invitation to his sacrifice of victory I refused yesterday, fearing a crowd, but promising that I would come today instead; and so I have put on my finery, because he is such a fine man. What say you to going with me unasked?"

"I will do as you bid me," I replied.

"Follow then," he said, "and let us demolish the proverb:

To the feasts of inferior men the good unbidden go;

instead of which our proverb will run:

To the feasts of the good the good unbidden go; [2]

and this alteration may be supported by the authority of Homer him-

2 In the Greek, the change in the proverb consists in substituting the word "Agathon" for the word that is here translated "of inferior men." "Agathon" is both the name of their host and the genitive plural of the adjective meaning "good."

self,[3] who not only demolishes but literally outrages the proverb. For, after picturing Agamemnon as the most valiant of men, he makes Menelaus, who is but a faint-hearted warrior, come unbidden to the banquet of Agamemnon, who is feasting and offering sacrifices, not the better to the worse, but the worse to the better."

"I rather fear, Socrates," said Aristodemus, "lest this may still be my case; and that, like Menelaus in Homer, I shall be the inferior person, who

to the feasts of the wise unbidden goes.

But I shall say that I was bidden of you, and then you will have to make an excuse."

" 'Two going together,' " he replied, in Homeric fashion,[4] "one or other of them may invent an excuse by the way."

This was the style of their conversation as they went along. Socrates dropped behind in a fit of abstraction, and desired Aristodemus, who was waiting, to go on before him. When he reached the house of Agathon he found the doors wide open, and a comical thing happened. A servant coming out met him, and led him at once into the banqueting hall in which the guests were reclining, for the banquet was about to begin.

"Welcome, Aristodemus," said Agathon, as soon as he appeared; "you are just in time to sup with us; if you come on any other matter put it off, and make one of us, as I was looking for you yesterday and meant to have asked you, if I could have found you. But what have you done with Socrates?"

I turned round, but Socrates was nowhere to be seen; and I had to explain that he had been with me a moment before, and that I came by his invitation to the supper.

"You were quite right in coming," said Agathon; "but where is he himself?"

3 *Iliad*, XVII 587, 588, and II, 408.
4 *Iliad*, X, 224, 225.

"He was behind me just now, as I entered," he said, "and I cannot think what has become of him."

"Go and look for him, boy," said Agathon, "and bring him in; and do you, Aristodemus, meanwhile take the place by Eryximachus."

The servant then assisted him to wash, and he lay down, and presently another servant came in and reported that our friend Socrates had retired into the portico of the neighboring house. "There he is fixed," said he, "and when I call to him he will not stir."

"How strange," said Agathon; "then you must call him again, and keep calling him."

"Let him alone," said my informant; "he has a way of stopping anywhere and losing himself without any reason. I believe that he will soon appear; do not therefore disturb him."

"Well, if you think so, I will leave him," said Agathon. And then, turning to the servants, he added, "Let us have supper without waiting for him. Serve up whatever you please, for there is no one to give you orders; hitherto I have never left you to yourselves. But on this occasion imagine that you are our hosts, and that I and the company are your guests; treat us well, and then we shall commend you."

After this, supper was served, but still no Socrates; and during the meal Agathon several times expressed a wish to send for him, but Aristodemus objected; and at last when the feast was about half over —for the fit, as usual, was not of long duration—Socrates entered. Agathon, who was reclining alone at the end of the table, begged that he would take the place next to him; that "I may touch you," he said, "and have the benefit of that wise thought which came into your mind in the portico, and is now in your possession; for I am certain that you would not have come away until you had found what you sought."

"How I wish," said Socrates, taking his place as he was desired, "that wisdom could be infused by touch, out of the fuller into the emptier man, as water runs through wool out of a fuller cup into an emptier one; if that were so, how greatly should I value the privilege of reclining at your side! For you would have filled me full with a stream of wisdom plenteous and fair; whereas my own is of a very mean and questionable sort, no better than a dream. But yours is bright and full of promise, and was manifested forth in all the splendor of youth the day before yesterday, in the presence of more than thirty thousand Hellenes."

"You are mocking, Socrates," said Agathon, "and ere long you and I will have to determine who bears off the palm of wisdom—of this Dionysus [5] shall be the judge; but at present you are better occupied with supper."

Socrates took his place on the couch, and supped with the rest; and then libations were offered, and after a hymn had been sung to the god, and there had been the usual ceremonies, they were about to commence drinking, when Pausanias said, "And now, my friends, how can we drink with least injury to ourselves? I can assure you that I feel severely the effect of yesterday's potations, and must have time to recover; and I suspect that most of you are in the same predicament, for you were of the party yesterday. Consider then: How can the drinking be made easiest?"

"I entirely agree," said Aristophanes, "that we should, by all means, avoid hard drinking, for I was myself one of those who were yesterday drowned in drink."

"I think that you are right," said Eryximachus, the son of Acumenus; "but I should still like to hear one other person speak. Is Agathon able to drink hard?"

"I am not equal to it," said Agathon.

"Then," said Eryximachus, "the weak heads like myself, Aristodemus, Phaedrus, and others who never can drink, are fortunate in finding that the stronger ones are not in a drinking mood. (I do not include Socrates, who is able either to drink or to abstain, and will not mind, whichever we do.) Well, as none of the company seems disposed to drink much, I may be forgiven for saying, as a physician, that drinking deep is a bad practice, which I never follow, if I can help, and certainly do not recommend to another, least of all to anyone who still feels the effects of yesterday's carouse."

5 The god of wine and the ecstasy of Nature, also known as Bacchus.

"I always do what you advise, and especially what you prescribe as a physician," rejoined Phaedrus the Myrrhinusian, "and the rest of the company, if they are wise, will do the same."

It was agreed that drinking was not to be the order of the day, but that they were all to drink only so much as they pleased.

"Then," said Eryximachus, "as you are all agreed that drinking is to be voluntary, and that there is to be no compulsion, I move, in the next place, that the flute-girl, who has just made her appearance, be told to go away and play to herself, or, if she likes, to the women who are within. Today let us have conversation instead; and, if you will allow me, I will tell you what sort of conversation."

This proposal having been accepted, Eryximachus proceeded as follows:

"I will begin," he said, after the manner of Melanippe in Euripides: " 'Not mine the word' [6] which I am about to speak, but that of Phaedrus. For often he says to me in an indignant tone: 'What a strange thing it is, Eryximachus, that, whereas other gods have poems and hymns made in their honor, the great and glorious god, Love, has no encomiast among all the poets who are so many. There are the worthy sophists too—the excellent Prodicus, for example—who have descanted in prose on the virtues of Heracles [7] and other heroes; and, what is still more extraordinary, I have met with a philosophical work in which the utility of salt has been made the theme of an eloquent discourse; and many other like things have had a like honor bestowed upon them. And only to think that there should have been an eager interest created about them, and yet that to this day no one has ever dared worthily to hymn Love's praises! So entirely has this great deity been neglected.' Now in this Phaedrus seems to me to be quite right, and therefore I want to offer him a contribution; also I think that at the present moment we who are here assembled cannot do better than honor the god Love. If you agree with me, there will

---

[6] *The Wise Melanippe* of Euripides in which this line occurs is lost but we have the line in Fragment 487.

[7] The Sophist Prodicus was author of a popular moral tale called *The Choice of Heracles.*

be no lack of conversation; for I mean to propose that each of us in turn, going from left to right, shall make a speech in honor of Love. Let him give us the best which he can; and Phaedrus, because he is sitting first on the left hand, and because he is the father of the thought, shall begin."

"No one will vote against you, Eryximachus," said Socrates. "How can I oppose your motion, who profess to understand nothing but matters of love; nor, I presume, will Agathon and Pausanias; and there can be no doubt of Aristophanes, whose whole concern is with Dionysus and Aphrodite; [8] nor will anyone disagree of those whom I see around me. The proposal, as I am aware, may seem rather hard upon us whose place is last; but we shall be contented if we hear some good speeches first. Let Phaedrus begin the praise of Love, and good luck to him." All the company expressed their assent, and desired him to do as Socrates bade him.

Aristodemus did not recollect all that was said, nor do I recollect all that he related to me; but I will tell you what I thought most worthy of remembrance, and what the chief speakers said.

Phaedrus began by affirming that: "Love is a mighty god, and wonderful among gods and men, but especially wonderful in his birth. For he is the eldest of the gods, which is an honor to him; and a proof of his claim to this honor is, that of his parents there is no memorial; neither poet nor prose-writer has ever affirmed that he had any. As Hesiod says:

> *First Chaos came, and then broad-bosomed Earth,*
> *The everlasting seat of all that is,*
> *And Love.*[9]

In other words, after Chaos, the Earth and Love, these two, came into being. Also Parmenides sings of Generation:

> *First in the train of gods, he fashioned Love.*[10]

8 The Greek goddess of love, whom the Romans identified with their goddess Venus.

9 Hesiod, *Theogony,* 116-120.

10 We have only fragments of the famous poem of the philosopher Parmenides on Nature. The line Phaedrus quotes here is in our Fragment 13.

And Acusilaus [11] agrees with Hesiod. Thus numerous are the witnesses who acknowledge Love to be the eldest of the gods. And not only is he the eldest, he is also the source of the greatest benefits to us. For I know not any greater blessing to a young man who is beginning life than a virtuous lover, or to the lover than a beloved youth. For the principle which ought to be the guide of men who would nobly live—that principle, I say, neither kindred, nor honor, nor wealth, nor any other motive is able to implant so well as love. Of what am I speaking? Of the sense of honor and dishonor, without which neither states nor individuals ever do any good or great work. And I say that a lover who is detected in doing any dishonorable act, or submitting through cowardice when any dishonor is done to him by another, will be more pained at being detected by his beloved than at being seen by his father, or by his companions, or by anyone else. The beloved too, when he is found in any disgraceful situation, has the same feeling about his lover. And if there were only some way of contriving that a state or an army should be made up of lovers and their loves, they would be the very best governors of their own city, abstaining from all dishonor, and emulating one another in honor; and when fighting at each other's side, although a mere handful, they would overcome the world. For what lover would not choose rather to be seen by all mankind than by his beloved, either when abandoning his post or throwing away his arms? He would be ready to die a thousand deaths rather than endure this. Or who would desert his beloved or fail him in the hour of danger? The veriest coward would become an inspired hero, equal to the bravest, at such a time; Love would inspire him. That courage which, as Homer says, the god breathes into the souls of some heroes,[12] Love of his own nature infuses into the lover.

"Love will make men dare to die for their beloved—love alone;

11 Acusilaus of Argos was a fifth century compiler of chronicles and genealogies, whose work has entirely disappeared.

12 *Iliad*, X, 482; XV, 262.

and women as well as men. Of this, Alcestis,[13] the daughter of Pelias, is a monument to all Hellas; for she was willing to lay down her life on behalf of her husband, when no one else would, although he had a father and mother; but the tenderness of her love so far exceeded theirs, that she made them seem to be strangers in blood to their own son, and in name only related to him; and so noble did this action of hers appear to the gods, as well as to men, that among the many who have done virtuously she is one of the very few to whom, in admiration of her noble action, they have granted the privilege of returning alive to earth; such exceeding honor is paid by the gods to the devotion and virtue of love. But Orpheus,[14] the son of Oeagrus, the harper, they sent empty away, and presented to him an apparition only of her whom he sought, but herself they would not give up, because he showed no spirit; he was only a harp-player, and did not dare like Alcestis to die for love, but was contriving how he might enter Hades alive; moreover, they afterwards caused him to suffer death at the hands of women, as the punishment of his cowardliness. Very different was the reward of the true love of Achilles towards his lover Patroclus [15]—his lover and not his love (the notion that Patroclus was the beloved one is a foolish error into which Aeschylus [16] has fallen, for Achilles was surely the fairer of the two, fairer also than all the other heroes; and, as Homer [17] informs us, he was still beardless, and younger far). And greatly as the gods honor the virtue of love, still the return of love on the part of the beloved to the lover is more admired and valued and rewarded by them, for the lover is more divine; because he is inspired by God. Now Achilles was quite aware, for he had been told by his mother, that he might avoid death

13 Alcestis laid down her life to ransom her husband Admetus from death and, as a reward for her selfless courage, was brought back from the lower world by the hero Heracles. Her story was known to every Greek.

14 The tale of Orpheus, who went down alive to Hades to rescue his lost wife Eurydice and failed, was also familiar to everyone.

15 The vengeance taken by Achilles for the death of his friend Patroclus is the theme of the last six books of the *Iliad*. His mother Thetis warns him in Book XVIII, 95-96. Socrates in his *Apology* also recalls the bravery of Achilles. Page 46.

16 A reference to the missing play of the *Myrmidons*. See Fragments 135-136.

17 *Iliad*, XI, 786, 787.

and return home, and live to a good old age, if he abstained from slaying Hector. Nevertheless he gave his life to revenge his friend, and dared to die, not only in his defense, but after he was dead. Wherefore the gods honored him even above Alcestis, and sent him to the Islands of the Blest.[18] These are my reasons for affirming that Love is the eldest and noblest and mightiest of the gods, and the chiefest author and giver of virtue in life, and of happiness after death."

This, or something like this, was the speech of Phaedrus; and some other speeches followed which Aristodemus did not remember; the next which he repeated was that of Pausanias. "Phaedrus," he said, "the argument has not been set before us, I think, quite in the right form: we should not be called upon to praise Love in such an indiscriminate manner. If there were only one Love, then what you said would be well enough; but since there are more Loves than one, you should have begun by determining which of them was to be the theme of our praises. I will amend this defect; and first of all I will tell you which Love is deserving of praise, and then try to hymn the praiseworthy one in a manner worthy of him. For we all know that Love is inseparable from Aphrodite, and if there were only one Aphrodite there would be only one Love; but as there are two goddesses there must be two Loves. And am I not right in asserting that there are two goddesses? The elder one, having no mother, who is called the heavenly Aphrodite—she is the daughter of Uranus; [19] the younger, who is the daughter of Zeus and Dione—her we call common; and the Love who is her fellow worker is rightly named common, as the other love is called heavenly. All the gods ought to have praise given to them, but not without distinction of their natures; and therefore I must try to distinguish the characters of the two Loves.

"Now actions vary according to the manner of their performance.

18 Pindar, *Olympian*, II, 79-82.
19 The primeval god of Heaven, father of Cronus, who in turn was father of Zeus. A daughter of Uranus would therefore be far older and more queenly than a daughter of Zeus and a mortal maid Dione.

Take, for example, that which we are now doing, drinking, singing and talking—these actions are not in themselves either good or evil, but they turn out in this or that way according to the mode of performing them; and when well done they are good, and when wrongly done they are evil; and in like manner not every love, but only that which has a noble purpose, is noble and worthy of praise. The Love who is the offspring of the common Aphrodite is essentially common, and has no discrimination, being such as the meaner sort of men feel, and is apt to be of women as well as of youths, and is of the body rather than of the soul—the most foolish beings are the objects of this love which desires only to gain an end, but never thinks of accomplishing the end nobly, and therefore does good and evil quite indiscriminately. The goddess who is his mother is far younger than the other, and she was born of the union of the male and female, and partakes of both. But the offspring of the heavenly Aphrodite is derived from a mother in whose birth the female has no part—she is from the male only; this is that love which is of youths, and the goddess being older, there is nothing of wantonness in her. Those who are inspired by this love turn to the male, and delight in him who is the more valiant and intelligent nature; anyone may recognize the pure enthusiasts in the very character of their attachments. For they love not boys, but intelligent beings whose reason is beginning to be developed, much about the time at which their beards begin to grow. And in choosing young men to be their companions, they mean to be faithful to them, and pass their whole life in company with them, not to take them in their inexperience, and deceive them, and play the fool with them, or run away from one to another of them. But the love of young boys should be forbidden by law, because their future is uncertain; they may turn out good or bad, either in body or soul, and much noble enthusiasm may be thrown away upon them; in this matter the good are a law to themselves, and the coarser sort of lovers ought to be restrained by force, as we restrain or attempt to restrain them from fixing their affections on women of free birth. These are the persons who bring a reproach on love; and some have been led to deny the lawfulness of such attachments because they see the impropriety and evil of them; for surely nothing that is decorously and lawfully done can justly be censured. Now here and in Lacedaemon the rules about love are perplexing, but in most cities they are simple and easily intelligible; in Elis and Boeotia, and in countries having no gifts of eloquence, they are very straightforward; the law is simply in favor of these connections, and no one, whether young or old, has anything to say to their discredit; the reason being, as I suppose, that they are men of few words in those parts, and therefore the lovers do not like the trouble of pleading their suit. In Ionia and other places, and generally in countries which are subject to the barbarians, the custom is held to be dishonorable; loves of youths share the evil repute in which philosophy and gymnastics are held, because they are inimical to tyranny; for the interests of rulers require that their subjects should be poor in spirit, and that there should be no strong bond of friendship or society among them, which love, above all other motives, is likely to inspire, as our Athenian tyrants learned by experience; for the love of Aristogeiton and the constancy of Harmodius [20] had a strength which undid their power. And, therefore, the ill repute into which these attachments have fallen is to be ascribed to the evil condition of those who make them to be ill-reputed; that is to say, to the self-seeking of the governors and the cowardice of the governed; on the other hand, the indiscriminate honor which is given to them in some countries is attributable to the laziness of those who hold this opinion of them.

"In our own country a far better principle prevails, but, as I was saying, the explanation of it is rather perplexing. For, observe that open loves are held to be more honorable than secret ones, and that the love of the noblest and highest, even if their persons are less beautiful than others, is especially honorable. Consider, too, how great is the encouragement which all the world gives to the lover; neither is he supposed to be doing anything dishonorable; but if he succeeds he is praised, and if he fail he is blamed. And in the pur-

20 In 510 B.C. the two friends, Harmodius and Aristogeiton, at the cost of their own lives, started the revolt that overthrew the tyranny of the sons of Peisistratus and opened the way for democracy in Athens.

suit of his love the custom of mankind allows him to do many strange things, which philosophy would bitterly censure if they were done from any motive of interest, or wish for office or power. He may pray, and entreat, and supplicate, and swear, and lie on a mat at the door, and endure a slavery worse than that of any slave—in any other case friends and enemies would be equally ready to prevent him, but now there is no friend who will be ashamed of him and admonish him, and no enemy will charge him with meanness or flattery; the actions of a lover have a grace which ennobles them; and custom has decided that they are highly commendable and that there is no loss of character in them; and, what is strangest of all, he only may swear and forswear himself (so men say), and the gods will forgive his transgression, for there is no such thing as a lover's oath. Such is the entire liberty which gods and men have allowed the lover, according to the custom which prevails in our part of the world.

"From this point of view a man fairly argues that in Athens to love and to be loved is held to be a very honorable thing. But when parents forbid their sons to talk with their lovers, and place them under a tutor's care, who is appointed to see to these things, and their companions and equals cast in their teeth anything of the sort which they may observe, and their elders refuse to silence the reprovers and do not rebuke them—anyone who reflects on all this will, on the contrary, think that we hold these practices to be most disgraceful. But, as I was saying at first, the truth as I imagine is, that whether such practices are honorable or whether they are dishonorable is not a simple question; they are honorable to him who follows them honorably, dishonorable to him who follows them dishonorably. There is dishonor in yielding to the evil, or in an evil manner; but there is honor in yielding to the good, or in an honorable manner. Evil is the vulgar lover who loves the body rather than the soul, inasmuch as he is not even stable, because he loves a thing which is in itself unstable, and therefore when the bloom of youth which he was desiring is over, he takes wing and flies away, in spite of all his words and promises; whereas the love of the noble disposition is lifelong, for

it becomes one with the everlasting. The custom of our country would
have both of them proven well and truly, and would have us yield to
the one sort of lover and avoid the other, and therefore encourages
some to pursue, and others to fly; testing both the lover and beloved
in contests and trials, until they show to which of the two classes they
respectively belong. And this is the reason why, in the first place, a
hasty attachment is held to be dishonorable, because time is the true
test of this as of most other things; and secondly there is a dishonor
in being overcome by the love of money, or of wealth, or of political
power, whether a man is frightened into surrender by the loss of
them, or, having experienced the benefits of money and political
corruption, is unable to rise above the seductions of them. For none
of these things are of a permanent or lasting nature; not to mention
that no generous friendship ever sprang from them. There remains,
then, only one way of honorable attachment which custom allows
in the beloved, and this is the way of virtue; for as we admitted that
any service which the lover does to him is not to be accounted flattery
or a dishonor to himself, so the beloved has one way only of voluntary service which is not dishonorable, and this is virtuous service.

"For we have a custom, and according to our custom anyone who
does service to another under the idea that he will be improved by
him either in wisdom, or in some other particular of virtue—such a
voluntary service, I say, is not to be regarded as a dishonor, and is not
open to the charge of flattery. And these two customs, one the love
of youth, and the other the practice of philosophy and virtue in
general, ought to meet in one, and then the beloved may honorably
indulge the lover. For when the lover and beloved come together,
having each of them a law, and the lover thinks that he is right in
doing any service which he can to his gracious loving one; and the
other that he is right in showing any kindness which he can to him
who is making him wise and good; the one capable of communicating
wisdom and virtue, the other seeking to acquire them with a view to
education and wisdom; when the two laws of love are fulfilled and
meet in one—then, and then only, may the beloved yield with honor
to the lover. Nor when love is of this disinterested sort is there any

disgrace in being deceived, but in every other case there is equal disgrace in being or not being deceived. For he who is gracious to his lover under the impression that he is rich, and is disappointed of his gains because he turns out to be poor, is disgraced all the same: for he has done his best to show that he would give himself up to anyone's 'uses base' for the sake of money; but this is not honorable. And on the same principle, he who gives himself to a lover because he is a good man, and in the hope that he will be improved by his company, shows himself to be virtuous, even though the object of his affection turn out to be a villain, and to have no virtue; and if he is deceived he has committed a noble error. For he has proved that for his part he will do anything for anybody with a view to virtue and improvement, than which there can be nothing nobler. Thus noble in every case is the acceptance of another for the sake of virtue. This is that love which is the love of the heavenly goddess, and is heavenly, and of great price to individuals and cities, making the lover and the beloved alike eager in the work of their own improvement. But all other loves are the offspring of the other, who is the common goddess. To you, Phaedrus, I offer this my contribution in praise of love, which is as good as I could make extempore."

Pausanias came to a pause—this is the balanced way in which I have been taught by the wise to speak; and Aristodemus said that the turn of Aristophanes was next, but either he had eaten too much, or from some other cause he had the hiccough, and was obliged to change turns with Eryximachus the physician, who was reclining on the couch below him.

"Eryximachus," he said, "you ought either to stop my hiccough, or to speak in my turn until I have left off."

"I will do both," said Eryximachus: "I will speak in your turn, and do you speak in mine; and while I am speaking let me recommend you to hold your breath, and if after you have done so for some time the hiccough is no better, then gargle with a little water; and if it still continues, tickle your nose with something and sneeze; and if you sneeze once or twice, even the most violent hiccough is sure to go."

"I will do as you prescribe," said Aristophanes, "and now get on."

Eryximachus spoke as follows: "Seeing that Pausanias made a fair beginning, and but a lame ending, I must endeavor to supply his deficiency. I think that he has rightly distinguished two kinds of love. But my art further informs me that the double love is not merely an affection of the soul of man towards the fair, or towards anything, but is to be found in the bodies of all animals and in productions of the earth, and I may say in all that is; such is the conclusion which I seem to have gathered from my own art of medicine, whence I learn how great and wonderful and universal is the deity of love, whose empire extends over all things, divine as well as human.[21] And from medicine I will begin, that I may do honor to my art. There are in the human body these two kinds of love, which are confessedly different and unlike, and being unlike, they have loves and desires which are unlike; and the desire of the healthy is one, and the desire of the diseased is another; and as Pausanias was just now saying that to indulge good men is honorable, and bad men dishonorable: so too in the body the good and healthy elements are to be indulged, and the bad elements and the elements of disease are not to be indulged, but discouraged. And this is what the physician has to do, and in this the art of medicine consists: for medicine may be regarded generally as the knowledge of the loves and desires of the body, and how to satisfy them or not; and the best physician is he who is able to separate fair love from foul, or to convert one into the other; and he who knows how to eradicate and how to implant love, whichever is required, and can reconcile the most hostile elements in the constitution and make them loving friends, is a skillful practitioner.

"Now the most hostile are the most opposite, such as hot and cold, bitter and sweet, moist and dry, and the like. And my ancestor, Asclepius,[22] knowing how to implant friendship and accord in these elements, was the creator of our art, as our friends the poets here tell

---

21 The philosopher Empedocles (c. 440 B.C.) had given the name of Love to the creative, cohesive forces pervading the universe and of Strife to the forces of decay and disruption.

22 See *Phaedo*, note 23.

us, and I believe them; and not only medicine in every branch, but the arts of gymnastic and husbandry are under his dominion. Anyone who pays the least attention to the subject will also perceive that in music there is the same reconciliation of opposites; and I suppose that this must have been the meaning of Heraclitus,[23] although his words are not accurate; for he says that the One is united by disunion, like the harmony of the bow and the lyre. Now there is an absurdity in saying that harmony is discord or is composed of elements which are still in a state of discord. But what he probably meant was, that harmony is composed of differing notes of higher or lower pitch which disagreed once, but are now reconciled by the art of music; for if the higher and lower notes still disagreed, there could be no harmony—clearly not. For harmony is a symphony, and symphony is an agreement; but an agreement of disagreements while they disagree there cannot be; you cannot harmonize that which disagrees. In like manner rhythm is compounded of elements short and long, once differing and now in accord; which accordance, as in the former instance, medicine, so in all these other cases, music implants, making love and unison to grow up among them; and thus music, too, is concerned with the principles of love in their application to harmony and rhythm. Again, in the essential nature of harmony and rhythm there is no difficulty in discerning love which has not yet become double. But when you want to use them in actual life, either in the composition of songs or in the correct performance of airs or meters composed already, which latter is called education, then the difficulty begins, and the good artist is needed. Then the old tale has to be repeated of fair and heavenly love—the love of Urania [24] the fair and heavenly muse—and of the duty of accepting the temperate, and those who are as yet intemperate only that they may become temperate, and of preserving their love; and again, of the vulgar

23 The poet and philosopher Heraclitus (c. 500 B.C.) had dwelt upon the principles of flux, change, and conflict in the universe. The world, he seems to say here, is held together by the combination of forces pulling opposite ways, as the harmony of bow and lyre is produced by the blending of discordant notes. Fragment 45.

24 The muse of astronomy.

Polyhymnia,[25] who must be used with circumspection that the
pleasure be enjoyed, but may not generate licentiousness; just as in
my own art it is a great matter so to regulate the desires of the epicure
that he may gratify his tastes without the attendant evil of disease. Whence I infer that in music, in medicine, in all other things
human as well as divine, both loves ought to be noted as far as may
be, for they are both present.

"The course of the seasons is also full of both these principles; and
when, as I was saying, the elements of hot and cold, moist and dry,
attain the harmonious love of one another and blend in temperance
and harmony, they bring to men, animals, and plants health and
plenty, and do them no harm; whereas the wanton love, getting the
upper hand and affecting the seasons of the year, is very destructive
and injurious, being the source of pestilence, and bringing many
other kinds of diseases on animals and plants; for hoar-frost and hail
and blight spring from the excesses and disorders of these elements
of love, which to know in relation to the revolutions of the heavenly
bodies and the seasons of the year is termed astronomy. Furthermore
all sacrifices and the whole province of divination, which is the art of
communion between gods and men—these, I say, are concerned only
with the preservation of the good and the cure of the evil love. For
all manner of impiety is likely to ensue if, instead of accepting and
honoring and reverencing the harmonious love in all his actions, a
man honors the other love, whether in his feelings towards gods or
parents, towards the living or the dead. Wherefore the business of
divination is to see to these loves and to heal them, and divination is
the peacemaker of gods and men, working by a knowledge of the
religious or irreligious tendencies which exist in human loves. Such
is the great and mighty, or rather omnipotent force of love in general.
And the love, more especially, which is concerned with the good,
and which is perfected in company with temperance and justice,
whether among gods or men, has the greatest power, and is the source
of all our happiness and harmony, and makes us friends with the

25 The muse of songs and solemn hymns.

gods who are above us, and with one another. I dare say that I too have omitted several things which might be said in praise of Love, but this was not intentional, and you, Aristophanes, may now supply the omission or take some other line of commendation; for I perceive that you are rid of the hiccough."

"Yes," said Aristophanes, who followed, "the hiccough is gone; not, however, until I applied the sneezing; and I wonder whether the harmony of the body has a love of such noises and ticklings, for I no sooner applied the sneezing than I was cured."

Eryximachus said: "Beware, friend Aristophanes, although you are going to speak, you are making fun of me; and I shall have to watch and see whether I cannot have a laugh at your expense, when you might speak in peace."

"You are quite right," said Aristophanes, laughing. "I will unsay my words; but do you please not to watch me, as I fear that in the speech which I am about to make, instead of others laughing with me, which is to the manner born of our muse and would be all the better, I shall only be laughed at by them."

"Do you expect to shoot your bolt and escape, Aristophanes? Well, perhaps if you are very careful and bear in mind that you will be called to account, I may be induced to let you off."

Aristophanes professed to open another vein of discourse; he had a mind to praise Love in another way, unlike that either of Pausanias or Eryximachus. "Mankind," he said, "judging by their neglect of him, have never, as I think, at all understood the power of Love. For if they had understood him they would surely have built noble temples and altars, and offered solemn sacrifices in his honor; but this is not done, and most certainly ought to be done: since of all the gods he is the best friend of men, the helper and the healer of the ills which are the great impediment to the happiness of the race. I will try to describe his power to you, and you shall teach the rest of the world what I am teaching you. In the first place, let me treat of the nature of man and what has happened to it; for the original human nature was not like the present, but different. The sexes were not two as they are now, but originally three in number; there was man,

woman, and the union of the two, having a name corresponding to
this double nature. which had once a real existence, but is now lost,
and the word "androgynous" [26] is only preserved as a term of reproach. In the second place, the primeval man was round, his back
and sides forming a circle; and he had four hands and four feet, one
head with two faces, looking opposite ways, set on a round neck and
precisely alike; also four ears, two privy members, and the remainder
to correspond. He could walk upright as men now do, backwards or
forwards as he pleased, and he could also roll over and over at a great
pace, turning on his four hands and four feet, eight in all, like
tumblers going over and over with their legs in the air; this was when
he wanted to run fast. Now the sexes were three, and such as I have
described them; because the sun, moon, and earth are three; and the
man was originally the child of the sun, the woman of the earth, and
the man-woman of the moon, which is made up of sun and earth, and
they were all round and moved round and round like their parents.
Terrible was their might and strength, and the thoughts of their
hearts were great, and they made an attack upon the gods; of them
is told the tale of Otys and Ephialtes [27] who, as Homer says, dared
to scale heaven, and would have laid hands upon the gods. Doubt
reigned in the celestial councils. Should they kill them and annihilate
the race with thunderbolts, as they had done the giants, then there
would be an end of the sacrifices and worship which men offered to
them; but, on the other hand, the gods could not suffer their insolence to be unrestrained.

"At last, after a good deal of reflection, Zeus discovered a way. He
said: Methinks I have a plan which will humble their pride and
improve their manners; men shall continue to exist, but I will cut
them in two and then they will be diminished in strength and in-
creased in numbers; this will have the advantage of making them
more profitable to us. They shall walk upright on two legs, and if

26 A compound of the Greek words meaning "man" and "woman"—*i.e.*, a creature of two sexes, bisexual.
27 Homer speaks twice of these giants, who tried to scale heaven and subjugate
the gods. *Iliad*, V, 385-391; *Odyssey*, XI, 305-320.

they continue insolent and will not be quiet, I will split them again and they shall hop about on a single leg. He spoke and cut men in two, like a sorb-apple which is halved for pickling, or as you might divide an egg with a hair; and as he cut them one after another, he bade Apollo give the face and the half of the neck a turn in order that the man might contemplate the section of himself: he would thus learn a lesson of humility. Apollo was also bidden to heal their wounds and compose their forms. So he gave a turn to the face and pulled the skin from the sides all over that which in our language is called the belly, like the purses which draw in, and he made one mouth at the center, which he fastened in a knot (the same which is called the navel); he also molded the breast and took out most of the wrinkles, much as a shoemaker might smooth leather upon a last; he left a few, however, in the region of the belly and navel, as a memorial of the primeval state. After the division the two parts of man, each desiring his other half, came together, and throwing their arms about one another, entwined in mutual embraces, longing to grow into one; they were on the point of dying from hunger and self-neglect, because they did not like to do anything apart; and when one of the halves died and the other survived, the survivor sought another mate, man or woman as we call them—being the sections of entire men or women—and clung to that. They were being destroyed, when Zeus in pity of them invented a new plan: he turned the parts of generation round to the front, for this had not been always their position, and they sowed the seed no longer as hitherto like grass-hoppers in the ground, but in one another; and after the transposition the male generated in the female in order that by the mutual embraces of man and woman they might breed, and the race might continue; or if man came to man they might be satisfied, and rest, and go their ways to the business of life: so ancient is the desire of one another which is implanted in us, reuniting our original nature, making one of two, and healing the state of man.

"Each of us when separated, having one side only, like a flat fish, is but the indenture of a man, and he is always looking for his other half. Men who are a section of that double nature which was once

called androgynous are lovers of women; adulterers are generally
of this breed, and also adulterous women who lust after men: the
women who are a section of the woman do not care for men, but
have female attachments; the female companions are of this sort.
But they who are a section of the male follow the male, and while
they are young, being slices of the original man, they hang about
men and embrace them, and they are themselves the best of boys
and youths, because they have the most manly nature. Some indeed
assert that they are shameless, but this is not true; for they do not act
thus from any want of shame, but because they are valiant and
manly, and have a manly countenance, and they embrace that which
is like them. And these when they grow up become our statesmen,
and these only, which is a great proof of the truth of what I am saying. When they reach manhood they are lovers of youth, and are not
naturally inclined to marry or beget children—if at all, they do so
only in obedience to the law; but they are satisfied if they may be
allowed to live with one another unwedded; and such a nature is
prone to love and ready to return love, always embracing that which
is akin to him. And when one of them meets with his other half, the
actual half of himself, whether he be a lover of youth or a lover of
another sort, the pair are lost in an amazement of love and friendship
and intimacy, and one will not be out of the other's sight, as I may
say, even for a moment: these are the people who pass their whole
lives together; yet they could not explain what they desire of one
another. For the intense yearning which each of them has towards the
other does not appear to be the desire of lover's intercourse, but of
something else which the soul of either evidently desires and cannot
tell, and of which she has only a dark and doubtful presentiment.
Suppose Hephaestus,[28] with his instruments, to come to the pair
who are lying side by side and to say to them, 'What do you people
want of one another?' they would be unable to explain. And suppose
further, that when he saw their perplexity he said: 'Do you desire to
be wholly one; always day and night to be in one another's com-

28 The Greek god of fire and metallurgy, whom the Romans later knew as Vulcan.
His instruments were the anvil, bellows, and hammer.

pany? for if this is what you desire, I am ready to melt you into one and let you grow together, so that being two you shall become one, and while you live live a common life as if you were a single man, and after your death in the world below still be one departed soul instead of two; I ask whether this is what you lovingly desire, and whether you are satisfied to attain this?'—there is not a man of them who when he heard the proposal would deny or would not acknowledge that this meeting and melting into one another, this becoming one instead of two, was the very expression of his ancient need.

"And the reason is that human nature was originally one and we were a whole, and the desire and pursuit of the whole is called love. There was a time, I say, when we were one, but now because of the wickedness of mankind God has dispersed us, as the Arcadians were dispersed into villages by the Lacedaemonians.[29] And if we are not obedient to the gods, there is a danger that we shall be split up again and go about in basso-relievo, like the profile figures having only half a nose which are sculptured on monuments, and that we shall be like tallies. Wherefore let us exhort all men to piety, that we may avoid evil, and obtain the good, of which Love is to us the lord and minister; and let no one oppose him—he is the enemy of the gods who opposes him. For if we are friends of the god and at peace with him we shall find our own true loves, which rarely happens in this world at present. I am serious, and therefore I must beg Eryximachus not to make fun or to find any allusion in what I am saying to Pausanias and Agathon, who, as I suspect, are both of the manly nature, and belong to the class which I have been describing. But my words have a wider application—they include men and women everywhere; and I believe that if our loves were perfectly accomplished, and each one returning to his primeval nature had his original true love, then our race would be happy. And if this would be best of all, the best in the next degree and under present circumstances must be the nearest approach to such an union; and that will be the attainment of a con-

---

29 In 385 B.C. the Spartans, in order to crush a revolt of the subject Arcadians, destroyed their chief town, Mantinea, and scattered its inhabitants among the villages.

genial love. Wherefore, if we would praise him who has given to us the benefit, we must praise the god Love, who is our greatest benefactor, both leading us in this life back to our own nature, and giving us high hopes for the future, for he promises that if we are pious, he will restore us to our original state, and heal us and make us happy and blessed. This, Eryximachus, is my discourse of love, which, although different to yours, I must beg you to leave unassailed by the shafts of your ridicule, in order that each may have his turn; each, or rather either, for Agathon and Socrates are the only ones left."

"Indeed, I am not going to attack you," said Eryximachus, "for I thought your speech charming, and did I not know that Agathon and Socrates are masters in the art of love, I should be really afraid that they would have nothing to say, after the world of things which have been said already. But, for all that, I am not without hopes."

Socrates said: "You played your part well, Eryximachus; but if you were as I am now, or rather as I shall be when Agathon has spoken, you would, indeed, be in a great strait."

"You want to cast a spell over me, Socrates," said Agathon, "in the hope that I may be disconcerted at the expectation raised among the audience that I shall speak well."

"I should be strangely forgetful, Agathon," replied Socrates, "of the courage and magnanimity which you showed when your own compositions were about to be exhibited, and you came upon the stage with the actors and faced the vast theater altogether undismayed, if I thought that your nerves could be fluttered at a small party of friends."

"Do you think, Socrates," said Agathon, "that my head is so full of the theater as not to know how much more formidable to a man of sense a few good judges are than many fools?"

"Nay," replied Socrates, "I should be very wrong in attributing to you, Agathon, that or any other want of refinement. And I am quite aware that if you happened to meet with any whom you thought wise, you would care for their opinion much more than for that of the many. But then we, having been a part of the foolish many in the theater, cannot be regarded as the select wise; though I know that if you chanced to be in the presence, not of one of ourselves, but of some really wise man, you would be ashamed of disgracing yourself before him—would you not?"

"Yes," said Agathon.

"But before the many you would not be ashamed, if you thought that you were doing something disgraceful in their presence?"

Here Phaedrus interrupted them, saying: "Do not answer him, my dear Agathon; for if he can only get a partner with whom he can talk, especially a good-looking one, he will no longer care about the completion of our plan. Now I love to hear him talk; but just at present I must not forget the encomium on Love which I ought to receive from him and from everyone. When you and he have paid your tribute to the god, then you may talk."

"Very good, Phaedrus," said Agathon; "I see no reason why I should not proceed with my speech, as I shall have many other opportunities of conversing with Socrates. Let me say first how I ought to speak, and then speak:

"The previous speakers, instead of praising the god Love, or unfolding his nature, appear to have congratulated mankind on the benefits which he confers upon them. But I would rather praise the god first, and then speak of his gifts; this is always the right way of praising everything. May I say without impiety or offense, that of all the blessed gods he is the most blessed because he is the fairest and best? And he is the fairest: for, in the first place, he is the youngest, and of his youth he is himself the witness, fleeing out of the way of age, who is swift enough, swifter truly than most of us like. Love hates him and will not come near him; but youth and love live and move together—like to like, as the proverb says. Many things were said by Phaedrus about Love in which I agree with him; but I cannot agree that he is older than Iapetus and Cronus [30]—not so; I maintain him to be the youngest of the gods, and youthful ever. The ancient

---

30 On Cronus, see *Symposium*, note 19. Iapetus was the brother of Cronus and like him, a Titan. In the myth the two were the first inhabitants of the earth.

doings among the gods of which Hesiod and Parmenides [31] spoke, if
the tradition of them be true, were done of Necessity and not of
Love; had Love been in those days, there would have been no chain-
ing or mutilation of the gods, or other violence, but peace and sweetness, as there is now in heaven, since the rule of Love began. Love is
young and also tender; he ought to have a poet like Homer to describe his tenderness, as Homer says of Ate,[32] that she is a goddess
and tender:

> Her feet are tender, for she sets her steps,
> Not on the ground but on the heads of men.

Herein is an excellent proof of her tenderness—that she walks not
upon the hard but upon the soft. Let us adduce a similar proof of the
tenderness of Love; for he walks not upon the earth, nor yet upon
the skulls of men, which are not so very soft, but in the hearts and
souls of both gods and men, which are of all things the softest: in
them he walks and dwells and makes his home. Not in every soul
without exception, for where there is hardness he departs, where
there is softness there he dwells; and nestling always with his feet
and in all manner of ways in the softest of soft places, how can he be
other than the softest of all things? Of a truth he is the tenderest as
well as the youngest, and also he is of flexile form; for if he were hard
and without flexure he could not enfold all things, or wind his way
into and out of every soul of man undiscovered. And a proof of his
flexibility and symmetry of form is his grace, which is universally
admitted to be in an especial manner the attribute of Love; ungrace
and love are always at war with one another. The fairness of his complexion is revealed by his habitation among the flowers; for he dwells
not amid bloomless or fading beauties, whether of body or soul or
aught else, but in the place of flowers and scents, there he sits and
abides. Concerning the beauty of the god I have said enough; and

31 The *Theogony* of Hesiod contains some primitive, savage tales of gods cruel to
one another. 176-182, 453-462, 853-868, 886-900. None of Parmenides' tales have
come down to us.

32 Ate, the goddess of bane and destruction, is described in the *Iliad*, XIX, 91-94.

yet there remains much more which I might say. Of his virtue I have now to speak: his greatest glory is that he can neither do nor suffer wrong to or from any god or any man; for he suffers not by force if he suffers; force comes not near him, neither when he acts does he act by force. For all men in all things serve him of their own free will, and where there is voluntary agreement, there, as the laws which are the lords of the city say, is justice. And not only is he just but exceedingly temperate, for Temperance is the acknowledged ruler of the pleasures and desires, and no pleasure ever masters Love; he is their master and they are his servants; and if he conquers them he must be temperate indeed. As to courage, even the God of War is no match for him; he is the captive and Love is the lord, for love, the love of Aphrodite, masters him, as the tale runs; [33] and the master is stronger than the servant. And if he conquers the bravest of all others, he must be himself the bravest.

"Of his courage and justice and temperance I have spoken, but I have yet to speak of his wisdom; [34] and according to the measure of my ability I must try to do my best. In the first place he is a poet (and here, like Eryximachus, I magnify my art), and he is also the source of poesy in others, which he could not be if he were not himself a poet. And at the touch of him everyone becomes a poet, even though he had no music in him before; this also is a proof that Love is a good poet and accomplished in all the fine arts; for no one can give to another that which he has not himself, or teach that of which he has no knowledge. Who will deny that the creation of the animals is his doing? Are they not all the works of his wisdom, born and begotten of him? And as to the artists, do we not know that he only of them whom love inspires has the light of fame?—he whom Love touches not walks in darkness. The arts of medicine and archery and divination were discovered by Apollo, under the guidance of love and desire; so that he too is a disciple of Love. Also the melody of the

33 Ares, god of war, was in the Greek myth the husband of Aphrodite, goddess of love, as in the imitative Latin myth Mars was the husband of Venus.

34 Love is endowed by Agathon with the four great Greek virtues, justice, temperance, courage, and wisdom.

Muses, the metallurgy of Hephaestus, the weaving of Athene,[35] the empire of Zeus over gods and men, are all due to Love, who was the inventor of them. And so Love set in order the empire of the gods— the love of beauty, as is evident, for with deformity Love has no concern. In the days of old, as I began by saying, dreadful deeds were done among the gods, for they were ruled by Necessity; but now since the birth of Love, and from the love of the beautiful, has sprung every good in heaven and earth. Therefore, Phaedrus, I say of Love that he is the fairest and best in himself, and the cause of what is fairest and best in all other things. And there comes into my mind a line of poetry in which he is said to be the god who

> Gives peace on earth and calms the stormy deep,
> Who stills the winds and bids the sufferer sleep.[36]

This is he who empties men of disaffection and fills them with affection, who makes them to meet together at banquets such as these: in sacrifices, feasts, dances, he is our lord—who sends courtesy and sends away discourtesy, who gives kindness ever and never gives unkindness; the friend of the good, the wonder of the wise, the amazement of the gods; desired by those who have no part in him, and precious to those who have the better part in him; parent of delicacy, luxury, desire, fondness, softness, grace; regardful of the good, regardless of the evil: in every word, work, wish, fear—savior, pilot, comrade, helper; glory of gods and men, leader best and brightest: in whose footsteps let every man follow, sweetly singing in his honor and joining in that sweet strain with which love charms the souls of gods and men. Such is the speech, Phaedrus, half-playful, yet having a certain measure of seriousness, which, according to my ability, I dedicate to the god."

When Agathon had done speaking, Aristodemus said that there was a general cheer; the young man was thought to have spoken in

35 Athene, the virgin patroness of Athens, was goddess of intelligence and various crafts and skills. Among the Romans her place was filled by Minerva.
36 Agathon is here apparently quoting a line of some composition of his own, with an echo in it of *Odyssey*, V, 391, 392.

a manner worthy of himself, and of the god. And Socrates, looking at Eryximachus, said: "Tell me, son of Acumenus, was there not reason in my fears? and was I not a true prophet when I said that Agathon would make a wonderful oration, and that I should be in a strait?"

"The part of the prophecy which concerns Agathon," replied Eryximachus, "appears to me to be true; but not the other part—that you will be in a strait."

"Why, my dear friend," said Socrates, "must not I or anyone be in a strait who has to speak after he has heard such a rich and varied discourse? I am especially struck with the beauty of the concluding words—who could listen to them without amazement? When I reflected on the immeasurable inferiority of my own powers, I was ready to run away for shame, if there had been a possibility of escape. For I was reminded of Gorgias, and at the end of his speech I fancied that Agathon was shaking at me the Gorginian or Gorgonian head of the great master of rhetoric, which was simply to turn me and my speech into stone, as Homer says,[37] and strike me dumb. And then I perceived how foolish I had been in consenting to take my turn with you in praising love, and saying that I too was a master of the art, when I really had no conception how anything ought to be praised. For in my simplicity I imagined that the topics of praise should be true, and that this being presupposed, out of the true the speaker was to choose the best and set them forth in the best manner. And I felt quite proud, thinking that I knew the nature of true praise, and should speak well. Whereas I now see that the intention was to attribute to Love every species of greatness and glory, whether really belonging to him or not, without regard to truth or falsehood—that was no matter; for the original proposal seems to have been not that each of you should really praise Love, but only that you should appear to praise him. And so you attribute to Love every imaginable form of praise which can be gathered anywhere; and you say that 'he

---

37 The Sophist Gorgias, under whom Agathon may have studied, was known as an elegant speaker. Socrates pretends to be as terrified as Odysseus was at the entrance to Hades, when he thought he might meet the Gorgon Medusa's head, which turned everyone who looked on it into stone. *Odyssey*, XI, 632-635.

is all this,' and 'the cause of all that,' making him appear the fairest and best of all to those who know him not, for you cannot impose upon those who know him. And a noble and solemn hymn of praise have you rehearsed. But as I misunderstood the nature of the praise when I said that I would take my turn, I must beg to be absolved from the promise which I made in ignorance, and which (as Euripides would say) [38] was a promise of the lips and not of the mind. Farewell then to such a strain: for I do not praise in that way; no, indeed, I cannot. But if you like to hear the truth about love, I am ready to speak in my own manner, though I will not make myself ridiculous by entering into any rivalry with you. Say then, Phaedrus, whether you would like to have the truth about love, spoken in any words and in any order which may happen to come into my mind at the time. Will that be agreeable to you?"

Aristodemus said that Phaedrus and the company bade him speak in any manner which he thought best. "Then," he added, "let me have your permission first to ask Agathon a few more questions, in order that I may take his admissions as the premises of my discourse."

"I grant the permission," said Phaedrus; "put your questions." Socrates then proceeded as follows:

"In the magnificent oration which you have just uttered, I think that you were right, my dear Agathon, in proposing to speak of the nature of Love first and afterwards of his works—that is a way of beginning which I very much approve. And as you have spoken so eloquently of his nature, may I ask you further, Whether love is the love of something or of nothing? And here I must explain myself: I do not want you to say that love is the love of a father or the love of a mother—that would be ridiculous; but to answer as you would, if I asked is a father a father of something? to which you would find no difficulty in replying, of a son or daughter: and the answer would be right."

"Very true," said Agathon.

"And you would say the same of a mother?"

---

38 Euripides, *Hippolytus*, 612. "My tongue hath sworn; my mind is yet unsworn."

He assented.

"Yet let me ask you one more question in order to illustrate my meaning: Is not a brother to be regarded essentially as a brother of something?"

"Certainly," he replied.

"That is, of a brother or sister?"

"Yes," he said.

"And now," said Socrates, "I will ask about Love: Is Love of something or of nothing?"

"Of something, surely," he replied.

"Keep in mind what this is, and tell me what I want to know—whether Love desires that of which love is."

"Yes, surely."

"And does he possess, or does he not possess, that which he loves and desires?"

"Probably not, I should say."

"Nay," replied Socrates, "I would have you consider whether 'necessarily' is not rather the word. The inference that he who desires something is in want of something, and that he who desires nothing is in want of nothing, is in my judgment, Agathon, absolutely and necessarily true. What do you think?"

"I agree with you," said Agathon.

"Very good. Would he who is great, desire to be great, or he who is strong, desire to be strong?"

"That would be inconsistent with our previous admissions."

"True. For he who is anything cannot want to be that which he is?"

"Very true."

"And yet," added Socrates, "if a man being strong desired to be strong, or being swift desired to be swift, or being healthy desired to be healthy, in that case he might be thought to desire something which he already has or is. I give the example in order that we may avoid misconception. For the possessors of these qualities, Agathon, must be supposed to have their respective advantages at the time, whether they choose or not; and who can desire that which he has?

Therefore, when a person says, I am well and wish to be well, or I am rich and wish to be rich, and I desire simply to have what I have —to him we shall reply: You, my friend, having wealth and health and strength, want to have the continuance of them; for at this moment, whether you choose or no, you have them. And when you say, I desire that which I have and nothing else, is not your meaning that you want to have what you now have in the future? He must agree with us—must he not?"

"He must," replied Agathon.

"Then," said Socrates, "he desires that what he has at present may be preserved to him in the future, which is equivalent to saying that he desires something which is nonexistent to him, and which as yet he has not got."

"Very true," he said.

"Then he and everyone who desires, desires that which he has not already, and which is future and not present, and which he has not, and is not, and of which he is in want; these are the sort of things which love and desire seek?"

"Very true," he said.

"Then now," said Socrates, "let us recapitulate the argument. First, is not love of something, and of something too which is wanting to a man?"

"Yes," he replied.

"Remember further what you said in your speech, or if you do not remember I will remind you: you said that the love of the beautiful set in order the empire of the gods, for that of deformed things there is no love—did you not say something of that kind?"

"Yes," said Agathon.

"Yes, my friend, and the remark was a just one. And if this is true, Love is the love of beauty and not of deformity?"

He assented.

"And the admission has been already made that Love is of something which a man wants and has not?"

"True," he said.

"Then Love wants and has not beauty?"

"Certainly," he replied.

"And would you call that beautiful which wants and does not possess beauty?"

"Certainly not."

"Then would you still say that love is beautiful?"

Agathon replied: "I fear that I did not understand what I was saying."

"You made a very good speech, Agathon," replied Socrates; "but there is yet one small question which I would fain ask: Is not the good also the beautiful?"

"Yes."

"Then in wanting the beautiful, love wants also the good?"

"I cannot refute you, Socrates," said Agathon. "Let us assume that what you say is true."

"Say rather, beloved Agathon, that you cannot refute the truth; for Socrates is easily refuted.

"And now, taking my leave of you, I will rehearse a tale of love which I heard from Diotima of Mantinea,[39] a woman wise in this and in many other kinds of knowledge, who in the days of old, when the Athenians offered sacrifice before the coming of the plague, delayed the disease ten years. She was my instructress in the art of love, and I shall repeat to you what she said to me, beginning with the admissions made by Agathon, which are nearly if not quite the same which I made to the wise woman when she questioned me: I think that this will be the easiest way, and I shall take both parts myself as well as I can. As you, Agathon, suggested, I must speak first of the being and nature of Love, and then of his works. First I said to her in nearly the same words which he used to me, that Love was a mighty god, and likewise fair; and she proved to me as I proved to him that, by my own showing, Love was neither fair nor good. 'What do you mean, Diotima,' I said, 'is love then evil and foul?' 'Hush,

---

39 To a Greek these names would suggest something divinely favored in the woman and prophetic in the place from which she came. Whether Diotima was a real woman or a figment of Socrates' or, more probably, Plato's imagination, we do not know.

she cried; 'must that be foul which is not fair?' 'Certainly,' I said. 'And is that which is not wise, ignorant? do you not see that there is a mean between wisdom and ignorance?' 'And what may that be?' I said. 'Right opinion,' she replied; 'which, as you know, being incapable of giving a reason, is not knowledge (for how can knowledge be devoid of reason?) nor again, ignorance (for neither can ignorance attain the truth), but is clearly something which is a mean between ignorance and wisdom.' 'Quite true,' I replied. 'Do not then insist,' she said, 'that what is not fair is of necessity foul, or what is not good evil; or infer that because love is not fair and good he is therefore foul and evil; for he is in a mean between them.' 'Well,' I said, 'Love is surely admitted by all to be a great god.' 'By those who know or by those who do not know?' 'By all.' 'And now, Socrates,' she said with a smile, 'can Love be acknowledged to be a great god by those who say that he is not a god at all?' 'And who are they?' I said. 'You and I are two of them,' she replied. 'How can that be?' I said. 'It is quite intelligible,' she replied; 'for you yourself would acknowledge that the gods are happy and fair—of course you would —would you dare to say that any god was not?' 'Certainly not,' I replied. 'And you mean by the happy, those who are the possessors of things good or fair?' 'Yes.' 'And you admitted that Love, because he was in want, desires those good and fair things of which he is in want?' 'Yes, I did.' 'But how can he be a god who has no portion in what is either good or fair?' 'Impossible.' 'Then you see that you also deny the divinity of Love.'

" 'What then is Love?' I asked; 'is he mortal?' 'No.' 'What then?' 'As in the former instance, he is neither mortal nor immortal, but in a mean between the two.' 'What is he, Diotima?' 'He is a great spirit (δαίμων), and like all spirits he is intermediate between the divine and the mortal.' 'And what,' I said, 'is his power?' 'He interprets,' she replied, 'between gods and men, conveying and taking across to the gods the prayers and sacrifices of men, and to men the commands and replies of the gods; he is the mediator who spans the chasm which divides them, and therefore in him all is bound together, and through him the arts of the prophet and the priest, their sacrifices and mys-

teries and charms, and all prophecy and incantation, find their way.
For God mingles not with man; but through Love all the intercourse
and converse of God with man, whether awake or asleep, is carried
on. The wisdom which understands this is spiritual; all other wisdom,
such as that of arts and handicrafts, is mean and vulgar. Now these
spirits or intermediate powers are many and diverse, and one of them
is Love.' 'And who,' I said, 'was his father, and who his mother?'
'The tale,' she said, 'will take time; nevertheless I will tell you. On
the birthday of Aphrodite there was a feast of the gods, at which the
god Poros or Plenty, who is the son of Metis or Discretion, was one of
the guests. When the feast was over, Penia or Poverty, as the manner
is on such occasions, came about the doors to beg. Now Plenty, who
was the worse for nectar (there was no wine in those days), went into
the garden of Zeus and fell into a heavy sleep; and Poverty, considering her own straitened circumstances, plotted to have a child by him,
and accordingly she lay down at his side and conceived Love, who
partly because he is naturally a lover of the beautiful, and because
Aphrodite is herself beautiful, and also because he was born on her
birthday, is her follower and attendant. And as his parentage is, so
also are his fortunes. In the first place he is always poor, and anything but tender and fair, as the many imagine him; and he is rough
and squalid, and has no shoes, nor a house to dwell in; on the bare
earth exposed he lies under the open heaven, in the streets, or at the
doors of houses, taking his rest; and like his mother he is always in
distress. Like his father too, whom he also partly resembles, he is
always plotting against the fair and good; he is bold, enterprising,
strong, a mighty hunter, always weaving some intrigue or other, keen
in the pursuit of wisdom, fertile in resources; a philosopher at all
times, terrible as an enchanter, sorcerer, sophist. He is by nature
neither mortal nor immortal, but alive and flourishing at one moment when he is in plenty, and dead at another moment, and again
alive by reason of his father's nature. But that which is always flowing in is always flowing out, and so he is never in want and never in
wealth; and, further, he is in a mean between ignorance and knowledge. The truth of the matter is this: No god is a philosopher or

seeker after wisdom, for he is wise already; nor does any man who is wise seek after wisdom. Neither do the ignorant seek after wisdom. For herein is the evil of ignorance, that he who is neither good nor wise is nevertheless satisfied with himself: he has no desire for that of which he feels no want.'

" 'But who then, Diotima,' I said, 'are the lovers of wisdom, if they are neither the wise nor the foolish?' 'A child may answer that question,' she replied; 'they are those who are in a mean between the two; Love is one of them. For wisdom is a most beautiful thing, and Love is of the beautiful; and therefore Love is also a philosopher or lover of wisdom, and being a lover of wisdom is in a mean between the wise and the ignorant. And of this too his birth is the cause; for his father is wealthy and wise, and his mother poor and foolish. Such, my dear Socrates, is the nature of the spirit Love. The error in your conception of him was very natural, and as I imagine from what you say, has arisen out of a confusion of love and the beloved, which made you think that love was all beautiful. For the beloved is the truly beautiful, and delicate, and perfect, and blessed; but the principle of love is of another nature, and is such as I have described.'

"I said: 'O thou stranger woman, thou sayest well; but, assuming Love to be such as you say, what is the use of him to men?' 'That, Socrates,' she replied, 'I will attempt to unfold: of his nature and birth I have already spoken; and you acknowledge that love is of the beautiful. But someone will say: Of the beautiful in what, Socrates and Diotima?—or rather let me put the question more clearly, and ask: When a man loves the beautiful, what does he desire?' I answered her: 'That the beautiful may be his.' 'Still,' she said, 'the answer suggests a further question: What is given by the possession of beauty?' 'To what you have asked,' I replied, 'I have no answer ready.' 'Then,' she said, 'let me put the word "good" in the place of the beautiful, and repeat the question once more: If he who loves loves the good, what is it then that he loves?' 'The possession of the good,' I said. 'And what does he gain who possesses the good?' 'Happiness,' I replied; 'there is less difficulty in answering that question.' 'Yes,' she said, 'the happy are made happy by the acquisition of good

things. Nor is there any need to ask why a man desires happiness;
the answer is already final.' 'You are right,' I said. 'And is this wish
and this desire common to all? and do all men always desire their
own good, or only some men?—what say you?' 'All men,' I replied;
'the desire is common to all.' 'Why, then,' she rejoined, 'are not all
men, Socrates, said to love, but only some of them? Whereas you say
that all men are always loving the same things.' 'I myself wonder,' I
said, 'why this is.' 'There is nothing to wonder at,' she replied; 'the
reason is that one part of love is separated off and receives the name
of the whole, but the other parts have other names.' 'Give an illustration,' I said.

"She answered me as follows: 'There is poetry, which, as you
know, is complex and manifold. All creation or passage of non-being
into being is poetry or making,[40] and the processes of all art are creative; and the masters of arts are all poets or makers.' 'Very true.'
'Still,' she said, 'you know that they are not called poets, but have
other names; only that portion of the art which is separated off from
the rest, and is concerned with music and meter, is termed poetry,
and they who possess poetry in this sense of the word are called poets.'
'Very true,' I said. 'And the same holds of love. For you may say
generally that all desire of good and happiness is only the great and
subtle power of love; but they who are drawn towards him by any
other path, whether the path of money-making or gymnastics or
philosophy, are not called lovers—the name of the whole is appro-
priated to those whose affection takes one form only—they alone are
said to love, or to be lovers.' 'I dare say,' I replied, 'that you are right.'
'Yes,' she added, 'and you hear people say that lovers are seeking for
their other half;[41] but I say that they are seeking neither for the half
of themselves, nor for the whole, unless the half or the whole be also a
good. And they will cut off their own hands and feet and cast them
away, if they are evil; for they love not what is their own, unless per-

40 The Greek word meaning "poetry," poiesis, comes like our own word from
the Greek verb that means "to make." Hence the earliest meaning of poetry was a
making, a creating, and a poet might be a maker of other things besides verse.
Diotima chooses to recall the old meaning.
41 An allusion to Aristophanes' speech.

chance there be someone who calls what belongs to him the good, and what belongs to another the evil. For there is nothing which men love but the good. Is there anything?' 'Certainly, I should say, that there is nothing.' 'Then,' she said, 'the simple truth is, that men love the good.' 'Yes,' I said. 'To which must be added that they love the possession of the good?' 'Yes, that must be added.' 'And not only the possession, but the everlasting possession of the good?' 'That must be added too.' 'Then love,' she said, 'may be described generally as the love of the everlasting possession of the good?' 'That is most true.'

" 'Then if this be the nature of love, can you tell me further,' she said, 'what is the manner of the pursuit? what are they doing who show all this eagerness and heat which is called love? and what is the object which they have in view? Answer me.' 'Nay, Diotima,' I replied, 'if I had known, I should not have wondered at your wisdom, neither should I have come to learn from you about this very matter.' 'Well,' she said, 'I will teach you: The object which they have in view is birth in beauty, whether of body or soul.' 'I do not understand you,' I said; 'the oracle requires an explanation.' 'I will make my meaning clearer,' she replied. 'I mean to say, that all men are bringing to birth in their bodies and in their souls. There is a certain age at which human nature is desirous of procreation—procreation which must be in beauty and not in deformity; and this procreation is the union of man and woman, and is a divine thing; for conception and generation are an immortal principle in the mortal creature, and in the inharmonious they can never be. But the deformed is always inharmonious with the divine, and the beautiful harmonious. Beauty, then, is the destiny or goddess of parturition who presides at birth, and therefore, when approaching beauty, the conceiving power is propitious, and diffusive, and benign, and begets and bears fruit: at the sight of ugliness she frowns and contracts and has a sense of pain, and turns away, and shrivels up, and not without a pang refrains from conception. And this is the reason why, when the hour of conception arrives, and the teeming nature is full, there is such a flutter and ecstasy about beauty, whose approach is the alleviation of the pain of travail. For love, Socrates, is not, as you imagine, the love of the beautiful only.' 'What then?' 'The love of generation and of birth in beauty.' 'Yes,' I said. 'Yes, indeed,' she replied. 'But why of generation?' 'Because to the mortal creature, generation is a sort of eternity and immortality,' she replied; 'and if, as has been already admitted, love is of the everlasting possession of the good, all men will necessarily desire immortality together with good: wherefore love is of immortality.'

"All this she taught me at various times when she spoke of love. And I remember her once saying to me, 'What is the cause, Socrates, of love, and the attendant desire? See you not how all animals, birds, as well as beasts, in their desire of procreation, are in agony when they take the infection of love, which begins with the desire of union; whereto is added the care of offspring, on whose behalf the weakest are ready to battle against the strongest even to the uttermost, and to die for them, and will let themselves be tormented with hunger or suffer anything in order to maintain their young. Man may be supposed to act thus from reason; but why should animals have these passionate feelings? Can you tell me why?' Again I replied that I did not know. She said to me: 'And do you expect ever to become a master in the art of love, if you do not know this?' 'But I have told you already, Diotima, that my ignorance is the reason why I come to you; for I am conscious that I want a teacher; tell me then the cause of this and of the other mysteries of love.' 'Marvel not,' she said, 'if you believe that love is of the immortal, as we have several times acknowledged; for here again, and on the same principle too, the mortal nature is seeking as far as is possible to be everlasting and immortal: and this is only to be attained by generation, because generation always leaves behind a new existence in the place of the old. Nay, even in the life of the same individual there is succession and not absolute unity: a man is called the same, and yet in the short interval which elapses between youth and age, and in which every animal is said to have life and identity, he is undergoing a perpetual process of loss and reparation—hair, flesh, bones, blood, and the whole body are always changing. Which is true not only of the body, but also of the soul, whose habits, tempers, opinions, desires, pleasures, pains, fears, never remain the same in any one of us, but are always coming and going; and equally true of knowledge, and what is still more surprising to us mortals, not only do the sciences in general spring up and decay, so that in respect of them we are never the same; but each of them individually experiences a like change.[42] For what is implied in the word "recollection," but the departure of knowledge, which is ever being forgotten, and is renewed and preserved by recollection, and appears to be the same although in reality new, according to that law of succession by which all mortal things are preserved, not absolutely the same, but by substitution, the old worn-out mortality leaving another new and similar existence behind—unlike the divine, which is always the same and not another? And in this way, Socrates, the mortal body, or mortal anything, partakes of immortality; but the immortal in another way. Marvel not then at the love which all men have of their offspring; for that universal love and interest is for the sake of immortality.'

"I was astonished at her words, and said: 'Is this really true, O thou wise Diotima?' And she answered with all the authority of an accomplished sophist: 'Of that, Socrates, you may be assured; think only of the ambition of men, and you will wonder at the senselessness of their ways, unless you consider how they are stirred by the love of an immortality of fame. They are ready to run all risks greater far than they would have run for their children, and to spend money and undergo any sort of toil, and even to die, for the sake of leaving behind them a name which shall be eternal. Do you imagine that Alcestis [43] would have died to save Admetus, or Achilles to avenge Patroclus, or your own Codrus in order to preserve the kingdom for

42 A clearer rendering of this passage is: "And stranger far than this, our knowledge changes. Some of it grows and some is lost, so that we are never the same even in what we know and each separate piece of our knowledge undergoes the same change."

43 The examples of Alcestis and Achilles have already been cited by Phaedrus in his speech. Codrus, a legendary king of Athens, offered himself to be slain because an oracle had said that only after the invading enemy had killed the Athenian king would they be driven out.

his sons, if they had not imagined that the memory of their virtues, which still survives among us, would be immortal? Nay,' she said, 'I am persuaded that all men do all things, and the better they are the more they do them, in hope of the glorious fame of immortal virtue; for they desire the immortal.

" 'Those who are pregnant in the body only betake themselves to women and beget children—this is the character of their love; their offspring, as they hope, will preserve their memory and give them the blessedness and immortality which they desire in the future. But souls which are pregnant—for there certainly are men who are more cre- ative in their souls than in their bodies—conceive that which is proper for the soul to conceive or contain. And what are these conceptions? —wisdom and virtue in general. And such creators are poets and all artists who are deserving of the name inventor. But the greatest and fairest sort of wisdom by far is that which is concerned with the ordering of states and families, and which is called temperance and justice. And he who in youth has the seed of these implanted in him and is himself inspired, when he comes to maturity desires to beget and generate. He wanders about seeking beauty that he may beget offspring—for in deformity he will beget nothing—and naturally em- braces the beautiful rather than the deformed body; above all, when he finds a fair and noble and well-nurtured soul, he embraces the two in one person, and to such a one he is full of speech about virtue and the nature and pursuits of a good man; and he tries to educate him; and at the touch of the beautiful which is ever present to his memory, even when absent, he brings forth that which he had conceived long before, and in company with him tends that which he brings forth; and they are married by a far nearer tie and have a closer friendship than those who beget mortal children, for the children who are their common offspring are fairer and more immortal. Who, when he thinks of Homer and Hesiod and other great poets, would not rather have their children than ordinary human ones? Who would not emulate them in the creation of children such as theirs, which have preserved their memory and given them everlasting glory? Or who would not have such children as Lycurgus [44] left behind him to be the saviors, not only of Lacedaemon, but of Hellas, as one may say? There is Solon, too, who is the revered father of Athenian laws; and many others there are in many other places, both among Hellenes and barbarians, who have given to the wo.ld many noble works, and have been the parents of virtue of every kind; and many temples have been raised in their honor for the sake of children such as theirs; which were never raised in honor of anyone, for the sake of his mortal children.

" 'These are the lesser mysteries of love, into which even you, Socrates, may enter; to the greater and more hidden ones which are the crown of these, and to which, if you pursue them in a right spirit, they will lead, I know not whether you will be able to attain. But I will do my utmost to inform you, and do you follow if you can. For he who would proceed aright in this matter should begin in youth to visit beautiful forms; and first, if he be guided by his instructor aright, to love one such form only—out of that he should create fair thoughts; and soon he will of himself perceive that the beauty of one form is akin to the beauty of another; and then if beauty of form in general is his pursuit, how foolish would he be not to recognize that the beauty in every form is one and the same! And when he perceives this he will abate his violent love of the one, which he will despise and deem a small thing, and will become a lover of all beautiful forms; in the next stage he will consider that the beauty of the mind is more honorable than the beauty of the outward form. So that if a virtuous soul have but a little comeliness, he will be content to love and tend him, and will search out and bring to the birth thoughts which may improve the young, until he is compelled to contemplate and see the beauty of institutions and laws, and to understand that the beauty of them all is of one family, and that personal beauty is a trifle; and after laws and institutions he will go on to the sciences, that he may see their beauty, being not like a servant in love with the beauty of one youth or man or institution, himself a

---

[44] The legendary founder of the Spartan laws and constitution. Solon (c. 600 B.C.) was the great lawgiver and statesman of early Athenian history.

slave mean and narrow-minded, but drawing towards and contemplating the vast sea of beauty, he will create many fair and noble thoughts and notions in boundless love of wisdom; until on that shore he grows and waxes strong, and at last the vision is revealed to him of a single science, which is the science of beauty everywhere. To this I will proceed; please to give me your very best attention:

" 'He who has been instructed thus far in the things of love, and who has learned to see the beautiful in due order and succession, when he comes toward the end will suddenly perceive a nature of wondrous beauty (and this, Socrates, is the final cause of all our former toils)—a nature which in the first place is everlasting, not growing and decaying, or waxing and waning; secondly, not fair in one point of view and foul in another, or at one time or in one relation or at one place fair, at another time or in another relation or at another place foul, as if fair to some and foul to others, or in the likeness of a face or hands or any other part of the bodily frame, or in any form of speech or knowledge, or existing in any other being, as for example, in an animal, or in heaven, or in earth, or in any other place; but beauty absolute, separate, simple, and everlasting, which without diminution and without increase, or any change, is imparted to the ever-growing and perishing beauties of all other things. He who, from these ascending under the influence of true love, begins to perceive that beauty is not far from the end. And the true order of going, or being led by another, to the things of love, is to begin from the beauties of earth and mount upwards for the sake of that other beauty, using these as steps only, and from one going on to two, and from two to all fair forms, and from fair forms to fair practices, and from fair practices to fair notions, until from fair notions he arrives at the notion of absolute beauty, and at last knows what the essence of beauty is. This, my dear Socrates,' said the stranger of Mantinea, 'is that life above all others which man should live, in the contemplation of beauty absolute; a beauty which if you once beheld, you would see not to be after the measure of gold, and garments, and fair boys and youths, whose presence now entrances you; and you and many a one would be content to live seeing them only and conversing with them without meat or drink, if that were possible—you only want to look at them and to be with them. But what if man had eyes to see the true beauty—the divine beauty, I mean, pure and clear and unalloyed, not clogged with the pollutions of mortality and all the colors and vanities of human life—thither looking, and holding converse with the true beauty simple and divine? Remember how in that communion only, beholding beauty with the eye of the mind, he will be enabled to bring forth, not images of beauty, but realities (for he has hold not of an image but of a reality), and bringing forth and nourishing true virtue to become the friend of God and immortal, if mortal man may. Would that be an ignoble life?'

"Such, Phaedrus—and I speak not only to you, but to all of you—were the words of Diotima; and I am persuaded of their truth. And being persuaded of them, I try to persuade others, that in the attainment of this end human nature will not easily find a helper better than love. And therefore, also, I say that every man ought to honor him as I myself honor him, and walk in his ways, and exhort others to do the same, and praise the power and spirit of love according to the measure of my ability now and ever.

"The words which I have spoken, you, Phaedrus, may call an encomium of love, or anything else which you please."

When Socrates had done speaking, the company applauded, and Aristophanes was beginning to say something in answer to the allusion which Socrates had made to his own speech, when suddenly there was a great knocking at the door of the house, as of revelers, and the sound of a flute-girl was heard. Agathon told the attendants to go and see who were the intruders. "If they are friends of ours," he said, "invite them in, but if not, say that the drinking is over."

A little while afterwards they heard the voice of Alcibiades resounding in the court; he was in a great state of intoxication, and kept roaring and shouting, "Where is Agathon? Lead me to Agathon," and at length, supported by the flute-girl and some of his attendants, he found his way to them.

"Hail, friends," he said, appearing at the door crowned with a massive garland of ivy and violets, his head flowing with ribands: "Will you have a very drunken man as a companion of your revels? Or shall I crown Agathon, which was my intention in coming, and go away? For I was unable to come yesterday, and therefore I am here today, carrying on my head these ribands, that taking them from my own head, I may crown the head of this fairest and wisest of men, as I may be allowed to call him. Will you laugh at me because I am drunk? Yet I know very well that I am speaking the truth, although you may laugh. But first tell me: if I come in shall we have the understanding of which I spoke? Will you drink with me or not?"

The company were vociferous in begging that he would take his place among them, and Agathon specially invited him. Thereupon he was led in by the people who were with him; and as he was being led, intending to crown Agathon, he took the ribands from his own head and held them in front of his eyes; he was thus prevented from seeing Socrates, who made way for him, and Alcibiades took the vacant place between Agathon and Socrates, and in taking the place he embraced Agathon and crowned him.

"Take off his sandals," said Agathon, "and let him make a third on the same couch."

"By all means; but who makes the third partner in our revels?" said Alcibiades, turning round and starting up as he caught sight of Socrates. "By Heracles," he said, "what is this? Here is Socrates always lying in wait for me, and always, as his way is, coming out at all sorts of unsuspected places: and now, what have you to say for yourself, and why are you lying here, where I perceive that you have contrived to find a place, not by a joker or lover of jokes, like Aristophanes, but by the fairest of the company?"

Socrates turned to Agathon and said: "I must ask you to protect me, Agathon; for the passion of this man has grown quite a serious matter to me. Since I became his admirer I have never been allowed to speak to any other fair one, or so much as to look at them. If I do, he goes wild with envy and jealousy, and not only abuses me but can hardly keep his hands off me, and at this moment he may do me some harm. Please to see to this, and either reconcile me to him, or, if he attempts violence, protect me, as I am in bodily fear of his mad and passionate attempts."

"There can never be reconciliation between you and me," said Alcibiades; "but for the present I will defer your chastisement. And I must beg you, Agathon, to give me back some of the ribands that I may crown the marvelous head of this universal despot—I would not have him complain of me for crowning you, and neglecting him—who in conversation is the conqueror of all mankind; and this not only once, as you were the day before yesterday, but always." Whereupon, taking some of the ribands, he crowned Socrates, and again reclined.

Then he said: "You seem, my friends, to be sober, which is a thing not to be endured; you must drink—for that was the agreement under which I was admitted—and I elect myself master of the feast until you are well drunk. Let us have a large goblet, Agathon, or rather," he said, addressing the attendant, "bring me that wine-cooler." The wine-cooler which had caught his eye was a vessel holding more than two quarts—this he filled and emptied, and bade the attendant fill it again for Socrates.

"Observe, my friends," said Alcibiades, "that this ingenious trick of mine will have no effect on Socrates, for he can drink any quantity of wine and not be at all nearer being drunk."

Socrates drank the cup which the attendant filled for him.

Eryximachus said: "What is this, Alcibiades? Are we to have neither conversation nor singing over our cups; but simply to drink as if we were thirsty?"

Alcibiades replied: "Hail, worthy son of a most wise and worthy sire!"

"The same to you," said Eryximachus; "but what shall we do?"

"That I leave to you," said Alcibiades.

   "The wise physician skilled our wounds to heal [45]

shall prescribe and we will obey. What do you want?"

"Well," said Eryximachus, "before you appeared we had passed

[45] Iliad, XI, 514.

a resolution that each one of us in turn should make a speech in praise
of love, and as good a one as he could: the turn was passed round
from left to right; and as all of us have spoken, and you have not
spoken but have well drunken, you ought to speak, and then impose
upon Socrates any task which you please, and he on his right hand
neighbor, and so on."

"That is good, Eryximachus," said Alcibiades; "and yet the comparison of a drunken man's speech with those of sober men is hardly
fair; and I should like to know, sweet friend, whether you really believe what Socrates was just now saying; for I can assure you that
the very reverse is the fact, and that if I praise anyone but himself in
his presence, whether God or man, he will hardly keep his hands off
me."

"For shame," said Socrates.

"Hold your tongue," said Alcibiades, "for, by Poseidon, there is
no one else whom I will praise, when you are of the company."

"Well then," said Eryximachus, "if you like, praise Socrates."

"What do you think, Eryximachus?" said Alcibiades. "Shall I attack him and inflict the punishment before you all?"

"What are you about?" said Socrates; "are you going to raise a
laugh at my expense? Is that the meaning of your praise?"

"I am going to speak the truth, if you will permit me."

"I not only permit, but exhort you to speak the truth."

"Then I will begin at once," said Alcibiades, "and if I say anything which is not true, you may interrupt me if you will, and say
'that is a lie,' though my intention is to speak the truth. But you
must not wonder if I speak anyhow, as things come into my mind;
for the fluent and orderly enumeration of all your singularities is not
a task which is easy to a man in my condition.

"And now, my boys, I shall praise Socrates in a figure which will
appear to him to be a caricature, and yet I speak, not to make fun of
him, but only for the truth's sake. I say, that he is exactly like the
busts of Silenus,[46] which are set up in the statuaries' shops, holding

---

46 Silenus was the leader of the satyrs, half human, half woodland beast, companions of the god Bacchus or Dionysus in his revels.

pipes and flutes in their mouths; and they are made to open in the middle, and have images of gods inside them. I say also that he is like Marsyas [47] the satyr. You yourself will not deny, Socrates, that your face is like that of a satyr. Aye, and there is a resemblance in other points too. For example, you are a bully, as I can prove by witnesses, if you will not confess. And are you not a flute-player? That you are, and a performer far more wonderful than Marsyas. He indeed with instruments used to charm the souls of men by the power of his breath, and the players of his music do so still: for the melodies of Olympus are derived from Marsyas who taught them, and these, whether they are played by a great master or by a miserable flute-girl, have a power which no others have; they alone possess the soul and reveal the wants of those who have need of gods and mysteries, because they are divine. But you produce the same effect with your words only, and do not require the flute: that is the difference between you and him. When we hear any other speaker, even a very good one, he produces absolutely no effect upon us, or not much, whereas the mere fragments of you and your words, even at second-hand, and however imperfectly repeated, amaze and possess the souls of every man, woman, and child who comes within hearing of them. And if I were not afraid that you would think me hopelessly drunk, I would have sworn as well as spoken to the influence which they have always had and still have over me. For my heart leaps within me more than that of any Corybantian reveler,[48] and my eyes rain tears when I hear them. And I observe that many others are affected in the same manner. I have heard Pericles and other great orators, and I thought that they spoke well, but I never had any similar feeling; my soul was not stirred by them, nor was I angry at the thought of my own slavish state. But this Marsyas has often brought me to such a pass, that I have felt as if I could hardly endure the life which I am leading (this, Socrates, you will admit); and I am conscious that

47 A satyr who played the flute with such ravishing charm that he challenged Apollo to a musical contest.
48 The Corybantes were priests of the Asiatic goddess Cybele, who worshiped her with wild and violent dancing.

if I did not shut my ears against him, and fly as from the voice of the siren, my fate would be like that of others—he would transfix me, and I should grow old sitting at his feet. For he makes me confess that I ought not to live as I do, neglecting the wants of my own soul, and busying myself with the concerns of the Athenians; therefore I hold my ears and tear myself away from him. And he is the only person who ever made me ashamed, which you might think not to be in my nature, and there is no one else who does the same. For I know that I cannot answer him or say that I ought not to do as he bids, but when I leave his presence the love of popularity gets the better of me. And therefore I run away and fly from him, and when I see him I am ashamed of what I have confessed to him. Many a time have I wished that he were dead, and yet I know that I should be much more sorry than glad, if he were to die: so that I am at my wit's end.

"And this is what I and many others have suffered from the flute-playing of this satyr. Yet hear me once more while I show you how exact the image is, and how marvelous his power. For let me tell you; none of you know him; but I will reveal him to you; having begun, I must go on. See you how fond he is of the fair? He is always with them and is always being smitten by them, and then again he knows nothing and is ignorant of all things—such is the appearance which he puts on. Is he not like a Silenus in this? To be sure he is: his outer mask is the carved head of the Silenus; but, O my companions in drink, when he is opened, what temperance there is residing within! Know you that beauty and wealth and honor, at which the many wonder, are of no account with him, and are utterly despised by him: he regards not at all the persons who are gifted with them; mankind are nothing to him; all his life is spent in mocking and flouting at them. But when I opened him, and looked within at his serious purpose, I saw in him divine and golden images of such fascinating beauty that I was ready to do in a moment whatever Socrates commanded: they may have escaped the observation of others, but I saw them. Now I fancied that he was seriously en-amoured of my beauty, and I thought that I should therefore have a grand opportunity of hearing him tell what he knew, for I had a wonderful opinion of the attractions of my youth. In the prosecution of this design, when I next went to him, I sent away the attendant who usually accompanied me (I will confess the whole truth, and beg you to listen; and if I speak falsely, do you, Socrates, expose the falsehood). Well, he and I were alone together, and I thought that when there was nobody with us, I should hear him speak the language which lovers use to their loves when they are by themselves, and I was delighted. Nothing of the sort; he conversed as usual, and spent the day with me and then went away. Afterwards I challenged him to the palaestra; [49] and he wrestled and closed with me several times when there was no one present; I fancied that I might succeed in this manner. Not a bit; I made no way with him. Lastly, as I had failed hitherto, I thought that I must take stronger measures and attack him boldly, and, as I had begun, not give him up, but see how matters stood between him and me. So I invited him to sup with me, just as if he were a fair youth, and I a designing lover. He was not easily persuaded to come; he did, however, after a while accept the invitation, and when he came the first time, he wanted to go away at once as soon as supper was over, and I had not the face to detain him. The second time, still in pursuance of my design, after we had supped, I went on conversing far into the night, and when he wanted to go away, I pretended that the hour was late and that he had much better remain. So he lay down on the couch next to me, the same on which he had supped, and there was no one but ourselves sleeping in the apartment. All this may be told without shame to anyone. But what follows I could hardly tell you if I were sober. Yet as the proverb says, 'In vino veritas,' whether with boys, or without them; [50] and therefore I must speak. Nor, again, should I be justified in concealing the lofty actions of Socrates when I come to praise him. Moreover, I have felt the serpent's sting; and he who has suffered, as they say,

---

49 Training school for wrestling and other athletic sports.

50 The Greeks had a familiar proverb, "Wine speaks the truth," for which Professor Jowett gives here the Latin equivalent. It was sometimes apparently expanded to "Wine and children speak the truth."

is willing to tell his fellow sufferers only, as they alone will be likely
to understand him, and will not be extreme in judging of the sayings
or doings which have been wrung from his agony. For I have been
bitten by a more than viper's tooth; I have known in my soul, or in
my heart, or in some other part, that worst of pangs, more violent in
ingenuous youth than any serpent's tooth, the pang of philosophy,
which will make a man say or do anything. And you whom I see
around me, Phaedrus and Agathon and Eryximachus and Pausanias
and Aristodemus and Aristophanes, all of you, and I need not say
Socrates himself, have had experience of the same madness and
passion in your longing after wisdom. Therefore listen and excuse my doings then and my sayings now. But let the attendants
and other profane and unmannered persons close up the doors of
their ears.

"When the lamp was put out and the servants had gone away, I
thought that I must be plain with him and have no more ambiguity.
So I gave him a shake, and I said: 'Socrates, are you asleep?' 'No,' he
said. 'Do you know what I am meditating?' 'What are you meditating?' he said. 'I think,' I replied, 'that of all the lovers whom I have
ever had you are the only one who is worthy of me, and you appear
to be too modest to speak. Now I feel that I should be a fool to refuse
you this or any other favor, and therefore I come to lay at your feet all
that I have and all that my friends have, in the hope that you will
assist me in the way of virtue, which I desire above all things, and in
which I believe that you can help me better than anyone else. And I
should certainly have more reason to be ashamed of what wise men
would say if I were to refuse a favor to such as you, than of what
the world, who are mostly fools, would say of me if I granted it.' To
these words he replied in the ironical manner which is so characteristic of him: 'Alcibiades, my friend, you have indeed an elevated aim
if what you say is true, and if there really is in me any power by which
you may become better; truly you must see in me some rare beauty of
a kind infinitely higher than any which I see in you. And therefore,
if you mean to share with me and to exchange beauty for beauty,

you will have greatly the advantage of me; you will gain true beauty in return for appearance—like Diomed, gold in exchange for brass.[51] But look again, sweet friend, and see whether you are not deceived in me. The mind begins to grow critical when the bodily eye fails, and it will be a long time before you get old.' Hearing this, I said: 'I have told you my purpose, which is quite serious, and do you consider what you think best for you and me.' 'That is good,' he said; 'at some other time then we will consider and act as seems best about this and about other matters.' Whereupon, I fancied that he was smitten, and that the words which I had uttered like arrows had wounded him, and so without waiting to hear more I got up, and throwing my coat about him crept under his threadbare cloak, as the time of year was winter, and there I lay during the whole night having this wonderful monster in my arms. This again, Socrates, will not be denied by you. And yet, notwithstanding all, he was so superior to my solicitations, so contemptuous and derisive and disdainful of my beauty, which really, as I fancied, had some attractions—hear, O judges; for judges you shall be of the haughty virtue of Socrates—nothing more happened, but in the morning when I awoke (let all the gods and goddesses be my witnesses) I arose as from the couch of a father or an elder brother.

"What do you suppose must have been my feelings, after this rejection, at the thought of my own dishonor? And yet I could not help wondering at his natural temperance and self-restraint and manliness. I never imagined that I could have met with a man such as he is in wisdom and endurance. And therefore I could not be angry with him or renounce his company, any more than I could hope to win him. For I well knew that if Ajax could not be wounded by steel,[52] much less he by money; and my only chance of captivating him by my personal attractions had failed. So I was at my wit's end; no one was ever more hopelessly enslaved by another. All this happened be-

51 Homer relates how the warrior Diomed cleverly exchanged his bronze armor for gold. *Iliad*, VI, 234-236.
52 The great warrior Ajax had a sevenfold shield that no spear could pierce. Sophocles, *Ajax*, 576.

fore he and I went on the expedition to Potidaea; [53] there we messed together, and I had the opportunity of observing his extraordinary power of sustaining fatigue. His endurance was simply marvelous when, being cut off from our supplies, we were compelled to go without food. On such occasions, which often happen in time of war, he was superior not only to me but to everybody; there was no one to be compared to him. Yet at a festival he was the only person who had any real powers of enjoyment; though not willing to drink, he could if compelled beat us all at that; wonderful to relate, no human being had ever seen Socrates drunk; and his powers, if I am not mistaken, will be tested before long. His fortitude in enduring cold was also surprising. There was a severe frost, for the winter in that region is really tremendous, and everybody else either remained indoors, or if they went out had on an amazing quantity of clothes, and were well shod, and had their feet swathed in felt and fleeces; in the midst of this, Socrates with his bare feet on the ice and in his ordinary dress marched better than the other soldiers who had shoes, and they looked daggers at him because he seemed to despise them.

"I have told you one tale, and now I must tell you another, which is worth hearing,

> *Of the doings and sufferings of the enduring man* [54]

while he was on the expedition. One morning he was thinking about something which he could not resolve; he would not give it up, but continued thinking from early dawn until noon—there he stood fixed in thought; and at noon attention was drawn to him, and the rumor ran through the wondering crowd that Socrates had been standing and thinking about something ever since the break of day. At last, in the evening after supper, some Ionians out of curiosity (I should explain that this was not in winter but in summer), brought out their mats and slept in the open air that they might watch him and see whether he would stand all night. There he stood until the follow-

---

53 In his *Apology*, Socrates refers to the campaigns at Potidaea and Delium. See page 47, note 13.
54 *Odyssey*, IV, 241-242.

ing morning; and with the return of light he offered up a prayer to the sun, and went his way.

"I will also tell, if you please—and indeed I am bound to tell—of his courage in battle; for who but he saved my life? Now this was the engagement in which I received the prize of valor: for I was wounded and he would not leave me, but he rescued me and my arms; and he ought to have received the prize of valor which the generals wanted to confer on me partly on account of my rank, and I told them so (this, again, Socrates will not impeach or deny), but he was more eager than the generals that I and not he should have the prize. There was another occasion on which his behavior was very remarkable—in the flight of the army after the battle of Delium, where he served among the heavy armed—I had a better opportunity of seeing him than at Potidaea, for I was myself on horseback, and therefore comparatively out of danger. He and Laches were retreating, for the troops were in flight, and I met them and told them not to be discouraged, and promised to remain with them; and there you might see him, Aristophanes, as you describe,[55] just as he is in the streets of Athens, stalking like a pelican, and rolling his eyes, calmly contemplating enemies as well as friends, and making very intelligible to anybody, even from a distance, that whoever attacked him would be likely to meet with a stout resistance; and in this way he and his companion escaped—for this is the sort of man who is never touched in war; those only are pursued who are running away headlong. I particularly observed how superior he was to Laches in presence of mind.

"Many are the marvels which I might narrate in praise of Socrates; most of his ways might perhaps be paralleled in another man, but his absolute unlikeness to any human being that is or ever has been is perfectly astonishing. You may imagine Brasidas and others to have been like Achilles; or you may imagine Nestor and Antenor to have been like Pericles;[56] and the same may be said of other famous men, but of this strange being you will never be able to find

55 Aristophanes, *Clouds*, 362.

56 That is, other brave men have been like Achilles, other wise men like Pericles.

any likeness, however remote, either among men who now are or who ever have been—other than that which I have already suggested of Silenus and the satyrs; and they represent in a figure not only himself, but his words. For, although I forgot to mention this to you before, his words are like the images of Silenus which open; they are ridiculous when you first hear them; he clothes himself in language that is like the skin of the wanton satyr—for his talk is of pack-asses and smiths and cobblers and curriers, and he is always repeating the same things in the same words, so that any ignorant or inexperienced person might feel disposed to laugh at him; but he who opens the bust and sees what is within will find that they are the only words which have a meaning in them, and also the most divine, abounding in fair images of virtue, and of the widest comprehension, or rather extending to the whole duty of a good and honorable man.

"This, friends, is my praise of Socrates. I have added my blame of him for his ill treatment of me; and he has ill treated not only me, but Charmides the son of Glaucon, and Euthydemus the son of Diocles, and many others in the same way—beginning as their lover he has ended by making them pay their addresses to him. Wherefore I say to you, Agathon: 'Be not deceived by him; learn from me and take warning, and do not be a fool and learn by experience, as the proverb says.' "

When Alcibiades had finished, there was a laugh at his outspokenness; for he seemed to be still in love with Socrates.

"You are sober, Alcibiades," said Socrates, "or you would never have gone so far about to hide the purpose of your satyr's praises, for all this long story is only an ingenious circumlocution, of which the point comes in by the way at the end; you want to get up a quarrel between me and Agathon, and your notion is that I ought to love you and nobody else, and that you and you only ought to love Agathon. But the plot of this satyric or Silenic drama has been detected, and you must not allow him, Agathon, to set us at variance."

"I believe you are right," said Agathon, "and I am disposed to think that his intention in placing himself between you and me was

only to divide us; but he shall gain nothing by that move; for I will
go and lie on the couch next to you."

"Yes, yes," replied Socrates, "by all means come here and lie on
the couch below me."

"Alas," said Alcibiades, "how I am fooled by this man; he is determined to get the better of me at every turn. I do beseech you, allow
Agathon to lie between us."

"Certainly not," said Socrates; "as you praised me, and I in turn
ought to praise my neighbor on the right, he will be out of order in
praising me again when he ought rather to be praised by me, and I
must entreat you to consent to this, and not be jealous, for I have a
great desire to praise the youth."

"Hurrah!" cried Agathon. "I will rise instantly, that I may be
praised by Socrates."

"The usual way," said Alcibiades; "where Socrates is, no one else
has any chance with the fair; and now how readily has he invented a
specious reason for attracting Agathon to himself."

Agathon arose in order that he might take his place on the couch
by Socrates, when suddenly a band of revelers entered, and spoiled
the order of the banquet. Someone who was going out having left the
door open, they had found their way in, and made themselves at
home; great confusion ensued, and everyone was compelled to drink
large quantities of wine. Aristodemus said that Eryximachus,
Phaedrus, and others went away—he himself fell asleep, and as the
nights were long took a good rest: he was awakened towards day-
break by a crowing of cocks, and when he awoke, the others were
either asleep, or had gone away; there remained only Socrates, Aristophanes, and Agathon, who were drinking out of a large goblet
which they passed round, and Socrates was discoursing to them. Aristodemus was only half awake, and he did not hear the beginning of
the discourse; the chief thing which he remembered was Socrates
compelling the other two to acknowledge that the genius of comedy
was the same with that of tragedy, and that the true artist in tragedy
was an artist in comedy also. To this they were constrained to assent,
being drowsy, and not quite following the argument. And first of all

Aristophanes dropped off, then, when the day was already dawning, Agathon. Socrates, having laid them to sleep, rose to depart; Aristodemus, as his manner was, following him. At the Lyceum he took a bath, and passed the day as usual. In the evening he retired to rest at his own home.

REPUBLIC

THE *Republic* is both the greatest and the longest, save one, of all Plato's dialogues, too long unfortunately to be reprinted here in full. No other has the same breadth of sweep, from earth to sky and back again, or attempts so earnestly to bring philosophy, the pursuit of ideal wisdom and goodness, into active, useful connection with the everyday life of humanity. No other sets out so clearly the perennial problems that beset every planner of a better social order, problems of morals, education, eugenics, relationship of the sexes, government, ownership of property, which keep us still puzzled two thousand years later.

The *Republic* was written probably between 380 and 370 B.C., though the conversation of which it professes to be a record is imagined as taking place only a few years apparently after the banquet of the *Symposium*. No information is given by which to date it, but the sky seems darker than it was over the *Symposium*. Democracy, we hear, makes a wretched farce of government. The lawless citizen mob has ears only for unprincipled, flattering demagogues, and the just man who longs to serve his country is reviled and thrust aside.

The setting of the conversation is simple. Socrates himself relates how on his way home from a trip to the Peiraeus to watch the festival of the Thracian goddess worshiped there, he was stopped by a young friend, who insisted on taking him to his house for supper. There he found his friend's benign old father, Cephalus, resting in his cushioned chair, and a group of young men ready for talk. Cephalus greets Socrates with some pleasant remarks on the comforts of peaceful old age fortified by memories of a life spent doing justice. It is the signal for Socrates to begin catechizing. But at this Cephalus excuses himself, deputing his son Polemarchus to answer for him.

Polemarchus, asked to define justice, gives thoughtless, conventional replies, which Socrates easily proves to be absurd. A Sophist, Thrasymachus, full of fight, breaks impatiently in with his cynical definition. Justice is a fine name for the interest of the stronger. Might makes anything right and always has. The successful in this world are in fact the unscrupulous and unjust. But Socrates disposes shortly of Thrasymachus too. The dishonesty of unjust men makes everyone distrust them and eventually brings them to ruin.

Two more serious young thinkers, however, Glaucon and Adeimantus, brothers of Plato, start the discussion off again by refusing to be satisfied with what Socrates has said. He has failed to tell them what justice itself is, apart from its effects, or why, if the life of justice is as profitable as he makes out, young men must be bribed to choose it with promises of honor and reward. If a good reputation is so important, why not merely keep up a façade of just and honorable dealing, while at the same time secretly getting away with murder? Is there anything in justice, regardless of consequences, that makes the life of every just man, simply because he is just, happier than that of an unjust man can ever be?

With these questions of Glaucon and Adeimantus the real hunt for justice is on and fills the rest of the book. No more is heard of supper or the fine torch-race that was to follow after. It is easier, Socrates begins, to grasp the true nature of justice when writ in large letters than in small, when expressed, that is, in the constitution of a state than in the acts of a lone individual. So first he will construct a just state. What would be the ideal state? What its organization and government? How would its children be educated and the best selected and trained to become its wise rulers? Could we find in such a state the justice for which we are looking? Can an analogy now be drawn between the peace and harmony of this well-balanced and nobly administered community and the inner peace of a man whose faculties are governed by the same great principles of wisdom, courage, temperateness, and, at last, justice? What, next, of our present world, as it actually exists? How far do any of its types of government approach in excellence the ideal state? What of the corresponding types of individuals? If a people enslaved to a tyrant lives in continual torment, is the tyrant himself, faithless, fearful, jealous, violent, a slave to his own greeds and passions, anything but the most miserable of them all? Can anyone who subjects the best in himself to the beast, who has never known what pure pleasures are, be counted happy, no matter how high his station? Through life after life the soul of man will go on learning by trial and pain that in goodness lies its happiness here and hereafter.

BOOK I

What is justice? Is the just life happier than the unjust?

PERSONS OF THE DIALOGUE: *Socrates
(the narrator), Glaucon, Adeimantus,
Polemarchus, Cephalus, Thrasymachus, Cleitophon*

SCENE: *In the house of Cephalus at the Peiraeus*

*Socrates speaks to his friends of the Dialogue
which had taken place the day before.*

I WENT down yesterday to the Peiraeus [1] with Glaucon the son of Ariston, that I might offer up my prayers to the goddess; [2] and also because I wanted to see in what manner they would celebrate the festival, which was a new thing. I was delighted with the procession of the inhabitants; but that of the Thracians was equally, if not more, beautiful. When we had finished our prayers and viewed the spectacle, we turned in the direction of the city; and at that instant Polemarchus the son of Cephalus chanced to catch sight of us from a distance as we were starting on our way home, and told his servant to run and bid us wait for him. The servant took hold of me by the cloak behind, and said: "Polemarchus desires you to wait."

1 The distance from Athens to the harbor of Peiraeus is about five miles.
2 Bendis, the Thracian moon-goddess.

I turned round, and asked him where his master was.

"There he is," said the youth, "coming after you, if you will only wait."

"Certainly we will," said Glaucon; and in a few minutes Polemarchus appeared, and with him Adeimantus, Glaucon's brother, Niceratus the son of Nicias, and several others who had been at the procession.

Polemarchus said to me: "I perceive, Socrates, that you and your companion are already on your way to the city."

"You are not far wrong," I said.

"But do you see," he rejoined, "how many we are?"

"Of course."

"And are you stronger than all these? for if not, you will have to remain where you are."

"May there not be the alternative," I said, "that we may persuade you to let us go?"

"But can you persuade us, if we refuse to listen to you?" he said.

"Certainly not," replied Glaucon.

"Then we are not going to listen; of that you may be assured."

Adeimantus added: "Has no one told you of the torch-race on horseback in honor of the goddess which will take place in the evening?"

"With horses!" I replied. "That is a novelty. Will horsemen carry torches and pass them one to another during the race?"

"Yes," said Polemarchus, "and not only so, but a festival will be celebrated at night, which you certainly ought to see. Let us rise soon after supper and see this festival; there will be a gathering of young men, and we will have a good talk. Stay then, and do not be perverse."

Glaucon said: "I suppose, since you insist, that we must."

"Very good," I replied.

Accordingly we went with Polemarchus to his house; and there we found his brothers Lysias and Euthydemus, and with them Thrasymachus the Chalcedonian, Charmantides the Paeanian, and Cleitophon the son of Aristonymus. There too was Cephalus the father of Polemarchus, whom I had not seen for a long time, and I thought him very much aged. He was seated on a cushioned chair, and had a garland on his head, for he had been sacrificing in the court; and there were some other chairs in the room arranged in a semicircle, upon which we sat down by him. He saluted me eagerly, and then he said:

"You don't come to see me, Socrates, as often as you ought. If I were still able to go and see you I would not ask you to come to me. But at my age I can hardly get to the city, and therefore you should come oftener to the Peiraeus. For let me tell you, that the more the pleasures of the body fade away, the greater to me is the pleasure and charm of conversation. Do not then deny my request, but make our house your resort and keep company with these young men; we are old friends, and you will be quite at home with us."

I replied: "There is nothing which for my part I like better, Cephalus, than conversing with aged men; for I regard them as travelers who have gone a journey which I too may have to go, and of whom I ought to inquire, whether the way is smooth and easy, or rugged and difficult. And this is a question which I should like to ask of you who have arrived at that time which the poets call the 'threshold of old age': Is life harder towards the end, or what report do you give of it?"

"I will tell you, Socrates," he said, "what my own feeling is. Men of my age flock together; we are birds of a feather, as the old proverb says; and at our meetings the tale of my acquaintance commonly is: I cannot eat, I cannot drink; the pleasures of youth and love are fled away; there was a good time once, but now that is gone, and life is no longer life. Some complain of the slights which are put upon them by relations, and they will tell you sadly of how many evils their old age is the cause. But to me, Socrates, these complainers seem to blame that which is not really in fault. For if old age were the cause, I too being old, and every other old man, would have felt as they do. But this is not my own experience, nor that of others whom I have known. How well I remember the aged poet Sophocles, when in answer to the question, 'How does love suit with age, Sophocles; are you still the man you were?' 'Peace,' he replied; 'most gladly have I escaped the thing of which you speak; I feel as if I had escaped from a mad and furious master.' His words have often occurred to my mind since, and they seem as good to me now as at the time when he uttered them. For certainly old age has a great sense of calm and freedom; when the passions relax their hold, then, as Sophocles says, we are freed from the grasp not of one mad master only, but of many. The truth is, Socrates, that these regrets, and also the complaints about relations, are to be attributed to the same cause, which is not old age, but men's characters and tempers; for he who is of a calm and happy nature will hardly feel the pressure of age, but to him who is of an opposite disposition youth and age are equally a burden."

I listened in admiration, and wanting to draw him out, that he might go on, "Yes, Cephalus," I said; "but I rather suspect that people in general are not convinced by you when you speak thus; they think that old age sits lightly upon you, not because of your happy disposition, but because you are rich, and wealth is well known to be a great comforter."

"You are right," he replied; "they are not convinced: and there is something in what they say; not, however, so much as they imagine. I might answer them as Themistocles [3] answered the Seriphian who was abusing him and saying that he was famous not for his own merits but because he was an Athenian: 'If you had been a native of my country or I of yours, neither of us would have been famous.' And to those who are not rich and are impatient of old age, the same reply may be made; for to the good poor man old age cannot be a light burden, nor can a bad rich man ever have peace with himself."

"May I ask, Cephalus, whether your fortune was for the most part inherited or acquired by you?"

"Acquired! Socrates, do you want to know how much I acquired? In the art of making money I have been midway between my father and grandfather: for my grandfather, whose name I bear, doubled and trebled the value of his patrimony, that which he inherited being

3 Plato gets this anecdote from the historian Herodotus (c. 450 B.C.), VIII, 125.

much what I possess now; but my father Lysanias reduced the property below what it is at present: and I shall be satisfied if I leave to these my sons not less but a little more than I received."

"That was why I asked you the question," I replied, "because I see that you are indifferent about money, which is a characteristic rather of those who have inherited their fortunes than of those who have acquired them; the makers of fortunes have a second love of money as a creation of their own, resembling the affection of authors for their own poems, or of parents for their children, besides that natural love of it for the sake of use and profit which is common to them and all men. And hence they are very bad company, for they can talk about nothing but the praises of wealth."

"That is true," he said.

"Yes, that is very true, but may I ask another question? What do you consider to be the greatest blessing which you have reaped from your wealth?"

"One," he said, "of which I could not expect easily to convince others. For let me tell you, Socrates, that when a man thinks himself to be near death, fears and cares enter into his mind which he never had before; the tales of a world below and the punishment which is exacted there of deeds done here were once a laughing matter to him, but now he is tormented with the thought that they may be true: either from the weakness of age, or because he is now drawing nearer to that other place, he has a clearer view of these things; suspicions and alarms crowd thickly upon him, and he begins to reflect and consider what wrongs he has done to others. And when he finds that the sum of his transgressions is great he will many a time like a child start up in his sleep for fear, and he is filled with dark forebodings. But to him who is conscious of no sin, sweet hope, as Pindar charmingly says, is the kind nurse of his age: *Hope* (he says), *cherishes the soul of him who lives in justice and holiness, and is the nurse of his age and the companion of his journey; hope which is mightiest to sway the restless soul of man.*[4] How admirable are his words! And

4 These lines are a fragment of a lost poem of the great singer of odes, Pindar (*c.* 480 B.C.). Fragment 214, Loeb edition.

the great blessing of riches, I do not say to every man, but to a good man, is, that he has had no occasion to deceive or to defraud others, either intentionally or unintentionally; and when he departs to the world below he is not in any apprehension about offerings due to the gods or debts which he owes to men. Now to this peace of mind the possession of wealth greatly contributes; and therefore I say, that, setting one thing against another, of the many advantages which wealth has to give, to a man of sense this is in my opinion the greatest."

"Well said, Cephalus," I replied; "but as concerning justice, what is it? To speak the truth and to pay your debts—no more than this? And even to this are there not exceptions? Suppose that a friend when in his right mind has deposited arms with me and he asks for them when he is not in his right mind, ought I to give them back to him? No one would say that I ought or that I should be right in doing so, any more than they would say that I ought always to speak the truth to one who is in his condition."

"You are quite right," he replied.

"But then," I said, "speaking the truth and paying your debts is not a correct definition of justice."

"Quite correct, Socrates, if Simonides is to be believed," said Polemarchus, interposing.

"I fear," said Cephalus, "that I must go now, for I have to look after the sacrifices, and I hand over the argument to Polemarchus and the company."

"Is not Polemarchus your heir?" I said.

"To be sure," he answered, and went away laughing to the sacrifices.

"Tell me then, O thou heir of the argument, what did Simonides say, and according to you truly say, about justice?"

"He said that the repayment of a debt is just,[5] and in saying so he appears to me to be right."

"I should be sorry to doubt the word of such a wise and inspired

---

[5] This definition is not in any of the surviving fragments of the caustic poet Simonides (c. 500 B.C.). It represents evidently an average business man's idea of decency: one should keep one's word and pay one's debts.

man, but his meaning, though probably clear to you, is the reverse of clear to me. For he certainly does not mean, as we were just now saying, that I ought to return a deposit of arms or of anything else to one who asks for it when he is not in his right senses; and yet a deposit cannot be denied to be a debt."

"True."

"Then when the person who asks me is not in his right mind I am by no means to make the return?"

"Certainly not."

"When Simonides said that the repayment of a debt was justice, he did not mean to include that case?"

"Certainly not; for he thinks that a friend ought always to do good to a friend and never evil."

"You mean that the return of a deposit of gold which is to the injury of the receiver, if the two parties are friends, is not the repayment of a debt—that is what you would imagine him to say?"

"Yes."

"And are enemies also to receive what we owe to them?"

"To be sure," he said, "they are to receive what we owe them, and an enemy, as I take it, owes to an enemy that which is due or proper to him—that is to say, evil."

"Simonides, then, after the manner of poets, would seem to have spoken darkly of the nature of justice; for he really meant to say that justice is the giving to each man what is proper to him, and this he termed a debt."

"That must have been his meaning," he said.

"By heaven!" I replied; "and if we asked him what due or proper thing is given by medicine, and to whom, what answer do you think that he would make to us?"

"He would surely reply that medicine gives drugs and meat and drink to human bodies."

"And what due or proper thing is given by cookery, and to what?"

"Seasoning to food."

"And what is that which justice gives, and to whom?"

"If, Socrates, we are to be guided at all by the analogy of the pre-ceding instances, then justice is the art which gives good to friends and evil to enemies." [6]

"That is his meaning then?"

"I think so."

"And who is best able to do good to his friends and evil to his enemies in time of sickness?"

"The physician."

"Or when they are on a voyage, amid the perils of the sea?"

"The pilot."

"And in what sort of actions or with a view to what result is the just man most able to do harm to his enemy and good to his friend?"

"In going to war against the one and in making alliances with the other."

"But when a man is well, my dear Polemarchus, there is no need of a physician?"

"No."

"And he who is not on a voyage has no need of a pilot?"

"No."

"Then in time of peace justice will be of no use?"

"I am very far from thinking so."

"You think that justice may be of use in peace as well as in war?"

"Yes."

"Like husbandry for the acquisition of corn?"

"Yes."

"Or like shoemaking for the acquisition of shoes—that is what you mean?"

"Yes."

"And what similar use or power of acquisition has justice in time of peace?"

"In contracts, Socrates, justice is of use."

"And by contracts you mean partnerships?"

"Exactly."

---

6 The definition is now extended and clarified until it seems to meet all the demands of popular morality. Even so, Socrates is not satisfied with it.

"But is the just man or the skillful player a more useful and better partner at a game of draughts?"

"The skillful player."

"And in the laying of bricks and stones is the just man a more useful or better partner than the builder?"

"Quite the reverse."

"Then in what sort of partnership is the just man a better partner than the harp-player, as in playing the harp the harp-player is certainly a better partner than the just man?"

"In a money partnership."

"Yes, Polemarchus, but surely not in the use of money; for you do not want a just man to be your counselor in the purchase or sale of a horse; a man who is knowing about horses would be better for that, would he not?"

"Certainly."

"And when you want to buy a ship, the shipwright or the pilot would be better?"

"True."

"Then what is that joint use of silver or gold in which the just man is to be preferred?"

"When you want a deposit to be kept safely."

"You mean when money is not wanted, but allowed to lie?"

"Precisely."

"That is to say, justice is useful when money is useless?"

"That is the inference."

"And when you want to keep a pruning-hook safe, then justice is useful to the individual and to the state; but when you want to use it, then the art of the vine-dresser?"

"Clearly."

"And when you want to keep a shield or a lyre, and not to use them, you would say that justice is useful; but when you want to use them, then the art of the soldier or of the musician?"

"Certainly."

"And so of all other things; justice is useful when they are useless, and useless when they are useful?"

"That is the inference."

"Then justice is not good for much. But let us consider this further point: Is not he who can best strike a blow in a boxing match or in any kind of fighting best able to ward off a blow?"

"Certainly."

"And he who is most skillful in preventing or escaping from a disease is best able to create one?"

"True."

"And he is the best guard of a camp who is best able to steal a march upon the enemy?"

"Certainly."

"Then he who is a good keeper of anything is also a good thief?"

"That, I suppose, is to be inferred."

"Then if the just man is good at keeping money, he is good at stealing it."

"That is implied in the argument."

"Then, after all, the just man has turned out to be a thief. And this is a lesson which I suspect you must have learnt out of Homer; for he, speaking of Autolycus, the maternal grandfather of Odysseus, who is a favorite of his, affirms that

He was excellent above all men in theft and perjury.[7]

And so, you and Homer and Simonides are agreed that justice is an art of theft; to be practiced however 'for the good of friends and for the harm of enemies,'—that was what you were saying?"

"No, certainly not that, though I do not now know what I did say; but I still stand by the latter words."

"Well, there is another question: By friends and enemies do we mean those who are so really, or only in seeming?"

"Surely," he said, "a man may be expected to love those whom he thinks good, and to hate those whom he thinks evil."

"Yes, but do not persons often err about good and evil: many who are not good seem to be so, and conversely?"

7 *Odyssey*, XIX, 395-396.

"That is true."

"Then to them the good will be enemies and the evil will be their friends?"

"True."

"And in that case they will be right in doing good to the evil and evil to the good?"

"Clearly."

"But the good are just and would not do an injustice?"

"True."

"Then according to your argument it is just to injure those who do no wrong?"

"Nay, Socrates; the doctrine is immoral."

"Then I suppose that we ought to do good to the just and harm to the unjust?"

"I like that better."

"But see the consequence: Many a man who is ignorant of human nature has friends who are bad friends, and in that case he ought to do harm to them; and he has good enemies whom he ought to benefit; but, if so, we shall be saying the very opposite of that which we affirmed to be the meaning of Simonides."

"Very true," he said; "and I think that we had better correct an error into which we seem to have fallen in the use of the words 'friend' and 'enemy.' "

"What was the error, Polemarchus?" I asked.

"We assumed that he is a friend who seems to be or who is thought good."

"And how is the error to be corrected?"

"We should rather say that he is a friend who is, as well as seems, good; and that he who seems only, and is not good, only seems to be and is not a friend; and of an enemy the same may be said."

"You would argue that the good are our friends and the bad our enemies?"

"Yes."

"And instead of saying simply as we did at first, that it is just to do good to our friends and harm to our enemies, we should further say:

It is just to do good to our friends when they are good and harm to our enemies when they are evil?"

"Yes, that appears to me to be the truth."

"But ought the just to injure anyone at all?"

"Undoubtedly he ought to injure those who are both wicked and his enemies."

"When horses are injured, are they improved or deteriorated?"

"The latter."

"Deteriorated, that is to say, in the good qualities of horses, not of dogs?"

"Yes, of horses."

"And dogs are deteriorated in the good qualities of dogs, and not of horses?"

"Of course."

"And will not men who are injured be deteriorated in that which is the proper virtue of man?"

"Certainly."

"And that human virtue is justice?"

"To be sure."

"Then men who are injured are of necessity made unjust?"

"That is the result."

"But can the musician by his art make men unmusical?"

"Certainly not."

"Or the horseman by his art make them bad horsemen?"

"Impossible."

"And can the just by justice make men unjust, or, speaking generally, can the good by virtue make them bad?"

"Assuredly not."

"Any more than heat can produce cold?"

"It cannot."

"Or drought moisture?"

"Clearly not."

"Nor can the good harm anyone?"

"Impossible."

"And the just is the good?"

"Certainly."

"Then to injure a friend or anyone else is not the act of a just man, but of the opposite, who is the unjust?" [8]

"I think that what you say is quite true, Socrates."

"Then if a man says that justice consists in the repayment of debts, and that good is the debt which a just man owes to his friends, and evil the debt which he owes to his enemies—to say this is not wise; for it is not true, if, as has been clearly shown, the injuring of another can be in no case just."

"I agree with you," said Polemarchus.

"Then you and I are prepared to take up arms against anyone who attributes such a saying to Simonides or Bias or Pittacus,[9] or any other wise man or seer?"

"I am quite ready to do battle at your side," he said.

"Shall I tell you whose I believe the saying to be?"

"Whose?"

"I believe that Periander [10] or Perdiccas or Xerxes or Ismenias the Theban, or some other rich and mighty man, who had a great opinion of his own power, was the first to say that justice is 'doing good to your friends and harm to your enemies.' "

"Most true," he said.

"Yes," I said; "but if this definition of justice also breaks down, what other can be offered?"

Several times in the course of the discussion Thrasymachus [11] had made an attempt to get the argument into his own hands, and had been put down by the rest of the company, who wanted to hear the end. But when Polemarchus and I had done speaking and there was a pause, he could no longer hold his peace; and, gathering himself

8 Plato was, as far as we know, the first European to declare that a good man would not return evil for evil nor do injury even to his enemies.

9 Bias and Pittacus were two of the Seven Wise Men of ancient Greece.

10 Periander (c. 600 B.C.) was also one of the Seven Wise Men as well as a firm and able ruler of Corinth.

11 The cocksure Sophist now gives bluntly the cynical answer to Socrates' question. There is no such thing as absolute right or wrong. In any state the governing party makes the moral code and they are out to get what they can for themselves. So right is whatever suits the strong.

up, he came at us like a wild beast, seeking to devour us. We were quite panic-stricken at the sight of him.

He roared out to the whole company: "What folly, Socrates, has taken possession of you all? And why, sillybillies, do you knock under to one another? I say that if you want really to know what justice is, you should not only ask but answer, and you should not seek honor to yourself from the refutation of an opponent, but have your own answer; for there is many a one who can ask and cannot answer. And now I will not have you say that justice is duty or advantage or profit or gain or interest, for this sort of nonsense will not do for me; I must have clearness and accuracy."

I was panic-stricken at his words, and could not look at him without trembling. Indeed I believe that if I had not fixed my eye upon him, I should have been struck dumb: but when I saw his fury rising, I looked at him first, and was therefore able to reply to him.

"Thrasymachus," I said, with a quiver, "don't be hard upon us. Polemarchus and I may have been guilty of a little mistake in the argument, but I can assure you that the error was not intentional. If we were seeking for a piece of gold, you would not imagine that we were 'knocking under to one another,' and so losing our chance of finding it. And why, when we are seeking for justice, a thing more precious than many pieces of gold, do you say that we are weakly yielding to one another and not doing our utmost to get at the truth? Nay, my good friend, we are most willing and anxious to do so, but the fact is that we cannot. And if so, you people who know all things should pity us and not be angry with us."

"How characteristic of Socrates!" he replied, with a bitter laugh; "that's your ironical style! Did I not foresee—have I not already told you, that whatever he was asked he would refuse to answer, and try irony or any other shuffle, in order that he might avoid answering?"

"You are a philosopher, Thrasymachus," I replied, "and well know that if you ask a person what numbers make up twelve, taking care to prohibit him whom you ask from answering twice six, or three times four, or six times two, or four times three, 'for this sort of nonsense will not do for me,' then obviously, if that is your way of putting the question, no one can answer you. But suppose that he were to retort, 'Thrasymachus, what do you mean? If one of these numbers which you interdict [12] be the true answer to the question, am I falsely to say some other number which is not the right one? Is that your meaning?'—How would you answer him?"

"Just as if the two cases were at all alike!" he said.

"Why should they not be?" I replied; "and even if they are not, but only appear to be so to the person who is asked, ought he not to say what he thinks, whether you and I forbid him or not?"

"I presume then that you are going to make one of the interdicted answers?"

"I dare say that I may, notwithstanding the danger, if upon reflection I approve of any of them."

"But what if I give you an answer about justice other and better," he said, "than any of these? What do you deserve to have done to you?"

"Done to me! As becomes the ignorant, I must learn from the wise —that is what I deserve to have done to me."

"What, and no payment! A pleasant notion!"

"I will pay when I have the money," I replied.

"But you have, Socrates," said Glaucon; "and you, Thrasymachus, need be under no anxiety about money, for we will all make a contribution for Socrates."

"Yes," he replied, "and then Socrates will do as he always does— refuse to answer himself, but take and pull to pieces the answer of someone else."

"Why, my good friend," I said, "how can anyone answer who knows, and says that he knows, just nothing; and who, even if he has some faint notions of his own, is told by a man of authority not to utter them? The natural thing is, that the speaker should be some- one like yourself who professes to know and can tell what he knows.

12 Forbid.

Will you then kindly answer, for the edification of the company and of myself?"

Glaucon and the rest of the company joined in my request, and Thrasymachus, as anyone might see, was in reality eager to speak; for he thought that he had an excellent answer, and would distinguish himself. But at first he affected to insist on my answering; at length he consented to begin. "Behold," he said, "the wisdom of Socrates; he refuses to teach himself, and goes about learning of others, to whom he never even says Thank you."

"That I learn of others," I replied, "is quite true; but that I am ungrateful I wholly deny. Money I have none, and therefore I pay in praise, which is all I have; and how ready I am to praise anyone who appears to me to speak well you will very soon find out when you answer; for I expect that you will answer well."

"Listen, then," he said. "I proclaim that justice is nothing else than the interest of the stronger. And now why do you not praise me? But of course you won't."

"Let me first understand you," I replied. "Justice, as you say, is the interest of the stronger. What, Thrasymachus, is the meaning of this? You cannot mean to say that because Polydamas, the pancratiast,[13] is stronger than we are, and finds the eating of beef conducive to his bodily strength, that to eat beef is therefore equally for our good who are weaker than he is, and right and just for us?"

"That's abominable of you, Socrates; you take the words in the sense which is most damaging to the argument."

"Not at all, my good sir," I said; "I am trying to understand them; and I wish that you would be a little clearer."

"Well," he said, "have you never heard that forms of government differ; there are tyrannies, and there are democracies, and there are aristocracies?" [14]

13 The winner in a "pancratium" or all-out trial of strength in a wrestling or boxing match. The ordinary Athenian ate little meat.

14 The three forms of government, autocracy or monarchy, democracy, and aristocracy, had been listed about a century earlier by the poet Pindar: "Where the tyrant's court or where the boisterous mob or where the wise have charge of the city." *Pythian Ode*, II, 86-88.

"Yes, I know."

"And the government is the ruling power in each state?"

"Certainly."

"And the different forms of government make laws democratical, aristocratical, tyrannical, with a view to their several interests; and these laws, which are made by them for their own interests, are the justice which they deliver to their subjects, and him who transgresses them they punish as a breaker of the law, and unjust. And that is what I mean when I say that in all states there is the same principle of justice, which is the interest of the government; and as the government must be supposed to have power, the only reasonable conclusion is that everywhere there is one principle of justice, which is the interest of the stronger."

"Now I understand you," I said; "and whether you are right or not I will try to discover. But let me remark, that in defining justice you have yourself used the word 'interest' which you forbade me to use. It is true, however, that in your definition the words 'of the stronger' are added."

"A small addition, you must allow," he said.

"Great or small, never mind about that: we must first inquire whether what you are saying is the truth. Now we are both agreed that justice is interest of some sort, but you go on to say 'of the stronger'; about this addition I am not so sure, and must therefore consider further."

"Proceed."

"I will; and first tell me, do you admit that it is just for subjects to obey their rulers?"

"I do."

"But are the rulers of states absolutely infallible, or are they sometimes liable to err?"

"To be sure," he replied, "they are liable to err."

"Then in making their laws they may sometimes make them rightly, and sometimes not?"

"True."

"When they make them rightly, they make them agreeably to

their interest; when they are mistaken, contrary to their interest; you admit that?"

"Yes."

"And the laws which they make must be obeyed by their subjects —and that is what you call justice?"

"Doubtless."

"Then justice, according to your argument, is not only obedience to the interest of the stronger but the reverse?"

"What is that you are saying?" he asked.

"I am only repeating what you are saying, I believe. But let us consider: Have we not admitted that the rulers may be mistaken about their own interest in what they command, and also that to obey them is justice? Has not that been admitted?"

"Yes."

"Then you must also have acknowledged justice not to be for the interest of the stronger, when the rulers unintentionally command things to be done which are to their own injury. For if, as you say, justice is the obedience which the subject renders to their commands, in that case, O wisest of men, is there any escape from the conclusion that the weaker are commanded to do, not what is for the interest, but what is for the injury of the stronger?"

"Nothing can be clearer, Socrates," said Polemarchus.

"Yes," said Cleitophon, interposing, "if you are allowed to be his witness."

"But there is no need of any witness," said Polemarchus, "for Thrasymachus himself acknowledges that rulers may sometimes command what is not for their own interest, and that for subjects to obey them is justice."

"Yes, Polemarchus, Thrasymachus said that for subjects to do what was commanded by their rulers is just."

"Yes, Cleitophon, but he also said that justice is the interest of the stronger, and, while admitting both these propositions, he further acknowledged that the stronger may command the weaker who are his subjects to do what is not for his own interest; whence follows that justice is the injury quite as much as the interest of the stronger."

"But," said Cleitophon, "he meant by the interest of the stronger what the stronger thought to be his interest—this was what the weaker had to do; and this was affirmed by him to be justice."

"Those were not his words," rejoined Polemarchus.

"Never mind," I replied, "if he now says that they are, let us accept his statement. Tell me, Thrasymachus," I said, "did you mean by justice what the stronger thought to be his interest, whether really so or not?"

"Certainly not," he said. "Do you suppose that I call him who is mistaken the stronger at the time when he is mistaken?"

"Yes," I said, "my impression was that you did so, when you admitted that the ruler was not infallible but might be sometimes mistaken."

"You argue like an informer, Socrates. Do you mean, for example, that he who is mistaken about the sick is a physician in that he is mistaken? or that he who errs in arithmetic or grammar is an arithmetician or grammarian at the time when he is making the mistake, in respect of the mistake? True, we say that the physician or arithmetician or grammarian has made a mistake, but this is only a way of speaking; for the fact is that neither the grammarian nor any other person of skill ever makes a mistake in so far as he is what his name implies; they none of them err unless their skill fails them, and then they cease to be skilled artists. No artist or sage or ruler errs at the time when he is what his name implies; though he is commonly said to err, and I adopted the common mode of speaking. But to be perfectly accurate, since you are such a lover of accuracy, we should say that the ruler, in so far as he is a ruler, is unerring, and, being unerring, always commands that which is for his own interest; and the subject is required to execute his commands; and therefore, as I said at first and now repeat, justice is the interest of the stronger."

"Indeed, Thrasymachus, and do I really appear to you to argue like an informer?"

"Certainly," he replied.

"And do you suppose that I ask these questions with any design of injuring you in the argument?"

"Nay," he replied, " 'suppose' is not the word—I know it; but you will be found out, and by sheer force of argument you will never prevail."

"I shall not make the attempt, my dear man; but to avoid any misunderstanding occurring between us in future, let me ask, in what sense do you speak of a ruler or stronger whose interest, as you were saying, he being the superior, it is just that the inferior should execute—is he a ruler in the popular or in the strict sense of the term?"

"In the strictest of all senses," he said. "And now cheat and play the informer if you can; I ask no quarter at your hands. But you never will be able, never."

"And do you imagine," I said, "that I am such a madman as to try and cheat Thrasymachus? I might as well shave a lion."

"Why," he said, "you made the attempt a minute ago, and you failed."

"Enough," I said, "of these civilities. It will be better that I should ask you a question: Is the physician, taken in that strict sense of which you are speaking, a healer of the sick or a maker of money? And remember that I am now speaking of the true physician."

"A healer of the sick," he replied.

"And the pilot—that is to say, the true pilot—is he a captain of sailors or a mere sailor?"

"A captain of sailors."

"The circumstance that he sails in the ship is not to be taken into account; neither is he to be called a sailor; the name pilot by which he is distinguished has nothing to do with sailing, but is significant of his skill and of his authority over the sailors."

"Very true," he said.

"Now," I said, "every art has an interest?"

"Certainly."

"For which the art has to consider and provide?"

"Yes, that is the aim of art."

"And the interest of any art is the perfection of it—this and nothing else?"

"What do you mean?"

"I mean what I may illustrate negatively by the example of the body. Suppose you were to ask me whether the body is self-sufficing or has wants, I should reply: Certainly the body has wants; for the body may be ill and require to be cured, and has therefore interests to which the art of medicine ministers; and this is the origin and intention of medicine, as you will acknowledge. Am I not right?"

"Quite right," he replied.

"But is the art of medicine or any other art faulty or deficient in any quality in the same way that the eye may be deficient in sight or the ear fail of hearing, and therefore requires another art to provide for the interests of seeing and hearing—has art in itself, I say, any similar liability to fault or defect, and does every art require another supplementary art to provide for its interests, and that another and another without end? Or have the arts to look only after their own interests? Or have they no need either of themselves or of another? —having no faults or defects, they have no need to correct them, either by the exercise of their own art or of any other; they have only to consider the interest of their subject-matter. For every art remains pure and faultless while remaining true—that is to say, while perfect and unimpaired. Take the words in your precise sense, and tell me whether I am not right."

"Yes, clearly."

"Then medicine does not consider the interest of medicine, but the interest of the body?"

"True," he said.

"Nor does the art of horsemanship consider the interests of the art of horsemanship, but the interests of the horse; neither do any other arts care for themselves, for they have no needs; they care only for that which is the subject of their art?"

"True," he said.

"But surely, Thrasymachus, the arts are the superiors and rulers of their own subjects?"

To this he assented with a good deal of reluctance.

"Then," I said, "no science or art considers or enjoins the interest of the stronger or superior, but only the interest of the subject and weaker?"

He made an attempt to contest this proposition also, but finally acquiesced.

"Then," I continued, "no physician, in so far as he is a physician, considers his own good in what he prescribes, but the good of his patient; for the true physician is also a ruler having the human body as a subject, and is not a mere money-maker; that has been admitted?"

"Yes."

"And the pilot likewise, in the strict sense of the term, is a ruler of sailors and not a mere sailor?"

"That has been admitted."

"And such a pilot and ruler will provide and prescribe for the interest of the sailor who is under him, and not for his own or the ruler's interest?"

He gave a reluctant "Yes."

"Then," I said, "Thrasymachus, there is no one in any rule who, in so far as he is a ruler, considers or enjoins what is for his own interest, but always what is for the interest of his subject or suitable to his art; to that he looks, and that alone he considers in everything which he says and does."

When we had got to this point in the argument, and everyone saw that the definition [15] of justice had been completely upset, Thrasymachus, instead of replying to me, said: "Tell me, Socrates, have you got a nurse?"

"Why do you ask such a question," I said, "when you ought rather to be answering?"

"Because she leaves you to snivel, and never wipes your nose: she has not even taught you to know the shepherd from the sheep."

"What makes you say that?" I replied.

"Because you fancy that the shepherd or neatherd fattens or tends the sheep or oxen with a view to their own good and not to the good

15 Thrasymachus' definition.

of himself or his master; and you further imagine that the rulers of states, if they are true rulers, never think of their subjects as sheep, and that they are not studying their own advantage day and night. Oh, no; and so entirely astray are you in your ideas about the just and unjust as not even to know that justice and the just are in reality another's good; that is to say, the interest of the ruler and stronger, and the loss of the subject and servant; and injustice the opposite; for the unjust is lord over the truly simple and just: he is the stronger, and his subjects do what is for his interest, and minister to his happiness, which is very far from being their own. Consider further, most foolish Socrates, that the just is always a loser in comparison with the unjust.[16] First of all, in private contracts: wherever the unjust is the partner of the just you will find that, when the partnership is dissolved, the unjust man has always more and the just less. Secondly, in their dealings with the State: when there is an income-tax, the just man will pay more and the unjust less on the same amount of income; and when there is anything to be received the one gains nothing and the other much. Observe also what happens when they take an office; there is the just man neglecting his affairs and perhaps suffering other losses, and getting nothing out of the public, because he is just; moreover he is hated by his friends and acquaintance for refusing to serve them in unlawful ways. But all this is reversed in the case of the unjust man. I am speaking, as before, of injustice on a large scale in which the advantage of the unjust is most apparent; and my meaning will be most clearly seen if we turn to that highest form of injustice in which the criminal is the happiest of men, and the sufferers or those who refuse to do injustice are the most miserable —that is to say tyranny, which by fraud and force takes away the property of others, not little by little but wholesale; comprehending in one, things sacred as well as profane, private and public; for which acts of wrong, if he were detected perpetrating any one of them singly, he would be punished and incur great disgrace—they who do

16 Thrasymachus now broadens out his position by adding the assertion that the good man, in contrast to the bad, is always the loser in everything that makes life attractive.

such wrong in particular cases are called robbers of temples, and man-stealers and burglars and swindlers and thieves. But when a man besides taking away the money of the citizens has made slaves of them, then, instead of these names of reproach, he is termed happy and blessed, not only by the citizens but by all who hear of his having achieved the consummation of injustice. For mankind censure injustice, fearing that they may be the victims of it and not because they shrink from committing it. And thus, as I have shown, Socrates, injustice, when on a sufficient scale, has more strength and freedom and mastery than justice; and, as I said at first, justice is the interest of the stronger, whereas injustice is a man's own profit and interest."

Thrasymachus, when he had thus spoken, having, like a bathman, deluged our ears with his words, had a mind to go away. But the company would not let him; they insisted that he should remain and defend his position; and I myself added my own humble request that he would not leave us.

"Thrasymachus," I said to him, "excellent man, how suggestive are your remarks! And are you going to run away before you have fairly taught or learned whether they are true or not? Is the attempt to determine the way of man's life so small a matter in your eyes—to determine how life may be passed by each one of us to the greatest advantage?"

"And do I differ from you," he said, "as to the importance of the inquiry?"

"You appear rather," I replied, "to have no care or thought about us, Thrasymachus—whether we live better or worse from not knowing what you say you know is to you a matter of indifference.[17] Prithee, friend, do not keep your knowledge to yourself; we are a large party; and any benefit which you confer upon us will be amply rewarded. For my own part I openly declare that I am not convinced, and that I do not believe injustice to be more gainful than justice,

17 Better translated: "You seem to," I replied, "or else to care nothing for us and be quite indifferent whether we live better or worse from not knowing what you say you know."

even if uncontrolled and allowed to have free play. For, granting that there may be an unjust man who is able to commit injustice either by fraud or force, still this does not convince me of the superior advantage of injustice, and there may be others who are in the same predicament with myself. Perhaps we may be wrong; if so, you in your wisdom should convince us that we are mistaken in preferring justice to injustice."

"And how am I to convince you," he said, "if you are not already convinced by what I have just said; what more can I do for you? Would you have me put the proof bodily into your souls?" [18]

"Heaven forbid!" I said; "I would only ask you to be consistent; or, if you change, change openly and let there be no deception. For I must remark, Thrasymachus, if you will recall what was previously said, that although you began by defining the true physician in an exact sense, you did not observe a like exactness when speaking of the shepherd; you thought that the shepherd as a shepherd tends the sheep not with a view to their own good, but like a mere diner or banqueter with a view to the pleasures of the table; or, again, as a trader for sale in the market, and not as a shepherd. Yet surely the art of the shepherd is concerned only with the good of his subjects; he has only to provide the best for them, since the perfection of the art is already insured whenever all the requirements of it are satisfied. And that was what I was saying just now about the ruler. I conceived that the art of the ruler, considered as ruler, whether in a state or in private life, could only regard the good of his flock or subjects; whereas you seem to think that the rulers in states, that is to say, the true rulers, like being in authority."

"Think! Nay, I am sure of it."

"Then why in the case of lesser offices do men never take them willingly without payment, unless under the idea that they govern for the advantage not of themselves but of others?

Government, which means the reformation of evils in society, is a hard task. Officials have either to be paid for their labors in

---

[18] Or "Shall I take the proof and ram it into your head?"

money and honor or else be induced to serve by the fear that
otherwise they will be ruled by men worse than themselves.

There is reason to think that if a city were composed entirely of good men, then to avoid office would be as much an object of contention as to obtain office is at present; then we should have plain proof that the true ruler is not meant by nature to regard his own interest, but that of his subjects; and everyone who knew this would choose rather to receive a benefit from another than to have the trouble of conferring one. So far am I from agreeing with Thrasymachus that justice is the interest of the stronger. This latter question need not be further discussed at present; but when Thrasymachus says that the life of the unjust is more advantageous than that of the just, his new statement appears to me to be of a far more serious character.[19] Which of us has spoken truly? And which sort of life, Glaucon, do you prefer?"

"I for my part deem the life of the just to be the more advantageous," he answered.

"Did you hear all the advantages of the unjust which Thrasymachus was rehearsing?"

"Yes, I heard him," he replied, "but he has not convinced me."

"Then shall we try to find some way of convincing him, if we can, that he is saying what is not true?"

"Most certainly," he replied.

"If," I said, "he makes a set speech and we make another recounting all the advantages of being just, and he answers and we rejoin, there must be a numbering and measuring of the goods which are claimed on either side, and in the end we shall want judges to decide; but if we proceed in our inquiry as we lately did, by making admissions to one another, we shall unite the offices of judge and advocate in our own persons."

"Very good," he said.

"And which method do I understand you to prefer?" I said.

19 Socrates arrives now at the main question of the *Republic*. Is the unjust life really happier and more profitable than the just?

"That which you propose."

"Well, then, Thrasymachus," I said, "suppose you begin at the beginning and answer me. You say that perfect injustice is more gainful than perfect justice?"

"Yes, that is what I say, and I have given you my reasons."

"And what is your view about them? Would you call one of them virtue and the other vice?"

"Certainly."

"I suppose that you would call justice virtue and injustice vice?"

"What a charming notion! So likely too, seeing that I affirm injustice to be profitable and justice not."

"What else then would you say?"

"The opposite," he replied.

"And would you call justice vice?"

"No, I would rather say sublime simplicity."

"Then would you call injustice malignity?"

"No; I would rather say discretion."

"And do the unjust appear to you to be wise and good?"

"Yes," he said; "at any rate those of them who are able to be perfectly unjust, and who have the power of subduing states and nations; but perhaps you imagine me to be talking of cutpurses. Even this profession if undetected has advantages, though they are not to be compared with those of which I was just now speaking."

"I do not think that I misapprehend your meaning, Thrasymachus," I replied; "but still I cannot hear without amazement that you class injustice with wisdom and virtue, and justice with the opposite."

"Certainly, I do so class them."

"Now," I said, "you are on more substantial and almost unanswerable ground; for if the injustice which you were maintaining to be profitable had been admitted by you as by others to be vice and deformity, an answer might have been given to you on received principles; but now I perceive that you will call injustice honorable and strong, and to the unjust you will attribute all the qualities which were attributed by us before to the just, seeing that you do not hesitate to rank injustice with wisdom and virtue."

"You have guessed most infallibly," he replied.

"Then I certainly ought not to shrink from going through with the argument so long as I have reason to think that you, Thrasymachus, are speaking your real mind; for I do believe that you are now in earnest and are not amusing yourself at our expense."

"I may be in earnest or not, but what is that to you?—to refute the argument is your business."

"Very true," I said; "that is what I have to do.

Socrates argues that a wise and good craftsman does not try to over-reach or get the better of his fellow craftsmen but that the unjust man tries to get the better of everybody, even his unjust comrades. Hence he is neither wise nor good.

You would not deny that a state may be unjust and may be unjustly attempting to enslave other states, or may have already enslaved them, and may be holding many of them in subje tion?"

"True," he replied; "and I will add that the best and most perfectly unjust state will be most likely to do so."

"I know," I said, "that such was your position; but what I would further consider is, whether this power which is possessed by the superior state can exist or be exercised without justice or only with justice."

"If you are right in your view, and justice is wisdom, then only with justice; but if I am right, then without justice."

"I am delighted, Thrasymachus, to see you not only nodding assent and dissent, but making answers which are quite excellent."

"That is out of civility to you," he replied.

"You are very kind," I said; "and would you have the goodness also to inform me, whether you think that a state, or an army, or a band of robbers and thieves, or any other gang of evil-doers could act at all if they injured one another?"

"No indeed," he said, "they could not."

"But if they abstained from injuring one another, then they might act together better?"

"Yes."

"And this is because injustice creates divisions and hatreds and fighting, and justice imparts harmony and friendship; is not that true, Thrasymachus?"

"I agree," he said, "because I do not wish to quarrel with you."

"How good of you," I said; "but I should like to know also whether injustice, having this tendency to arouse hatred, wherever existing, among slaves or among freemen, will not make them hate one another and set them at variance and render them incapable of common action?"

"Certainly."

"And even if injustice be found in two only, will they not quarrel and fight, and become enemies to one another and to the just?"

"They will."

"And suppose injustice abiding in a single person, would your wisdom say that she loses or that she retains her natural power?"

"Let us assume that she retains her power."

"Yet is not the power which injustice exercises of such a nature that wherever she takes up her abode, whether in a city, in an army, in a family, or in any other body, that body is, to begin with, rendered incapable of united action by reason of sedition and distraction; and does it not become its own enemy and at variance with all that opposes it, and with the just? Is not this the case?"

"Yes, certainly."

"And is not injustice equally fatal when existing in a single person; in the first place rendering him incapable of action because he is not at unity with himself, and in the second place making him an enemy to himself and the just? Is not that true, Thrasymachus?"

"Yes."

"And O my friend," I said, "surely the gods are just?"

"Granted that they are."

"But if so, the unjust will be the enemy of the gods, and the just will be their friend?"

"Feast away in triumph, and take your fill of the argument; I will not oppose you, lest I should displease the company."

"Well then, proceed with your answers, and let me have the remainder of my repast. For we have already shown that the just are clearly wiser and better and abler than the unjust, and that the unjust are incapable of common action; nay more, that to speak as we did of men who are evil acting at any time vigorously together is not strictly true, for if they had been perfectly evil, they would have laid hands upon one another; but it is evident that there must have been some remnant of justice in them, which enabled them to combine; if there had not been they would have injured one another as well as their victims; they were but half-villains in their enterprises; for had they been whole villains, and utterly unjust, they would have been utterly incapable of action. That, as I believe, is the truth of the matter, and not what you said at first. But whether the just have a better and happier life than the unjust is a further question which we also proposed to consider.[20] I think that they have, and for the reasons which I have given; but still I should like to examine further, for no light matter is at stake, nothing less than the rule of human life."

"Proceed."

"I will proceed by asking a question: Would you not say that a horse has some end?"

"I should."

"And the end or use of a horse or of anything would be that which could not be accomplished, or not so well accomplished, by any other thing?"

"I do not understand," he said.

"Let me explain. Can you see, except with the eye?"

"Certainly not."

"Or hear, except with the ear?"

"No."

"These then may be truly said to be the ends of these organs?"

20 Having shown that even the fiercest and most unjust men are compelled to practice some justice among themselves in order to survive, Socrates returns to the central question of the dialogue.

"They may."

"But you can cut off a vine-branch with a dagger or with a chisel, and in many other ways?"

"Of course."

"And yet not so well as with a pruning-hook made for the purpose?"

"True."

"May we not say that this is the end of a pruning-hook?"

"We may."

"Then now I think you will have no difficulty in understanding my meaning when I asked the question whether the end of anything would be that which could not be accomplished, or not so well accomplished, by any other thing?"

"I understand your meaning," he said, "and assent."

"And that to which an end is appointed has also an excellence? Need I ask again whether the eye has an end?"

"It has."

"And has not the eye an excellence?"

"Yes."

"And the ear has an end and an excellence also?"

"True."

"And the same is true of all other things; they have each of them an end and a special excellence?"

"That is so."

"Well, and can the eyes fulfill their end if they are wanting in their own proper excellence and have a defect instead?"

"How can they," he said, "if they are blind and cannot see?"

"You mean to say, if they have lost their proper excellence, which is sight; but I have not arrived at that point yet. I would rather ask the question more generally, and only inquire whether the things which fulfill their ends fulfill them by their own proper excellence, and fail of fulfilling them by their own defect?"

"Certainly," he replied.

"I might say the same of the ears; when deprived of their own proper excellence they cannot fulfill their end?"

"True."

"And the same observation will apply to all other things?"

"I agree."

"Well; and has not the soul an end which nothing else can fulfill? For example, to superintend and command and deliberate and the like. Are not these functions proper to the soul, and can they rightly be assigned to any other?"

"To no other."

"And is not life to be reckoned among the ends of the soul?"

"Assuredly," he said.

"And has not the soul an excellence also?"

"Yes."

"And can she or can she not fulfill her own ends when deprived of that excellence?"

"She cannot."

"Then an evil soul [21] must necessarily be an evil ruler and superintendent, and the good soul a good ruler?"

"Yes, necessarily."

"And we have admitted that justice is the excellence of the soul, and injustice the defect of the soul?"

"That has been admitted."

"Then the just soul and the just man will live well, and the unjust man will live ill?"

"That is what your argument proves."

"And he who lives well is blessed and happy, and he who lives ill the reverse of happy?"

"Certainly."

"Then the just is happy, and the unjust miserable?"

"So be it."

"But happiness and not misery is profitable."

"Of course."

---

21 Socrates here passes too hastily from the physical to the moral sphere. He assumes without proof that evil in the soul is like a physical defect in the body, which deprives it of the ability to function normally and intelligently. Hence his promptly expressed dissatisfaction with his own argument at this point. He deals with the subject more adequately later.

"Then, my blessed Thrasymachus, injustice can never be more profitable than justice."

"Let this, Socrates," he said, "be your entertainment at the Bendidea." [22]

"For which I am indebted to you," I said, "now that you have grown gentle towards me and have left off scolding. Nevertheless, I have not been well entertained; but that was my own fault and not yours. As an epicure snatches a taste of every dish which is successively brought to table, he not having allowed himself time to enjoy the one before, so have I gone from one subject to another without having discovered what I sought at first, the nature of justice. I left that inquiry and turned away to consider whether justice is virtue and wisdom or evil and folly; and when there arose a further question about the comparative advantages of justice and injustice, I could not refrain from passing on to that. And the result of the whole discussion has been that I know nothing at all. For I know not what justice is, and therefore I am not likely to know whether it is or is not a virtue, nor can I say whether the just man is happy or unhappy."

BOOK II

The life of a well-ordered state and education of its soldier citizens in music and gymnastics, and in right ideas of God.

WITH these words I was thinking that I had made an end of the discussion; but the end, in truth, proved to be only a beginning. For Glaucon, who is always the most pugnacious of men, was dissatisfied at Thrasymachus' retirement; he wanted to have the battle out. So he said to me: "Socrates, do you wish really to persuade us, or only

22 Festival of the goddess Bendis.

to seem to have persuaded us, that to be just is always better than to be unjust?"

"I should wish really to persuade you," I replied, "if I could."

"Then you certainly have not succeeded. Let me ask you now: How would you arrange [1] goods—are there not some which we welcome for their own sakes, and independently of their consequences, as, for example, harmless pleasures and enjoyments, which delight us at the time, although nothing follows from them?"

"I agree in thinking that there is such a class," I replied.

"Is there not also a second class of goods, such as knowledge, sight, health, which are desirable not only in themselves, but also for their results?"

"Certainly," I said.

"And would you not recognize a third class, such as gymnastic, and the care of the sick, and the physician's art; also the various ways of money-making—these do us good but we regard them as disagreeable; and no one would choose them for their own sakes, but only for the sake of some reward or result which flows from them?"

"There is," I said, "this third class also. But why do you ask?"

"Because I want to know in which of the three classes you would place justice?"

"In the highest class," I replied, "among those goods which he who would be happy desires both for their own sake and for the sake of their results."

"Then the many are of another mind; they think that justice is to be reckoned in the troublesome class, among goods which are to be pursued for the sake of rewards and of reputation, but in themselves are disagreeable and rather to be avoided."

"I know," I said, "that this is their manner of thinking, and that this was the thesis which Thrasymachus was maintaining just now, when he censured justice and praised injustice. But I am too stupid to be convinced by him."

"I wish," he said, "that you would hear me as well as him, and

1 Or classify.

then I shall see whether you and I agree. For Thrasymachus seems to me, like a snake, to have been charmed by your voice sooner than he ought to have been; but to my mind the nature of justice and injustice have not yet been made clear.[2] Setting aside their rewards and results, I want to know what they are in themselves, and how they inwardly work in the soul. If you please, then, I will revive the argument of Thrasymachus. And first I will speak of the nature and origin of justice according to the common view of them. Secondly, I will show that all men who practice justice do so against their will, of necessity, but not as a good. And thirdly, I will argue that there is reason in this view, for the life of the unjust is after all better far than the life of the just—if what they say is true, Socrates, since I myself am not of their opinion. But still I acknowledge that I am perplexed when I hear the voices of Thrasymachus and myriads of others dinning in my ears; and, on the other hand, I have never yet heard the superiority of justice to injustice maintained by anyone in a satisfactory way. I want to hear justice praised in respect of itself; then I shall be satisfied, and you are the person from whom I think that I am most likely to hear this; and therefore I will praise the unjust life to the utmost of my power, and my manner of speaking will indicate the manner in which I desire to hear you too praising justice and censuring injustice. Will you say whether you approve of my proposal?"

"Indeed I do; nor can I imagine any theme about which a man of sense would oftener wish to converse."

"I am delighted," he replied, "to hear you say so, and shall begin by speaking, as I proposed, of the nature and origin of justice.

"They say that to do injustice is, by nature, good; to suffer injustice, evil; but that the evil is greater than the good. And so when men have both done and suffered injustice and have had experience of both, not being able to avoid the one and obtain the other, they think

2 The theory of Thrasymachus is now to be restated by Plato's brothers far more powerfully than that blustering Sophist was able to do it. They demand a thoroughgoing refutation of the cynic's idea that the good man's life is an abnormal life, that naturally every man is out for himself, to get whatever he can without being found out.

that they had better agree among themselves to have neither; [3] hence there arise laws and mutual covenants; and that which is ordained by law is termed by them lawful and just. This they affirm to be the origin and nature of justice; it is a mean or compromise, between the best of all, which is to do injustice and not be punished, and the worst of all, which is to suffer injustice without the power of retaliation; and justice, being at a middle point between the two, is tolerated not as a good, but as the lesser evil, and honored by reason of the inability of men to do injustice. For no man who is worthy to be called a man would ever submit to such an agreement if he were able to resist; he would be mad if he did. Such is the received account, Socrates, of the nature and origin of justice.

"Now that those who practice justice do so involuntarily and because they have not the power to be unjust will best appear if we imagine something of this kind: having given both to the just and the unjust power to do what they will, let us watch and see whither desire will lead them; then we shall discover in the very act the just and unjust man to be proceeding along the same road, following their interest, which all natures deem to be their good, and are only diverted into the path of justice by the force of law. The liberty which we are supposing may be most completely given to them in the form of such a power as is said to have been possessed by Gyges,[4] the ancestor of Croesus the Lydian. According to the tradition, Gyges was a shepherd in the service of the king of Lydia; there was a great storm, and an earthquake made an opening in the earth at the place where he was feeding his flock. Amazed at the sight, he descended into the opening, where, among other marvels, he beheld a hollow brazen horse, having doors, at which he stooping and looking in saw a dead

3 A better translation is: "Those who have not enough power to avoid the one and enjoy the other conclude they would better make a compact between themselves that they will neither commit nor suffer injustice." Plato is here the originator of the theory that governments began first with social contracts by which bands of men pledged themselves to refrain from harming one another in order to make possible an advantageous life together.

4 A different story of Gyges and how he won the queen and the kingdom of Lydia, with no word of a magic ring, had been told by the historian Herodotus (c. 450 B.C.), I, 8-13.

body of stature, as appeared to him, more than human, and having
nothing on but a gold ring; this he took from the finger of the dead
and reascended. Now the shepherds met together, according to custom, that they might send their monthly report about the flocks to
the king; into their assembly he came having the ring on his finger,
and as he was sitting among them he chanced to turn the collet [5] of
the ring inside his hand, when instantly he became invisible to the
rest of the company and they began to speak of him as if he were no
longer present. He was astonished at this, and again touching the
ring he turned the collet outwards and reappeared; he made several
trials of the ring, and always with the same result—when he turned
the collet inwards he became invisible, when outwards he reappeared. Whereupon he contrived to be chosen one of the messengers
who were sent to the court; where as soon as he arrived he seduced
the queen, and with her help conspired against the king and slew
him, and took the kingdom. Suppose now that there were two such
magic rings, and the just put on one of them and the unjust the
other; no man can be imagined to be of such an iron nature that he
would stand fast in justice. No man would keep his hands off what
was not his own when he could safely take what he liked out of the
market, or go into houses and lie with anyone at his pleasure, or kill
or release from prison whom he would, and in all respects be like a
god among men. Then the actions of the just would be as the actions
of the unjust; they would both come at last to the same point. And
this we may truly affirm to be a great proof that a man is just, not
willingly or because he thinks that justice is any good to him individually, but of necessity, for wherever anyone thinks that he can
safely be unjust, there he is unjust. For all men believe in their hearts
that injustice is far more profitable to the individual than justice, and
he who argues as I have been supposing, will say that they are right.
If you could imagine anyone obtaining this power of becoming invisible, and never doing any wrong or touching what was another's,
he would be thought by the lookers-on to be a most wretched idiot,

5 Or setting.

although they would praise him to one another's faces, and keep up appearances with one another from a fear that they too might suffer injustice. Enough of this.

"Now, if we are to form a real judgment of the life of the just and unjust, we must isolate them; there is no other way; and how is the isolation to be effected? I answer: Let the unjust man be entirely unjust, and the just man entirely just; [6] nothing is to be taken away from either of them, and both are to be perfectly furnished for the work of their respective lives. First, let the unjust be like other distinguished masters of craft; like the skillful pilot or physician, who knows intuitively his own powers and keeps within their limits, and who, if he fails at any point, is able to recover himself. So let the unjust make his unjust attempts in the right way, and lie hidden if he means to be great in his injustice (he who is found out is nobody); for the highest reach of injustice is to be deemed just when you are not. Therefore I say that in the perfectly unjust man we must assume the most perfect injustice; there is to be no deduction, but we must allow him, while doing the most unjust acts, to have acquired the greatest reputation for justice. If he have taken a false step he must be able to recover himself; he must be one who can speak with effect, if any of his deeds come to light, and who can force his way where force is required by his courage and strength, and command of money and friends. And at his side let us place the just man in his nobleness and simplicity, wishing, as Aeschylus says, to be and not to seem good. There must be no seeming, for if he seem to be just he will be honored and rewarded, and then we shall not know whether he is just for the sake of justice or for the sake of honors and rewards; therefore, let him be clothed in justice only, and have no other covering; and he must be imagined in a state of life the opposite of the former. Let him be the best of men, and let him be thought the worst; then he will have been put to the proof; and we shall see

6 The question is now to be put in its most extreme form. Let the unjust man have it all his own way, be never found out, and get everything he wants. Let the just man make a failure of living, be poor and utterly despised by everyone. Which of them will be the happier?

whether he will be affected by the fear of infamy and its consequences. And let him continue thus to the hour of death; being just
and seeming to be unjust. When both have reached the uttermost
extreme, the one of justice and the other of injustice, let judgment be
given which of them is the happier of the two."

"Heavens! my dear Glaucon," I said, "how energetically you polish
them up for the decision, first one and then the other, as if they were
two statues."

"I do my best," he said. "And now that we know what they are
like there is no difficulty in tracing out the sort of life which awaits
either of them. This I will proceed to describe; but as you may think
the description a little too coarse, I ask you to suppose, Socrates, that
the words which follow are not mine. Let me put them into the
mouths of the eulogists of injustice. They will tell you that the just
man who is thought unjust will be scourged, racked, bound—will
have his eyes burnt out; and, at last, after suffering every kind of evil,
he will be impaled.[7] Then he will understand that he ought to seem
only, and not to be, just; the words of Aeschylus may be more truly
spoken of the unjust than of the just. For the unjust is pursuing a
reality; he does not live with a view to appearances—he wants to be
really unjust and not to seem only:

> His mind has a soil deep and fertile,
> Out of which spring his prudent counsels.[8]

In the first place, he is thought just, and therefore bears rule in the
city; he can marry whom he will, and give in marriage to whom he
will; also he can trade and deal where he likes, and always to his own
advantage, because he has no misgivings about injustice; and at
every contest, whether in public or private, he gets the better of his
antagonists, and gains at their expense, and is rich, and out of his
gains he can benefit his friends, and harm his enemies; moreover, he
can offer sacrifices, and dedicate gifts to the gods abundantly and

7 Or crucified. The fate of Plato's just man was often in later centuries compared
with that of Christ.
8 Aeschylus, *Seven Against Thebes*, 580, 581.

magnificently, and can honor the gods or any man whom he wants to honor in a far better style than the just, and therefore he is likely to be dearer than they are to the gods. And thus, Socrates, gods and men are said to unite in making the life of the unjust better than the life of the just."

I was going to say something in answer to Glaucon, when Adeimantus, his brother, interposed: "Socrates," he said, "you do not suppose that there is nothing more to be urged?"

"Why, what else is there?" I answered.

"The strongest point of all has not been even mentioned," he replied.

"Well, then, according to the proverb, 'Let brother help brother,' if he fails in any part do you assist him; although I must confess that Glaucon has already said quite enough to lay me in the dust, and take from me the power of helping justice."

"Nonsense," he replied. "But let me add something more: There is another side to Glaucon's argument about the praise and censure of justice and injustice, which is equally required in order to bring out what I believe to be his meaning. Parents and tutors are always telling their sons and their wards that they are to be just; but why? not for the sake of justice, but for the sake of character and reputation; in the hope of obtaining for him who is reputed just some of those offices, marriages, and the like which Glaucon has enumerated among the advantages accruing to the unjust from the reputation of justice. More, however, is made of appearances by this class of persons than by the others; for they throw in the good opinion of the gods, and will tell you of a shower of benefits which the heavens, as they say, rain upon the pious; and this accords with the testimony of the noble Hesiod and Homer, the first of whom says, that the gods make the oaks of the just—

> *To bear acorns at their summit, and bees in the middle;*
> *And the sheep are bowed down with the weight of their fleeces,* [9]

[9] Hesiod, *Works and Days*, 232-4.

aying, and praying and sinning, the gods will be propitiated, and
shall not be punished.—But there is a world below in which either
or our posterity will suffer for our unjust deeds.—Yes, my friend,
ll be the reflection, but there are mysteries and atoning deities, and
ese have great power. That is what mighty cities declare; and the
ildren of the gods, who were their poets and prophets, bear a like
timony.

"On what principle, then, shall we any longer choose justice
her than the worst injustice? when, if we only unite the latter with
eceitful regard to appearances, we shall fare to our mind both with
ds and men, in life and after death, as the most numerous and the
ghest authorities tell us. Knowing all this, Socrates, how can a man
o has any superiority of mind or person or rank or wealth, be
lling to honor justice; or indeed to refrain from laughing when he
ars justice praised? And even if there should be someone who is
le to disprove the truth of my words, and who is satisfied that jus-
e is best, still he is not angry with the unjust, but is very ready to
rgive them, because he also knows that men are not just of their
n free will; unless, peradventure, there be someone whom the
vinity within him may have inspired with a hatred of injustice, or
o has attained knowledge of the truth—but no other man. He only
ames injustice who, owing to cowardice or age or some weakness,
s not the power of being unjust. And this is proved by the fact that
en he obtains the power, he immediately becomes unjust as far as
can be.

"The cause of all this, Socrates, was indicated by us at the begin-
ng of the argument, when my brother and I told you how aston-
hed we were to find that of all the professing panegyrists of justice
beginning with the ancient heroes of whom any memorial has been
eserved to us, and ending with the men of our own time—no one
s ever blamed injustice or praised justice except with a view to the
ories, honors, and benefits which flow from them. No one has ever
equately described either in verse or prose the true essential nature
either of them abiding in the soul, and invisible to any human or
vine eye; or shown that of all the things of a man's soul which he

and many other blessings of a like kind are provided for them. And
Homer has a very similar strain; for he speaks of one whose fame is—

> As the fame of some blameless king who, like a god,
> Maintains justice; to whom the black earth brings forth
> Wheat and barley, whose trees are bowed with fruit,
> And his sheep never fail to bear, and the sea gives him fish.[10]

Still grander are the gifts of heaven which Musaeus [11] and his son
vouchsafe to the just; they take them down into the world below,
where they have the saints lying on couches at a feast, everlastingly
drunk, crowned with garlands; their idea seems to be that an immortality of drunkenness is the highest meed of virtue. Some extend
their rewards yet further; the posterity, as they say, of the faithful and
just shall survive to the third and fourth generation. This is the style
in which they praise justice. But about the wicked there is another
strain; they bury them in a slough in Hades, and make them carry
water in a sieve; also while they are yet living they bring them to infamy, and inflict upon them the punishments which Glaucon described as the portion of the just who are reputed to be unjust; nothing else does their invention supply. Such is their manner of praising
the one and censuring the other.

"Once more, Socrates, I will ask you to consider another way of
speaking about justice and injustice, which is not confined to the
poets, but is found in prose writers. The universal voice of mankind
is always declaring that justice and virtue are honorable, but grievous
and toilsome; and that the pleasures of vice and injustice are easy of
attainment, and are only censured by law and opinion. They say
also that honesty is for the most part less profitable than dishonesty;
and they are quite ready to call wicked men happy, and to honor
them both in public and private when they are rich or in any other
way influential, while they despise and overlook those who may be
weak and poor, even though acknowledging them to be better than

10 *Odyssey*, XIX, 109-113.
11 A mythical poet and seer, son of the divinely gifted Orpheus. He was said to
have been the first composer of priestly poetry and hymns of solemn purification.

the othe.s. But most extraordinary of all is their mode of speaking about virtue and the gods: they say that the gods apportion calamity and misery to many good men, and good and happiness to the wicked. And mendicant prophets go to rich men's doors and persuade them that they have a power committed to them by the gods of making an atonement for a man's own or his ancestor's sins by sacrifices or charms, with rejoicings and feasts; and they promise to harm an enemy, whether just or unjust, at a small cost; with magic arts and incantations binding heaven, as they say, to execute their will. And the poets are the authorities to whom they appeal, now smoothing the path of vice with the words of Hesiod: *Vice may be had in abundance without trouble; the way is smooth and her dwelling-place is near. But before virtue the gods have set toil,*[12] and a tedious and uphill road: then citing Homer as a witness that the gods may be influenced by men; for he also says: *The gods, too, may be turned from their purpose; and men pray to them and avert their wrath by sacrifices and soothing entreaties, and by libations and the odor of fat, when they have sinned and transgressed.*[13] And they produce a host of books written by Musaeus and Orpheus, who were children of the Moon and the Muses—that is what they say—according to which they perform their ritual, and persuade not only individuals, but whole cities, that expiations and atonements for sin may be made by sacrifices and amusements which fill a vacant hour, and are equally at the service of the living and the dead; the latter sort they call mysteries, and they redeem us from the pains of hell, but if we neglect them no one knows what awaits us."

He proceeded: "And now when the young hear all this said about virtue and vice, and the way in which gods and men regard them, how are their minds likely to be affected, my dear Socrates—those of them, I mean, who are quickwitted, and, like bees on the wing, light on every flower, and from all that they hear are prone to draw conclusions as to what manner of persons they should be and in what way they should walk if they would make the best of life? Probably

12 Hesiod, *Works and Days,* 287-289.
13 *Iliad,* IX, 497-501.

the youth will say to himself in the words of Pii or *by crooked ways of deceit ascend a loftier t fortress to me all my days?* [14] For what men say just and am not also thought just, profit th pain and loss on the other hand are unmistal unjust, I acquire the reputation of justice, a h ised to me. Since then, as philosophers prov nizes over truth and is lord of happiness, tc devote myself. I will describe around me a of virtue to be the vestibule and exterior of will trail the subtle and crafty fox, as Archi sages, recommends. But I hear someone exclaim ment of wickedness is often difficult; to which great is easy. Nevertheless, the argument indica be happy, to be the path along which we shou view to concealment we will establish secret bro ical clubs. And there are professors of rhetoric persuading courts and assemblies; and so, partl partly by force, I shall make unlawful gains ar Still I hear a voice saying that the gods cannot can they be compelled. But what if there are n them to have no care of human things—why in e mind about concealment? And even if there ar care about us, yet we know of them only fror genealogies of the poets; and these are the very p they may be influenced and turned by 'sacrifice treaties and by offerings.' Let us be consistent the or neither. If the poets speak truly, why then we h and offer of the fruits of injustice; for if we are ju escape the vengeance of heaven, we shall lose th but, if we are unjust, we shall keep the gains, and

14 Pindar, Fragment 213, Loeb edition.
15 An early Greek poet (650 B.C.) and inventor of new grave and sharply satiric verse which was much admired by statue was sometimes set up beside Homer's.

and many other blessings of a like kind are provided for them. And Homer has a very similar strain; for he speaks of one whose fame is—

As the fame of some blameless king who, like a god,
Maintains justice; to whom the black earth brings forth
Wheat and barley, whose trees are bowed with fruit,
And his sheep never fail to bear, and the sea gives him fish.[10]

Still grander are the gifts of heaven which Musaeus [11] and his son vouchsafe to the just; they take them down into the world below, where they have the saints lying on couches at a feast, everlastingly drunk, crowned with garlands; their idea seems to be that an immortality of drunkenness is the highest meed of virtue. Some extend their rewards yet further; the posterity, as they say, of the faithful and just shall survive to the third and fourth generation. This is the style in which they praise justice. But about the wicked there is another strain; they bury them in a slough in Hades, and make them carry water in a sieve; also while they are yet living they bring them to infamy, and inflict upon them the punishments which Glaucon described as the portion of the just who are reputed to be unjust; nothing else does their invention supply. Such is their manner of praising the one and censuring the other.

"Once more, Socrates, I will ask you to consider another way of speaking about justice and injustice, which is not confined to the poets, but is found in prose writers. The universal voice of mankind is always declaring that justice and virtue are honorable, but grievous and toilsome; and that the pleasures of vice and injustice are easy of attainment, and are only censured by law and opinion. They say also that honesty is for the most part less profitable than dishonesty; and they are quite ready to call wicked men happy, and to honor them both in public and private when they are rich or in any other way influential, while they despise and overlook those who may be weak and poor, even though acknowledging them to be better than

10 *Odyssey*, XIX, 109-113.
11 A mythical poet and seer, son of the divinely gifted Orpheus. He was said to have been the first composer of priestly poetry and hymns of solemn purification.

the othe.s. But most extraordinary of all is their mode of speaking about virtue and the gods: they say that the gods apportion calamity and misery to many good men, and good and happiness to the wicked. And mendicant prophets go to rich men's doors and persuade them that they have a power committed to them by the gods of making an atonement for a man's own or his ancestor's sins by sacrifices or charms, with rejoicings and feasts; and they promise to harm an enemy, whether just or unjust, at a small cost; with magic arts and incantations binding heaven, as they say, to execute their will. And the poets are the authorities to whom they appeal, now smoothing the path of vice with the words of Hesiod: *Vice may be had in abundance without trouble; the way is smooth and her dwelling-place is near. But before virtue the gods have set toil,*[12] and a tedious and uphill road: then citing Homer as a witness that the gods may be influenced by men; for he also says: *The gods, too, may be turned from their purpose; and men pray to them and avert their wrath by sacrifices and soothing entreaties, and by libations and the odor of fat, when they have sinned and transgressed.*[13] And they produce a host of books written by Musaeus and Orpheus, who were children of the Moon and the Muses—that is what they say—according to which they perform their ritual, and persuade not only individuals, but whole cities, that expiations and atonements for sin may be made by sacrifices and amusements which fill a vacant hour, and are equally at the service of the living and the dead; the latter sort they call mysteries, and they redeem us from the pains of hell, but if we neglect them no one knows what awaits us."

He proceeded: "And now when the young hear all this said about virtue and vice, and the way in which gods and men regard them, how are their minds likely to be affected, my dear Socrates—those of them, I mean, who are quickwitted, and, like bees on the wing, light on every flower, and from all that they hear are prone to draw conclusions as to what manner of persons they should be and in what way they should walk if they would make the best of life? Probably

12 Hesiod, *Works and Days*, 287-289.
13 *Iliad*, IX, 497-501.

the youth will say to himself in the words of Pindar: *Can I by justice or by crooked ways of deceit ascend a loftier tower which may be a fortress to me all my days?* [14] For what men say is that, if I am really just and am not also thought just, profit there is none, but the pain and loss on the other hand are unmistakable. But if, though unjust, I acquire the reputation of justice, a heavenly life is promised to me. Since then, as philosophers prove, appearance tyrannizes over truth and is lord of happiness, to appearance I must devote myself. I will describe around me a picture and shadow of virtue to be the vestibule and exterior of my house; behind I will trail the subtle and crafty fox, as Archilochus,[15] greatest of sages, recommends. But I hear someone exclaiming that the concealment of wickedness is often difficult; to which I answer, Nothing great is easy. Nevertheless, the argument indicates this, if we would be happy, to be the path along which we should proceed. With a view to concealment we will establish secret brotherhoods and political clubs. And there are professors of rhetoric who teach the art of persuading courts and assemblies; and so, partly by persuasion and partly by force, I shall make unlawful gains and not be punished. Still I hear a voice saying that the gods cannot be deceived, neither can they be compelled. But what if there are no gods? or, suppose them to have no care of human things—why in either case should we mind about concealment? And even if there are gods, and they do care about us, yet we know of them only from tradition and the genealogies of the poets; and these are the very persons who say that they may be influenced and turned by 'sacrifices and soothing entreaties and by offerings.' Let us be consistent then, and believe both or neither. If the poets speak truly, why then we had better be unjust, and offer of the fruits of injustice; for if we are just, although we may escape the vengeance of heaven, we shall lose the gains of injustice; but, if we are unjust, we shall keep the gains, and by our sinning and

---

14 Pindar, Fragment 213, Loeb edition.

15 An early Greek poet (650 B.C.) and inventor of new meters, author of both grave and sharply satiric verse which was much admired by his contemporaries. His statue was sometimes set up beside Homer's.

praying, and praying and sinning, the gods will be propitiated, and we shall not be punished.—But there is a world below in which either we or our posterity will suffer for our unjust deeds.—Yes, my friend, will be the reflection, but there are mysteries and atoning deities, and these have great power. That is what mighty cities declare; and the children of the gods, who were their poets and prophets, bear a like testimony.

"On what principle, then, shall we any longer choose justice rather than the worst injustice? when, if we only unite the latter with a deceitful regard to appearances, we shall fare to our mind both with gods and men, in life and after death, as the most numerous and the highest authorities tell us. Knowing all this, Socrates, how can a man who has any superiority of mind or person or rank or wealth, be willing to honor justice; or indeed to refrain from laughing when he hears justice praised? And even if there should be someone who is able to disprove the truth of my words, and who is satisfied that justice is best, still he is not angry with the unjust, but is very ready to forgive them, because he also knows that men are not just of their own free will; unless, peradventure, there be someone whom the divinity within him may have inspired with a hatred of injustice, or who has attained knowledge of the truth—but no other man. He only blames injustice who, owing to cowardice or age or some weakness, has not the power of being unjust. And this is proved by the fact that when he obtains the power, he immediately becomes unjust as far as he can be.

"The cause of all this, Socrates, was indicated by us at the beginning of the argument, when my brother and I told you how astonished we were to find that of all the professing panegyrists of justice —beginning with the ancient heroes of whom any memorial has been preserved to us, and ending with the men of our own time—no one has ever blamed injustice or praised justice except with a view to the glories, honors, and benefits which flow from them. No one has ever adequately described either in verse or prose the true essential nature of either of them abiding in the soul, and invisible to any human or divine eye; or shown that of all the things of a man's soul which he

has within him, justice is the greatest good, and injustice the greatest
evil. Had this been the universal strain, had you sought to persuade
us of this from our youth upwards, we should not have been on the
watch to keep one another from doing wrong, but everyone would
have been his own watchman, because afraid, if he did wrong, of
harboring in himself the greatest of evils. I dare say that Thrasymachus and others would seriously hold the language which I have
been merely repeating, and words even stronger than these about
justice and injustice, grossly, as I conceive, perverting their true
nature. But I speak in this vehement manner, as I must frankly confess to you, because I want to hear from you the opposite side; and I
would ask you to show not only the superiority which justice has
over injustice, but what effect they have on the possessor of them
which makes the one to be a good and the other an evil to him. And
please, as Glaucon requested of you, to exclude reputations; for unless you take away from each of them his true reputation and add on
the false, we shall say that you do not praise justice, but the appearance of it; we shall think that you are only exhorting us to keep
injustice dark, and that you really agree with Thrasymachus in
thinking that justice is another's good and the interest of the
stronger, and that injustice is a man's own profit and interest, though
injurious to the weaker. Now as you have admitted that justice is one
of that highest class of goods which are desired indeed for their results, but in a far greater degree for their own sakes—like sight or
hearing or knowledge or health, or any other real and natural and
not merely conventional good—I would ask you in your praise of
justice to regard one point only: I mean the essential good and evil
which justice and injustice work in the possessors of them. Let others
praise justice and censure injustice, magnifying the rewards and
honors of the one and abusing the other; that is a manner of arguing
which, coming from them, I am ready to tolerate, but from you who
have spent your whole life in the consideration of this question, unless I hear the contrary from your own lips, I expect something better.
And therefore, I say, not only prove to us that justice is better than
injustice, but show what they either of them do to the possessor of

them, which makes the one to be a good and the other an evil, whether seen or unseen by gods and men."

I had always admired the genius of Glaucon and Adeimantus, but on hearing these words I was quite delighted, and said: "Sons of an illustrious father, that was not a bad beginning of the Elegiac verses which the admirer [16] of Glaucon made in honor of you after you had distinguished yourselves at the battle of Megara:

Sons of Ariston, (he sang,) *divine offspring of an illustrious hero.*

The epithet is very appropriate, for there is something truly divine in being able to argue as you have done for the superiority of injustice, and remaining unconvinced by your own arguments. And I do believe that you are not convinced—this I infer from your general character, for had I judged only from your speeches I should have mistrusted you. But now, the greater my confidence in you, the greater is my difficulty in knowing what to say. For I am in a strait between two; on the one hand I feel that I am unequal to the task; and my inability is brought home to me by the fact that you were not satisfied with the answer which I made to Thrasymachus, proving, as I thought, the superiority which justice has over injustice. And yet I cannot refuse to help, while breath and speech remain to me; I am afraid that there would be an impiety in being present when justice is evil spoken of and not lifting up a hand in her defense. And therefore I had best give such help as I can."

Glaucon and the rest entreated me by all means not to let the question drop, but to proceed in the investigation. They wanted to arrive at the truth, first, about the nature of justice and injustice, and secondly, about their relative advantages. I told them, what I really thought, that the inquiry would be of a serious nature, and would require very good eyes. "Seeing then," I said, "that we are no great wits, I think that we had better adopt a method which I may illustrate thus; suppose that a short-sighted person had been asked by someone to

16 Who this "admirer" was we do not know.

read small letters from a distance; and it occurred to someone else that they might be found in another place which was larger and in which the letters were larger—if they were the same and he could read the larger letters first, and then proceed to the lesser—this would have been thought a rare piece of good fortune."

"Very true," said Adeimantus; "but how does the illustration apply to our inquiry?"

"I will tell you," I replied; "justice, which is the subject of our inquiry, is, as you know, sometimes spoken of as the virtue of an individual, and sometimes as the virtue of a State." [17]

"True," he replied..

"And is not a State larger than an individual?"

"It is."

"Then in the larger the quantity of justice is likely to be larger and more easily discernible. I propose therefore that we inquire into the nature of justice and injustice, first as they appear in the State, and secondly in the individual, proceeding from the greater to the lesser and comparing them."

"That," he said, "is an excellent proposal."

"And if we imagine the State in process of creation, we shall see the justice and injustice of the State in process of creation also."

"I dare say."

"When the State is completed there may be a hope that the object of our search will be more easily discovered."

"Yes, far more easily."

"But ought we to attempt to construct one?" I said; "for to do so, as I am inclined to think, will be a very serious task. Reflect therefore."

"I have reflected," said Adeimantus, "and am anxious that you should proceed."

"A State," I said, "arises,' as I conceive, out of the needs of mankind; no one is self-sufficing, but all of us have many wants. Can any other origin of a State be imagined?"

---

[17] With this Socrates launches on the serious argument of the dialogue, showing first what ideal justice would be, if realized in the outward life of the community, and then how the same principles would work in the inner life of an individual.

"There can be no other."

"Then', as we have many wants, and many persons are needed tc supply them, one takes a helper for one purpose and another for another; and when these partners and helpers are gathered together in one habitation the body of inhabitants is termed a State."

"True," he said.

"And they exchange with one another, and one gives, and another receives, under the idea that the exchange will be for their good."

"Very true."

"Then," I said, "let us begin and create in idea a State; and yet the true creator is necessity, who is the mother of our invention."

"Of course," he replied.

"Now the first and greatest of necessities is food, which is the condition of life and existence."

"Certainly."

"The second is a dwelling, and the third clothing and the like."

"True."

"And now let us see how our city will be able to supply this great demand: We may suppose that one man is a husbandman, another a builder, someone else a weaver—shall we add to them a shoemaker, or perhaps some other purveyor to our bodily wants?"

"Quite right."

"The barest notion of a State must include four or five men."

"Clearly."

"And how will they proceed? Will each bring the result of his labors into a common stock?—the individual husbandman, for example, producing for four, and laboring four times as long and as much as he need in the provision of food with which he supplies others as well as himself; or will he have nothing to do with others and not be at the trouble of producing for them, but provide for himself alone a fourth of the food in a fourth of the time, and in the remaining three fourths of his time be employed in making a house or a coat or a pair of shoes, having no partnership with others, but supplying himself all his own wants?"

Adeimantus thought that he should aim at producing food only and not at producing everything.

"Probably," I replied, "that would be the better way; and when I hear you say this, I am myself reminded that we are not all alike; there are diversities of natures among us which are adapted to different occupations."

"Very true."

"And will you have a work better done when the workman has many occupations, or when he has only one?"

"When he has only one."

"Further, there can be no doubt that a work is spoilt when not done at the right time?"

"No doubt."

"For business is not disposed to wait until the doer of the business is at leisure; but the doer must follow up what he is doing, and make the business his first object."

"He must."

"And if so, we must infer that all things are produced more plentifully and easily and of a better quality when one man does one thing which is natural to him and does it at the right time, and leaves other things."

"Undoubtedly."

"Then more than four citizens will be required; for the husbandman will not make his own plow or mattock, or other implements of agriculture, if they are to be good for anything. Neither will the builder make his tools—and he too needs many; and in like manner the weaver and shoemaker."

"True."

"Then carpenters, and smiths, and many other artisans, will be sharers in our little State, which is already beginning to grow?"

"True."

"Yet even if we add neatherds, shepherds, and other herdsmen, in order that our husbandmen may have oxen to plow with, and builders as well as husbandmen may have draught cattle, and curriers and weavers fleeces and hides—still our State will not be very large."

"That is true; yet neither will it be a very small State which contains all these."

"Then, again, there is the situation of the city—to find a place where nothing need be imported is wellnigh impossible."

"Impossible."

"Then there must be another class of citizens who will bring the required supply from another city?"

"There must."

"But if the trader goes empty-handed, having nothing which they require who would supply his need, he will come back empty-handed."

"That is certain."

"And therefore what they produce at home must be not only enough for themselves, but such both in quantity and quality as to accommodate those from whom their wants are supplied."

"Very true."

"Then more husbandmen and more artisans will be required?"

"They will."

"Not to mention the importers and exporters, who are called merchants?"

"Yes."

"Then we shall want merchants?"

"We shall."

"And if merchandise is to be carried over the sea, skillful sailors will also be needed, and in considerable numbers?"

"Yes, in considerable numbers."

"Then, again, within the city, how will they exchange their productions? To secure such an exchange was, as you will remember, one of our principal objects when we formed them into a society and constituted a State."

"Clearly they will buy and sell."

"Then they will need a market place, and a money-token for purposes of exchange."

"Certainly."

"Suppose now that a husbandman, or an artisan, brings some production to market, and he comes at a time when there is no one to exchange with him—is he to leave his calling and sit idle in the market place?"

"Not at all; he will find people there who, seeing the want, undertake the office of salesmen. In well-ordered states they are commonly those who are the weakest in bodily strength, and therefore of little use for any other purpose; their duty is to be in the market, and to give money in exchange for goods to those who desire to sell and to take money from those who desire to buy."

"This want, then, creates a class of retail traders in our State. Is not 'retailer' the term which is applied to those who sit in the market place engaged in buying and selling, while those who wander from one city to another are called merchants?"

"Yes," he said.

"And there is another class of servants, who are intellectually hardly on the level of companionship; still they have plenty of bodily strength for labor, which accordingly they sell, and are called, if I do not mistake, hirelings, hire being the name which is given to the price of their labor."

"True."

"Then hirelings will help to make up our population?"

"Yes."

"And now, Adeimantus, is our State matured and perfected?"

"I think so."

"Where, then, is justice, and where is injustice, and in what part of the State did they spring up?"

"Probably in the dealings of these citizens with one another. I cannot imagine that they are more likely to be found anywhere else."

"I dare say that you are right in your suggestion," I said; "we had better think the matter out, and not shrink from the inquiry.

"Let us then consider, first of all, what will be their way of life, now that we have thus established them. Will they not produce corn, and wine, and clothes, and shoes, and build houses for themselves? And when they are housed, they will work, in summer, commonly, stripped and barefoot. but in winter substantially clothed and shod.

They will feed on barley-meal and flour of wheat, baking and kneading them, making noble cakes and loaves; these they will serve up on a mat of reeds or on clean leaves, themselves reclining the while upon beds strewn with yew or myrtle. And they and their children will feast, drinking of the wine which they have made, wearing garlands on their heads, and hymning the praises of the gods, in happy converse with one another. And they will take care that their families do not exceed their means; having an eye to poverty or war."

"But," said Glaucon, interposing, you have not given them a relish to their meal."

"True," I replied, "I had forgotten; of course they must have a relish—salt, and olives, and cheese, and they will boil roots and herbs such as country people prepare; for a dessert we shall give them figs, and peas, and beans; and they will roast myrtle-berries and acorns at the fire, drinking in moderation. And with such a diet they may be expected to live in peace and health to a good old age, and bequeath a similar life to their children after them."

"Yes, Socrates," he said, "and if you were providing for a city of pigs, how else would you feed the beasts?"

"But what would you have, Glaucon?" I replied.

"Why," he said, "you should give them the ordinary conveniences of life. People who are to be comfortable are accustomed to lie on sofas, and dine off tables, and they should have sauces and sweets in the modern style."

"Yes," I said, "now I understand: the question which you would have me consider is, not only how a State, but how a luxurious State is created; and possibly there is no harm in this, for in such a State we shall be more likely to see how justice and injustice originate. In my opinion the true and healthy constitution of the State is the one which I have described. But if you wish also to see a State at feverheat, I have no objection. For I suspect that many will not be satisfied with the simpler way of life. They will be for adding sofas, and tables, and other furniture; also dainties, and perfumes, and incense, and courtesans, and cakes, all these not of one sort only, but in every variety; we must go beyond the necessaries of which I was at first speaking, such as houses, and clothes, and shoes; the arts of the painter and the embroiderer will have to be set in motion, and gold and ivory and all sorts of materials must be procured."

"True," he said.

"Then we must enlarge our borders; for the original healthy State is no longer sufficient. Now will the city have to fill and swell with a multitude of callings which are not required by any natural want; such as the whole tribe of hunters and actors, of whom one large class have to do with forms and colors; another will be the votaries of music —poets and their attendant train of rhapsodists, players, dancers, contractors; also makers of divers kinds of articles, including women's dresses. And we shall want more servants. Will not tutors be also in request, and nurses wet and dry, tirewomen and barbers, as well as confectioners and cooks; and swineherds, too, who were not needed and therefore had no place in the former edition of our State, but are needed now? They must not be forgotten: and there will be animals of many other kinds, if people eat them."

"Certainly."

"And living in this way we shall have much greater need of physicians than before?"

"Much greater."

"And the country which was enough to support the original inhabitants will be too small now, and not enough?"

"Quite true."

"Then a slice of our neighbors' land [18] will be wanted by us for pasture and tillage, and they will want a slice of ours, if, like ourselves, they exceed the limit of necessity, and give themselves up to the unlimited accumulation of wealth?"

"That, Socrates, will be inevitable."

"And so we shall go to war, Glaucon. Shall we not?"

"Most certainly," he replied.

"Then, without determining as yet whether war does good or harm, thus much we may affirm, that now we have discovered war

---

[18] The state that becomes rich will inevitably sooner or later be involved in war.

to be derived from causes which are also the causes of almost all the evils in States, private as well as public."

"Undoubtedly."

"And our State must once more enlarge; and this time the enlargement will be nothing short of a whole army, which will have to go out and fight with the invaders for all that we have, as well as for the things and persons whom we were describing above."

"Why?" he said; "are they not capable of defending themselves?"

"No," I said; "not if we were right in the principle which was acknowledged by all of us when we were framing the State: the principle, as you will remember, was that one man cannot practice many arts with success."

"Very true," he said.

"But is not war an art?"

"Certainly."

"And an art requiring as much attention as shoemaking?"

"Quite true."

"And the shoemaker was not allowed by us to be a husbandman, or a weaver, or a builder—in order that we might have our shoes well made; but to him and to every other worker was assigned one work for which he was by nature fitted, and at that he was to continue working all his life long and at no other; he was not to let opportunities slip, and then he would become a good workman. Now nothing can be more important than that the work of a soldier should be well done. But is war an art so easily acquired that a man may be a warrior who is also a husbandman, or shoemaker, or other artisan; although no one in the world would be a good dice or draught player who merely took up the game as a recreation, and had not from his earliest years devoted himself to this and nothing else? No tools will make a man a skilled workman, or master of defense, nor be of any use to him who has not learned how to handle them, and has never bestowed any attention upon them. How then will he who takes up a shield or other implement of war become a good fighter all in a day, whether with heavy-armed or any other kind of troops?"

"Yes," he said, "the tools which would teach men their own use would be beyond price."

"And the higher the duties of the guardian," I said, "the more time, and skill, and art, and application will be needed by him?"

"No doubt," he replied.

"Will he not also require natural aptitude for his calling?"

"Certainly."

"Then it will be our duty to select, if we can, natures which are fitted for the task of guarding the city?"

"It will."

"And the selection will be no easy matter," I said; "but we must be brave and do our best."

"We must."

"Is not the noble youth very like a well-bred dog in respect of guarding and watching?"

"What do you mean?"

"I mean that both of them ought to be quick to see, and swift to overtake the enemy when they see him; and strong too if, when they have caught him, they have to fight with him."

"All these qualities," he replied, "will certainly be required by them."

"Well, and your guardian must be brave if he is to fight well?"

"Certainly."

"And is he likely to be brave who has no spirit, whether horse or dog or any other animal? Have you never observed how invincible and unconquerable is spirit and how the presence of it makes the soul of any creature to be absolutely fearless and indomitable?"

"I have."

"Then now we have a clear notion of the bodily qualities which are required in the guardian."

"True."

"And also of the mental ones; his soul is to be full of spirit?"

"Yes."

"But are not these spirited natures apt to be savage with one another, and with everybody else?"

"A difficulty by no means easy to overcome," he replied.

"Whereas," I said, "they ought to be dangerous to their enemies, and gentle to their friends; if not, they will destroy themselves without waiting for their enemies to destroy them."

"True," he said.

"What is to be done then?" I said; "how shall we find a gentle nature which has also a great spirit, for the one is the contradiction of the other?"

"True."

"He will not be a good guardian who is wanting in either of these two qualities; and yet the combination of them appears to be impossible; and hence we must infer that to be a good guardian is impossible."

"I am afraid that what you say is true," he replied.

Here feeling perplexed I began to think over what had preceded. "My friend," I said, "no wonder that we are in a perplexity; for we have lost sight of the image which we had before us."

"What do you mean?" he said.

"I mean to say that there do exist natures gifted with those opposite qualities."

"And where do you find them?"

"Many animals," I replied, "furnish examples of them; our friend the dog is a very good one: you know that well-bred dogs are perfectly gentle to their familiars and acquaintances, and the reverse to strangers."

"Yes, I know."

"Then there is nothing impossible or out of the order of nature in our finding a guardian who has a similar combination of qualities?"

"Certainly not."

"Would not he who is fitted to be a guardian, besides the spirited nature, need to have the qualities of a philosopher?"

"I do not apprehend your meaning."

"The trait of which I am speaking," I replied, "may be also seen in the dog, and is remarkable in the animal."

"What trait?"

"Why, a dog, whenever he sees a stranger, is angry; when an acquaintance, he welcomes him, although the one has never done him any harm, nor the other any good. Did this never strike you as curious?"

"The matter never struck me before; but I quite recognize the truth of your remark."

"And surely this instinct of the dog is very charming; your dog is a true philosopher."

"Why?"

"Why, because he distinguishes the face of a friend and of an enemy only by the criterion of knowing and not knowing. And must not an animal be a lover of learning who determines what he likes and dislikes by the test of knowledge and ignorance?"

"Most assuredly."

"And is not the love of learning the love of wisdom, which is philosophy?"

"They are the same," he replied.

"And may we not say confidently of man also, that he who is likely to be gentle to his friends and acquaintances must by nature be a lover of wisdom and knowledge?"

"That we may safely affirm."

"Then he who is to be a really good and noble guardian of the State will require to unite in himself philosophy and spirit and swiftness and strength?"

"Undoubtedly."

"Then we have found the desired natures; and now that we have found them, how are they to be reared and educated? Is not this an inquiry which may be expected to throw light on the greater inquiry which is our final end: How do justice and injustice grow up in States? for we do not want either to omit what is to the point or to draw out the argument to an inconvenient length."

Adeimantus thought that the inquiry would be of great service to us.

"Then," I said, "my dear friend, the task must not be given up, even if somewhat long."

"Certainly not."

"Come then, and let us pass a leisure hour in story telling, and our story shall be the education of our heroes."

"By all means."

"And what shall be their education? [19] Can we find a better than the traditional sort? And this has two divisions, gymnastic for the body, and music for the soul."

"True."

"Shall we begin education with music, and go on to gymnastic afterwards?"

"By all means."

"And when you speak of music, do you include literature or not?" [20]

"I do."

"And literature may be either true or false?"

"Yes."

"And the young should be trained in both kinds, and we begin with the false?"

"I do not understand your meaning," he said.

"You know," I said, "that we begin by telling children stories which, though not wholly destitute of truth, are in the main fictitious; and these stories are told them when they are not of an age to learn gymnastics."

"Very true."

"That was my meaning when I said that we must teach music before gymnastics."

"Quite right," he said.

"You know also that the beginning is the most important part of any work, especially in the case of a young and tender thing; for

19 The program of music and gymnastics which Socrates now lays down as required education for the guardian or soldier class is the normal curriculum of Athenian schools, freed of a few defects. Further on Socrates will describe the higher education of the boys and girls selected to become rulers.

20 Under the heading of music the Greeks included not only the study of harmony and musical theory and skill in playing the lyre, but also the reading of poetry and other literature, and a general grounding in the culture of the age.

that is the time at which the character is being formed and the desired impression is more readily taken."

"Quite true."

"And shall we just carelessly allow children to hear any casual tales which may be devised by casual persons, and to receive into their minds ideas for the most part the very opposite of those which we should wish them to have when they are grown up?"

"We cannot."

"Then the first thing will be to establish a censorship of the writers of fiction, and let the censors receive any tale of fiction which is good, and reject the bad; and we will desire mothers and nurses to tell their children the authorized ones only. Let them fashion the mind with such tales, even more fondly than they mold the body with their hands; but most of those which are now in use must be discarded."

"Of what tales are you speaking?" he said.

"You may find a model of the lesser in the greater," I said; "for they are necessarily of the same type, and there is the same spirit in both of them."

"Very likely," he replied; "but I do not as yet know what you would term the greater."

"Those," I said, "which are narrated by Homer and Hesiod, and the rest of the poets, who have ever been the great storytellers of mankind."

"But which stories do you mean," he said; "and what fault do you find with them?"

"A fault which is most serious," I said; "the fault of telling a lie, and, what is more, a bad lie."

"But when is this fault committed?"

"Whenever an erroneous representation is made of the nature of gods and heroes, as when a painter paints a portrait not having the shadow of a likeness to the original.

"Yes," he said, "that sort of thing is certainly very blameable; but what are the stories which you mean?"

"First of all," I said, "there was that greatest of all lies in high places, which the poet told about Uranus, and which was a bad lie too—I mean what Hesiod says that Uranus did, and how Cronus re-taliated on him.[21] The doings of Cronus, and the sufferings which in turn his son inflicted upon him, even if they were true, ought certainly not to be lightly told to young and thoughtless persons; if possible, they had better be buried in silence. But if there is an absolute necessity for their mention, a chosen few might hear them in a mystery, and they should sacrifice not a common [Eleusinian] pig,[22] but some huge and unprocurable victim; and then the number of the hearers will be very few indeed."

"Why, yes," said he, "those stories are extremely objectionable."

"Yes, Adeimantus, they are stories not to be repeated in our State; the young man should not be told that in committing the worst of crimes he is far from doing anything outrageous; and that even if he chastises his father when he does wrong, in whatever manner, he will only be following the example of the first and greatest among the gods."

"I entirely agree with you," he said; "in my opinion those stories are quite unfit to be repeated."

"Neither, if we mean our future guardians to regard the habit of quarreling among themselves as of all things the basest, should any word be said to them of the wars in heaven, and of the plots and fightings of the gods against one another, for they are not true. No, we shall never mention the battles of the giants, or let them be embroidered on garments; and we shall be silent about the innumerable other quarrels of gods and heroes with their friends and relatives. If they would only believe us we would tell them that quarreling is unholy, and that never up to this time has there been any quarrel between citizens; this is what old men and old women should begin by telling children; and when they grow up, the poets also should be told to compose for them in a similar spirit. But the narrative of Hephaestus binding Hera his mother, or how on another occasion

21 Hesiod, *Theogony*, 154-182, 496. Uranus was the oldest of the nature deities of Greece, Cronus his son, and Zeus the son of Cronus. Each father in turn maltreated his son and was in the end brutally mutilated or crushed by him.

22 A pig was the usual sacrifice at the mystery worship of the earth goddess Demeter, held in her temple at Eleusis, not far from Athens.

Zeus sent him flying for taking her part when she was being beaten,[23] and all the battles of the gods in Homer [24]—these tales must not be admitted into our State, whether they are supposed to have an allegorical meaning or not. For a young person cannot judge what is allegorical and what is literal; anything that he receives into his mind at that age is likely to become indelible and unalterable; and therefore it is most important that the tales which the young first hear should be models of virtuous thoughts."

"There you are right," he replied; "but if anyone asks where are such models to be found and of what tales are you speaking—how shall we answer him?"

I said to him, "You and I, Adeimantus, at this moment are not poets, but founders of a State: now the founders of a State ought to know the general forms in which poets should cast their tales, and the limits which must be observed by them, but to make the tales is not their business."

"Very true," he said; "but what are these forms of theology which you mean?"

"Something of this kind," I replied: "God is always to be represented as he truly is, whatever be the sort of poetry, epic, lyric or tragic, in which the representation is given."

"Right."

"And is he not truly good? and must he not be represented as such?"

"Certainly."

"And no good thing is hurtful?"

"No, indeed."

"And that which is not hurtful hurts not?"

"Certainly not."

"And that which hurts not does no evil?"

"No."

"And can that which does no evil be a cause of evil?"

"Impossible."

"And the good is advantageous?"

"Yes."

"And therefore the cause of well-being?"

"Yes."

"It follows therefore that the good is not the cause of all things, but of the good only?"

"Assuredly."

"Then God, if he be good, is not the author of all things, as the many assert, but he is the cause of a few things only, and not of most things that occur to men. For few are the goods of human life, and many are the evils, and the good is to be attributed to God alone; of the evils the causes are to be sought elsewhere, and not in him."

"That appears to me to be most true," he said.

"Then we must not listen to Homer or to any other poet who is guilty of the folly of saying that two casks

> Lie at the threshold of Zeus, full of lots, one of good, the other
> of evil lots, [25]

and that he to whom Zeus gives a mixture of the two

> Sometimes meets with evil fortune, at other times with good;

but that he to whom is given the cup of unmingled ill,

> Him wild hunger drives o'er the beauteous earth.

And again—

> Zeus, who is the dispenser of good and evil to us. [26]

And if anyone asserts that the violation of oaths and treaties, which was really the work of Pandarus,[27] was brought about by Athene and Zeus, or that the strife and contention of the gods was instigated by

---

[25] This and the two following poetic lines are quoted from the *Iliad*, XXIV, 527-537.

[26] This line is not to be found in our Homer.

[27] Pandarus shot the arrow that broke the pledged truce between Greeks and Trojans. *Iliad*, IV, 68-126. Homer tells us, however, that the goddess Athene put the idea into his mind.

Themis and Zeus,[28] he shall not have our approval; neither will we allow our young men to hear the words of Aeschylus, that

God plants guilt among men when he desires utterly to destroy a house.[29]

And if a poet writes of the sufferings of Niobe—the subject of the tragedy in which these iambic verses occur—or of the house of Pelops,[30] or of the Trojan war or on any similar theme, either we must not permit him to say that these are the works of God, or if they are of God, he must devise some explanation of them such as we are seeking: he must say that God did what was just and right, and they were the better for being punished; but that those who are punished are miserable, and that God is the author of their misery— the poet is not to be permitted to say; though he may say that the wicked are miserable because they require to be punished, and are benefited by receiving punishment from God; but that God being good is the author of evil to anyone is to be strenuously denied, and not to be said or sung or heard in verse or prose by anyone whether old or young in any well-ordered commonwealth. Such a fiction is suicidal, ruinous, impious."

"I agree with you," he replied, "and am ready to give my assent to the law."

"Let this then be one of our rules and principles concerning the gods, to which our poets and reciters will be expected to conform— that God is not the author of all things, but of good only."

"That will do," he said.

"And what do you think of a second principle? Shall I ask you whether God is a magician, and of a nature to appear insidiously now in one shape, and now in another—sometimes himself changing and

28 In the *Iliad*, XX, 4-32, the gods are summoned by Themis at command of Zeus to a council at which Zeus knows they will disagree.

29 Aeschylus' tragedy of the unhappy Niobe, whose children were all slain by the god Apollo, is lost.

30 The workings of the curse on the descendants of Pelops—Atreus, Agamemnon, Electra, and Orestes—were the subject of several great series of tragedies by Aeschylus, Sophocles, and Euripides.

passing into many forms, sometimes deceiving us with the semblance of such transformations; or is he one and the same immutably fixed in his own proper image?"

"I cannot answer you," he said, "without more thought."

"Well," I said; "but if we suppose a change in anything, that change must be effected either by the thing itself, or by some other thing?"

"Most certainly."

"And things which are at their best are also least liable to be altered or discomposed; for example, when healthiest and strongest, the human frame is least liable to be affected by meats and drinks, and the plant which is in the fullest vigor also suffers least from winds or the heat of the sun or any similar causes."

"Of course."

"And will not the bravest and wisest soul be least confused or deranged by any external influence?"

"True."

"And the same principle, as I should suppose, applies to all composite things—furniture, houses, garments: when good and well made, they are least altered by time and circumstances."

"Very true."

"Then everything which is good, whether made by art or nature, or both, is least liable to suffer change from without?"

"True."

"But surely God and the things of God are in every way perfect?"

"Of course they are."

"Then he can hardly be compelled by external influence to take many shapes?"

"He cannot."

"But may he not change and transform himself?"

"Clearly," he said, "that must be the case if he is changed at all."

"And will he then change himself for the better and fairer, or for the worse and more unsightly?"

"If he change at all he can only change for the worse, for we cannot suppose him to be deficient either in virtue or beauty."

"Very true, Adeimantus; but then, would anyone, whether God or man, desire to make himself worse?"

"Impossible."

"Then it is impossible that God should ever be willing to change; being, as is supposed, the fairest and best that is conceivable, every God remains absolutely and forever in his own form."

"That necessarily follows," he said, "in my judgment."

"Then," I said, "my dear friend, let none of the poets tell us that

The gods, taking the disguise of strangers from other lands,
Walk up and down cities in all sorts of forms; [31]

and let no one slander Proteus and Thetis,[32] neither let anyone, either in tragedy or in any other kind of poetry, introduce Hera disguised in the likeness of a priestess asking an alms

For the life-giving daughters of Inachus the river of Argos; [33]

—let us have no more lies of that sort. Neither must we have mothers under the influence of the poets scaring their children with a bad version of these myths—telling how certain gods, as they say, 'go about by night in the likeness of so many strangers and in divers forms'; but let them take heed lest they make cowards of their children, and at the same time speak blasphemy against the gods."

"Heaven forbid," he said.

"But although the gods are themselves unchangeable, still by witchcraft and deception they may make us think that they appear in various forms?"

"Perhaps," he replied.

"Well, but can you imagine that God will be willing to lie, whether in word or deed, or to put forth a phantom of himself?"

"I cannot say," he replied.

31 Homer, *Odyssey*, XVII, 485, 486.
32 The god Proteus was distinguished for his ability to slide from one shape into another. The goddess Thetis transformed herself to escape the pursuit of the mortal Peleus, by whom eventually she had her son Achilles.
33 From another lost tragedy of Aeschylus.

"Do you not know," I said, "that the true lie, if such an expression may be allowed, is hated of gods and men?"

"What do you mean?" he said.

"I mean that no one is willingly deceived in that which is the truest and highest part of himself, or about the truest and highest matters; there, above all, he is most afraid of a lie having possession of him."

"Still," he said, "I do not comprehend you."

"The reason is," I replied, "that you attribute some profound meaning to my words; but I am only saying that deception, or being deceived or uninformed about the highest realities in the highest part of themselves, which is the soul, and in that part of them to have and to hold the lie, is what mankind least like; that, I say, is what they utterly detest.'

"There is nothing more hateful to them."

"And, as I was just now remarking, this ignorance in the soul of him who is deceived may be called the true lie; for the lie in words is only a kind of imitation and shadowy image of a previous affection c' the soul, not pure unadulterated falsehood. Am I not right?"

"Perfectly right."

"The true lie is hated not only by the gods, but also by men?"

"Yes."

"Whereas the lie in words is in certain cases useful and not hateful; in dealing with enemies—that would be an instance; or again, when those whom we call our friends in a fit of madness or illusion are going to do some harm, then it is useful and is a sort of medicine or preventive; also in the tales of mythology, of which we were just now speaking—because we do not know the truth about ancient times, we make falsehood as much like truth as we can, and so turn it to account."

"Very true," he said.

"But can any of these reasons apply to God? Can we suppose that he is ignorant of antiquity, and therefore has recourse to invention?"

"That would be ridiculous," he said.

"Then the lying poet has no place in our idea of God?"

"I should say not."

"Or perhaps he may tell a lie because he is afraid of enemies?"

"That is inconceivable."

"But he may have friends who are senseless or mad?"

"But no mad or senseless person can be a friend of God."

"Then no motive can be imagined why God should lie?"

"None whatever."

"Then the superhuman and divine is absolutely incapable of falsehood?"

"Yes."

"Then is God perfectly simple and true both in word and deed; he changes not; he deceives not, either by sign or word, by dream or waking vision."

"Your thoughts," he said, "are the reflection of my own."

"You agree with me then," I said, "that this is the second type or form in which we should write and speak about divine things. The gods are not magicians who transform themselves, neither do they deceive mankind in any way."

"I grant that."

"Then, although we are admirers of Homer, we do not admire the lying dream which Zeus sends to Agamemnon; [34] neither will we praise the verses of Aeschylus in which Thetis says that Apollo at her nuptials *was celebrating in song her fair progeny whose days were to be long, and to know no sickness. And when he had spoken of my lot as in all things blessed of heaven he raised a note of triumph and cheered my soul. And I thought that the word of Phoebus, being divine and full of prophecy, would not fail. And now he himself who uttered the strain, he who was present at the banquet, and who said this—he it is who has slain my son.*[35] These are the kind of sentiments about the gods which will arouse our anger; and he who utters them shall be refused a chorus; neither shall we allow teachers to make use of them in the instruction of the young, meaning, as we

34 *Iliad*, II, 1-34. The lying dream promised a quick and easy victory over Troy.
35 From a lost tragedy. Thetis' son Achilles was slain in his youth at Troy.

do, that our guardians, as far as men can be, should be true worshipers of the gods and like them."

"I entirely agree," he said, "in these principles, and promise to make them my laws."

BOOK III

Exclusion of the poets from the schools. Value of the right sort of music and gymnastics. Selection of the best boys and girls for training as rulers.

Socrates goes on proving in more detail the harmful effect on the young of the old poets' tales of the gods and the spirit world. He does the same for drama and music that are frivolous, ignoble, or sensuous.

BUT shall our superintendence go no further, and are the poets only to be required by us to express the image of the good in their works, on pain, if they do anything else, of expulsion from our State? Or is the same control to be extended to other artists, and are they also to be prohibited from exhibiting the opposite forms of vice and intemperance and meanness and indecency in sculpture and building and the other creative arts; and is he who cannot conform to this rule of ours to be prevented from practicing his art in our State, lest the taste of our citizens be corrupted by him? We would not have our guardians grow up amid images of moral deformity, as in some noxious pasture, and there browse and feed upon many a baneful herb and flower day by day, little by little, until they silently gather a festering mass of corruption in their own soul. Let our artists rather be those who are gifted to discern the true nature of the beautiful and graceful; then will our youth dwell in a land of health, amid fair sights and sounds, and receive the good in everything; and beauty, the effluence of fair works, shall flow into the eye and ear, like a health-giving breeze from a purer region, and insensibly draw the soul from earliest years into likeness and sympathy with the beauty of reason."

"There can be no nobler training than that," he replied.

"And therefore," I said, "Glaucon, musical training is a more potent instrument than any other, because rhythm and harmony find their way into the inward places of the soul, on which they mightily fasten, imparting grace, and making the soul of him who is rightly educated graceful, or of him who is ill-educated ungraceful; and also because he who has received this true education of the inner being will most shrewdly perceive omissions or faults in art and nature, and with a true taste, while he praises and rejoices over and receives into his soul the good, and becomes noble and good, he will justly blame and hate the bad, now in the days of his youth, even before he is able to know the reason why; and when reason comes he will recognize and salute the friend with whom his education has made him long familiar."

"Yes," he said, "I quite agree with you in thinking that our youth should be trained in music and on the grounds which you mention."

"Just as in learning to read," I said, "we were satisfied when we knew the letters of the alphabet, which are very few, in all their recurring sizes and combinations; not slighting them as unimportant whether they occupy a space large or small, but everywhere eager to make them out; and not thinking ourselves perfect in the art of reading until we recognize them wherever they are found."

"True."

"Or, as we recognize the reflection of letters in the water, or in a mirror, only when we know the letters themselves; the same art and study giving us the knowledge of both."

"Exactly."

"Even so, as I maintain, neither we nor our guardians, whom we have to educate, can ever become musical until we and they know the essential forms of temperance, courage, liberality, magnificence, and their kindred, as well as the contrary forms, in all their combinations, and can recognize them and their images wherever they

are found, not slighting them either in small things or great, but believing them all to be within the sphere of one art and study."

"Most assuredly."

"And when a beautiful soul harmonizes with a beautiful form,
and the two are cast in one mold, that will be the fairest of sights to
him who has an eye to see it?"

"The fairest indeed."

"And the fairest is also the loveliest?"

"That may be assumed."

"And the man who has the spirit of harmony will be most in love
with the loveliest; but he will not love him who is of an inharmonious
soul?"

"That is true," he replied, "if the deficiency be in his soul; but if
there be any merely bodily defect in another he will be patient of it,
and will love all the same."

"I perceive," I said, "that you have or have had experiences of this
sort, and I agree. But let me ask you another question: Has excess
of pleasure any affinity to temperance?"

"How can that be?" he replied; "pleasure deprives a man of the
use of his faculties quite as much as pain."

"Or any affinity to virtue in general?"

"None whatever."

"Any affinity to wantonness and intemperance?"

"Yes, the greatest."

"And is there any greater or keener pleasure than that of sensual
love?"

"No, nor a madder."

"Whereas true love is a love of beauty and order—temperate and
harmonious?"

"Quite true," he said.

"Then no intemperance or madness should be allowed to approach
true love?"

"Certainly not."

"Then mad or intemperate pleasure must never be allowed to come near the lover and his beloved; neither of them can have any part in it if their love is of the right sort?"

"No, indeed, Socrates, it must never come near them."

"Then I suppose that in the city which we are founding you would make a law to the effect that a friend should use no other familiarity to his love than a father would use to his son, and then only for a noble purpose, and he must first have the other's consent; and this rule is to limit him in all his intercourse, and he is never to be seen going further, or, if he exceeds, he is to be deemed guilty of coarseness and bad taste."

"I quite agree," he said.

"Thus much of music, which makes a fair ending; for what should be the end of music if not the love of beauty?"

"I agree," he said.

"After music comes gymnastic, in which our youth are next to be trained."

"Certainly."

"Gymnastic as well as music should begin in early years; the training in it should be careful and should continue through life. Now my belief is—and this is a matter upon which I should like to have your opinion in confirmation of my own, but my own belief is —not that the good body by any bodily excellence improves the soul, but, on the contrary, that the good soul, by her own excellence, improves the body as far as this may be possible. What do you say?"

"Yes, I agree."

"Then, to the mind when adequately trained, we shall be right in handing over the more particular care of the body; and in order to avoid prolixity we will now only give the general outlines of the subject."

"Very good."

"That they must abstain from intoxication has been already remarked by us; for of all persons a guardian should be the last to get drunk and not know where in the world he is."

"Yes," he said; "that a guardian should require another guardian to take care of him is ridiculous indeed."

"But next, what shall we say of their food; for the men are in training for the great contest of all—are they not?"

"Yes," he said.

"And will the habit of body of our ordinary athletes be suited to them?"

"Why not?"

"I am afraid," I said, "that a habit of body such as they have is but a sleepy sort of thing, and rather perilous to health. Do you not observe that these athletes sleep away their lives, and are liable to most dangerous illnesses if they depart, in ever so slight a degree, from their customary regimen?"

"Yes, I do."

"Then," I said, "a finer sort of training will be required for our warrior athletes, who are to be like wakeful dogs, and to see and hear with the utmost keenness; amid the many changes of water and also of food, of summer heat and winter cold, which they will have to endure when on a campaign, they must not be liable to break down in health."

"That is my view."

"The really excellent gymnastic is twin sister of that simple music which we were just now describing."

"How so?"

"Why, I conceive that there is a gymnastic which, like our music, is simple and good; and especially the military gymnastic."

"What do you mean?"

"My meaning may be learned from Homer; he, you know, feeds his heroes at their feasts, when they are campaigning, on soldiers' fare; they have no fish, although they are on the shores of the Hellespont, and they are not allowed boiled meats but only roast, which is the food most convenient for soldiers, requiring only that they should light a fire, and not involving the trouble of carrying about pots and pans."

"True."

"And I can hardly be mistaken in saying that sweet sauces are nowhere mentioned in Homer. In proscribing them, however, he is not singular; all professional athletes are well aware that a man who is to be in good condition should take nothing of the kind."

"Yes," he said; "and knowing this, they are quite right in not taking them."

"Then you would not approve of Syracusan dinners, and the refinements of Sicilian cookery?"

"I think not."

"Nor, if a man is to be in condition, would you allow him to have a Corinthian girl as his fair friend?"

"Certainly not."

"Neither would you approve of the delicacies, as they are thought, of Athenian confectionery?"

"Certainly not."

"All such feeding and living may be rightly compared by us to melody and song composed in the panharmonic style,[1] and in all the rhythms."

"Exactly."

"There complexity engendered license, and here disease; whereas simplicity in music was the parent of temperance in the soul; and simplicity in gymnastic of health in the body."

"Most true," he said.

"But when intemperance and diseases multiply in a State, halls of justice and medicine are always being opened; and the arts of the doctor and the lawyer give themselves airs, finding how keen is the interest which not only the slaves but the freemen of a city take about them."

"Of course."

"And yet what greater proof can there be of a bad and disgraceful state of education than this, that not only artisans and the meaner sort of people need the skill of first-rate physicians and judges, but

---

1 In the passage omitted above Socrates has just said that the only melodies he would admit into his state were those austere and serious airs in the simple Dorian and Phrygian modes that required comparatively few notes to play and called for neither complicated instruments nor a "panharmonic" scale.

also those who would profess to have had a liberal education? Is it not disgraceful, and a great sign of the want of good breeding, that a man should have to go abroad for his law and physic because he has none of his own at home, and must therefore surrender himself into the hands of other men whom he makes lords and judges over him?"

"Of all things," he said, "the most disgraceful."

"Would you say 'most,' " I replied, "when you consider that there is a further stage of the evil in which a man is not only a life-long litigant, passing all his days in the courts, either as plaintiff or defendant, but is actually led by his bad taste to pride himself on his litigiousness; he imagines that he is a master in dishonesty; able to take every crooked turn, and wriggle into and out of every hole, bending like a withy and getting out of the way of justice: and all for what?—in order to gain small points not worth mentioning, he not knowing that so to order his life as to be able to do without a napping judge is a far higher and nobler sort of thing. Is not that still more disgraceful?"

"Yes," he said, "that is still more disgraceful."

"Well," I said, "and to require the help of medicine, not when a wound has to be cured, or on occasion of an epidemic, but just because, by indolence and a habit of life such as we have been describing, men fill themselves with waters and winds, as if their bodies were a marsh, compelling the ingenious sons of Asclepius [2] to find more names for diseases, such as flatulence and catarrh; is not this, too, a disgrace?"

"Yes," he said, "they do certainly give very strange and new-fangled names to diseases."

"Yes," I said, "and I do not believe that there were any such diseases in the days of Asclepius; and this I infer from the circumstance that the hero Eurypylus, after he has been wounded in Homer, drinks a posset of Pramnian wine well besprinkled with barley-meal and grated cheese, which are certainly inflammatory, and yet the sons of Asclepius who were at the Trojan war do not blame the damsel

2 "Sons of Asclepius" was a name for physicians. See *Phaedo*, note 23.

who gives him the drink, or rebuke Patroclus, who is treating his case." [3]

"Well," he said; "that was surely an extraordinary drink to be given to a person in his condition."

"Not so extraordinary," I replied, "if you bear in mind that in former days, as is commonly said, before the time of Herodicus, the guild of Asclepius did not practice our present system of medicine, which may be said to educate diseases. But Herodicus,[4] being a trainer, and himself of a sickly constitution, by a combination of training and doctoring found out a way of torturing first and chiefly himself, and secondly the rest of the world."

"How was that?" he said.

"By the invention of lingering death; for he had a mortal disease which he perpetually tended, and as recovery was out of the question, he passed his entire life as a valetudinarian; he could do nothing but attend upon himself, and he was in constant torment whenever he departed in anything from his usual regimen, and so dying hard, by the help of science he struggled on to old age."

"A rare reward of his skill!"

"Yes," I said; "a reward which a man might fairly expect who never understood that, if Asclepius did not instruct his descendants in valetudinarian arts, the omission arose, not from ignorance or inexperience of such a branch of medicine, but because he knew that in all well-ordered states every individual has an occupation to which he must attend, and has therefore no leisure to spend in continually being ill. This we remark in the case of the artisan, but, ludicrously enough, do not apply the same rule to people of the richer sort."

"How do you mean?" he said.

"I mean this: When a carpenter is ill he asks the physician for a rough and ready cure; an emetic or a purge or a cautery or the knife —these are his remedies. And if someone prescribes for him a course

3 Plato is quoting inaccurately from memory. In the *Iliad*, XI, 624-641, this treatment is given to the wounded Machaon and the aged Nestor.

4 A Greek physician of the fifth century B.C., teacher of the so-called Father of Medicine, Hippocrates. He is said to have stressed the value of gymnastics and massage coupled with proper diet.

of dietetics, and tells him that he must swathe and swaddle his head, and all that sort of thing, he replies at once that he has no time to be ill, and that he sees no good in a life which is spent in nursing his disease to the neglect of his customary employment; and therefore bidding good-bye to this sort of physician, he resumes his ordinary habits, and either gets well and lives and does his business, or, if his constitution fails, he dies and has no more trouble."

"Yes," he said, "and a man in his condition of life ought to use the art of medicine thus far only."

"Has he not," I said, "an occupation; and what profit would there be in his life if he were deprived of his occupation?"

"Quite true," he said.

"But with the rich man this is otherwise; of him we do not say that he has any specially appointed work which he must perform, if he would live."

"He is generally supposed to have nothing to do."

"Then you never heard of the saying of Phocylides,[5] that as soon as a man has a livelihood he should practice virtue?"

"Nay," he said, "I think that he had better begin somewhat sooner."

"Let us not have a dispute with him about this," I said; "but rather ask ourselves: Is the practice of virtue obligatory on the rich man, or can he live without it? And if obligatory on him, then let us raise a further question, whether this dieting of disorders, which is an impediment to the application of the mind in carpentering and the mechanical arts, does not equally stand in the way of the sentiment of Phocylides?"

"Of that," he replied, "there can be no doubt; such excessive care of the body, when carried beyond the rules of gymnastic, is most inimical to the practice of virtue."

"Yes, indeed," I replied, "and equally incompatible with the management of a house, an army, or an office of state; and, what is most important of all, irreconcilable with any kind of study or thought or

---

5 The author of moral maxims in verse, a few fragments of which have come down to us. He wrote about 530 B.C.

self-reflection—there is a constant suspicion that headache and gid-
diness are to be ascribed to philosophy, and hence all practicing or
making trial of virtue in the higher sense is absolutely stopped; for a
man is always fancying that he is being made ill, and is in constant
anxiety about the state of his body."

"Yes, likely enough."

"And therefore our politic Asclepius may be supposed to have
exhibited the power of his art only to persons who, being generally
of healthy constitution and habits of life, had a definite ailment;
such as these he cured by purges and operations, and bade them live
as usual, herein consulting the interests of the State; but bodies which
disease had penetrated through and through he would not have attempted to cure by gradual processes of evacuation and infusion; he
did not want to lengthen out good-for-nothing lives, or to have weak
fathers begetting weaker sons; if a man was not able to live in the
ordinary way he had no business to cure him; for such a cure would
have been of no use either to himself, or to the State.

*The best physicians are those who both know their art and have
had the greatest experience of disease. They would better not
be themselves too robust in health.*

This is the sort of medicine, and this is the sort of law, which you will
sanction in your state. They will minister to better natures, giving
health both of soul and of body; but those who are diseased in their
bodies they will leave to die, and the corrupt and incurable souls they
will put an end to themselves."

"That is clearly the best thing both for the patients and for the
State."

"And thus our youth, having been educated only in that simple
music which, as we said, inspires temperance, will be reluctant to
go to law."

"Clearly."

"And the musician, who, keeping to the same track, is content to
practice the simple gymnastic, will have nothing to do with medicine
unless in some extreme case."

"That I quite believe."

"The very exercises and toils which he undergoes are intended to stimulate the spirited element of his nature, and not to increase his strength; he will not, like common athletes, use exercise and regimen to develop his muscles."

"Very right," he said.

"Neither are the two arts of music and gymnastic really designed, as is often supposed, the one for the training of the soul, the other for the training of the body."

"What then is the real object of them?"

"I believe," I said, "that the teachers of both have in view chiefly the improvement of the soul."

"How can that be?" he asked.

"Did you never observe," I said, "the effect on the mind itself of exclusive devotion to gymnastic, or the opposite effect of an exclusive devotion to music?"

"In what way shown?" he said.

"The one producing a temper of hardness and ferocity, the other of softness and effeminacy," I replied.

"Yes," he said, "I am quite aware that the mere athlete becomes too much of a savage, and that the mere musician is melted and softened beyond what is good for him."

"Yet surely," I said, "this ferocity only comes from spirit, which, if rightly educated, would give courage, but, if too much intensified, is liable to become hard and brutal."

"That I quite think."

"On the other hand, the philosopher will have the quality of gentleness. And this also, when too much indulged, will turn to softness, but, if educated rightly, will be gentle and moderate."

"True."

"And in our opinion the guardians ought to have both these qualities?"

"Assuredly."

"And both should be in harmony?"

"Beyond question."

"And the harmonious soul is both temperate and courageous?"

"Yes."

"And the inharmonious is cowardly and boorish?"

"Very true."

"And, when a man allows music to play upon him and to pour into his soul through the funnel of his ears those sweet and soft and melancholy airs of which we were just now speaking, and his whole life is passed in warbling and the delights of song; in the first stage of the process the passion or spirit which is in him is tempered like iron, and made useful, instead of brittle and useless. But, if he carries on the softening and soothing process, in the next stage he begins to melt and waste, until he has wasted away his spirit and cut out the sinews of his soul; and he becomes a feeble warrior."

"Very true."

"If the element of spirit is naturally weak in him the change is speedily accomplished, but if he have a good deal, then the power of music weakening the spirit renders him excitable;—on the least provocation he flames up at once, and is speedily extinguished; instead of having spirit he grows irritable and passionate and is quite impracticable."

"Exactly."

"And so in gymnastics, if a man takes violent exercise and is a great feeder, and the reverse of a great student of music and philosophy, at first the high condition of his body fills him with pride and spirit, and he becomes twice the man that he was."

"Certainly."

"And what happens? if he do nothing else, and holds no converse with the Muses, does not even that intelligence which there may be in him, having no taste of any sort of learning or inquiry or thought or culture, grow feeble and dull and blind, his mind never waking up or receiving nourishment, and his senses not being purged of their mists?"

"True," he said.

"And he ends by becoming a hater of philosophy, uncivilized, never using the weapon of persuasion—he is like a wild beast, all violence and fierceness, and knows no other way of dealing; and he lives in all ignorance and evil conditions, and has no sense of propriety and grace."

"That is quite true," he said.

"And as there are two principles of human nature,[6] one the spirited and the other the philosophical, some God, as I should say, has given mankind two arts answering to them (and only indirectly to the soul and body), in order that these two principles (like the strings of an instrument) may be relaxed or drawn tighter until they are duly harmonized."

"That appears to be the intention."

"And he who mingles music with gymnastic in the fairest proportions, and best attempers them to the soul, may be rightly called the true musician and harmonist in a far higher sense than the tuner of the strings."

"You are quite right, Socrates."

"And such a presiding genius will be always required in our State if the government is to last."

"Yes, he will be absolutely necessary."

"Such, then, are our principles of nurture and education. Where would be the use of going into further details about the dances of our citizens, or about their hunting and coursing, their gymnastic and equestrian contests? For these all follow the general principle, and having found that, we shall have no difficulty in discovering them."

"I dare say that there will be no difficulty."

"Very good, I said; then what is the next question? Must we not ask who are to be rulers and who subjects?"

"Certainly."

"There can be no doubt that the elder must rule the younger."

"Clearly."

"And that the best of these must rule."[7]

6 Later Socrates enlarges more fully on these two elements in human nature, the spirited and energetic will and the rational and understanding mind.

7 At this point Socrates begins the selection of the best soldier lads and lasses for training in the higher task of ruling the state.

"That is also clear."

"Now, are not the best husbandmen those who are most devoted to husbandry?"

"Yes,"

"And as we are to have the best of guardians for our city, must they not be those who have most the character of guardians?"

"Yes."

"And to this end they ought to be wise and efficient, and to have a special care of the State?"

"True."

"And a man will be most likely to care about that which he loves?"

"To be sure."

"And he will be most likely to love that which he regards as having the same interests with himself, and that of which the good or evil fortune is supposed by him at any time most to affect his own?"

"Very true," he replied.

"Then there must be a selection. Let us note among the guardians those who in their whole life show the greatest eagerness to do what is for the good of their country, and the greatest repugnance to do what is against her interests."

"Those are the right men."

"And they will have to be watched at every age, in order that we may see whether they preserve their resolution, and never, under the influence either of force or enchantment, forget or cast off their sense of duty to the State. * * * * * We must watch them from their youth upwards, and make them perform actions in which they are most likely to forget or to be deceived, and he who remembers and is not deceived is to be selected, and he who fails in the trial is to be rejected. That will be the way?"

"Yes."

"And there should also be toils and pains and conflicts prescribed for them, in which they will be made to give further proof of the same qualities."

"Very right," he replied.

"And then," I said, "we must try them with enchantments—that is

the third sort of test—and see what will be their behavior: like those
who take colts amid noise and tumult to see if they are of a timid
nature, so must we take our youth amid terrors of some kind, and
again pass them into pleasures, and prove them more thoroughly
than gold is proved in the furnace, that we may discover whether
they are armed against all enchantments, and of a noble bearing always, good guardians of themselves and of the music which they
have learned, and retaining under all circumstances a rhythmical
and harmonious nature, such as will be most serviceable to the individual and to the State. And he who at every age, as boy and youth
and in mature life, has come out of the trial victorious and pure, shall
be appointed a ruler and guardian of the State; he shall be honored in
life and death, and shall receive sepulture and other memorials of
honor, the greatest that we have to give. But him who fails, we must
reject. I am inclined to think that this is the sort of way in which our
rulers and guardians should be chosen and appointed. I speak generally, and not with any pretension to exactness."

"And, speaking generally, I agree with you," he said.

"And perhaps the word 'guardian' in the fullest sense ought to be
applied to this higher class only who preserve us against foreign
enemies and maintain peace among our citizens at home, that the
one may not have the will, or the others the power, to harm us. The
young men whom we before called guardians may be more properly
designated auxiliaries and supporters of the principles of the rulers."

"I agree with you," he said.

"How then may we devise one of those needful falsehoods of
which we lately spoke—just one royal lie which may deceive the
rulers, if that be possible, and at any rate the rest of the city?"

"What sort of lie?" he said.

"Nothing new," I replied; "only an old Phoenician tale [8] of what
has often occurred before now in other places (as the poets say, and
have made the world believe), though not in our time, and I do not

[8] In the form of a fanciful allegory Socrates states his belief in the natural inequality of human beings. A "Phoenician tale" meant something extraordinary and
incredible.

know whether such an event could ever happen again, or could now even be made probable, if it did."

"How your words seem to hesitate on your lips!"

"You will not wonder," I replied, "at my hesitation when you have heard."

"Speak," he said, "and fear not."

"Well then, I will speak, although I really know not how to look you in the face, or in what words to utter the audacious fiction, which I propose to communicate gradually, first to the rulers, then to the soldiers, and lastly to the people. They are to be told that their youth was a dream, and the education and training which they received from us, an appearance only; in reality during all that time they were being formed and fed in the womb of the earth, where they themselves and their arms and appurtenances were manufactured; when they were completed, the earth, their mother, sent them up; and so, their country being their mother and also their nurse, they are bound to advise for her good, and to defend her against attacks, and her citizens they are to regard as children of the earth and their own brothers."

"You had good reason," he said, "to be ashamed of the lie which you were going to tell."

"True," I replied, "but there is more coming; I have only told you half. Citizens, we shall say to them in our tale, you are brothers, yet God has framed you differently. Some of you have the power of command, and in the composition of these he has mingled gold, wherefore also they have the greatest honor; others he has made of silver, to be auxiliaries; others again who are to be husbandmen and craftsmen he has composed of brass and iron; and the species will generally be preserved in the children. But as all are of the same original stock, a golden parent will sometimes have a silver son, or a silver parent a golden son. And God proclaims as a first principle to the rulers, and above all else, that there is nothing which they should so anxiously guard, or of which they are to be such good guardians, as of the purity of the race. They should observe what elements mingle in their offspring; for if the son of a golden or silver parent has an admixture

of brass and iron, then nature orders a transposition of ranks, and the
eye of the ruler must not be pitiful towards the child because he has
to descend in the scale and become a husbandman or artisan, just as
there may be sons of artisans who having an admixture of gold or
silver in them are raised to honor, and become guardians or auxiliaries. For an oracle says that when a man of brass or iron guards the
State, it will be destroyed. Such is the tale; is there any possibility of
making our citizens believe in it?"

"Not in the present generation," he replied; "there is no way of
accomplishing this; but their sons may be made to believe in the tale,
and their sons' sons, and posterity after them."

"I see the difficulty," I replied; "yet the fostering of such a belief
will make them care more for the city and for one another. Enough,
however, of the fiction, which may now fly abroad upon the wings
of rumor, while we arm our earth-born heroes, and lead them forth
under the command of their rulers. Let them look round and
select a spot whence they can best suppress insurrection, if any
prove refractory within, and also defend themselves against enemies,
who like wolves may come down on the fold from without; there let
them encamp, and whe ı they have encamped, let them sacrifice to
the proper Gods and prepare their dwellings."

"Just so," he said.

"And their dwellings must be such as will shield them against the
cold of winter and the heat of summer."

"I suppose that you mean houses," he replied.

"Yes," I said; "but they must be the houses of soldiers, and not of
shopkeepers."

"What is the difference?" he said.

"That I will endeavor to explain," I replied. "To keep watchdogs,
who, from want of discipline or hunger, or some evil habit or other,
would turn upon the sheep and worry them, and behave not like
dogs but wolves, would be a foul and monstrous thing in a shepherd?"

"Truly monstrous," he said.

"And therefore every care must be taken that our auxiliaries, being stronger than our citizens, may not grow to be too much for them and become savage tyrants instead of friends and allies?"

"Yes, great care should be taken."

"And would not a really good education furnish the best safeguard?"

"But they are well educated already," he replied.

"I cannot be so confident, my dear Glaucon," I said; "I am much more certain that they ought to be, and that true education, whatever that may be, will have the greatest tendency to civilize and humanize them in their relations to one another, and to those who are under their protection."

"Very true," he replied.

"And not only their education, but their habitations, and all that belongs to them, should be such as will neither impair their virtue as guardians, nor tempt them to prey upon the other citizens. Any man of sense must acknowledge that."

"He must."

"Then now let us consider what will be their way of life, if they are to realize our idea of them. In the first place, none of them should have any property of his own beyond what is absolutely necessary; 9 neither should they have a private house or store closed against any one who has a mind to enter; their provisions should be only such as are required by trained warriors, who are men of temperance and courage; they should agree to receive from the citizens a fixed rate of pay, enough to meet the expenses of the year and no more; and they will go to mess and live together like soldiers in a camp. Gold and silver we will tell them that they have from God; the diviner metal is within them, and they have therefore no need of the dross which is current among men, and ought not to pollute the divine by any such earthly admixture; for that commoner metal has been the source of many unholy deeds, but their own is undefiled. And they alone of all the citizens may not touch or handle silver or gold, or be under the same roof with them, or wear them, or drink from them. And this

9 The soldier guardians and rulers of the state live apart from the mass of common folk, under a system of communism.

will be their salvation, and they will be the saviors of the State. But should they ever acquire homes or lands or moneys of their own, they will become housekeepers and husbandmen instead of guardians, enemies and tyrants instead of allies of the other citizens; hating and being hated, plotting and being plotted against, they will pass their whole life in much greater terror of internal than of external enemies, and the hour of ruin, both to themselves and to the rest of the State, will be at hand. For all which reasons may we not say that thus shall our State be ordered, and that these shall be the regulations appointed by us for our guardians concerning their houses and all other matters?"

"Yes," said Glaucon.

BOOK IV

The virtues of such a state—wisdom, courage, and temperance. Justice also to be found there. The same virtues appear in the life of a well-ordered individual.

HERE Adeimantus interposed a question: "How would you answer, Socrates," said he, "if a person were to say that you are making these people miserable, and that they are the cause of their own unhappiness; the city in fact belongs to them, but they are none the better for it; whereas other men acquire lands, and build large and handsome houses, and have everything handsome about them, offering sacrifices to the gods on their own account, and practicing hospitality; moreover, as you were saying just now, they have gold and silver, and all that is usual among the favorites of fortune; but our poor citizens are no better than mercenaries who are quartered in the city and are always mounting guard?"

"Yes," I said; "and you may add that they are only fed, and not paid in addition to their food, like other men; and therefore they cannot, if they would, take a journey of pleasure; they have no money to spend on a mistress or any other luxurious fancy, which, as the world goes, is thought to be happiness; and many other accusations of the same nature might be added."

"But," said he, "let us suppose all this to be included in the charge."

"You mean to ask," I said, "what will be our answer?"

"Yes."

"If we proceed along the old path, my belief," I said, "is that we shall find the answer. And our answer will be that, even as they are, our guardians may very likely be the happiest of men; but that our aim in founding the State was not the disproportionate happiness of any one class, but the greatest happiness of the whole; we thought that in a State which is ordered with a view to the good of the whole we should be most likely to find justice, and in the ill-ordered State injustice: and, having found them, we might then decide which of the two is the happier. At present, I take it, we are fashioning the happy State, not piecemeal, or with a view of making a few happy citizens, but as a whole; and by and by we will proceed to view the opposite kind of State. Suppose that we were painting a statue, and someone came up to us and said, 'Why do you not put the most beautiful colors on the most beautiful parts of the body? The eyes ought to be purple, but you have made them black.' To him we might fairly answer, 'Sir, you would not surely have us beautify the eyes to such a degree that they are no longer eyes; consider rather whether, by giving this and the other features their due proportion, we make the whole beautiful.' And so I say to you, do not compel us to assign to the guardians a sort of happiness which will make them anything but guardians; for we too can clothe our husbandmen in royal apparel, and set crowns of gold on their heads, and bid them till the ground as much as they like, and no more. Our potters also might be allowed to repose on couches, and feast by the fireside, passing round the wine cup, while their wheel is conveniently at hand, and working at pottery only as much as they like; in this way we might make every class happy—and then, as you imagine, the whole State would be happy. But do not put this idea into our heads; for, if we listen to you, the husbandman will be no longer a husbandman, the potter will cease to be a potter, and no one will have the character of any distinct class in the State. Now this is not of much consequence where the corruption of society, and pretension to be what you are not, is confined to cobblers; but when the guardians of the laws and of the government are only seeming and not real guardians, then see how they turn the State upside down; and on the other hand they alone have the power of giving order and happiness to the State. We mean our guardians to be true saviors and not the destroyers of the State, whereas our opponent is thinking of peasants at a festival, who are enjoying a life of revelry, not of citizens who are doing their duty to the State. But, if so, we mean different things, and he is speaking of something which is not a State. And therefore we must consider whether in appointing our guardians we would look to their greatest happiness individually, or whether this principle of happiness does not rather reside in the State as a whole. But if the latter be the truth, then the guardians and auxiliaries, and all others equally with them, must be compelled or induced to do their own work in the best way. And thus the whole State will grow up in a noble order, and the several classes will receive the proportion of happiness which nature assigns to them."

"I think that you are quite right."

"I wonder whether you will agree with another remark which occurs to me."

"What may that be?"

"There seem to be two causes of the deterioration of the arts."

"What are they?"

"Wealth," I said, "and poverty."

"How do they act?"

"The process is as follows: When a potter becomes rich, will he, think you, any longer take the same pains with his art?"

"Certainly not."

"He will grow more and more indolent and careless?"

"Very true."

"And the result will be that he becomes a worse potter?"

"Yes; he greatly deteriorates."

"But, on the other hand, if he has no money, and cannot provide himself with tools or instruments, he will not work equally well himself, nor will he teach his sons or apprentices to work equally well."

"Certainly not."

"Then, under the influence either of poverty or of wealth, workmen and their work are equally liable to degenerate?"

"That is evident."

"Here, then, is a discovery of new evils," I said, "against which the guardians will have to watch, or they will creep into the city unobserved."

"What evils?"

"Wealth," I said, "and poverty; the one is the parent of luxury and indolence, and the other of meanness and viciousness, and both of discontent."

"That is very true," he replied; "but still I should like to know, Socrates, how our city will be able to go to war, especially against an enemy who is rich and powerful, if deprived of the sinews of war."

"There would certainly be a difficulty," I replied, "in going to war with one such enemy; but there is no difficulty where there are two of them."

"How so?" he asked.

"In the first place," I said, "if we have to fight, our side will be trained warriors fighting against an army of rich men."

"That is true," he said.

"And do you not suppose, Adeimantus, that a single boxer who was perfect in his art would easily be a match for two stout and well-to-do gentlemen who were not boxers?"

"Hardly, if they came upon him at once."

"What, not," I said, "if he were able to run away and then turn and strike at the one who first came up? And supposing he were to do this several times under the heat of a scorching sun, might he not, being an expert, overturn more than one stout personage?"

"Certainly," he said, "there would be nothing wonderful in that."

"And yet rich men probably have a greater superiority in the science and practice of boxing than they have in military qualities."

"Likely enough."

"Then we may assume that our athletes will be able to fight with two or three times their own number?"

"I agree with you, for I think you right."

"And suppose that, before engaging, our citizens send an embassy to one of the two cities, telling them what is the truth: Silver and gold we neither have nor are permitted to have, but you may; do you therefore come and help us in war, and take the spoils of the other city. Who, on hearing these words, would choose to fight against lean wiry dogs, rather than, with the dogs on their side, against fat and tender sheep?"

"That is not likely; and yet there might be a danger to the poor State if the wealth of many States were to be gathered into one."

"But how simple of you to use the term State at all of any but our own!"

"Why so?"

"You ought to speak of other States in the plural number; not one of them is a city, but many cities, as they say in the game. For indeed any city, however small, is in fact divided into two, one the city of the poor, the other of the rich; these are at war with one another; and in either there are many smaller divisions, and you would be altogether beside the mark if you treated them all as a single State. But if you deal with them as many, and give the wealth or power or persons of the one to the others, you will always have a great many friends and not many enemies. And your State, while the wise order which has now been prescribed continues to prevail in her, will be the greatest of States, I do not mean to say in reputation or appearance, but in deed and truth, though she number not more than a thousand defenders. A single State which is her equal you will hardly find, either among Hellenes or barbarians, though many that appear to be as great and many times greater."

"That is most true," he said.

"And what," I said, "will be the best limit for our rulers to fix when they are considering the size of the State and the amount of territory which they are to include, and beyond which they will not go?"

"What limit would you propose?"

"I would allow the State to increase so far as is consistent with unity; that, I think, is the proper limit."

"Very good," he said.

"Here then," I said, "is another order which will have to be conveyed to our guardians: Let our city be accounted neither large nor small, but one and self-sufficing."

"And surely," said he, "this is not a very severe order which we impose upon them."

"And the other," said I, "of which we were speaking before is lighter still—I mean the duty of degrading the offspring of the guardians when inferior, and of elevating into the rank of guardians the offspring of the lower classes, when naturally superior. The intention was, that, in the case of the citizens generally, each individual should be put to the use for which nature intended him, one to one work, and then every man would do his own business, and be one and not many; and so the whole city would be one and not many."

"Yes," he said; "that is not so difficult."

"The regulations which we are prescribing, my good Adeimantus, are not, as might be supposed, a number of great principles, but trifles all, if care be taken, as the saying is, of the one great thing— a thing, however, which I would rather call not great, but sufficient for our purpose."

"What may that be?" he asked.

"Education," I said, "and nurture: If our citizens are well educated, and grow into sensible men, they will easily see their way through all these, as well as other matters which I omit; such, for example, as marriage, the possession of women and the procreation of children, which will all follow the general principle that friends have all things in common, as the proverb says."

"That will be the best way of settling them."

"Also," I said, "the State, if once started well, moves **with accumu-**

lating force like a wheel. For good nurture and education implant good constitutions, and these good constitutions taking root in a good education improve more and more, and this improvement affects the breed in man as in other animals."

"Very possibly," he said.

"Then to sum up: This is the point to which, above all, the attention of our rulers should be directed—that music and gymnastic be preserved in their original form, and no innovation made. They must do their utmost to maintain them intact. And when anyone says that mankind most regard

The newest song which the singers have,[1]

they will be afraid that he may be praising, not new songs, but a new kind of song; and this ought not to be praised, or conceived to be the meaning of the poet; for any musical innovation is full of danger to the whole State, and ought to be prohibited. So Damon tells me, and I can quite believe him; he says that when modes of music change, the fundamental laws of the State always change with them."

"Yes," said Adeimantus; "and you may add my suffrage to Damon's and your own."

"Then," I said, "our guardians must lay the foundations of their fortress in music?"

"Yes," he said; "the lawlessness of which you speak too easily steals in."

"Yes," I replied, "in the form of amusement; and at first sight it appears harmless."

"Why, yes," he said, "and there is no harm; were it not that little by little this spirit of license, finding a home, imperceptibly penetrates into manners and customs; whence, issuing with greater force, it invades contracts between man and man, and from contracts goes on to laws and constitutions, in utter recklessness, ending at last, Socrates, by an overthrow of all rights, private as well as public."

"Is that true?" I said.

1 Homer, *Odyssey,* I, 352.

"That is my belief," he replied.

"Then, as I was saying, our youth should be trained from the first in a stricter system, for if amusements become lawless, and the youths themselves become lawless, they can never grow up into well-conducted and virtuous citizens."

"Very true," he said.

"And when they have made a good beginning in play, and by the help of music have gained the habit of good order, then this habit of order, in a manner how unlike the lawless play of the others! will accompany them in all their actions and be a principle of growth to them, and if there be any fallen places in the State will raise them up again."

"Very true," he said.

"Thus educated, they will invent for themselves any lesser rules which their predecessors have altogether neglected."

"What do you mean?"

"I mean such things as these: when the young are to be silent be fore their elders; how they are to show respect to them by standing and making them sit; what honor is due to parents; what garments or shoes are to be worn; the mode of dressing the hair; deportment and manners in general. You would agree with me?"

"Yes."

"But there is, I think, small wisdom in legislating about such matters—I doubt if it is ever done; nor are any precise written enactments about them likely to be lasting."

"Impossible."

"It would seem, Adeimantus, that the direction in which education starts a man, will determine his future life. Does not like always attract like?"

"To be sure."

"Until some one rare and grand result is reached which may be good, and may be the reverse of good?"

"That is not to be denied."

"And for this reason," I said, "I shall not attempt to legislate further about them."

"Naturally enough," he replied.

"Well, and about the business of the agora, and the ordinary dealings between man and man, or again about agreements with artisans; about insult and injury, or the commencement of actions, and the appointment of juries, what would you say? there may also arise questions about any impositions and exactions of market and harbor dues which may be required, and in general about the regulations of markets, police, harbors, and the like. But, oh heavens! shall we condescend to legislate on any of these particulars?"

"I think," he said, "that there is no need to impose laws about them on good men; what regulations are necessary they will find out soon enough for themselves."

"Yes," I said, "my friend, if God will only preserve to them the laws which we have given them."

It is useless to try by endless reform legislation to cure rascality in a state when its fundamental order is wrong.

"What, then," he said, "is still remaining to us of the work of legislation?"

"Nothing to us," I replied; "but to Apollo, the god of Delphi, there remains the ordering of the greatest and noblest and chiefest things of all."

"Which are they?" he said.

"The institution of temples and sacrifices, and the entire service of gods, demigods, and heroes; also the ordering of the repositories of the dead, and the rites which have to be observed by him who would propitiate the inhabitants of the world below. These are matters of which we are ignorant ourselves, and as founders of a city we should be unwise in trusting them to any interpreter but our ancestral deity. He is the god who sits in the center, on the navel of the earth, and he is the interpreter of religion to all mankind."

"You are right, and we will do as you propose."

"But where, amid all this, is justice? son of Ariston, tell me where. Now that our city has been made habitable, light a candle and search, and get your brother and Polemarchus and the rest of our friends to help, and let us see where in it we can discover justice and where injustice, and in what they differ from one another, and which of them the man who would be happy should have for his portion, whether seen or unseen by gods and men."

"Nonsense," said Glaucon: "did you not promise to search yourself, saying that for you not to help justice in her need would be an impiety?"

"I do not deny that I said so; and as you remind me, I will be as good as my word; but you must join."

"We will," he replied.

"Well, then, I hope to make the discovery in this way: I mean to begin with the assumption that our State, if rightly ordered, is perfect."

"That is most certain."

"And being perfect, is therefore wise and valiant and temperate and just." [2]

"That is likewise clear."

"And whichever of these qualities we find in the State, the one which is not found will be the residue?"

"Very good."

"If there were four things, and we were searching for one of them, wherever it might be, the one sought for might be known to us from the first, and there would be no further trouble; or we might know the other three first, and then the fourth would clearly be the one left."

"Very true," he said.

"And is not a similar method to be pursued about the virtues, which are also four in number?"

"Clearly."

"First among the virtues found in the State, wisdom comes into view, and in this I detect a certain peculiarity."

2 Here Plato lists, as he does in other dialogues, what to him are the four great virtues—wisdom, courage, temperance or self-control, and justice. From this time on they were accepted as the standard virtues of the ancient world.

"What is that?"

"The State which we have been describing is said to be wise as being good in counsel?"

"Very true."

"And good counsel is clearly a kind of knowledge, for not by ignorance, but by knowledge, do men counsel well?"

"Clearly."

"And the kinds of knowledge in a State are many and diverse?"

"Of course."

"There is the knowledge of the carpenter; but is that the sort of knowledge which gives a city the title of wise and good in counsel?"

"Certainly not; that would only give a city the reputation of skill in carpentering."

"Then a city is not to be called wise because possessing a knowledge which counsels for the best about wooden implements?"

"Certainly not."

"Nor by reason of a knowledge which advises about brazen pots, nor as possessing any other similar knowledge?"

"Not by reason of any of them," he said.

"Nor yet by reason of a knowledge which cultivates the earth; that would give the city the name of agricultural?"

"Yes."

"Well," I said, "and is there any knowledge in our recently-founded State among any of the citizens which advises, not about any particular thing in the State, but about the whole, and considers how a State can best deal with itself and with other States?"

"There certainly is."

"And what is this knowledge, and among whom is it found?" I asked.

"It is the knowledge of the guardians," he replied, "and is found among those whom we were just now describing as perfect guardians."

"And what is the name which the city derives from the possession of this sort of knowledge?"

"The name of good in counsel and truly wise."

"And will there be in our city more of these true guardians or more smiths?"

"The smiths," he replied, "will be far more numerous."

"Will not the guardians be the smallest of all the classes who receive a name from the profession of some kind of knowledge?"

"Much the smallest."

"And so by reason of the smallest part or class, and of the knowledge which resides in this presiding and ruling part of itself, the whole State, being thus constituted according to nature, will be wise; and this, which has the only knowledge worthy to be called wisdom, has been ordained by nature to be of all classes the least."

"Most true."

"Thus, then," I said, "the nature and place in the State of one of the four virtues has somehow or other been discovered."

"And, in my humble opinion, very satisfactorily discovered," he replied.

"Again," I said, "there is no difficulty in seeing the nature of courage, and in what part that quality resides which gives the name of courageous to the State."

"How do you mean?"

"Why," I said, "everyone who calls any State courageous or cowardly, will be thinking of the part which fights and goes out to war on the State's behalf."

"No one," he replied, "would ever think of any other."

"The rest of the citizens may be courageous or may be cowardly, but their courage or cowardice will not, as I conceive, have the effect of making the city either the one or the other."

"Certainly not."

"The city will be courageous in virtue of a portion of herself which preserves under all circumstances that opinion about the nature of things to be feared and not to be feared in which our legislator educated them; and this is what you term courage."

"I should like to hear what you are saying once more, for I do not think that I perfectly understand you."

"I mean that courage is a kind of salvation."

"Salvation of what?"

"Of the opinion respecting things to be feared, what they are and of what nature, which the law implants through education; and I mean by the words 'under all circumstances' to intimate that in pleasure or in pain, or under the influence of desire or fear, a man preserves, and does not lose this opinion. Shall I give you an illustration?"

"If you please."

"You know," I said, "that dyers, when they want to dye wool for making the true sea-purple, begin by selecting their white color first; this they prepare and dress with much care and pains, in order that the white ground may take the purple hue in full perfection. The dyeing then proceeds; and whatever is dyed in this manner becomes a fast color, and no washing either with lyes or without them can take away the bloom. But, when the ground has not been duly prepared, you will have noticed how poor is the look either of purple or of any other color."

"Yes," he said; "I know that they have a washed-out and ridiculous appearance."

"Then now," I said, "you will understand what our object was in selecting our soldiers, and educating them in music and gymnastic; we were contriving influences which would prepare them to take the dye of the laws in perfection, and the color of their opinion about dangers and of every other opinion was to be indelibly fixed by their nurture and training, not to be washed away by such potent lyes as pleasure—mightier agent far in washing the soul than any soda or lye; or by sorrow, fear, and desire, the mightiest of all other solvents. And this sort of universal saving power of true opinion in conformity with law about real and false dangers I call and maintain to be courage, unless you disagree."

"But I agree," he replied; "for I suppose that you mean to exclude mere uninstructed courage, such as that of a wild beast or of a slave—this, in your opinion, is not the courage which the law ordains, and ought to have another name."

"Most certainly."

"Then I may infer courage to be such as you describe?"

"Why, yes," said I, "you may, and if you add the words 'of a citizen,' you will not be far wrong; hereafter, if you like, we will carry the examination further, but at present we are seeking not for courage but justice; and for the purpose of our inquiry we have said enough."

"You are right," he replied.

"Two virtues remain to be discovered in the State—first, temperance, and then justice which is the end of our search."

"Very true."

"Now, can we find justice without troubling ourselves about temperance?"

"I do not know how that can be accomplished," he said, "nor do I desire that justice should be brought to light and temperance lost sight of; and therefore I wish that you would do me the favor of considering temperance first."

"Certainly," I replied, "I should not be justified in refusing your request."

"Then consider," he said.

"Yes," I replied; "I will; and as far as I can at present see, the virtue of temperance has more of the nature of harmony and symphony than the preceding."

"How so?" he asked.

"Temperance," I replied, "is the ordering or controlling of certain pleasures and desires; this is curiously enough implied in the saying of 'a man being his own master'; and other traces of the same notion may be found in language."

"No doubt," he said.

"There is something ridiculous in the expression 'master of himself'; for the master is also the servant and the servant the master; and in all these modes of speaking the same person is denoted."

"Certainly."

"The meaning is," I believe, "that in the human soul there is a better and also a worse principle; and when the better has the worse under control, then a man is said to be master of himself; and this is a term of praise: but when, owing to evil education or association, the better principle, which is also the smaller, is overwhelmed by the greater mass of the worse—in this case he is blamed and is called the slave of self and unprincipled."

"Yes, there is reason in that."

"And now," I said, "look at our newly-created State, and there you will find one of these two conditions realized; for the State, as you will acknowledge, may be justly called master of itself, if the words 'temperance' and 'self-mastery' truly express the rule of the better part over the worse."

"Yes," he said, "I see that what you say is true."

"Let me further note that the manifold and complex pleasures and desires and pains are generally found in children and women and servants, and in the freemen so called who are of the lowest and more numerous class."

"Certainly," he said.

"Whereas the simple and moderate desires which follow reason, and are under the guidance of mind and true opinion, are to be found only in a few, and those the best born and best educated."

"Very true."

"These two, as you may perceive, have a place in our State; and the meaner desires of the many are held down by the virtuous desires and wisdom of the few."

"That I perceive," he said.

"Then if there be any city which may be described as master of its own pleasures and desires, and master of itself, ours may claim such a designation?"

"Certainly," he replied.

"It may also be called temperate, and for the same reasons?"

"Yes."

"And if there be any State in which rulers and subjects will be agreed as to the question who are to rule, that again will be our State?"

"Undoubtedly."

"And the citizens being thus agreed among themselves, in which class will temperance be found—in the rulers or in the subjects?"

"In both, as I should imagine," he replied.

"Do you observe that we were not far wrong in our guess that temperance was a sort of harmony?"

"Why so?"

"Why, because temperance is unlike courage and wisdom, each of which resides in a part only, the one making the State wise and the other valiant; not so temperance, which extends to the whole, and runs through all the notes of the scale, and produces a harmony of the weaker and the stronger and the middle class, whether you suppose them to be stronger or weaker in wisdom or power or numbers or wealth, or anything else. Most truly then may we deem temperance to be the agreement of the naturally superior and inferior, as to the right to rule of either, both in states and individuals."

"I entirely agree with you."

"And so," I said, "we may consider three out of the four virtues to have been discovered in our State. The last of those qualities which make a state virtuous must be justice, if we only knew what that was."

"The inference is obvious."

"The time then has arrived, Glaucon, when, like huntsmen, we should surround the cover, and look sharp that justice does not steal away, and pass out of sight and escape us; for beyond a doubt she is somewhere in this country: watch therefore and strive to catch a sight of her, and if you see her first, let me know."

"Would that I could! but you should regard me rather as a follower who has just eyes enough to see what you show him—that is about as much as I am good for."

"Offer up a prayer with me and follow."

"I will, but you must show me the way."

"Here is no path," I said, "and the wood is dark and perplexing; still we must push on."

"Let us push on."

Here I saw something: "Halloo!" I said, "I begin to perceive a track, and I believe that the quarry will not escape."

"Good news," he said.

"Truly," I said, "we are stupid fellows."

"Why so?"

"Why, my good sir, at the beginning of our inquiry, ages ago, there was justice tumbling out at our feet, and we never saw her; nothing could be more ridiculous. Like people who go about looking for what they have in their hands—that was the way with us—we looked not at what we were seeking, but at what was far off in the distance; and therefore, I suppose, we missed her."

"What do you mean?"

"I mean to say that in reality for a long time past we have been talking of justice, and have failed to recognize her."

"I grow impatient at the length of your exordium."

"Well then, tell me," I said, "whether I am right or not: You remember the original principle which we were always laying down at the foundation of the State, that one man should practice one thing only, the thing to which his nature was best adapted; now justice is this principle or a part of it."

"Yes, we often said that one man should do one thing only."

"Further, we affirmed that justice was doing one's own business, and not being a busybody; we said so again and again, and many others have said the same to us."

"Yes, we said so."

"Then to do one's own business in a certain way may be assumed to be justice. Can you tell me whence I derive this inference?"

"I cannot, but I should like to be told."

"Because I think that this is the only virtue which remains in the State when the other virtues of temperance and courage and wisdom are abstracted; and, that this is the ultimate cause and condition of the existence of all of them, and while remaining in them is also their preservative; and we were saying that if the three were discovered by us, justice would be the fourth or remaining one."

"That follows of necessity."

"If we are asked to determine which of these four qualities by its presence contributes most to the excellence of the State, whether the agreement of rulers and subjects, or the preservation in the soldiers of the opinion which the law ordains about the true nature of dangers, or wisdom and watchfulness in the rulers, or whether this other which I am mentioning, and which is found in children and women, slave and freeman, artisan, ruler, subject—the quality, I mean, of every one doing his own work, and not being a busybody, would claim the palm—the question is not so easily answered."

"Certainly," he replied, "there would be a difficulty in saying which."

"Then the power of each individual in the State to do his own work appears to compete with the other political virtues, wisdom, temperance, courage."

"Yes," he said.

"And the virtue which enters into this competition is justice?"

"Exactly."

"Let us look at the question from another point of view: Are not the rulers in a State those to whom you would entrust the office of determining suits at law?"

"Certainly."

"And are suits decided on any other ground but that a man may neither take what is another's, nor be deprived of what is his own?"

"Yes; that is their principle."

"Which is a just principle?"

"Yes."

"Then on this view also justice will be admitted to be the having and doing what is a man's own, and belongs to him?" [3]

"Very true."

"Think, now, and say whether you agree with me or not. Sup-

---

3 Here at last Socrates arrives at the first acceptable definition of social justice, a condition in which every person has and does peacefully what it is his right to have and to do, fills the place for which he is fitted. The same definition, translated into psychological terms, is then applied to the state of the individual whose faculties are so fairly and harmoniously adjusted that each plays that part in his inner life that it rightfully should, neither more nor less.

pose a carpenter to be doing the business of a cobbler, or a cobbler of a carpenter; and suppose them to exchange their implements or their duties, or the same person to be doing the work of both, or whatever be the change; do you think that any great harm would result to the State?"

"Not much."

"But when the cobbler or any other man whom nature designed to be a trader, having his heart lifted up by wealth or strength or the number of his followers, or any like advantage, attempts to force· his way into the class of warriors, or a warrior into that of legislators and guardians, for which he is unfitted, and either to take the implements or the duties of the other; or when one man is trader, legislator, and warrior all in one, then I think you will agree with me in saying that this interchange and this meddling of one with another is the ruin of the State."

"Most true."

"Seeing then," I said, "that there are three distinct classes, any meddling of one with another, or the change of one into another, is the greatest harm to the State, and may be most justly termed evil-doing?"

"Precisely."

"And the greatest degree of evil-doing to one's own city would be termed by you injustice?"

"Certainly."

"This then is injustice; and on the other hand when the trader, the auxiliary, and the guardian each do their own business, that is justice, and will make the city just."

"I agree with you."

"We will not," I said, "be over-positive as yet; but if, on trial, this conception of justice be verified in the individual as well as in the State, there will be no longer any room for doubt; if it be not verified, we must have a fresh inquiry. First let us complete the old investigation, which we began, as you remember, under the impression that, if we could previously examine justice on the larger scale, there would be less difficulty in discerning her in the individual. That larger example appeared to be the State, and accordingly we constructed as good a one as we could, knowing well that in the good State justice would be found. Let the discovery which we made be now applied to the individual—if they agree, we shall be satisfied; or, if there be a difference in the individual, we will come back to the State and have another trial of the theory. The friction of the two when rubbed together may possibly strike a light in which justice will shine forth, and the vision which is then revealed we will fix in our souls."

"That will be in regular course; let us do as you say."

I proceeded to ask: "When two things, a greater and less, are called by the same name, are they like or unlike in so far as they are called the same?"

"Like," he replied.

"The just man then, if we regard the idea of justice only, will be like the just State?"

"He will."

"And a State was thought by us to be just when the three classes in the State severally did their own business; and also thought to be temperate and valiant and wise by reason of certain other affections and qualities of these same classes?"

"True," he said.

"And so of the individual; we may assume that he has the same three principles in his own soul which are found in the State; and he may be rightly described in the same terms, because he is affected in the same manner?"

"Certainly," he said.

Socrates develops more fully his theory of three principles or elements in each man's nature, corresponding to the three classes in the ideal state. The reasoning intellect matched the wise rulers, the courageous spirit the intrepid soldiery and the bodily desires and appetites the working classes that provide for the physical needs of the state.

"Must we not then infer that the individual is wise in the same way, and in virtue of the same quality which makes the State wise?"

"Certainly."

"Also that the same quality which constitutes courage in the State constitutes courage in the individual, and that both the State and the individual bear the same relation to all the other virtues?"

"Assuredly."

"And the individual will be acknowledged by us to be just in the same way in which the State is just?"

"That follows of course."

"We cannot but remember that the justice of the State consisted in each of the three classes doing the work of its own class?"

"We are not very likely to have forgotten," he said.

"We must recollect that the individual in whom the several qualities of his nature do their own work will be just, and will do his own work?"

"Yes," he said, "we must remember that too."

"And ought not the rational principle, which is wise, and has the care of the whole soul, to rule, and the passionate or spirited principle to be the subject and ally?"

"Certainly."

"And, as we were saying, the united influence of music and gymnastic will bring them into accord, nerving and sustaining the reason with noble words and lessons, and moderating and soothing and civilizing the wildness of passion by harmony and rhythm?"

"Quite true," he said.

"And these two, thus nurtured and educated, and having learned truly to know their own functions, will rule over the concupiscent, which in each of us is the largest part of the soul and by nature most insatiable of gain; over this they will keep guard, lest, waxing great and strong with the fullness of bodily pleasures, as they are termed, the concupiscent soul, no longer confined to her own sphere, should attempt to enslave and rule those who are not her natural-born subjects, and overturn the whole life of man?"

"Very true," he said.

"Both together will they not be the best defenders of the whole soul and the whole body against attacks from without; the one counseling, and the other fighting under his leader, and courageously executing his commands and counsels?"

"True."

"And he is to be deemed courageous whose spirit retains in pleasure and in pain the commands of reason about what he ought or ought not to fear?"

"Right," he replied.

"And him we call wise who has in him that little part which rules, and which proclaims these commands; that part too being supposed to have a knowledge of what is for the interest of each of the three parts and of the whole?"

"Assuredly."

"And would you not say that he is temperate who has these same elements in friendly harmony, in whom the one ruling principle of reason, and the two subject ones of spirit and desire are equally agreed that reason ought to rule, and do not rebel?"

"Certainly," he said, "that is the true account of temperance whether in the State or individual."

"And surely," I said, "we have explained again and again how and by virtue of what quality a man will be just."

"That is very certain."

"And is justice dimmer in the individual, and is her form different, or is she the same which we found her to be in the State?"

"There is no difference in my opinion," he said.

"Because, if any doubt is still lingering in our minds, a few commonplace instances will satisfy us of the truth of what I am saying."

"What sort of instances do you mean?"

"If the case is put to us, must we not admit that the just State, or the man who is trained in the principles of such a State, will be less likely than the unjust to make away with a deposit of gold or silver? Would anyone deny this?"

"No one," he replied.

"Will the just man or citizen ever be guilty of sacrilege or theft, or treachery either to his friends or to his country?"

"Never."

"Neither will he ever break faith where there have been oaths or agreements?"

"Impossible."

"No one will be less likely to commit adultery, or to dishonor his father and mother, or to fail in his religious duties?"

"No one."

"And the reason is that each part of him is doing its own business, whether in ruling or being ruled?"

"Exactly so."

"Are you satisfied then that the quality which makes such men and such states is justice, or do you hope to discover some other?"

"Not I, indeed."

"Then our dream has been realized; and the suspicion which we entertained at the beginning of our work of construction, that some divine power must have conducted us to a primary form of justice, has now been verified?"

"Yes, certainly."

"And the division of labor which required the carpenter and the shoemaker and the rest of the citizens to be doing each his own business, and not another's, was a shadow of justice, and for that reason it was of use?"

"Clearly."

"But in reality justice was such as we were describing, being concerned however, not with the outward man, but with the inward, which is the true self and concernment of man: for the just man does not permit the several elements within him to interfere with one another, or any of them to do the work of others—he sets in order his own inner life, and is his own master and his own law, and at peace with himself; and when he has bound together the three principles within him, which may be compared to the higher, lower, and middle notes of the scale, and the intermediate intervals—when he has bound all these together, and is no longer many, but has become one entirely temperate and perfectly adjusted nature, then he proceeds to act, if he has to act, whether in a matter of property, or in the treatment of the body, or in some affair of politics or private business; always thinking and calling that which preserves and co-operates with this harmonious condition, just and good action, and the knowledge which presides over it, wisdom, and that which at any time impairs this condition, he will call unjust action, and the opinion which presides over it ignorance."

"You have said the exact truth, Socrates."

"Very good; and if we were to affirm that we had discovered the just man and the just State, and the nature of justice in each of them, we should not be telling a falsehood?"

"Most certainly not."

"May we say so, then?"

"Let us say so."

"And now," I said, "injustice has to be considered."

"Clearly."

"Must not injustice be a strife which arises among the three principles—a meddlesomeness, and interference, and rising up of a part of the soul against the whole, an assertion of unlawful authority, which is made by a rebellious subject against a true prince, of whom he is the natural vassal—what is all this confusion and delusion but injustice and intemperance and cowardice and ignorance, and every form of vice?"

"Exactly so."

"And if the nature of justice and injustice be known, then the meaning of acting unjustly and being unjust, or, again, of acting justly, will also be perfectly clear?"

"What do you mean?" he said.

"Why," I said, "they are like disease and health; being in the soul just what disease and health are in the body."

"How so?" he said.

"Why," I said, "that which is healthy causes health, and that which is unhealthy causes disease."

"Yes."

"And just actions cause justice, and unjust actions cause injustice?"

"That is certain."

"And the creation of health is the institution of a natural order and government of one by another in the parts of the body; and the creation of disease is the production of a state of things at variance with this natural order?"

"True."

"And is not the creation of justice the institution of a natural order and government of one by another in the parts of the soul, and the creation of injustice the production of a state of things at variance with the natural order?"

"Exactly so," he said.

"Then virtue is the health and beauty and well-being of the soul, and vice the disease and weakness and deformity of the same?"

"True."

"And do not good practices lead to virtue, and evil practices to vice?"

"Assuredly."

"Still our old question of the comparative advantage of justice and injustice has not been answered: Which is the more profitable, to be just and act justly and practice virtue, whether seen or unseen of gods and men, cr to be unjust and act unjustly, if only unpunished and unreformed?"

"In my judgment, Socrates, the question has now become ridiculous. We know that, when the bodily constitution is gone, life is no longer endurable, though pampered with all kinds of meats and drinks, and having all wealth and all power; and shall we be told that when the very essence of the vital principle is undermined and corrupted, life is still worth having to a man, if only he be allowed to do whatever he likes with the single exception that he is not to acquire justice and virtue, or to escape from injustice and vice; assuming them both to be such as we have described?"

"Yes,"I said, "the question is, as you say, ridiculous. Still, as we are near the spot at which we may see the truth in the clearest manner with our own eyes, let us not faint by the way."

"Certainly not," he replied.

"Come up hither," I said, "and behold the various forms of vice, those of them, I mean, which are worth looking at."

"I am following you," he replied; "proceed."

I said, "The argument seems to have reached a height from which, as from some tower of speculation, a man may look down and see that virtue is one, but that the forms of vice are innumerable; there being four special ones [4] which are deserving of note."

"What do you mean?" he said.

"I mean," I replied, "that there appear to be as many forms of the soul as there are distinct forms of the State."

"How many?"

"There are five of the State, and five of the soul," I said.

"What are they?"

"The first," I said, "is that which we have been describing, and which may be said to have two names, monarchy and aristocracy,[5] accordingly as rule is exercised by one distinguished man or by many."

"True," he replied.

"But I regard the two names as describing one form only; for whether the government is in the hands of one or many, if the governors have been trained in the manner which we have supposed, the fundamental laws of the State will be maintained."

"That is true," he replied.

4 The description of the four inferior types of states and souls, together with the explanation of how the process of deterioration begins and continues down to the worst, does not, as we might expect, follow at once. Socrates is interrupted and forced by his audience to give a far more complete account of the workings of his ideal system before he is allowed to go on. He does not get back to the inferior systems until Book VIII, page 429.

5 The ideal system is hereafter spoken of sometimes as a monarchy, sometimes as an aristocracy. In both cases it is government by a ruler or rulers of the rare caliber described in the next four books.

BOOK V

Education of women. Community of wives and children in the governing classes. Humanity in war. Rulers must be philosophers.

"Such is the good and true City or State, and the good and true man is of the same pattern; and if this is right every other is wrong; and the evil is one which affects not only the ordering of the State, but also the regulation of the individual soul, and is exhibited in four forms."

"What are they?" he said.

I was proceeding to tell the order in which the four evil forms appeared to me to succeed one another, when Polemarchus, who was sitting a little way off, just beyond Adeimantus, began to whisper to him: stretching forth his hand, he took hold of the upper part of his coat by the shoulder, and drew him towards him, leaning forward himself so as to be quite close and saying something in his ear, of which I only caught the words, "Shall we let him off, or what shall we do?"

"Certainly not," said Adeimantus, raising his voice.

"Who is it," I said, "whom you are refusing to let off?"

"You," he said.

I repeated, "Why am I especially not to be let off?"

"Why," he said, "we think that you are lazy, and mean to cheat us out of a whole chapter which is a very important part of the story; and you fancy that we shall not notice your airy way of proceeding; as if it were self-evident to everybody, that in the matter of women and children 'friends have all things in common.' "

"And was I not right, Adeimantus?"

"Yes," he said; "but what is right in this particular case, like everything else, requires to be explained; for community may be of many kinds. Please, therefore, to say what sort of community you mean. We have been long expecting that you would tell us something about the family life of your citizens—how they will bring children into the world, and rear them when they have arrived, and, in general, what is the nature of this community of women and children—for we are of opinion that the right or wrong management of such matters will have a great and paramount influence on the State for good or for evil. And now, since the question is still undetermined, and you are taking in hand another State, we have resolved, as you heard, not to let you go until you give an account of all this."

"To that resolution," said Glaucon, "you may regard me as saying Agreed."

"And without more ado," said Thrasymachus, "you may consider us all to be equally agreed."

I said: "You know not what you are doing in thus assailing me. What an argument are you raising about the State! Just as I thought that I had finished, and was only too glad that I had laid this question to sleep, and was reflecting how fortunate I was in your acceptance of what I then said, you ask me to begin again at the very foundation, ignorant of what a hornet's nest of words you are stirring. Now I foresaw this gathering trouble, and avoided it."

"For what purpose do you conceive that we have come here," said Thrasymachus, "to look for gold, or to hear discourse?"

"Yes, but discourse should have a limit."

"Yes, Socrates," said Glaucon, "and the whole of life is the only limit which wise men assign to the hearing of such discourses. But never mind about us; take heart yourself and answer the question in your own way: What sort of community of women and children is this which is to prevail among our guardians? and how shall we manage the period between birth and education, which seems to require the greatest care? Tell us how these things will be."

"Yes, my simple friend, but the answer is the reverse of easy; many more doubts arise about this than about our previous conclusions. For the practicability of what is said may be doubted; and looked at in another point of view, whether the scheme, if ever so practicable, would be for the best, is also doubtful.[1] Hence I feel a reluctance to approach the subject, lest our aspiration, my dear friend, should turn out to be a dream only."

"Fear not," he replied, "for your audience will not be hard upon you; they are not skeptical or hostile."

I said: "My good friend, I suppose that you mean to encourage me by these words."

"Yes," he said.

"Then let me tell you that you are doing just the reverse; the encouragement which you offer would have been all very well had I myself believed that I knew what I was talking about: to declare the truth about matters of high interest which a man honors and loves among wise men who love him need occasion no fear or faltering in his mind; but to carry on an argument when you are yourself only a hesitating inquirer, which is my condition, is a dangerous and slippery thing; and the danger is not that I shall be laughed at (of which the fear would be childish), but that I shall miss the truth where I have most need to be sure of my footing, and drag my friends after me in my fall. And I pray Nemesis [2] not to visit upon me the words which I am going to utter. For I do indeed believe that to be an involuntary homicide is a less crime than to be a deceiver about beauty or goodness or justice in the matter of laws. And that is a risk which I would rather run among enemies than among friends, and therefore you do well to encourage me."

Glaucon laughed and said: "Well then, Socrates, in case you and your argument do us any serious injury you shall be acquitted beforehand of the homicide, and shall not be held to be a deceiver; take courage then and speak."

"Well," I said, "the law says that when a man is acquitted he is free from guilt, and what holds at law may hold in argument."

"Then why should you mind?"

---

1 Notice the hesitation of Socrates to dogmatize about the radical schemes he is about to propose. He offers what seems an ideal and visionary solution to an eternally perplexing problem and keeps his hearers from breaking out in violent opposition by reminding them that he is "only a hesitating inquirer."

2 The goddess who pursues with her vengeance men who have sinned.

"Well," I replied, "I suppose that I must retrace my steps and say what I perhaps ought to have said before in the proper place. The part of the men has been played out, and now properly enough comes the turn of the women. Of them I will proceed to speak, and the more readily since I am invited by you.

"For men born and educated like our citizens, the only way, in my opinion, of arriving at a right conclusion about the possession and use of women and children is to follow the path on which we originally started, when we said that the men were to be the guardians and watchdogs of the herd." [3]

"True."

"Let us further suppose the birth and education of our women to be subject to similar or nearly similar regulations; then we shall see whether the result accords with our design."

"What do you mean?"

"What I mean may be put into the form of a question," I said. "Are dogs divided into hes and shes, or do they both share equally in hunting and in keeping watch and in the other duties of dogs? or do we entrust to the males the entire and exclusive care of the flocks, while we leave the females at home, under the idea that the bearing and suckling their puppies is labor enough for them?"

"No," he said, "they share alike; the only difference between them is that the males are stronger and the females weaker."

"But can you use different animals for the same purpose, unless they are bred and fed in the same way?"

"You cannot."

"Then, if women are to have the same duties as men, they must have the same nurture and education?"

"Yes."

"The education which was assigned to the men was music and gymnastic."

3 Note that all that follows as to the life and sexual relations of women and the birth and nurture of children applies only to the women and children of the warrior and ruler classes, who live in community houses and own no private property. See page 301 ff. Ordinary people, business men, farmers, workers of all sorts, live in families under their own roofs just as people do everywhere else.

"Yes."

"Then women must be taught music and gymnastic and also the art of war, which they must practice like the men?"

"That is the inference, I suppose."

"I should rather expect," I said, "that several of our proposals, if they are carried out, being unusual, may appear ridiculous."

"No doubt of it."

"Yes, and the most ridiculous thing of all will be the sight of women naked in the palaestra,[4] exercising with the men, especially when they are no longer young; they certainly will not be a vision of beauty, any more than the enthusiastic old men who in spite of wrinkles and ugliness continue to frequent the gymnasia."

"Yes, indeed," he said; "according to present notions the proposal would be thought ridiculous."

"But then," I said, "as we have determined to speak our minds, we must not fear the jests of the wits which will be directed against this sort of innovation; how they will talk of women's attainments both in music and gymnastic, and above all about their wearing armor and riding upon horseback!"

"Very true," he replied.

"Yet having begun we must go forward to the rough places of the law; at the same time begging of these gentlemen for once in their life to be serious. Not long ago, as we shall remind them, the Hellenes were of the opinion, which is still generally received among the barbarians, that the sight of a naked man was ridiculous and improper; and when first the Cretans and then the Lacedaemonians introduced the custom, the wits of that day might equally have ridiculed the innovation."

"No doubt."

"But when experience showed that to let all things be uncovered was far better than to cover them up, and the ludicrous effect to the outward eye vanished before the better principle which reason asserted, then the man was perceived to be a fool who directs the shafts of his ridicule at any other sight but that of folly and vice, or seriously inclines to weigh the beautiful by any other standard but that of the good."

"Very true," he replied.

"First, then, whether the question is to be put in jest or in earnest, let us come to an understanding about the nature of woman: Is she capable of sharing either wholly or partially in the actions of men, or not at all? And is the art of war one of those arts in which she can or can not share? That will be the best way of commencing the inquiry, and will probably lead to the fairest conclusion."

"That will be much the best way."

"Shall we take the other side first and begin by arguing against ourselves; in this manner the adversary's position will not be undefended."

"Why not?" he said.

"Then let us put a speech into the mouths of our opponents. They will say: 'Socrates and Glaucon, no adversary need convict you, for you yourselves, at the first foundation of the State, admitted the principle that everybody was to do the one work suited to his own nature.' And certainly, if I am not mistaken, such an admission was made by us. 'And do not the natures of men and women differ very much indeed?' And we shall reply: 'Of course they do.' Then we shall be asked whether the tasks assigned to men and to women should not be different, and such as are agreeable to their different natures. Certainly they should. 'But if so, have you not fallen into a serious inconsistency in saying that men and women, whose natures are so entirely different, ought to perform the same actions?'—What defense will you make for us, my good sir, against anyone who offers these objections?"

"That is not an easy question to answer when asked suddenly; and I shall and I do beg of you to draw out the case on our side."

"These are the objections, Glaucon, and there are many others of a like kind, which I foresaw long ago; they made me afraid and reluctant to take in hand any law about the possession and nurture of women and children."

"By Zeus," he said, "the problem to be solved is anything but easy."

"Why yes," I said, "but the fact is that when a man is out of his depth, whether he has fallen into a little swimming bath or into mid-ocean, he has to swim all the same."

"Very true."

"And must not we swim and try to reach the shore—we will hope that Arion's dolphin [5] or some other miraculous help may save us?"

"I suppose so," he said.

"Well then, let us see if any way of escape can be found. We acknowledged—did we not? that different natures ought to have different pursuits, and that men's and women's natures are different. And now what are we saying? That different natures ought to have the same pursuits; this is the inconsistency which is charged upon us."

"Precisely."

"Verily, Glaucon," I said, "glorious is the power of the art of contradiction!"

"Why do you say so?"

"Because I think that many a man falls into the practice against his will. When he thinks that he is reasoning he is really disputing, just because he cannot define and divide, and so know that of which he is speaking; and he will pursue a merely verbal opposition in the spirit of contention and not of fair discussion."

"Yes," he replied, "such is very often the case; but what has that to do with us and our argument?"

"A great deal; for there is certainly a danger of our getting unintentionally into a verbal opposition."

"In what way?"

"Why we valiantly and pugnaciously insist upon the verbal truth, that different natures ought to have different pursuits, but we never considered at all what was the meaning of sameness or difference of

---

5 The tale of the sweet singer Arion, who was compelled by his wicked shipmates to throw himself into the sea and was saved by a dolphin that bore him to land on his back, is told by Herodotus, I, 24.

nature, or why we distinguished them when we assigned different pursuits to different natures and the same to the same natures."

"Why, no," he said, "that was never considered by us."

I said: "Suppose that by way of illustration we were to ask the question whether there is not an opposition in nature between bald men and hairy men; and if this is admitted by us, then, if bald men are cobblers, we should forbid the hairy men to be cobblers, and conversely?"

"That would be a jest," he said.

"Yes," I said, "a jest; and why? because we never meant when we constructed the State, that the opposition of natures should extend to every difference, but only to those differences which affected the pursuit in which the individual is engaged; we should have argued, for example, that a physician and one who is in mind a physician may be said to have the same nature."

"True."

"Whereas the physician and the carpenter have different natures?"

"Certainly."

"And if," I said, "the male and female sex appear to differ in their fitness for any art or pursuit, we should say that such pursuit or art ought to be assigned to one or the other of them; but if the difference consists only in women bearing and men begetting children, this does not amount to a proof that a woman differs from a man in respect of the sort of education she should receive; and we shall therefore continue to maintain that our guardians and their wives ought to have the same pursuits."

"Very true," he said.

"Next, we shall ask our opponent how, in reference to any of the pursuits or arts of civic life, the nature of a woman differs from that of a man?"

"That will be quite fair."

"And perhaps he, like yourself, will reply that to give a sufficient answer on the instant is not easy; but after a little reflection there is no difficulty."

"Yes, perhaps."

"Suppose then that we invite him to accompany us in the argument, and then we may hope to show him that there is nothing peculiar in the constitution of women which would affect them in the administration of the State."

"By all means."

"Let us say to him: Come now, and we will ask you a question: when you spoke of a nature gifted or not gifted in any respect, did you mean to say that one man will acquire a thing easily, another with difficulty; a little learning will lead the one to discover a great deal; whereas the other, after much study and application, no sooner learns than he forgets; or again, did you mean, that the one has a body which is a good servant to his mind, while the body of the other is a hindrance to him?—would not these be the sort of differences which distinguish the man gifted by nature from the one who is ungifted?"

"No one will deny that."

"And can you mention any pursuit of mankind in which the male sex has not all these gifts and qualities in a higher degree than the female? Need I waste time in speaking of the art of weaving, and the management of pancakes and preserves, in which womankind does really appear to be great, and in which for her to be beaten by a man is of all things the most absurd?"

"You are quite right," he replied, "in maintaining the general inferiority of the female sex: although many women are in many things superior to many men, yet on the whole what you say is true."

"And if so, my friend," I said, "there is no special faculty of administration in a state which a woman has because she is a woman, or which a man has by virtue of his sex, but the gifts of nature are alike diffused in both; all the pursuits of men are the pursuits of women also, but in all of them a woman is inferior to a man."

"Very true."

"Then are we to impose all our enactments on men and none of them on women?"

"That will never do."

"One woman has a gift of healing, another not; one is a musician, and another has no music in her nature?"

"Very true."

"And one woman has a turn for gymnastic and military exercises, and another is unwarlike and hates gymnastics?"

"Certainly."

"And one woman is a philosopher, and another is an enemy of philosophy; one has spirit, and another is without spirit?"

"That is also true."

"Then one woman will have the temper of a guardian, and another not. Was not the selection of the male guardians determined by differences of this sort?"

"Yes."

"Men and women alike possess the qualities which make a guardian; they differ only in their comparative strength or weakness."

"Obviously."

"And those women who have such qualities are to be selected as the companions and colleagues of men who have similar qualities and whom they resemble in capacity and in character?"

"Very true."

"And ought not the same natures to have the same pursuits?"

"They ought."

"Then, as we were saying before, there is nothing unnatural in assigning music and gymnastic to the wives of the guardians—to that point we come round again."

"Certainly not."

"The law which we then enacted was agreeable to nature, and therefore not an impossibility or mere aspiration; and the contrary practice, which prevails at present, is in reality a violation of nature."

"That appears to be true."

"We had to consider, first, whether our proposals were possible, and secondly whether they were the most beneficial?"

"Yes."

"And the possibility has been acknowledged?"

"Yes."

"The very great benefit has next to be established?"

"Quite so."

"You will admit that the same education which makes a man a good guardian will make a woman a good guardian; for their original nature is the same?"

"Yes."

"I should like to ask you a question."

"What is it?"

"Would you say that all men are equal in excellence, or is one man better than another?"

"The latter."

"And in the commonwealth which we were founding do you conceive the guardians who have been brought up on our model system to be more perfect men, or the cobblers whose education has been cobbling?"

"What a ridiculous question!"

"You have answered me," I replied: "Well, and may we not further say that our guardians are the best of our citizens?"

"By far the best."

"And will not their wives be the best women?"

"Yes, by far the best."

"And can there be anything better for the interests of the State than that the men and women of a State should be as good as possible?"

"There can be nothing better."

"And this is what the arts of music and gymnastic, when present in such manner as we have described, will accomplish?"

"Certainly."

"Then we have made an enactment not only possible but in the highest degree beneficial to the State?"

"True."

"Then let the wives of our guardians strip, for their virtue will be their robe, and let them share in the toils of war and the defense of their country; only in the distribution of labors the lighter are to be assigned to the women, who are the weaker natures, but in other respects their duties are to be the same. And as for the man who laughs at naked women exercising their bodies from the best of motives, in his laughter he is plucking 'A fruit of unripe wisdom,' [6] and he himself is ignorant of what he is laughing at, or what he is about; —for that is, and ever will be, the best of sayings, 'That the useful is the noble and the hurtful is the base.' "

"Very true."

"Here, then, is one difficulty in our law about women, which we may say that we have now escaped; the wave has not swallowed us up alive for enacting that the guardians of either sex should have all their pursuits in common; to the utility and also to the possibility of this arrangement the consistency of the argument with itself bears witness."

"Yes, that was a mighty wave which you have escaped."

"Yes," I said, "but a greater is coming; you will not think much of this when you see the next."

"Go on; let me see."

"The law," I said, "which is the sequel of this and of all that has preceded, is to the following effect: That the wives of our guardians are to be common,[7] and their children are to be common, and no parent is to know his own child, nor any child his parent."

"Yes," he said, "that is a much greater wave than the other; and the possibility as well as the utility of such a law are far more questionable."

"I do not think," I said, "that there can be any dispute about the very great utility of having wives and children in common; the possibility is quite another matter, and will be very much disputed."

"I think that a good many doubts may be raised about both."

"You imply that the two questions must be combined," I replied. "Now I meant that you should admit the utility; and in this way, as

6 Pindar, *Fragment* 209.

7 Some years before the appearance of the *Republic,* the comedy writer Aristophanes had produced a play, *Ecclesiazusae,* in which the women of Athens took over the city government. The men having made such a glaring failure of politics, it was not hard to convince them that women might perhaps do better and should be given a chance. One of the new laws set up a universal system of free love. There was nothing in this burlesque suggestion, however, remotely like Plato's carefully planned scheme of eugenics by which, breeding from the best, he would steadily raise the quality of his citizen stock.

I thought, I should escape from one of them, and then there would
remain only the possibility."

"But that little attempt is detected, and therefore you will please
to give a defense of both."

"Well," I said, "I submit to my fate. Yet grant me a little favor: let
me feast my mind with the dream as day dreamers are in the habit of
feasting themselves when they are walking alone; for before they
have discovered any means of effecting their wishes—that is a matter
which never troubles them—they would rather not tire themselves [8]
by thinking about possibilities; but assuming that what they desire is
already granted to them, they proceed with their plan, and delight in
detailing what they mean to do when their wish has come true—that
is a way which they have of not doing much good to a capacity which
was never good for much. Now I myself am beginning to lose heart,
and I should like, with your permission, to pass over the question of
possibility at present. Assuming therefore the possibility of the
proposal, I shall now proceed to inquire how the rulers will carry
out these arrangements, and I shall demonstrate that our plan, if
executed, will be of the greatest benefit to the State and to the
guardians. First of all, then, if you have no objection, I will endeavor
with your help to consider the advantages of the measure; and hereafter the question of possibility."

"I have no objection; proceed."

"First, I think that if our rulers and their auxiliaries are to be
worthy of the name which they bear, there must be willingness to
obey in the one and the power of command in the other; the
guardians must themselves obey the laws, and they must also imitate
the spirit of them in any details which are entrusted to their care."

"That is right," he said.

"You," I said, "who are their legislator, having selected the men,
will now select the women and give them to them; they must be as

8 The rest of this sentence is better translated: "By thinking about possibilities
and impossibilities, but assuming their wish fulfilled, proceed to work out the details, imagining happily what they will do when it comes true, thus making still
more idle a mind that was already idle."

far as possible of like natures with them; and they must live in common houses and meet at common meals. None of them will have anything specially his or her own; they will be together, and will be brought up together, and will associate at gymnastic exercises. And so they will be drawn by a necessity of their natures to have intercourse with each other—necessity is not too strong a word, I think?"

"Yes," he said; "necessity, not geometrical, but another sort of necessity which lovers know, and which is far more convincing and constraining to the mass of mankind."

"True," I said; "and this, Glaucon, like all the rest, must proceed after an orderly fashion; in a city of the blessed, licentiousness is an unholy thing which the rulers will forbid."

"Yes," he said, "and it ought not to be permitted."

"Then clearly the next thing will be to make matrimony sacred in the highest degree, and what is most beneficial will be deemed sacred?"

"Exactly."

"And how can marriages be made most beneficial? That is a question which I put to you, because I see in your house dogs for hunting, and of the nobler sort of birds not a few. Now, I beseech you, do tell me, have you ever attended to their pairing and breeding?"

"In what particulars?"

"Why, in the first place, although they are all of a good sort, are not some better than others?"

"True."

"And do you breed from them all indifferently, or do you take care to breed from the best only?"

"From the best."

"And do you take the oldest or the youngest, or only those of ripe age?"

"I choose only those of ripe age."

"And if care was not taken in the breeding, your dogs and birds would greatly deteriorate?"

"Certainly."

"And the same of horses and of animals in general?"

"Undoubtedly."

"Good heavens! my dear friend," I said, "what consummate skill will our rulers need if the same principle holds of the human species!"

"Certainly, the same principle holds; but why does this involve any particular skill?"

"Because," I said, "our rulers will often have to practice upon the body corporate with medicines. Now you know that when patients do not require medicines, but have only to be put under a regimen, the inferior sort of practitioner is deemed to be good enough; but when medicine has to be given, then the doctor should be more of a man."

"That is quite true," he said; "but to what are you alluding?"

"I mean," I replied, "that our rulers will find a considerable dose of falsehood and deceit necessary for the good of their subjects: we were saying that the use of all these things regarded as medicines might be of advantage."

"And we were very right."

"And this lawful use of them seems likely to be often needed in the regulations of marriages and births."

"How so?"

"Why," I said, "the principle has been already laid down that the best of either sex should be united with the best as often, and the inferior with the inferior, as seldom as possible; and that they should rear the offspring of the one sort of union, but not of the other, if the flock is to be maintained in first-rate condition. Now these goings-on must be a secret which the rulers only know, or there will be a further danger of our herd, as the guardians may be termed, breaking out into rebellion."

"Very true."

"Had we not better appoint certain festivals at which we will bring together the brides and bridegrooms, and sacrifices will be offered and suitable hymeneal songs composed by our poets: the number of weddings is a matter which must be left to the discretion of the rulers, whose aim will be to preserve the average of population? There are many other things which they will have to consider, such as the effects of wars and diseases and any similar agencies, in order as far as this is possible to prevent the State from becoming either too large or too small."

"Certainly," he replied.

"We shall have to invent some ingenious kind of lots which the less worthy may draw on each occasion of our bringing them together, and then they will accuse their own ill-luck and not the rulers."

"To be sure," he said.

"And I think that our braver and better youth, besides their other honors and rewards, might have greater facilities of intercourse with women given them; their bravery will be a reason, and such fathers ought to have as many sons as possible."

"True."

"And the proper officers, whether male or female or both, for offices are to be held by women as well as by men—"

"Yes—"

"The proper officers will take the offspring of the good parents to the pen or fold, and there they will deposit them with certain nurses who dwell in a separate quarter; but the offspring of the inferior, or of the better when they chance to be deformed, will be put away in some mysterious, unknown place, as they should be."

"Yes," he said, "that must be done if the breed of the guardians is to be kept pure."

"They will provide for their nurture, and will bring the mothers to the fold when they are full of milk, taking the greatest possible care that no mother recognizes her own child; and other wet-nurses may be engaged if more are required. Care will also be taken that the process of suckling shall not be protracted too long; and the mothers will have no getting up at night or other trouble, but will hand over all this sort of thing to the nurses and attendants."

"You suppose the wives of our guardians to have a fine easy time of it when they are having children."

"Why," said I, "and so they ought. Let us, however, proceed with our scheme. We were saying that the parents should be in the prime of life?"

"Very true."

"And what is the prime of life? May it not be defined as a period of about twenty years in a woman's life, and thirty in a man's?"

"Which years do you mean to include?"

"A woman," I said, "at twenty years of age may begin to bear children to the State, and continue to bear them until forty; a man may begin at five-and-twenty, when he has passed the point at which the pulse of life beats quickest, and continue to beget children until he be fifty-five."

"Certainly," he said, "both in men and women those years are the prime of physical as well as of intellectual vigor."

"Anyone above or below the prescribed ages who takes part in the public hymeneals shall be said to have done an unholy and unrighteous thing; the child of which he is the father, if it steals into life, will have been conceived under auspices very unlike the sacrifices and prayers, which at each hymeneal priestesses and priests and the whole city will offer, that the new generation may be better and more useful than their good and useful parents, whereas his child will be the offspring of darkness and strange lust."

"Very true," he replied.

"And the same law will apply to anyone of those within the prescribed age who forms a connection with any woman in the prime of life without the sanction of the rulers; for we shall say that he is raising up a bastard to the State, uncertified and unconsecrated."

"Very true," he replied.

"This applies, however, only to those who are within the specified age: after that we allow them to range at will, except that a man may not marry his daughter or his daughter's daughter, or his mother or his mother's mother; and women, on the other hand, are prohibited from marrying their sons or fathers, or son's son or father's father, and so on in either direction. And we grant all this, accompanying the permission with strict orders to prevent any embryo which may come into being from seeing the light; and if any force a way to the birth, the parents must understand that the offspring of such an union cannot be maintained, and arrange accordingly."

"That also," he said, "is a reasonable proposition. But how will they know who are fathers and daughters, and so on?"

"They will never know. The way will be this: dating from the day of the hymeneal, the bridegroom who was then married will call all the male children who are born in the seventh and the tenth month afterwards his sons, and the female children his daughters, and they will call him father, and he will call their children his grandchildren, and they will call the elder generation grandfathers and grandmothers. All who were begotten at the time when their fathers and mothers came together will be called their brothers and sisters, and these, as I was saying, will be forbidden to intermarry. This, however, is not to be understood as an absolute prohibition of the marriage of brothers and sisters; if the lot favors them, and they receive the sanction of the Pythian Oracle,[9] the law will allow them."

"Quite right," he replied.

"Such is the scheme, Glaucon, according to which the guardians of our State are to have their wives and families in common. And now you would have the argument show that this community is consistent with the rest of our polity, and also that nothing can be better—would you not?"

"Yes, certainly."

"Shall we try to find a common basis by asking of ourselves what ought to be the chief aim of the legislator in making laws and in the organization of a State—what is the greatest good, and what is the greatest evil, and then consider whether our previous description has the stamp of the good or of the evil?"

"By all means."

"Can there be any greater evil than discord and distraction and plurality where unity ought to reign? or any greater good than the bond of unity?"

"There cannot."

9 Apollo's oracle at Delphi. See *Apology*, note 7.

"And there is unity where there is community of pleasures and pains—where all the citizens are glad or grieved on the same occasions of joy and sorrow?"

"No doubt."

"Yes; and where there is no common but only private feeling a State is disorganized—when you have one half of the world triumphing and the other plunged in grief at the same events happening to the city or the citizens?"

"Certainly."

"Such differences commonly originate in a disagreement about the use of the terms 'mine' and 'not mine,' 'his' and 'not his.' "

"Exactly so."

"And is not that the best-ordered State in which the greatest number of persons apply the terms 'mine' and 'not mine' in the same way to the same thing?"

"Quite true."

"Or that again which most nearly approaches to the condition of the individual—as in the body, when but a finger of one of us is hurt, the whole frame, drawn towards the soul as a center and forming one kingdom under the ruling power therein, feels the hurt and sympathizes all together with the part affected, and we say that the man has a pain in his finger; and the same expression is used about any other part of the body, which has a sensation of pain at suffering or of pleasure at the alleviation of suffering."

"Very true," he replied; "and I agree with you that in the best-ordered State there is the nearest approach to this common feeling which you describe."

"Then when anyone of the citizens experiences any good or evil, the whole State will make his case their own, and will either rejoice or sorrow with him?"

"Yes," he said, "that is what will happen in a well-ordered State."

"It will now be time," I said, "for us to return to our State and see whether this or some other form is most in accordance with these fundamental principles."

"Very good."

"Our State like every other has rulers and subjects?"

"True."

"All of whom will call one another citizens?"

"Of course."

"But is there not another name which people give to their rulers in other States?"

"Generally they call them masters, but in democratic States they simply call them rulers."

"And in our State what other name besides that of citizens do the people give the rulers?"

"They are called saviors and helpers," he replied.

"And what do the rulers call the people?"

"Their maintainers and foster-fathers."

"And what do they call them in other States?"

"Slaves."

"And what do the rulers call one another in other States?"

"Fellow rulers."

"And what in ours?"

"Fellow guardians."

"Did you ever know an example in any other State of a ruler who would speak of one of his colleagues as his friend and of another as not being his friend?"

"Yes, very often."

"And the friend he regards and describes as one in whom he has an interest, and the other as a stranger in whom he has no interest?"

"Exactly."

"But would any of your guardians think or speak of any other guardian as a stranger?"

"Certainly he would not; for everyone whom they meet will be regarded by them either as a brother or sister, or father or mother, or son or daughter, or as the child or parent of those who are thus connected with him."

"Capital," I said; "but let me ask you once more: Shall they be a family in name only; or shall they in all their actions be true to the name? For example, in the use of the word 'father,' would the care

of a father be implied and the filial reverence and duty and obedience
to him which the law commands; and is the violator of these duties to
be regarded as an impious and unrighteous person who is not likely to
receive much good either at the hands of God or of man? Are these to
be or not to be the strains which the children will hear repeated in
their ears by all the citizens about those who are intimated to them to
be their parents and the rest of their kinsfolk?"

"These," he said, "and none other; for what can be more ridiculous than for them to utter the names of family ties with the lips
only and not to act in the spirit of them?"

"Then in our city the language of harmony and concord will be
more often heard than in any other. As I was describing before, when
anyone is well or ill, the universal word will be 'with me it is well' or
'it is ill.' "

"Most true."

"And agreeably to this mode of thinking and speaking, were we
not saying that they will have their pleasures and pains in common?"

"Yes, and so they will."

"And they will have a common interest in the same thing which
they will alike call 'my own,' and having this common interest they
will have a common feeling of pleasure and pain?"

"Yes, far more so than in other States."

"And the reason of this, over and above the general constitution
of the State, will be that the guardians will have a community of
women and children?"

"That will be the chief reason."

"And this unity of feeling we admitted to be the greatest good, as
was implied in our own comparison of a well-ordered State to the
relation of the body and the members, when affected by pleasure or
pain?"

"That we acknowledged, and very rightly."

"Then the community of wives and children among our citizens is
clearly the source of the greatest good to the State?"

"Certainly."

"And this agrees with the other principle which we were affirming—that the guardians were not to have houses or lands or any other property; their pay was to be their food, which they were to receive from the other citizens, and they were to have no private expenses; for we intended them to preserve their true character of guardians."

"Right," he replied.

"Both the community of property and the community of families, as I am saying, tend to make them more truly guardians; they will not tear the city in pieces by differing about 'mine' and 'not mine'; each man dragging any acquisition which he has made into a separate house of his own, where he has a separate wife and children and private pleasures and pains; but all will be affected as far as may be by the same pleasures and pains because they are all of one opinion about what is near and dear to them, and therefore they all tend towards a common end."

"Certainly," he replied.

"And as they have nothing but their persons which they can call their own, suits and complaints will have no existence among them; they will be delivered from all those quarrels of which money or children or relations are the occasion."

"Of course they will."

"Neither will trials for assault or insult ever be likely to occur among them. For that equals should defend themselves against equals we shall maintain to be honorable and right; we shall make the protection of the person a matter of necessity."

"That is good," he said.

"Yes; and there is a further good in the law; viz., that if a man has a quarrel with another he will satisfy his resentment then and there, and not proceed to more dangerous lengths."

"Certainly."

"To the elder shall be assigned the duty of ruling and chastising the younger."

"Clearly."

"Nor can there be a doubt that the younger will not strike or do any other violence to an elder, unless the magistrates command him; nor will he slight him in any way. For there are two guardians, shame and fear, mighty to prevent him: shame, which makes men refrain from laying hands on those who are to them in the relation of parents; fear, that the injured one will be succored by the others who are his brothers, sons, fathers."

"That is true," he replied.

"Then in every way the laws will help the citizens to keep the peace with one another?"

"Yes, there will be no want of peace."

"And as the guardians will never quarrel among themselves there will be no danger of the rest of the city being divided either against them or against one another."

"None whatever."

"I hardly like even to mention the little meannesses of which they will be rid, for they are beneath notice: such, for example, as the flattery of the rich by the poor, and all the pains and pangs which men experience in bringing up a family, and in finding money to buy necessaries for their household, borrowing and then repudiating, getting how they can, and giving the money into the hands of women and slaves to keep—the many evils of so many kinds which people suffer in this way are mean enough and obvious enough, and not worth speaking of."

"Yes," he said, "a man has no need of eyes in order to perceive that."

"And from all these evils they will be delivered, and their life will be blessed as the life of Olympic victors and yet more blessed."

"How so?"

"The Olympic victor," I said, "is deemed happy in receiving a part only of the blessedness which is secured to our citizens, who have won a more glorious victory and have a more complete maintenance at the public cost. For the victory which they have won is the salvation of the whole State; and the crown with which they and their children are crowned is the fullness of all that life needs; they receive rewards from the hands of their country while living, and after death have an honorable burial."

"Yes," he said, "and glorious rewards they are."

"Do you remember," I said, "how in the course of the previous discussion someone who shall be nameless accused us of making our guardians unhappy [10]—they had nothing and might have possessed all things—to whom we replied that, if an occasion offered, we might perhaps hereafter consider this question, but that, as at present advised, we would make our guardians truly guardians, and that we were fashioning the State with a view to the greatest happiness, not of any particular class, but of the whole?"

"Yes, I remember."

"And what do you say, now that the life of our protectors is made out to be far better and nobler than that of Olympic victors—is the life of shoemakers, or any other artisans, or of husbandmen, to be compared with it?"

"Certainly not."

"At the same time I ought here to repeat what I have said elsewhere, that if any of our guardians shall try to be happy in such a manner that he will cease to be a guardian, and is not content with this safe and harmonious life, which, in our judgment, is of all lives the best, but infatuated by some youthful conceit of happiness which gets up into his head shall seek to appropriate the whole state to himself, then he will have to learn how wisely Hesiod spoke, when he said, 'half is more than the whole.' " [11]

"If he were to consult me, I should say to him: Stay where you are, when you have the offer of such a life."

"You agree then," I said, "that men and women are to have a common way of life such as we have described—common education, common children; and they are to watch over the citizens in common whether abiding in the city or going out to war; they are to keep watch together, and to hunt together like dogs; and always and in all things, as far as they are able, women are to share with the men? And in so doing they will do what is best, and will not violate, but preserve the natural relation of the sexes."

"I agree with you," he replied.

10 This was at the beginning of Book IV, page 306.
11 Hesiod. *Works and Days*, 40.

"The inquiry," I said, "has yet to be made, whether such a community will be found possible—as among other animals, so also among men—and if possible, in what way possible?"

"You have anticipated the question which I was about to suggest."

"There is no difficulty," I said, "in seeing how war will be carried on by them."

"How?"

"Why, of course they will go on expeditions together; and will take with them any of their children who are strong enough, that, after the manner of the artisan's child, they may look on at the work which they will have to do when they are grown up; and besides looking on they will have to help and be of use in war, and to wait upon their fathers and mothers. Did you never observe in the arts how the potters' boys look on and help, long before they touch the wheel?"

"Yes, I have."

"And shall potters be more careful in educating their children and in giving them the opportunity of seeing and practicing their duties than our guardians will be?"

"The idea is ridiculous," he said.

Children who are allowed on the battlefield should be protected from undue risks. Honors are to be paid to brave soldiers.

"Next, how shall our soldiers treat their enemies? What about this?"

"In what respect do you mean?"

"First of all, in regard to slavery? Do you think it right that Hellenes should enslave Hellenic States,[12] or allow others to enslave them, if they can help? Should not their custom be to spare them, considering the danger which there is that the whole race may one day fall under the yoke of the barbarians?"

"To spare them is infinitely better."

"Then no Hellene should be owned by them as a slave; that is a

[12] The Greek national name for themselves was Hellenes. The Romans called them Greci, whence our Greeks. Socrates now prescribes a code of humanity in war, at least for Greeks fighting Greeks.

rule which they will observe and advise the other Hellenes to observe."

"Certainly," he said; "they will in this way be united against the
barbarians and will keep their hands off one another."

"Next as to the slain; ought the conquerors," I said, "to take anything but their armor? Does not the practice of despoiling an enemy
afford an excuse for not facing the battle? Cowards skulk about the
dead, pretending that they are fulfilling a duty, and many an army
before now has been lost from this love of plunder."

"Very true."

"And is there not illiberality and avarice in robbing a corpse, and
also a degree of meanness and womanishness in making an enemy
of the dead body when the real enemy has flown away and left only
his fighting gear behind him—is not this rather like a dog who cannot
get at his assailant, quarreling with the stones which strike him instead?"

"Very like a dog," he said.

"Then we must abstain from spoiling the dead or hindering their
burial?"

"Yes," he replied, "we most certainly must."

"Neither shall we offer up arms at the temples of the gods, least
of all the arms of Hellenes, if we care to maintain good feeling with
other Hellenes; and, indeed, we have reason to fear that the offering
of spoils taken from kinsmen may be a pollution unless commanded
by the god himself?"

"Very true."

"Again, as to the devastation of Hellenic territory or the burning
of houses, what is to be the practice?"

"May I have the pleasure," he said, "of hearing your opinion?"

"Both should be forbidden, in my judgment; I would take the
annual produce and no more. Shall I tell you why?"

"Pray do."

"Why, you see, there is a difference in the names 'discord' [13] and

13 Or faction.

PLATO

'war,' and I imagine that there is also a difference in their natures; the one is expressive of what is internal and domestic, the other of what is external and foreign; and the first of the two is termed discord, and only the second, war."

"That is a very proper distinction," he replied.

"And may I not observe with equal propriety that the Hellenic race is all united together by ties of blood and friendship, and alien and strange to the barbarians?"

"Very good," he said.

"And therefore when Hellenes fight with barbarians and barbarians with Hellenes, they will be described by us as being at war when they fight, and by nature enemies, and this kind of antagonism should be called war; but when Hellenes fight with one another we shall say that Hellas is then in a state of disorder and discord, they being by nature friends; and such enmity is to be called discord."

"I agree."

"Consider then," I said, "when that which we have acknowledged to be discord occurs, and a city is divided, if both parties destroy the lands and burn the houses of one another, how wicked does the strife appear! No true lover of his country would bring himself to tear in pieces his own nurse and mother: There might be reason in the conqueror depriving the conquered of their harvest, but still they would have the idea of peace in their hearts and would not mean to go on fighting forever."

"Yes," he said, "that is a better temper than the other."

"And will not the city, which you are founding, be an Hellenic city?"

"It ought to be," he replied.

"Then will not the citizens be good and civilized?"

"Yes, very civilized."

"And will they not be lovers of Hellas, and think of Hellas as their own land, and share in the common temples?"

"Most certainly."

"And any difference which arises among them will be regarded

by them as discord only—a quarrel among friends, which is not to be
called a war?"

"Certainly not."

"Then they will quarrel as those who intend some day to be
reconciled?"

"Certainly."

"They will use friendly correction, but will not enslave or destroy
their opponents; they will be correctors, not enemies?"

"Just so."

"And as they are Hellenes themselves they will not devastate
Hellas, nor will they burn houses, nor ever suppose that the whole
population of a city—men, women, and children—are equally their
enemies, for they know that the guilt of war is always confined to a
few persons and that the many are their friends. And for all these
reasons they will be unwilling to waste their lands and raze their
houses; their enmity to them will only last until the many innocent
sufferers have compelled the guilty few to give satisfaction?"

"I agree," he said, "that our citizens should thus deal with their
Hellenic enemies; and with barbarians as the Hellenes now deal with
one another."

"Then let us enact this law also for our guardians: that they are
neither to devastate the lands of Hellenes nor to burn their houses."

"Agreed; and we may agree also in thinking that these, like all our
previous enactments, are very good.

"But still I must say, Socrates, that if you are allowed to go on in
this way you will entirely forget the other question which at the
commencement of this discussion you thrust aside: Is such an order
of things possible, and how, if at all? For I am quite ready to acknowledge that the plan which you propose, if only feasible, would do all
sorts of good to the State. I will add, what you have omitted, that
your citizens will be the bravest of warriors, and will never leave their
ranks, for they will all know one another, and each will call the other
father, brother, son; and if you suppose the women to join their
armies, whether in the same rank or in the rear, either as a terror to
the enemy, or as auxiliaries in case of need, I know that they will then

be absolutely invincible; and there are many domestic advantages which might also be mentioned and which I also fully acknowledge; but, as I admit all these advantages and as many more as you please, if only this State of yours were to come into existence, we need say no more about them; assuming then the existence of the State, let us now turn to the question of possibility and ways and means—the rest may be left."

"If I loiter for a moment, you instantly make a raid upon me," I said, "and have no mercy; I have hardly escaped the first and second waves, and you seem not to be aware that you are now bringing upon me the third, which is the greatest and heaviest. When you have seen and heard the third wave, I think you will be more considerate and will acknowledge that some fear and hesitation was natural respecting a proposal so extraordinary as that which I have now to state and investigate."

"The more appeals of this sort which you make," he said, "the more determined are we that you shall tell us how such a State is possible: speak out and at once."

"Let me begin by reminding you that we found our way hither in the search after justice and injustice."

"True," he replied; "but what of that?"

"I was only going to ask whether, if we have discovered them, we are to require that the just man should in nothing fail of absolute justice; or may we be satisfied with an approximation, and the attainment in him of a higher degree of justice than is to be found in other men?"

"The approximation will be enough."

"We were inquiring into the nature of absolute justice and into the character of the perfectly just, and into injustice and the perfectly unjust, that we might have an ideal. We were to look at these in order that we might judge of our own happiness and unhappiness according to the standard which they exhibited and the degree in which we resembled them, but not with any view of showing that they could exist in fact."

"True," he said.

"Would a painter be any the worse because, after having delineated with consummate art an ideal of a perfectly beautiful man, he was unable to show that any such man could ever have existed?"

"He would be none the worse."

"Well, and were we not creating an ideal of a perfect State?"

"To be sure."

"And is our theory a worse theory because we are unable to prove the possibility of a city being ordered in the manner described?" [14]

"Surely not," he replied.

"That is the truth," I said. "But if, at your request, I am to try and show how and under what conditions the possibility is highest, I must ask you, having this in view, to repeat your former admissions."

"What admissions?"

"I want to know whether ideals are ever fully realized in language? Does not the word express more than the fact, and must not the actual, whatever a man may think, always, in the nature of things, fall short of the truth? What do you say?"

"I agree."

"Then you must not insist on my proving that the actual State will in every respect coincide with the ideal: if we are only able to discover how a city may be governed nearly as we proposed, you will admit that we have discovered the possibility which you demand; and will be contented. I am sure that I should be contented—will not you?"

"Yes, I will."

"Let me next endeavor to show what is that fault in States which is the cause of their present maladministration, and what is the least change which will enable a State to pass into the truer form; and let the change, if possible, be of one thing only, or, if not, of two; at any rate, let the changes be as few and slight as possible."

"Certainly," he replied.

"I think," I said, "that there might be a reform of the State if only

---

14 Socrates is justifying faith in an ideal, even if that ideal may never be fully realized on earth. He has more to say to the same effect at the end of Book IX, page 476.

one change were made, which is not a slight or easy though still a possible one."

"What is it?" he said.

"Now then," I said, "I go to meet that which I liken to the greatest of the waves; yet shall the word be spoken, even though the wave break and drown me in laughter and dishonor; and do you mark my words."

"Proceed."

I said: "*Until philosophers are kings, or the kings and princes of this world have the spirit and power of philosophy, and political greatness and wisdom meet in one, and those commoner natures who pursue either to the exclusion of the other are compelled to stand aside, cities will never have rest from their evils,—no, nor the human race, as I believe,—and then only will this our State have a possibility of life and behold the light of day.*[15] Such was the thought, my dear Glaucon, which I would fain have uttered if it had not seemed too extravagant; for to be convinced that in no other State can there be happiness private or public is indeed a hard thing."

"Socrates, what do you mean? I would have you consider that the word which you have uttered is one at which numerous persons, and very respectable persons too, in a figure pulling off their coats all in a moment, and seizing any weapon that comes to hand, will run at you might and main, before you know where you are, intending to do heaven knows what; and if you don't prepare an answer, and put yourself in motion, you will be 'pared by their fine wits,' and no mistake."

"You got me into the scrape," I said.

"And I was quite right; however, I will do all I can to get you out of it; but I can only give you good will and good advice, and, perhaps, I may be able to fit answers to your questions better than another—that is all. And now, having such an auxiliary, you must do your best to show the unbelievers that you are right."

"I ought to try," I said, "since you offer me such invaluable assist-

---

15 This is probably the most quoted sentence in all Plato's dialogues.

ance. And I think that, if there is to be a chance of our escaping, we must explain to them whom we mean when we say that philosophers are to rule in the State; then we shall be able to defend ourselves. There will be discovered to be some natures who ought to study philosophy and to be leaders in the State; and others who are not born to be philosophers, and are meant to be followers rather than leaders."

Socrates tells how the natural philosopher may be recognized in youth. He "has a taste for every sort of knowledge," is "curious to learn and never satisfied."

He said: "Who then are the true philosophers?"

"Those," I said, "who are lovers of the vision of truth."

"That is also good," he said; "but I should like to know what you mean?"

"To another," I replied, "I might have a difficulty in explaining; but I am sure that you will admit a proposition which I am about to make."

"What is the proposition?"

"That since beauty is the opposite of ugliness, they are two?"

"Certainly."

"And inasmuch as they are two, each of them is one?"

"True again."

"And of just and unjust, good and evil, and of every other class,[16] the same remark holds: taken singly, each of them is one; but from the various combinations of them with actions and things and with one another, they are seen in all sorts of lights and appear many?"

"Very true."

"And this is the distinction which I draw between the sight-loving,

16 Better translated "and of all ideas." Plato is putting into Socrates' mouth his own famous theory of Ideas or Absolute Reality. Absolute and perfect justice, goodness, and beauty exist in some invisible realm, each in itself a unity. But to him who sees only their varying influences and effects upon our world of natural objects and human acts they appear each as merely a shifting conglomerate of more or less just, good, or beautiful objects and acts. A true philosopher looks past this multitude of imperfectly beautiful things to the single perfect and eternal idea of beauty behind them.

art-loving, practical class and those of whom I am speaking, and who are alone worthy of the name of philosophers."

"How do you distinguish them?" he said.

"The lovers of sounds and sights," I replied, "are, as I conceive, fond of fine tones and colors and forms and all the artificial products that are made out of them, but their mind is incapable of seeing or loving absolute beauty."

"True," he replied.

"Few are they who are able to attain to the sight of this."

"Very true."

"And he who, having a sense of beautiful things has no sense of absolute beauty, or who, if another lead him to a knowledge of that beauty is unable to follow—of such an one I ask, Is he awake or in a dream only? Reflect: is not the dreamer, sleeping or waking, one who likens dissimilar things, who puts the copy in the place of the real object?"

"I should certainly say that such an one was dreaming."

"But take the case of the other, who recognizes the existence of absolute beauty and is able to distinguish the idea from the objects which participate in the idea, neither putting the objects in the place of the idea nor the idea in the place of the objects—is he a dreamer, or is he awake?"

"He is wide awake."

"And may we not say that the mind of the one who knows has knowledge, and that the mind of the other, who opines only, has opinion?"

"Certainly."

"But suppose that the latter should quarrel with us and dispute our statement, can we administer any soothing cordial or advice to him, without revealing to him that there is sad disorder in his wits?"

"We must certainly offer him some good advice," he replied.

"Come, then, and let us think of something to say to him. Shall we begin by assuring him that he is welcome to any knowledge which he may have, and that we are rejoiced at his having it? But we should like to ask him a question: Does he who has knowledge know something or nothing? (You must answer for him.)"

"I answer that he knows something."

"Something that is or is not?"

"Something that is; for how can that which is not ever be known?"

"And are we assured, after looking at the matter from many points of view, that absolute being is or may be absolutely known, but that the utterly non-existent is utterly unknown?"

"Nothing can be more certain."

"Good. But if there be anything which is of such a nature as to be and not to be, that will have a place intermediate between pure being and the absolute negation of being?"

"Yes, between them."

"And, as knowledge corresponded to being and ignorance of necessity to not-being, for that intermediate between being and not-being there has to be discovered a corresponding intermediate between ignorance and knowledge, if there be such?"

"Certainly."

Socrates explains that there are three stages of being. There are first the two extremes, one absolute, unchangeable, pure being, what Plato calls the Idea; the other, complete non-being or nothingness. In between them is our world of intermediate, material objects, that neither perfectly are nor are not. Corresponding to these three stages of being are the three stages of human intelligence. First is true knowledge, by which we know clearly what we can of absolute being or the world of Ideas. Second is ignorance, our state as regards non-being. Third is opinion, the faulty and uncertain knowledge we have of the shifting world of matter.

"And in that interval there has now been discovered something which we call opinion?"

"There has."

"Then what remains to be discovered is the object which partakes equally of the nature of being and not-being, and cannot rightly be termed either, pure and simple; this unknown term, when discovered, we may truly call the subject of opinion, and assign each to their proper faculty—the extremes to the faculties of the extremes and the mean to the faculty of the mean."

"True."

"This being premised, I would ask the gentleman who is of opinion that there is no absolute or unchangeable idea of beauty—in whose opinion the beautiful is the manifold—he, I say, your lover of beautiful sights, who cannot bear to be told that the beautiful is one, and the just is one, or that anything is one—to him I would appeal, saying, Will you be so very kind, sir, as to tell us whether, of all these beautiful things, there is one which will not be found ugly; or of the just, which will not be found unjust; or of the holy, which will not also be unholy?"

"No," he replied; "the beautiful will in some point of view be found ugly; and the same is true of the rest."

"And may not the many which are doubles be also halves?—doubles, that is of one thing, and halves of another?"

"Quite true."

"And things great and small, heavy and light, as they are termed, will not be denoted by these any more than by the opposite names?"

"True; both these and the opposite names will always attach to all of them."

"And can any one of those many things which are called by particular names be said to be this rather than not to be this?"

He replied: "They are like the punning riddles which are asked at feasts or the children's puzzle about the eunuch aiming at the bat, with what he hit him, as they say in the puzzle, and upon what the bat was sitting.[17] The individual objects of which I am speaking are

[17] The riddle is put into English by Shorey in the Loeb edition of the *Republic*, I, 531, note c.

> *A tale there is, a man, yet not a man,*
> *Seeing, saw not, a bird and not a bird,*
> *Perching upon a bough and not a bough,*
> *And hit it—not, with a stone and not a stone.*

The answer is contained in the words, "eunuch, bat, reed and pumice stone."

also a riddle, and have a double sense: nor can you fix them in your mind, either as being or not-being, or both, or neither."

"Then what will you do with them?" I said. "Can they have a better place than between being and not-being? For they are clearly not in greater darkness or negation than not-being, or more full of light and existence than being."

"That is quite true," he said.

"Thus then we seem to have discovered that the many ideas which the multitude entertain about the beautiful and about all other things are tossing about in some region which is half-way between pure being and pure not-being?" [18]

"We have."

"Yes; and we had before agreed that anything of this kind which we might find was to be described as matter of opinion, and not as matter of knowledge; being the intermediate flux which is caught and detained by the intermediate faculty."

"Quite true."

"Then those who see the many beautiful, and who yet neither see absolute beauty, nor can follow any guide who points the way thither; who see the many just, and not absolute justice, and the like —such persons may be said to have opinion but not knowledge?"

"That is certain."

"But those who see the absolute and eternal and immutable may be said to know, and not to have opinion only?"

"Neither can that be denied."

"The one love and embrace the subjects of knowledge, the other those of opinion? The latter are the same, as I dare say you will remember, who listened to sweet sounds and gazed upon fair colors, but would not tolerate the existence of absolute beauty."

"Yes, I remember."

"Shall we then be guilty of any impropriety in calling them lovers

18 In other words, the notions which men who know only the imperfect images of beauty and justice in this world form of beauty and justice themselves will be as unstable and variable as are the images on which they are based.

of opinion rather than lovers of wisdom, and will they be very angry with us for thus describing them?"

"I shall tell them not to be angry; no man should be angry at what is true."

"But those who love the truth in each thing are to be called lovers of wisdom and not lovers of opinion."

"Assuredly."

BOOK VI

Nature of the true philosopher, "spectator of all time and all existence." Contribution of the philosopher to the state. The Idea of the Good.

"AND thus, Glaucon, after the argument has gone a weary way, the true and the false philosophers have at length appeared in view."

"I do not think," he said, "that the way could have been shortened."

"I suppose not," I said; "and yet I believe that we might have had a better view of both of them if the discussion could have been confined to this one subject and if there were not many other questions awaiting us, which he who desires to see in what respect the life of the just differs from that of the unjust must consider."

"And what is the next question?" he asked.

"Surely," I said, "the one which follows next in order. Inasmuch as philosophers only are able to grasp the eternal and unchangeable, and those who wander in the region of the many and variable are not philosophers, I must ask you which of the two classes should be the rulers of our State?"

"And how can we rightly answer that question?"

"Whichever of the two are best able to guard the laws and institutions of our State—let them be our guardians."

"Very good."

"Neither," I said, "can there be any question that the guardian who is to keep anything should have eyes rather than no eyes?"

"There can be no question of that."

"And are not those who are verily and indeed wanting in the knowledge of the true being of each thing, and who have in their souls no clear pattern, and are unable as with a painter's eye to look at the absolute truth and to that original to repair, and having perfect vision of the other world to order the laws about beauty, goodness, justice in this, if not already ordered, and to guard and preserve the order of them—are not such persons, I ask, simply blind?"

"Truly," he replied, "they are much in that condition."

"And shall they be our guardians when there are others who, besides being their equals in experience and falling short of them in no particular of virtue, also know the very truth of each thing?"

"There can be no reason," he said, "for rejecting those who have this greatest of all great qualities; they must always have the first place unless they fail in some other respect."

"Suppose then," I said, "that we determine how far they can unite this and the other excellences."

"By all means."

"In the first place, as we began by observing, the nature of the philosopher has to be ascertained. We must come to an understanding about him, and, when we have done so, then, if I am not mistaken, we shall also acknowledge that such a union of qualities is possible, and that those in whom they are united, and those only, should be rulers in the State."

"What do you mean?"

"Let us suppose that philosophical minds always love knowledge of a sort which shows them the eternal nature not varying from generation and corruption."

"Agreed."

"And further," I said, "let us agree that they are lovers of all true being; there is no part whether greater or less, or more or less honorable, which they are willing to renounce; as we said before of the lover and the man of ambition."

"True."

"And if they are to be what we were describing, is there not another quality which they should also possess?"

"What quality?"

"Truthfulness: they will never intentionally receive into their mind falsehood, which is their detestation, and they will love the truth."

"Yes, that may be safely affirmed of them."

" 'May be,' my friend," I replied, "is not the word; say rather, 'must be affirmed': for he whose nature is amorous of anything cannot help loving all that belongs or is akin to the object of his affections."

"Right," he said.

"And is there anything more akin to wisdom than truth?"

"How can there be?"

"Can the same nature be a lover of wisdom and a lover of falsehood?"

"Never."

"The true lover of learning then must from his earliest youth, as far as in him lies, desire all truth?"

"Assuredly."

"But then again, as we know by experience, he whose desires are strong in one direction will have them weaker in others; they will be like a stream which has been drawn off into another channel."

"True."

"He whose desires are drawn towards knowledge in every form will be absorbed in the pleasures of the soul, and will hardly feel bodily pleasure—I mean, if he be a true philosopher and not a sham one."

"That is most certain."

"Such a one is sure to be temperate and the reverse of covetous; for the motives which make another man desirous of having and spending have no place in his character."

"Very true."

"Another criterion of the philosophical nature has also to be considered."

"What is that?"

"There should be no secret corner of illiberality; nothing can be more antagonistic than meanness to a soul which is ever longing after the whole of things both divine and human."

"Most true," he replied.

"Then how can he who has magnificence of mind and is the spectator of all time and all existence, think much of human life?"

"He cannot."

"Or can such a one account death fearful?"

"No indeed."

"Then the cowardly and mean nature has no part in true philosophy?"

"Certainly not."

"Or again: can he who is harmoniously constituted, who is not covetous or mean, or a boaster, or a coward—can he, I say, ever be unjust or hard in his dealings?"

"Impossible."

"Then you will soon observe whether a man is just and gentle, or rude and unsociable; these are the signs which distinguish even in youth the philosophical nature from the unphilosophical."

"True."

"There is another point which should be remarked."

"What point?"

"Whether he has or has not a pleasure in learning; for no one will love that which gives him pain, and in which after much toil he makes little progress."

"Certainly not."

"And again, if he is forgetful and retains nothing of what he learns, will he not be an empty vessel?"

"That is certain."

"Laboring in vain, he must end in hating himself and his fruitless occupation?"

"Yes."

"Then a soul which forgets cannot be ranked among genuine philosophic natures; we must insist that the philosopher should have a good memory?"

"Certainly."

"And once more, the inharmonious and unseemly nature can only tend to disproportion?"

"Undoubtedly."

"And do you consider truth to be akin to proportion or to disproportion?"

"To proportion."

"Then, besides other qualities, we must try to find a naturally well-proportioned and gracious mind, which will move spontaneously towards the true being of everything."

"Certainly."

"Well, and do not all these qualities, which we have been enumerating, go together, and are they not, in a manner, necessary to a soul, which is to have a full and perfect participation of being?"

"They are absolutely necessary," he replied.

"And must not that be a blameless study which he only can pursue who has the gift of a good memory, and is quick to learn,—noble, gracious, the friend of truth, justice, courage, temperance, who are his kindred?"

"The god of jealousy himself," he said, "could find no fault with such a study."

"And to men like him," I said, "when perfected by years and education, and to these only you will entrust the State." [1]

Here Adeimantus interposed and said: "To these statements, Socrates, no one can offer a reply; but when you talk in this way, a strange feeling passes over the minds of your hearers: They fancy that they are led astray a little at each step in the argument, owing to their own want of skill in asking and answering questions; these

---

1 Socrates has now drawn a portrait of the philosopher statesman to whom, in contrast to the grasping politician, his ideal state can be safely entrusted. Yet in another moment he will admit that philosophers can make a failure of politics.

littles accumulate, and at the end of the discussion they are found to have sustained a mighty overthrow and all their former notions appear to be turned upside down. And as unskillful players of draughts [2] are at last shut up by their more skillful adversaries and have no piece to move, so they too find themselves shut up at last; for they have nothing to say in this new game of which words are the counters; and yet all the time they are in the right. The observation is suggested to me by what is now occurring. For any one of us might say, that although in words he is not able to meet you at each step of the argument, he sees as a fact that the votaries of philosophy, when they carry on the study, not only in youth as a part of education, but as the pursuit of their maturer years, most of them become strange monsters, not to say utter rogues, and that those who may be considered the best of them are made useless to the world by the very study which you extol."

"Well, and do you think that those who say so are wrong?"

"I cannot tell," he replied; "but I should like to know what is your opinion."

"Hear my answer; I am of opinion that they are quite right."

"Then how can you be justified in saying that cities will not cease from evil until philosophers rule in them, when philosophers are acknowledged by us to be of no use to them?"

"You ask a question," I said, "to which a reply can only be given in a parable."

"Yes, Socrates; and that is a way of speaking to which you are not at all accustomed, I suppose."

"I perceive," I said, "that you are vastly amused at having plunged me into such a hopeless discussion; but now hear the parable, and then you will be still more amused at the meagerness of my imagination: for the manner in which the best men are treated in their own States is so grievous that no single thing on earth is comparable to it; and therefore, if I am to plead their cause, I must have recourse to fiction, and put together a figure made up of many things, like the

2 Or checkers.

fabulous unions of goats and stags which are found in pictures. Imagine then a fleet or a ship in which there is a captain [3] who is taller and stronger than any of the crew, but he is a little deaf and has a similar infirmity in sight, and his knowledge of navigation is not much better. The sailors are quarreling with one another about the steering—everyone is of opinion that he has a right to steer, though he has never learned the art of navigation and cannot tell who taught him or when he learned, and will further assert that it cannot be taught, and they are ready to cut in pieces anyone who says the contrary. They throng about the captain, begging and praying him to commit the helm to them; and if at any time they do not prevail, but others are preferred to them, they kill the others or throw them overboard, and having first chained up the noble captain's senses with drink or some narcotic drug, they mutiny and take possession of the ship and make free with the stores; thus, eating and drinking, they proceed on their voyage in such manner as might be expected of them. Him who is their partisan and cleverly aids them in their plot for getting the ship out of the captain's hands into their own whether by force or persuasion, they compliment with the name of sailor, pilot, able seaman, and abuse the other sort of man, whom they call a good-for-nothing; but that the true pilot must pay attention to the year and seasons and sky and stars and winds, and whatever else belongs to his art, if he intends to be really qualified for the command of a ship, and that he must and will be the steerer, whether other people like or not—the possibility of this union of authority with the steerer's art has never seriously entered into their thoughts or been made part of their calling. Now in vessels which are in a state of mutiny and by sailors who are mutineers, how will the true pilot [4] be regarded? Will he not be called by them a prater, a star-gazer, a good-for-nothing?"

3 The ship's captain, strong and tall but a little deaf and a little weaksighted and knowing not much about the art of navigation, is a figure of the Athenian democracy. The impudent, ungovernable sailors are the self-seeking, cheap politicians who plot to get control of the ship of state.

4 The trained, patriotic philosopher statesman.

"Of course," said Adeimantus.

"Then you will hardly need," I said, "to hear the interpretation of the figure, which describes the true philosopher in his relation to the State; for you understand already."

"Certainly."

"Then suppose you now take this parable to the gentleman who is surprised at finding that philosophers have no honor in their cities; explain it to him and try to convince him that their having honor would be far more extraordinary."

"I will."

"Say to him, that, in deeming the best votaries of philosophy to be useless to the rest of the world, he is right; but also tell him to attribute their uselessness to the fault of those who will not use them, and not to themselves. The pilot should not humbly beg the sailors to be commanded by him—that is not the order of nature; neither are 'the wise to go to the doors of the rich' [5]—the ingenious author of this saying told a lie—but the truth is, that, when a man is ill, whether he be rich or poor, to the physician he must go, and he who wants to be governed, to him who is able to govern. The ruler who is good for anything ought not to beg his subjects to be ruled by him; although the present governors of mankind are of a different stamp; they may be justly compared to the mutinous sailors, and the true helmsmen to those who are called by them good-for-nothings and star-gazers."

"Precisely so," he said.

"For these reasons, and among men like these, philosophy, the noblest pursuit of all, is not likely to be much esteemed by those of the opposite faction; not that the greatest and most lasting injury is done to her by her opponents, but by her own professing followers, the same of whom you suppose the accuser to say, that the greater number of them are arrant rogues, and the best are useless; in which opinion I agreed."

"Yes."

---

5 A saying ascribed to the poet Simonides.

"And the reason why the good [6] are useless has now been explained?"

"True."

*　　*　　*　　*　　*

"And we have next to consider the corruptions of the philosophic nature, why so many are spoiled and so few escape spoiling—I am speaking of those who were said to be useless but not wicked—and, when we have done with them, we will speak of the imitators of philosophy, what manner of men are they who aspire after a profession which is above them and of which they are unworthy, and then, by their manifold inconsistencies, bring upon philosophy, and upon all philosophers, that universal reprobation of which we speak."

"What are these corruptions?" he said.

"I will see if I can explain them to you. Everyone will admit that a nature having in perfection all the qualities which we required in a philosopher, is a rare plant which is seldom seen among men."

"Rare indeed."

"And what numberless and powerful causes tend to destroy these rare natures!"

"What causes?"

"In the first place there are their own virtues, their courage, temperance, and the rest of them, every one of which praiseworthy qualities (and this is a most singular circumstance) destroys and distracts from philosophy the soul which is the possessor of them."

"That is very singular," he replied.

"Then there are all the ordinary goods of life—beauty, wealth, strength, rank, and great connections in the State—you understand the sort of things—these also have a corrupting and distracting effect."

"I understand; but I should like to know more precisely what you mean about them."

"Grasp the truth as a whole," I said, "and in the right way; you

6 That is, the best, just mentioned.

will then have no difficulty in apprehending the preceding remarks, and they will no longer appear strange to you."

"And how am I to do so?" he asked.

"Why," I said, "we know that all germs or seeds, whether vegetable or animal, when they fail to meet with proper nutriment or climate or soil, in proportion to their vigor, are all the more sensitive to the want of a suitable environment,[7] for evil is a greater enemy to what is good than to what is not."

"Very true."

"There is reason in supposing that the finest natures, when under alien conditions, receive more injury than the inferior, because the contrast is greater."

"Certainly."

"And may we not say, Adeimantus, that the most gifted minds, when they are ill-educated, become pre-eminently bad? Do not great crimes and the spirit of pure evil spring out of a fullness of nature ruined by education rather than from any inferiority, whereas weak natures are scarcely capable of any very great good or very great evil?"

"There I think that you are right."

"And our philosopher follows the same analogy—he is like a plant which, having proper nurture, must necessarily grow and mature into all virtue, but, if sown and planted in an alien soil, becomes the most noxious of all weeds, unless he be preserved by some divine power. Do you really think, as people so often say, that our youth are corrupted by Sophists, or that private teachers of the art corrupt them in any degree worth speaking of? Are not the public who say these things the greatest of all Sophists? And do they not educate to perfection young and old, men and women alike, and fashion them after their own hearts?"

"When is this accomplished?" he said.

"When they meet together, and the world sits down at an assembly, or in a court of law, or a theater, or a camp, or in any other popu-

---

7 Or "the more vigorous they are, the more sensitive they are to a lack of suitable environment."

lar resort, and there is a great uproar, and they praise some things which are being said or done, and blame other things, equally exaggerating both, shouting and clapping their hands, and the echo of the rocks and the place in which they are assembled redoubles the sound of the praise or blame—at such a time will not a young man's heart, as they say, leap within him? Will any private training enable him to stand firm against the overwhelming flood of popular opinion? or will he be carried away by the stream? Will he not have the notions of good and evil which the public in general have—he will do as they do, and as they are, such will he be?"

"Yes, Socrates; necessity will compel him."

"And yet," I said, "there is a still greater necessity, which has not been mentioned."

"What is that?"

"The gentle force of attainder or confiscation or death, which, as you are aware, these new Sophists and educators, who are the public, apply when their words are powerless." [8]

"Indeed they do; and in right good earnest."

"Now what opinion of any other Sophist, or of any private person, can be expected to overcome in such an unequal contest?"

"None," he replied.

"No, indeed," I said, "even to make the attempt is a great piece of folly; there neither is, nor has been, nor is ever likely to be, any different type of character which has had no other training in virtue but that which is supplied by public opinion—I speak, my friend, of human virtue only; what is more than human, as the proverb says, is not included: for I would not have you ignorant that, in the present evil state of governments, whatever is saved and comes to good is saved by the power of God, as we may truly say."

"I quite assent," he replied.

"Then let me crave your assent also to a further observation."

"What are you going to say?"

"Why, that all those mercenary individuals, whom the many call

---

8 An apparently prophetic allusion by Socrates to his own future condemnation by a popular jury.

Sophists and whom they deem to be their adversaries, do, in fact, teach nothing but the opinion of the many, that is to say, the opinions of their assemblies; and this is their wisdom. I might compare them to a man who should study the tempers and desires of a mighty strong beast [9] who is fed by him—he would learn how to approach and handle him, also at what times and from what causes he is dangerous or the reverse, and what is the meaning of his several cries, and by what sounds, when another utters them, he is soothed or infuriated; and you may suppose further, that when, by continually attending upon him, he has become perfect in all this, he calls his knowledge wisdom, and makes of it a system or art, which he proceeds to teach, although he has no real notion of what he means by the principles or passions of which he is speaking, but calls this honorable and that dishonorable, or good or evil, or just or unjust, all in accordance with the tastes and tempers of the great brute. Good he pronounces to be that in which the beast delights and evil to be that which he dislikes; and he can give no other account of them except that the just and noble are the necessary, having never himself seen, and having no power of explaining to others the nature of either, or the difference between them, which is immense. By heaven, would not such a one be a rare educator?"

"Indeed he would."

"And in what way does he who thinks that wisdom is the discernment of the tempers and tastes of the motley multitude, whether in painting or music, or, finally, in politics, differ from him whom I have been describing? For when a man consorts with the many, and exhibits to them his poem or other work of art or the service which he has done the State, making them his judges when he is not obliged, the so-called necessity of Diomed [10] will oblige him to produce whatever they praise. And yet the reasons are utterly ludicrous which they give in confirmation of their own notions about the hon-

9 Another figure for the people of the Athenian democracy, the general mob.

10 An expression, apparently, for the compulsion a man may feel to keep on working at an almost impossible task. In the *Iliad*, XIV, 128, Diomed urges the Greeks to go on fighting, "wounded though we be, for it is necessary."

orable and good. Did you ever hear any of them which were not?"

"No, nor am I likely to hear."

"You recognize the truth of what I have been saying? Then let me ask you to consider further whether the world will ever be induced to believe in the existence of absolute beauty rather than of the many beautiful, or of the absolute in each kind rather than of the many in each kind?"

"Certainly not."

"Then the world cannot possibly be a philosopher?"

"Impossible."

"And therefore philosophers must inevitably fall under the censure of the world?"

"They must."

"And of individuals who consort with the mob and seek to please them?"

"That is evident."

"Then, do you see any way in which the philosopher can be preserved in his calling to the end? and remember what we were saying of him, that he was to have quickness and memory and courage and magnificence—these were admitted by us to be the true philosopher's gifts."

"Yes."

"Will not such a one from his early childhood be in all things first among all, especially if his bodily endowments are like his mental ones?"

"Certainly," he said.

"And his friends and fellow-citizens will want to use him as he gets older for their own purposes?"

"No question."

"Falling at his feet, they will make requests to him and do him honor and flatter him, because they want to get into their hands now the power which he will one day possess."

"That often happens," he said.

"And what will a man such as he is be likely to do under such circumstances, especially if he be a citizen of a great city, rich and noble, and a tall proper youth? Will he not be full of boundless aspirations, and fancy himself able to manage the affairs of Hellenes and of barbarians, and having got such notions into his head will he not dilate and elevate himself in the fullness of vain pomp and senseless pride?"

"To be sure he will."

"Now, when he is in this state of mind, if someone gently comes to him and tells him that he is a fool and must get understanding, which can only be got by slaving for it, do you think that, under such adverse circumstances, he will be easily induced to listen?"

"Far otherwise."

"And even if there be someone who through inherent goodness or natural reasonableness has had his eyes opened a little and is humbled and taken captive by philosophy, how will his friends behave when they think that they are likely to lose the advantage which they were hoping to reap from his companionship? Will they not do and say anything to prevent him from yielding to his better nature and to render his teacher powerless, using to this end private intrigues as well as public prosecutions?"

"There can be no doubt of it."

"And how can one who is thus circumstanced ever become a philosopher?"

"Impossible."

"Then were we not right in saying that even the very qualities which make a man a philosopher may, if he be ill-educated, divert him from philosophy, no less than riches and their accompaniments and the other so-called goods of life?"

"We were quite right."

"Thus, my excellent friend, is brought about all that ruin and failure which I have been describing of the natures best adapted to the best of all pursuits; they are natures which we maintain to be rare at any time; this being the class out of which come the men who are authors of the greatest evil to States and individuals; and also of the greatest good when the tide carries them in that direction; but a small man never was the doer of any great thing either to individuals or to States."

"That is most true," he said.

"And so philosophy is left desolate, with her marriage rite incomplete: for her own have fallen away and forsaken her, and while they are leading a false and unbecoming life, other unworthy persons, seeing that she has no kinsmen to be her protectors, enter in and dishonor her; and fasten upon her the reproaches which, as you say, her reprovers utter, who affirm of her votaries that some are good for nothing, and that the greater number deserve the severest punishment."

"That is certainly what people say."

"Yes; and what else would you expect," I said, "when you think of the puny creatures who, seeing this land open to them—a land well stocked with fair names and showy titles—like prisoners running out of prison into a sanctuary, take a leap out of their trades into philosophy; those who do so being probably the cleverest hands at their own miserable crafts? For, although philosophy be in this evil case, still there remains a dignity about her which is not to be found in the arts. And many are thus attracted by her whose natures are imperfect and whose souls are maimed and disfigured by their meannesses, as their bodies are by their trades and crafts. Is not this unavoidable?"

"Yes."

"Are they not exactly like a bald little tinker who has just got out of durance and come into a fortune; he takes a bath and puts on a new coat, and is decked out as a bridegroom going to marry his master's daughter, who is left poor and desolate?"

"A most exact parallel."

"What will be the issue of such marriages? Will they not be vile and bastard?"

"There can be no question of it."

"And when persons who are unworthy of education approach philosophy and make an alliance with her who is in a rank above them, what sort of ideas and opinions are likely to be generated?

Will they not be sophisms captivating to the ear, having nothing in them genuine, or worthy of or akin to true wisdom?"

"No doubt," he said.

"Then, Adeimantus," I said, "the worthy disciples of philosophy will be but a small remnant: perchance some noble and well-educated person, detained by exile in her service, who in the absence of corrupting influences remains devoted to her; or some lofty soul born in a mean city, the politics of which he contemns and neglects; and there may be a gifted few who leave the arts, which they justly despise, and come to her; or peradventure there are some who are restrained by our friend Theages' bridle; for everything in the life of Theages [11] conspired to divert him from philosophy; but ill-health kept him away from politics. My own case of the internal sign is hardly worth mentioning, for rarely, if ever, has such a monitor been given to any other man. Those who belong to this small class have tasted how sweet and blessed a possession philosophy is, and have also seen enough of the madness of the multitude; and they know that no politician is honest, nor is there any champion of justice at whose side they may fight and be saved. Such a one may be compared to a man who has fallen among wild beasts—he will not join in the wickedness of his fellows, but neither is he able singly to resist all their fierce natures, and therefore seeing that he would be of no use to the State or to his friends, and reflecting that he would have to throw away his life without doing any good either to himself or others, he holds his peace, and goes his own way. He is like one who, in the storm of dust and sleet which the driving wind hurries along, retires under the shelter of a wall; and seeing the rest of mankind full of wickedness, he is content, if only he can live his own life and be pure from evil or unrighteousness, and depart in peace and good will, with bright hopes."

"Yes," he said, "and he will have done a great work before he departs."

---

11 A former pupil of Socrates. See the *Apology*, page 52. The "bridle of Theages" was the poor health that kept him always out of politics in spite of many so-called temptations. It was evidently by now a proverbial expression in Socratic circles.

"A great work—yes; but not the greatest, unless he find a State suitable to him; for in a State which is suitable to him, he will have a larger growth and be the savior of his country, as well as of himself.

Socrates expatiates further on the inability of men under the present system to realize what philosophy can do for them. Hence, he says, the need of a better form of society, where true-born philosophers may receive the right education and the opportunity to use their gifts for the benefit of their fellow men.

"And this was what we foresaw, and this was the reason why truth forced us to admit, not without fear and hesitation, that neither cities nor States nor individuals will ever attain perfection until the small class of philosophers whom we termed useless but not corrupt are providentially compelled, whether they will or not, to take care of the State, and until a like necessity be laid on the State to obey them; or until kings, or if not kings, the sons of kings or princes, are divinely inspired with a true love of true philosophy. That either or both of these alternatives are impossible, I see no reason to affirm: if they were so, we might indeed be justly ridiculed as dreamers and visionaries. Am I not right?"

"Quite right."

"If then, in the countless ages of the past, or at the present hour in some foreign clime which is far away and beyond our ken, the perfected philosopher is or has been or hereafter shall [12] be compelled by a superior power to have the charge of the State, we are ready to assert to the death, that this our constitution has been, and is—yea, and will be whenever the Muse of Philosophy is queen. There is no impossibility in all this; that there is a difficulty, we acknowledge ourselves."

"My opinion agrees with yours," he said.

"But do you mean to say that this is not the opinion of the multitude?"

---

[12] In some future age, some faraway clime, the ideal may be realized.

"I should imagine not," he replied.

"O my friend," I said, "do not attack the multitude: they will change their minds, if, not in an aggressive spirit but gently and with the view of soothing them and removing their dislike of over-education, you show them your philosophers as they really are and describe as you were just now doing their character and profession, and then mankind will see that he of whom you are speaking is not such as they supposed—if they view him in this new light, they will surely change their notion of him, and answer in another strain. Who can be at enmity with one who loves them, who that is himself gentle and free from envy will be jealous of one in whom there is no jealousy? Nay, let me answer for you, that in a few this harsh temper may be found but not in the majority of mankind."

"I quite agree with you," he said.

"And do you not also think, as I do, that the harsh feeling which the many entertain towards philosophy originates in the pretenders, who rush in uninvited, and are always abusing them, and finding fault with them, who make persons instead of things the theme of their conversation? and nothing can be more unbecoming in philosophers than this."

"It is most unbecoming."

"For he, Adeimantus, whose mind is fixed upon true being, has surely no time to look down upon the affairs of earth, or to be filled with malice and envy, contending against men; his eye is ever directed towards things fixed and immutable, which he sees neither injuring nor injured by one another, but all in order moving according to reason; these he imitates, and to these he will, as far as he can, conform himself. Can a man help imitating that with which he holds reverential converse?"

"Impossible."

"And the philosopher holding converse with the divine order, becomes orderly and divine, as far as the nature of man allows; but like everyone else, he will suffer from detraction."

"Of course."

"And if a necessity be laid upon him of fashioning, not only himself, but human nature generally, whether in States or individuals, into that which he beholds elsewhere, will he, think you, be an unskillful artificer of justice, temperance, and every civil virtue?"

"Anything but unskillful."

"And if the world perceives that what we are saying about him is the truth, will they be angry with philosophy? Will they disbelieve us, when we tell them that no State can be happy which is not designed by artists who imitate the heavenly pattern?"

"They will not be angry if they understand," he said. "But how will they draw out the plan of which you are speaking?"

"They will begin by taking the State and the manners of men, from which, as from a tablet, they will rub out the picture, and leave a clean surface. This is no easy task. But whether easy or not, herein will lie the difference between them and every other legislator—they will have nothing to do either with individual or State, and will inscribe no laws, until they have either found, or themselves made, a clean surface."

"They will be very right," he said.

"Having effected this, they will proceed to trace an outline of the constitution?"

"No doubt."

"And when they are filling in the work, as I conceive, they will often turn their eyes upwards and downwards: I mean that they will first look at absolute justice and beauty and temperance, and again at the human copy; and will mingle and temper the various elements of life into the image of a man; and this they will conceive according to that other·image, which, when existing among men, Homer calls the form and likeness of God." [13]

"Very true," he said.

"And one feature they will erase, and another they will put in, until they have made the ways of men, as far as possible, agreeable to the ways of God?"

[13] Homer uses the epithet, "like to a god," of his greatest heroes, such as Achilles and Telemachus. *Iliad*, I, 131; XXIV, 630; *Odyssey*, III, 416.

"Indeed," he said, "in no way could they make a fairer picture."

"And now," I said, "are we beginning to persuade those whom you described as rushing at us with might and main, that the painter of constitutions is such a one as we were praising; at whom they were so very indignant because to his hands we committed the State; and are they growing a little calmer at what they have just heard?"

"Much calmer, if there is any sense in them."

"Why, where can they still find any ground for objection? Will they doubt that the philosopher is a lover of truth and being?"

"They would not be so unreasonable."

"Or that his nature, being such as we have delineated, is akin to the highest good?"

"Neither can they doubt this."

"But again, will they tell us that such a nature, placed under favorable circumstances, will not be perfectly good and wise if any ever was? Or will they prefer those whom we have rejected?"

"Surely not."

"Then will they still be angry at our saying, that, until philosophers bear rule, States and individuals will have no rest from evil, nor will this our imaginary State ever be realized?"

"I think that they will be less angry."

"Shall we assume that they are not only less angry but quite gentle, and that they have been converted and for very shame, if for no other reason, cannot refuse to come to terms?"

"By all means," he said.

"Then let us suppose that the reconciliation has been effected. Will anyone deny the other point, that there may be sons of kings or princes who are by nature philosophers?"

"Surely no man," he said.

"And when they have come into being will anyone say that they must of necessity be destroyed; that they can hardly be saved is not denied even by us; but that in the whole course of ages no single one of them can escape—who will venture to affirm this?"

"Who indeed!"

"But," said I, "one is enough; [14] let there be one man who has a city obedient to his will, and he might bring into existence the ideal polity about which the world is so incredulous."

"Yes, one is enough."

"The ruler may impose the laws and institutions which we have been describing, and the citizens may possibly be willing to obey them?"

"Certainly."

"And that others should approve of what we approve is no miracle or impossibility?"

"I think not."

"But we have sufficiently shown, in what has preceded, that all this, if only possible, is assuredly for the best."

"We have."

"And now we say not only that our laws, if they could be enacted, would be for the best, but also that the enactment of them, though difficult, is not impossible."

"Very good."

"And so with pain and toil we have reached the end of one subject, but more remains to be discussed; how and by what studies and pursuits will the saviors of the constitution be created, and at what ages are they to apply themselves to their several studies?"

"Certainly."

"I omitted the troublesome business of the possession of women, and the procreation of children, and the appointment of the rulers, because I knew that the perfect State would be eyed with jealousy and was difficult of attainment; but that piece of cleverness was not of much service to me, for I had to discuss them all the same. The women and children are now disposed of, but the other question of the rulers must be investigated from the very beginning. We were saying, as you will remember, that they were to be lovers of their country, tried by the test of pleasures and pains, and neither in hard-

---

14 For a moment Socrates sounds hopeful. One true statesman, with the power and the will to make the ways of men pleasing to God, could bring the ideal state into being.

ships, nor in dangers, nor at any other critical moment were to lose their patriotism—he was to be rejected who failed, but he who always came forth pure, like gold tried in the refiner's fire, was to be made a ruler, and to receive honors and rewards in life and after death. This was the sort of thing which was being said, and then the argument turned aside and veiled her face; not liking to stir the question which has now arisen."

"I perfectly remember," he said.

"Yes, my friend," I said, "and I then shrank from hazarding the bold word; but now let me dare to say—that the perfect guardian must be a philosopher."

"Yes," he said, "let that be affirmed."

"And do not suppose that there will be many of them; for the gifts which were deemed by us to be essential rarely grow together; they are mostly found in shreds and patches."

"What do you mean?" he said.

"You are aware," I replied, "that quick intelligence, memory, sagacity, cleverness, and similar qualities, do not often grow together, and that persons who possess them and are at the same time high-spirited and magnanimous are not so constituted by nature as to live orderly and in a peaceful and settled manner; they are driven any way by their impulses, and all solid principle goes out of them."

"Very true," he said.

"On the other hand, those steadfast natures which can better be depended upon, which in a battle are impregnable to fear and immovable, are equally immovable when there is anything to be learned; they are always in a torpid state, and are apt to yawn and go to sleep over any intellectual toil."

"Quite true."

"And yet we were saying that both qualities were necessary in those to whom the higher education is to be imparted, and who are to share in any office or command."

"Certainly," he said.

"And will they be a class which is rarely found?"

"Yes, indeed."

"Then the aspirant must not only be tested in those labors and dangers and pleasures which we mentioned before, but there is another kind of probation which we did not mention—he must be exercised also in many kinds of knowledge, to see whether the soul will be able to endure the highest of all, or will faint under them, as in any other studies and exercises."

"Yes," he said, "you are quite right in testing him. But what do you mean by the highest of all knowledge?"

"You may remember," I said, "that we divided the soul into three parts; and distinguished the several natures of justice, temperance, courage, and wisdom?"

"Indeed," he said, "if I had forgotten, I should not deserve to hear more."

"And do you remember the word of caution which preceded the discussion of them?"

"To what do you refer?"

"We were saying, if I am not mistaken, that he who wanted to see them in their perfect beauty must take a longer and more circuitous way, at the end of which they would appear; but that we could add on a popular exposition of them on a level with the discussion which had preceded. And you replied that such an exposition would be enough for you, and so the inquiry was continued in what to me seemed to be a very inaccurate manner; whether you were satisfied or not, it is for you to say."

"Yes," he said, "I thought and the others thought that you gave us a fair measure of truth."

"But, my friend," I said, "a measure of such things which in any degree falls short of the whole truth is not fair measure; for nothing imperfect is the measure of anything, although persons are too apt to be contented and think that they need search no further."

"Not an uncommon case when people are indolent."

"Yes," I said; "and there cannot be any worse fault in a guardian of the State and of the laws."

"True."

"The guardian then," I said, "must be required to take the longer circuit, and toil at learning [15] as well as at gymnastics, or he will never reach the highest knowledge of all which, as we were just now saying, is his proper calling."

"What," he said, "is there a knowledge still higher than this—higher than justice and the other virtues?"

"Yes," I said, "there is. And of the virtues too we must behold not the outline merely, as at present—nothing short of the most finished picture should satisfy us. When little things are elaborated with an infinity of pains, in order that they may appear in their full beauty and utmost clearness, how ridiculous that we should not think the highest truths worthy of attaining the highest accuracy!"

"A right noble thought; but do you suppose that we shall refrain from asking you what is this highest knowledge?"

"Nay," I said, "ask if you will; but I am certain that you have heard the answer many times, and now you either do not understand me or, as I rather think, you are disposed to be troublesome; for you have often been told that the idea of good [16] is the highest knowledge, and that all other things become useful and advantageous only by their use of this. You can hardly be ignorant that of this I was about to speak, concerning which, as you have often heard me say, we know so little; and, without which, any other knowledge or possession of any kind will profit us nothing. Do you think that the possession of all other things is of any value if we do not possess the good? or the knowledge of all other things if we have no knowledge of beauty and goodness?"

"Assuredly not."

15 The higher duties and education of the philosopher ruler are now to be described.

16 The Idea of the Good is, according to Plato, speaking here through Socrates' lips, the crowning Idea of all and the cause of every lesser idea, such as that of beauty, truth or justice. Through the light that radiates from it as from the sun in the sky we perceive these lesser lights. Towards the Idea of the Good as toward the goal of all his searching, the philosopher will press to catch in its light a vision of the perfect life for man. Some students of Plato take the Idea of the Good as another name for God. Others understand by it a pattern of supreme goodness existing apart from God, to which he looked when he created the universe.

"You are further aware that most people affirm pleasure to be the good, but the finer sort of wits say it is knowledge?"

"Yes."

"And you are aware too that the latter cannot explain what they mean by knowledge, but are obliged after all to say knowledge of the good?"

"How ridiculous!"

"Yes," I said, "that they should begin by reproaching us with our ignorance of the good, and then presume our knowledge of it—for the good they define to be knowledge of the good, just as if we understood them when they use the term 'good'—this is of course ridiculous."

"Most true," he said.

"And those who make pleasure their good are in equal perplexity; for they are compelled to admit that there are bad pleasures as well as good."

"Certainly."

"And therefore to acknowledge that bad and good are the same?"

"True."

"There can be no doubt about the numerous difficulties in which this question is involved."

"There can be none."

"Further, do we not see that many are willing to do or to have or to seem to be what is just and honorable without the reality; but no one is satisfied with the appearance of good—the reality is what they seek; in the case of the good, appearance is despised by everyone."

"Very true," he said.

"Of this then, which every soul of man pursues and makes the end of all his actions, having a presentiment that there is such an end, and yet hesitating because neither knowing the nature nor having the same assurance of this as of other things, and therefore losing whatever good there is in other things—of a principle such and so great as this ought the best men in our State, to whom everything is entrusted, to be in the darkness of ignorance?"

"Certainly not," he said.

"I am sure," I said, "that he who does not know how the beautiful and the just are likewise good will be but a sorry guardian of them; and I suspect that no one who is ignorant of the good will have a true knowledge of them."

"That," he said, "is a shrewd suspicion of yours."

"And if we only have a guardian who has this knowledge our State will be perfectly ordered?"

"Of course," he replied; "but I wish that you would tell me whether you conceive this supreme principle of the good to be knowledge or pleasure, or different from either?"

"Aye," I said, "I knew all along that a fastidious gentleman like you would not be contented with the thoughts of other people about these matters."

"True, Socrates; but I must say that one who like you has passed a lifetime in the study of philosophy should not be always repeating the opinions of others, and never telling his own."

"Well, but has anyone a right to say positively what he does not know?"

"Not," he said, "with the assurance of positive certainty; he has no right to do that: but he may say what he thinks, as a matter of opinion."

"And do you not know," I said, "that all mere opinions are bad, and the best of them blind? You would not deny that those who have any true notion without intelligence are only like blind men who feel their way along the road?"

"Very true."

"And do you wish to behold what is blind and crooked and base, when others will tell you of brightness and beauty?"

"Still, I must implore you, Socrates," said Glaucon, "not to turn away just as you are reaching the goal; if you will only give such an explanation of the good as you have already given of justice and temperance and the other virtues, we shall be satisfied."

"Yes, my friend, and I shall be at least equally satisfied, but I cannot help fearing that I shall fail, and that my indiscreet zeal will bring ridicule upon me. No, sweet sirs, let us not at present ask what is the actual nature of the good,[17] for to reach what is now in my thoughts would be an effort too great for me. But of the child of the good who is likest him, I would fain speak, if I could be sure that you wished to hear—otherwise, not."

"By all means," he said, "tell us about the child, and you shall remain in our debt for the account of the parent."

"I do indeed wish," I replied, "that I could pay, and you receive, the account of the parent, and not, as now, of the offspring only; take, however, this latter by way of interest, and at the same time have a care that I do not render a false account, although I have no intention of deceiving you."

"Yes, we will take all the care that we can: proceed."

"Yes," I said, "but I must first come to an understanding with you, and remind you of what I have mentioned in the course of this discussion, and at many other times."

"What?"

"The old story, that there is a many beautiful and a many good, and so of other things which we describe and define; to all of them the term 'many' is applied."

"True," he said.

"And there is an absolute beauty and an absolute good, and of other things to which the term 'many' is applied there is an absolute; for they may be brought under a single idea, which is called the essence of each."

"Very true."

"The many, as we say, are seen but not known, and the ideas are known but not seen."

"Exactly."

"And what is the organ with which we see the visible things?"

"The sight," he said.

"And with the hearing," I said, "we hear, and with the other senses perceive the other objects of sense?"

"True."

17 Socrates refuses to define by any formula that highest good "which every soul of man pursues" but of which the human mind can speak only in symbols.

"But have you remarked that sight is by far the most costly and complex piece of workmanship which the artificer of the senses ever contrived?"

"No, I never have," he said.

"Then reflect: has the ear or voice need of any third or additional nature in order that the one may be able to hear and the other to be heard?"

"Nothing of the sort."

"No, indeed," I replied; "and the same is true of most, if not all, the other senses—you would not say that any of them requires such an addition?"

"Certainly not."

"But you see that without the addition of some other nature there is no seeing or being seen?"

"How do you mean?"

"Sight being, as I conceive, in the eyes, and he who has eyes wanting to see; color being also present in them, still unless there be a third nature specially adapted to the purpose, the owner of the eyes will see nothing and the colors will be invisible."

"Of what nature are you speaking?"

"Of that which you term light," I replied.

"True," he said.

"Noble, then, is the bond which links together sight and visibility, and great beyond other bonds by no small difference of nature; for light is their bond, and light is no ignoble thing?"

"Nay," he said, "the reverse of ignoble."

"And which," I said, "of the gods in heaven would you say was the lord of this element? Whose is that light which makes the eye to see perfectly and the visible to appear?"

"You mean the sun, as you and all mankind say."

"May not the relation of sight to this deity be described as follows?"

"How?"

"Neither sight nor the eye in which sight resides is the sun?"

"No."

"Yet of all the organs of sense the eye is the most like the sun?"

"By far the most like."

"And the power which the eye possesses is a sort of effluence which is dispensed from the sun?"

"Exactly."

"Then the sun is not sight, but the author of sight who is recognized by sight?"

"True," he said.

"And this is he whom I call the child of the good, whom the good begat in his own likeness, to be in the visible world, in relation to sight and the things of sight, what the good is in the intellectual world in relation to mind and the things of mind."

"Will you be a little more explicit?" he said.

"Why, you know," I said, "that the eyes, when a person directs them towards objects on which the light of day is no longer shining, but the moon and stars only, see dimly, and are nearly blind; they seem to have no clearness of vision in them?"

"Very true."

"But when they are directed towards objects on which the sun shines, they see clearly and there is sight in them?"

"Certainly."

"And the soul is like the eye: when resting upon that on which truth and being shine, the soul perceives and understands, and is radiant with intelligence; but when turned towards the twilight of becoming and perishing, then she has opinion only, and goes blinking about, and is first of one opinion and then of another, and seems to have no intelligence?"

"Just so."

"Now, that which imparts truth to the known and the power of knowing to the knower is what I would have you term the idea of good, and this you will deem to be the cause of science, and of truth in so far as the latter becomes the subject of knowledge; beautiful too, as are both truth and knowledge, you will be right in esteeming this other nature as more beautiful than either; and, as in the previous instance, light and sight may be truly said to be like the sun, and yet not to be the sun, so in this other sphere, science and truth may be deemed to be like the good, but not the good; the good has a place of honor yet higher."

"What a wonder of beauty that must be," he said, "which is the author of science and truth, and yet surpasses them in beauty; for you surely cannot mean to say that pleasure is the good?"

"God forbid," I replied; "but may I ask you to consider the image in another point of view?"

"In what point of view?"

"You would say, would you not, that the sun is not only the author of visibility in all visible things, but of generation and nourishment and growth, though he himself is not generation?"

"Certainly."

"In like manner the good may be said to be not only the author of knowledge to all things known, but of their being and essence, and yet the good is not essence, but far exceeds essence in dignity and power."

Glaucon said, with a ludicrous earnestness: "By the light of heaven, how amazing!"

"Yes," I said, "and the exaggeration may be set down to you; for you made me utter my fancies."

Socrates analyzes the degree of reality in the objects of man's knowledge. Beginning with the most unsubstantial and transient, shadows and reflections in water, he goes on to the solid, material objects that fill our visible world, of which the shadows and reflections are only copies. Beyond them, however, is the invisible world of perfect ideas, of which this imperfect world and the mathematician's figures are but copies and shadows. Still above and beyond all multiplicity is the supreme principle of the One, to which only the most highly trained reason may soar.

BOOK VII

*Figure of mankind in the dark cave. Special education
and training of rulers in science, philosophy and practice
of government.*

"AND now," I said, "let me show in a figure [1] how far our nature is
enlightened or unenlightened. Behold! human beings living in an
underground den, which has a mouth open towards the light and
reaching all along the den; here they have been from their childhood,
and have their legs and necks chained so that they cannot move, and
can only see before them, being prevented by the chains from turning round their heads. Above and behind them a fire is blazing at a
distance, and between the fire and the prisoners there is a raised way;
and you will see, if you look, a low wall built along the way, like the
screen which marionette players have in front of them, over which
they show the puppets."

"I see."

"And do you see," I said, "men passing along the wall carrying all
sorts of vessels, and statues and figures of animals made of wood and
stone and various materials, which appear over the wall? Some of
them are talking, others silent."

"You have shown me a strange image, and they are strange
prisoners."

"Like ourselves," I replied; "and they see only their own shadows,[2]
or the shadows of one another, which the fire throws on the opposite
wall of the cave?"

---

1 The famous parable of the cave, in which Socrates is made to contrast again the
material world of our everyday sense experience and the spiritual world of pure
thought and truth.

2 The dwellers in the den see only the shadows of puppets, which are themselves
only imitations of really living things. That is, they see only the appearances of
material things, not their true nature.

"True," he said; "how could they see anything but the shadows if they were never allowed to move their heads?"

"And of the objects which are being carried in like manner they would only see the shadows?"

"Yes," he said.

"And if they were able to converse with one another, would they not suppose that they were naming what was actually before them?"

"Very true."

"And suppose further that the prison had an echo which came from the other side, would they not be sure to fancy when one of the passers-by spoke that the voice which they heard came from the passing shadow?"

"No question," he replied.

"To them," I said, "the truth would be literally nothing but the shadows of the images."

"That is certain."

"And now look again, and see what will naturally follow if the prisoners are released and disabused of their error. At first, when any of them is liberated and compelled suddenly to stand up and turn his neck round and walk and look towards the light, he will suffer sharp pains; the glare will distress him, and he will be unable to see the realities of which in his former state he had seen the shadows; and then conceive someone saying to him that what he saw before was an illusion, but that now, when he is approaching nearer to being and his eye is turned towards more real existence, he has a clearer vision—what will be his reply? And you may further imagine that his instructor is pointing to the objects as they pass and requiring him to name them,—will he not be perplexed? Will he not fancy that the shadows which he formerly saw are truer than the objects which are now shown to him?"

"Far truer."

"And if he is compelled to look straight at the light, will he not have a pain in his eyes which will make him turn away to take refuge in the objects of vision which he can see, and which he will conceive to be in reality clearer than the things which are now being shown to him?" [3]

"True," he said.

"And suppose once more, that he is reluctantly dragged up a steep and rugged ascent, and held fast until he is forced into the presence of the sun himself, is he not likely to be pained and irritated? When he approaches the light his eyes will be dazzled, and he will not be able to see anything at all of what are now called realities."

"Not all in a moment," he said.

"He will require to grow accustomed to the sight of the upper world. And first he will see the shadows best, next the reflections of men and other objects in the water, and then the objects themselves; then he will gaze upon the light of the moon and the stars and the spangled heaven; and he will see the sky and the stars by night better than the sun or the light of the sun by day?"

"Certainly."

"Last of all he will be able to see the sun, and not mere reflections of him in the water, but he will see him in his own proper place, and not in another; and he will contemplate him as he is."

"Certainly."

"He will then proceed to argue that this is he who gives the season and the years, and is the guardian of all that is in the visible world, and in a certain way the cause of all things which he and his fellows have been accustomed to behold?"

"Clearly," he said, "he would first see the sun and then reason about him."

"And when he remembered his old habitation, and the wisdom of the den and his fellow prisoners, do you not suppose that he would felicitate himself on the change, and pity them?"

"Certainly, he would."

"And if they were in the habit of conferring honors among them-

3 He will think the shadows to which he is accustomed more real than the puppets behind him that caused them. The puppets in turn he will find easier to look at than the living creatures in the world of sunlight outside, of which the puppets were but copies.

selves on those who were quickest to observe the passing shadows and to remark which of them went before, and which followed after, and which were together; and who were therefore best able to draw conclusions as to the future, do you think that he would care for such honors and glories, or envy the possessors of them? Would he not say with Homer, 'Better to be the poor servant of a poor master.' [4] and to endure anything, rather than think as they do and live after their manner?"

"Yes," he said, "I think that he would rather suffer anything than entertain these false notions and live in this miserable manner."

"Imagine once more," I said, "such a one coming suddenly out of the sun to be replaced in his old situation; [5] would he not be certain to have his eyes full of darkness?"

"To be sure," he said.

"And if there were a contest, and he had to compete in measuring the shadows with the prisoners who had never moved out of the den, while his sight was still weak, and before his eyes had become steady (and the time which would be needed to acquire this new habit of sight might be very considerable), would he not be ridiculous? Men would say of him that up he went and down he came without his eyes; and that it was better not even to think of ascending; and if any one tried to loose another and lead him up to the light, let them only catch the offender, and they would put him to death."

"No question," he said.

"This entire allegory," I said, "you may now append, dear Glaucon, to the previous argument; the prison house is the world of sight, the light of the fire is the sun, and you will not misapprehend me if you interpret the journey upwards to be the ascent of the soul into the intellectual world according to my poor belief, which, at your desire, I have expressed—whether rightly or wrongly, God knows. But, whether true or false, my opinion is that in the world of knowledge the idea of good appears last of all, and is seen only with an

4 Homer continues, "than to be lord of all the dead who have perished." *Odyssey,* XI, 489-491.
5 Or "such a one going down again and taking his old position."

effort; and, when seen, is also inferred to be the universal author of all things beautiful and right, parent of light and of the lord of light in this visible world, and the immediate source of reason and truth in the intellectual; and that this is the power upon which he who would act rationally either in public or private life must have his eye fixed."

"I agree," he said, "as far as I am able to understand you."

"Moreover," I said, "you must not wonder that those who attain to this beatific vision are unwilling to descend to human affairs; for their souls are ever hastening into the upper world where they desire to dwell; which desire of theirs is very natural, if our allegory may be trusted."

"Yes, very natural."

"And is there anything surprising in one who passes from divine contemplations to the evil state of man, misbehaving himself in a ridiculous manner; if, while his eyes are blinking and before he has become accustomed to the surrounding darkness, he is compelled to fight in courts of law, or in other places, about the images or the shadows of images of justice, and is endeavoring to meet the conceptions of those who have never yet seen absolute justice?"

"Anything but surprising," he replied.

"Anyone who has common sense will remember that the bewilderments of the eyes are of two kinds, and arise from two causes, either from coming out of the light or from going into the light, which is true of the mind's eye, quite as much as of the bodily eye; and he who remembers this when he sees anyone whose vision is perplexed and weak, will not be too ready to laugh; he will first ask whether that soul of man has come out of the brighter life, and is unable to see because unaccustomed to the dark, or having turned from darkness to the day is dazzled by excess of light. And he will count the one happy in his condition and state of being, and he will pity the other; or, if he have a mind to laugh at the soul which comes from below into the light, there will be more reason in this than in the laugh which greets him who returns from above out of the light into the den."

"That," he said, "is a very just distinction."

"But then, if I am right, certain professors of education must be wrong when they say that they can put a knowledge into the soul which was not there before, like sight into blind eyes."

"They undoubtedly say this," he replied.

"Whereas our argument shows that the power and capacity of learning exists in the soul already; and that just as the eye was unable to turn from darkness to light without the whole body, so too the instrument of knowledge can only by the movement of the whole soul be turned from the world of becoming into that of being, and learn by degrees to endure the sight of being, and of the brightest and best of being, or in other words, of the good."

"Very true."

"And must there not be some art which will effect conversion in the easiest and quickest manner; not implanting the faculty of sight, for that exists already, but has been turned in the wrong direction, and is looking away from the truth?"

"Yes," he said, "such an art may be presumed."

"And whereas the other so-called virtues of the soul seem to be akin to bodily qualities, for even when they are not originally innate they can be implanted later by habit and exercise, the virtue of wisdom more than anything else contains a divine element which always remains, and by this conversion is rendered useful and profitable; or, on the other hand, hurtful and useless. Did you never observe the narrow intelligence flashing from the keen eye of a clever rogue—how eager he is, how clearly his paltry soul sees the way to his end he is the reverse of blind, but his keen eyesight is forced into the service of evil, and he is mischievous in proportion to his cleverness?"

"Very true," he said.

"But what if there had been a circumcision of such natures in the days of their youth; and they had been severed from those sensual pleasures, such as eating and drinking, which, like leaden weights, were attached to them at their birth, and which drag them down and turn the vision of their souls upon the things that are below—if, I say, they had been released from these impediments and turned in the opposite direction, the very same faculty in them would have seen the truth as keenly as they see what their eyes are turned to now."

"Very likely."

"Yes," I said; "and there is another thing which is likely, or rather a necessary inference from what has preceded, that neither the uneducated and uninformed of the truth, nor yet those who never make an end of their education, will be able ministers of State; not the former, because they have no single aim of duty which is the rule of all their actions, private as well as public; nor the latter, because they will not act at all except upon compulsion, fancying that they are already dwelling apart in the islands of the blest."

"Very true," he replied.

"Then," I said, "the business of us who are the founders of the State will be to compel the best minds to attain that knowledge which we have already shown to be the greatest of all—they must continue to ascend until they arrive at the good; but when they have ascended and seen enough we must not allow them to do as they do now."

"What do you mean?"

"I mean that they remain in the upper world: but this must not be allowed; they must be made to descend again among the prisoners in the den, and partake of their labors and honors, whether they are worth having or not."

"But is not this unjust?" he said; "ought we to give them a worse life, when they might have a better?"

"You have again forgotten, my friend," I said, "the intention of the legislator, who did not aim at making any one class in the State happy above the rest; the happiness was to be in the whole State, and he held the citizens together by persuasion and necessity, making them benefactors of the State, and therefore benefactors of one another; to this end he created them, not to please themselves, but to be his instruments in binding up the State."

"True," he said, "I had forgotten."

"Observe, Glaucon, that there will be no injustice in compelling our philosophers to have a care and providence of others; we shall explain to them that in other States, men of their class are not obliged to share in the toils of politics: and this is reasonable, for they grow up at their own sweet will, and the government would rather not have them. Being self-taught, they cannot be expected to show any gratitude for a culture which they have never received. But we have brought you into the world to be rulers of the hive, kings of yourselves and of the other citizens, and have educated you far better and more perfectly than they have been educated, and you are better able to share in the double duty. Wherefore each of you, when his turn comes, must go down to the general underground abode, and get the habit of seeing in the dark. When you have acquired the habit, you will see ten thousand times better than the inhabitants of the den, and you will know what the several images are, and what they represent, because you have seen the beautiful and just and good in their truth. And thus our State, which is also yours, will be a reality, and not a dream only, and will be administered in a spirit unlike that of other States, in which men fight with one another about shadows only and are distracted in the struggle for power, which in their eyes is a great good. Whereas the truth is that the State in which the rulers are most reluctant to govern is always the best and most quietly governed, and the State in which they are most eager, the worst."

"Quite true," he replied.

"And will our pupils, when they hear this, refuse to take their turn at the toils of State, when they are allowed to spend the greater part of their time with one another in the heavenly light?"

"Impossible," he answered; "for they are just men, and the commands which we impose upon them are just; there can be no doubt that every one of them will take office as a stern necessity, and not after the fashion of our present rulers of State."

"Yes, my friend," I said; "and there lies the point. You must contrive for your future rulers another and a better life than that of a ruler, and then you may have a well-ordered State; for only in the

State which offers this, will they rule who are truly rich, not in silver and gold, but in virtue and wisdom, which are the true blessings of life. Whereas if they go to the administration of public affairs, poor and hungering after their own private advantage, thinking that hence they are to snatch the chief good, order there can never be; for they will be fighting about office, and the civil and domestic broils which thus arise will be the ruin of the rulers themselves and of the whole State."

"Most true," he replied.

"And the only life which looks down upon the life of political ambition is that of true philosophy. Do you know of any other?"

"Indeed, I do not," he said.

"And those who govern ought not to be lovers of the task? For, if they are, there will be rival lovers, and they will fight."

"No question."

"Who then are those whom we shall compel to be guardians? Surely they will be the men who are wisest about affairs of State, and by whom the State is best administered, and who at the same time have other honors and another and a better life than that of politics?"

"They are the men, and I will choose them," he replied.

"And now shall we consider in what way such guardians will be produced, and how they are to be brought from darkness to light—as some are said to have ascended from the world below to the gods?"

"By all means," he replied.

"The process," I said, "is not the turning over of an oyster shell,[6] but the turning round of a soul passing from a day which is little better than night to the true day of being, that is, the ascent from below, which we affirm to be true philosophy?"

"Quite so."

"And should we not inquire what sort of knowledge has the power of effecting such a change?"

"Certainly."

---

6 A reference to a game in which the players, divided into two sides, either chased their opponents or ran away according as an oyster shell, tossed into the air, fell with its dark or light side uppermost.

"What sort of knowledge is there which would draw the soul from becoming to being? [7] And another consideration has just occurred to me: You will remember that our young men are to be warrior athletes?"

"Yes, that was said."

"Then this new kind of knowledge must have an additional quality?"

"What quality?"

"Usefulness in war."

"Yes, if possible."

"There were two parts in our former scheme of education, were there not?"

"Just so."

"There was gymnastic which presided over the growth and decay of the body, and may therefore be regarded as having to do with generation and corruption?"

"True."

"Then that is not the knowledge which we are seeking to discover?"

"No."

"But what do you say of music, that also entered to a certain extent into our former scheme?"

"Music," he said, "as you will remember, was the counterpart of gymnastic, and trained the guardians by the influences of habit, by harmony making them harmonious, by rhythm rhythmical, but not giving them science; [8] and the words, whether fabulous or possibly true, had kindred elements of rhythm and harmony in them. But in music there was nothing which tended to that good which you are now seeking."

"You are most accurate," I said, "in your recollection; in music

7 That is, from the world of change and decay to the world of true, uncorruptible being. Socrates is looking now for a course of study that will develop in the finest boys and girls both the necessary practical skills and the power of abstract reasoned judgment, that will enable them to look at this world from the point of view of someone above it.

8 Or knowledge in the true sense as distinguished from mere habit.

there certainly was nothing of the kind. But what branch of knowledge is there, my dear Glaucon, which is of the desired nature; since all the useful arts were reckoned mean by us?"

"Undoubtedly; and yet if music and gymnastic are excluded, and the arts are also excluded, what remains?"

"Well," I said, "there may be nothing left of our special subjects; and then we shall have to take something which is not special, but of universal application."

"What may that be?"

"A something which all arts and sciences and intelligences use in common, and which everyone first has to learn among the elements of education."

"What is that?"

"The little matter of distinguishing one, two, and three—in a word, number and calculation: do not all arts and sciences necessarily partake of them?"

"Yes."

"Then the art of war partakes of them?"

"To be sure."

"Then Palamedes,[9] whenever he appears in tragedy, proves Agamemnon ridiculously unfit to be a general. Did you never remark how he declares that he had invented number, and had numbered the ships and set in array the ranks of the army at Troy; which implies that they had never been numbered before, and Agamemnon must be supposed literally to have been incapable of counting his own fleet—how could he if he was ignorant of number? And if that is true, what sort of general must he have been?"

"I should say a very strange one, if this was as you say."

"Can we deny that a warrior should have a knowledge of arithmetic?"

"Certainly he should, if he is to have the smallest understanding of

9 The hero of lost plays by Aeschylus and Euripides. In the story he was falsely accused by Agamemnon, Diomed, and Odysseus of treason to the Greek cause and stoned to death. He was said also to have been the inventor of the Greek alphabet, weights, and measures.

military tactics, or indeed, I should rather say, if he is to be a man at all."

"I should like to know whether you have the same notion which I have of this study?"

"What is your notion?"

"It appears to me to be a study of the kind which we are seeking, and which leads naturally to reflection, but never to have been rightly used; for the true use of it is simply to draw the soul towards being.[10]

> *Socrates uses the illustration of three fingers to show that there are aspects of any visible object which the mind understands at once, without further thinking, such as that the objects in this case are fingers. But other aspects, matters of size, of hardness and softness, of unity and number, these are all relative. Questions regarding them the mind cannot answer without reflecting.*

If simple unity could be adequately perceived by the sight or by any other sense, then, as we were saying in the case of the finger, there would be nothing to attract towards being; but when there is some contradiction always present, and one is the reverse of one and involves the conception of plurality, then thought begins to be aroused within us, and the soul perplexed and wanting to arrive at a decision asks, What is absolute unity? This is the way in which the study of the one has a power of drawing and converting the mind to the contemplation of true being."

"And surely," he said, "this occurs notably in the case of one; for we see the same thing to be both one and infinite in multitude?"

"Yes," I said; "and this being true of one must be equally true of all number?"

"Certainly."

"And all arithmetic and calculation have to do with number?"

"Yes."

---

10 Socrates proceeds to prove the value both for concrete use and as an incentive to abstract thinking of the comparatively new studies of arithmetic and geometry.

"And they appear to lead the mind towards truth?"

"Yes, in a very remarkable manner."

"Then this is knowledge of the kind for which we are seeking, having a double use, military and philosophical; for the man of war must learn the art of number or he will not know how to array his troops, and the philosopher also, because he has to rise out of the sea of change and lay hold of true being, and therefore he must be an arithmetician."

"That is true."

"And our guardian is both warrior and philosopher?"

"Certainly."

"Then this is a kind of knowledge which legislation may fitly prescribe; and we must endeavor to persuade those who are to be the principal men of our State to go and learn arithmetic, not as amateurs, but they must carry on the study until they see the nature of numbers with the mind only; nor again, like merchants or retail traders, with a view to buying or selling, but for the sake of their military use, and of the soul herself; and because this will be the easiest way for her to pass from becoming to truth and being."

"That is excellent," he said.

"Yes," I said, "and now having spoken of it, I must add how charming the science is! and in how many ways it conduces to our desired end, if pursued in the spirit of a philosopher, and not of a shopkeeper!"

"How do you mean?"

"I mean, as I was saying, that arithmetic has a very great and elevating effect, compelling the soul to reason about abstract number, and rebelling against the introduction of visible or tangible objects into the argument. You know how steadily the masters of the art repel and ridicule anyone who attempts to divide absolute unity when he is calculating, and if you divide, they multiply,[11] taking

---

11 Socrates' meaning seems to be that in a philosophical argument about things that are really units, the ordinary man tends to divide or split up the unity into numerous parts and to talk of them, whereat the expert will multiply or reduce the parts to one again.

care that one shall continue one and not become lost in fractions."

"That is very true."

"Now, suppose a person were to say to them: O my friends, what are these wonderful numbers about which you are reasoning, in which, as you say, there is a unity such as you demand, and each unit is equal, invariable, indivisible,—what would they answer?"

"They would answer, as I should conceive, that they were speaking of those numbers which can only be realized in thought."

"Then you see that this knowledge may be truly called necessary, necessitating as it clearly does the use of the pure intelligence in the attainment of pure truth?"

"Yes; that is a marked characteristic of it."

"And have you further observed, that those who have a natural talent for calculation are generally quick at every other kind of knowledge; and even the dull, if they have had an arithmetical training, although they may derive no other advantage from it, always become much quicker than they would otherwise have been."

"Very true," he said.

"And indeed, you will not easily find a more difficult study, and not many as difficult."

"You will not."

"And, for all these reasons, arithmetic is a kind of knowledge in which the best natures should be trained, and which must not be given up."

"I agree."

"Let this then be made one of our subjects of education. And next, shall we inquire whether the kindred science also concerns us?"

"You mean geometry?"

"Exactly so."

"Clearly," he said, "we are concerned with that part of geometry which relates to war; for in pitching a camp, or taking up a position, or closing or extending the lines of an army, or any other military maneuver, whether in actual battle or on a march, it will make all the difference whether a general is or is not a geometrician."

"Yes." I said, "but for that purpose a very little of either geometry or calculation will be enough; the question relates rather to the greater and more advanced part of geometry—whether that tends in any degree to make more easy the vision of the idea of good; and thither, as I was saying, all things tend which compel the soul to turn her gaze towards that place, where is the full perfection of being, which she ought, by all means, to behold."

"True," he said.

"Then if geometry compels us to view being, it concerns us; if becoming only, it does not concern us?"

"Yes, that is what we assert."

"Yet anybody who has the least acquaintance with geometry will not deny that such a conception of the science is in flat contradiction to the ordinary language of geometricians."

"How so?"

"They have in view practice only, and are always speaking, in a narrow and ridiculous manner, of squaring and extending and applying and the like—they confuse the necessities of geometry with those of daily life; whereas knowledge is the real object of the whole science."

"Certainly," he said.

"Then must not a further admission be made?"

"What admission?"

"That the knowledge at which geometry aims is knowledge of the eternal, and not of aught perishing and transient."

"That," he replied, "may be readily allowed, and is true."

"Then, my noble friend, geometry will draw the soul towards truth, and create the spirit of philosophy, and raise up that which is now unhappily allowed to fall down."

"Nothing will be more likely to have such an effect."

"Then nothing should be more sternly laid down than that the inhabitants of your fair city should by all means learn geometry. Moreover the science has indirect effects, which are not small."

"Of what kind?" he said.

"There are the military advantages of which you spoke," I said; "and in all departments of knowledge, as experience proves, anyone who has studied geometry is infinitely quicker of apprehension than one who has not."

"Yes, indeed," he said; "there is an infinite difference between them."

"Then shall we propose this as a second branch of knowledge which our youth will study?"

"Let us do so," he replied.

"And suppose we make astronomy the third—what do you say?"

"I am strongly inclined to it," he said; "the observation of the seasons and of months and years is as essential to the general as it is to the farmer or sailor."

"I am amused," I said, "at your fear of the world, which makes you guard against the appearance of insisting upon useless studies; and I quite admit the difficulty of believing that in every man there is an eye [12] of the soul which, when by other pursuits lost and dimmed, is by these purified and re-illumined; and is more precious far than ten thousand bodily eyes, for by it alone is truth seen. Now there are two classes of persons: one class of those who will agree with you and will take your words as a revelation; another class to whom they will be utterly unmeaning, and who will naturally deem them to be idle tales, for they see no sort of profit which is to be obtained from them. And therefore you had better decide at once with which of the two you are proposing to argue. You will very likely say with neither, and that your chief aim in carrying on the argument is your own improvement; at the same time you do not grudge to others any benefit which they may receive."

"I think that I should prefer to carry on the argument mainly on my own behalf."

"Then take a step backward, for we have gone wrong in the order of the sciences."

"What was the mistake?" he said.

"After plane geometry," I said, "we proceeded at once to solids in

12 Or "at your apparent fear that the public may think you are introducing useless studies; it is indeed difficult and not at all easy to realize that in every man there is an eye. . . ."

revolution, instead of taking solids in themselves; whereas after the -second dimension the third, which is concerned with cubes and dimensions of depth, ought to have followed." [13]

"That is true, Socrates; but so little seems to be known as yet about these subjects."

"Why, yes," I said, "and for two reasons: in the first place, no government patronizes them; this leads to a want of energy in the pursuit of them, and they are difficult; in the second place, students cannot learn them unless they have a director. But then a director can hardly be found, and even if he could, as matters now stand, the students, who are very conceited, would not attend to him. That, however, would be otherwise if the whole State became the director of these studies and gave honor to them; then disciples would want to come, and there would be continuous and earnest search, and discoveries would be made; since even now, disregarded as they are by the world, and maimed of their fair proportions, and although none of their votaries can tell the use of them, still these studies force their way by their natural charm, and very likely, if they had the help of the State, they would some day emerge into light."

"Yes," he said, "there is a remarkable charm in them. But I do not clearly understand the change in the order. First you began with a geometry of plane surfaces?"

"Yes," I said.

"And you placed astronomy next, and then you made a step backward?"

"Yes, and I have delayed you by my hurry; the ludicrous state of solid geometry, which, in natural order, should have followed, made me pass over this branch and go on to astronomy, or motion of solids."

"True," he said.

"Then assuming that the science now omitted would come into existence if encouraged by the State, let us go on to astronomy, which will be fourth."

---

13 That is, solid geometry should come next after plane. In Plato's day the spread of geometry from plane surfaces to solids was just taking place, in part, perhaps, under his direction.

"The right order," he replied. "And now, Socrates, as you rebuked the vulgar manner in which I praised astronomy before, my praise shall be given in your own spirit. For everyone, as I think, must see that astronomy compels the soul to look upwards and leads us from this world to another."

"Everyone but myself," I said; "to everyone else this may be clear, but not to me."

"And what then would you say?"

"I should rather say that those who elevate astronomy into philosophy appear to me to make us look downwards and not upwards."

"What do you mean?" he asked.

"You," I replied, "have in your mind a truly sublime conception of our knowledge of the things above. And I dare say that if a person were to throw his head back and study the fretted ceiling, you would still think that his mind was the percipient, and not his eyes.[14] And you are very likely right, and I may be a simpleton; but, in my opinion, that knowledge only which is of being and of the unseen can make the soul look upwards, and whether a man gapes àt the heavens or blinks on the ground, seeking to learn some particular of sense, I would deny that he can learn, for nothing of that sort is matter of science; his soul is looking downwards, not upwards, whether his way to knowledge is by water or by land, whether he floats, or only lies on his back."

"I acknowledge," he said, "the justice of your rebuke. Still, I should like to ascertain how astronomy can be learned in any manner more conducive to that knowledge of which we are speaking?"

"I will tell you," I said: "The starry heaven which we behold is wrought upon a visible ground, and therefore, although the fairest and most perfect of visible things, must necessarily be deemed inferior far to the true motions of absolute swiftness and absolute slowness, which are relative to each other, and carry with them that which is contained in them, in the true number and in every true figure.

14 Glaucon is taking the idea of higher in a literal sense, as if gazing at physical objects on the ceiling or in the sky were itself a nobler form of study than gazing at similar objects on the ground.

Now, these are to be apprehended by reason and intelligence, but not by sight."

"True," he replied.

"The spangled heavens should be used as a pattern and with a view to that higher knowledge; their beauty is like the beauty of figures or pictures excellently wrought by the hand of Daedalus, or some other great artist, which we may chance to behold; any geometrician who saw them would appreciate the exquisiteness of their workmanship, but he would never dream of thinking that in them he could find the true equal or the true double, or the truth of any other proportion."

"No," he replied, "such an idea would be ridiculous."

"And will not a true astronomer have the same feeling when he looks at the movements of the stars? Will he not think that heaven and the things in heaven are framed by the Creator of them in the most perfect manner? But he will never imagine that the proportions of night and day, or of both to the month, or of the month to the year, or of the stars to these and to one another, and any other things that are material and visible can also be eternal and subject to no deviation—that would be absurd; and it is equally absurd to take so much pains in investigating their exact truth."

"I quite agree, though I never thought of this before."

"Then," I said, "in astronomy, as in geometry, we should employ problems,[15] and let the heavens alone if we would approach the subject in the right way and so make the natural gift of reason to be of any real use."

"That," he said, "is a work infinitely beyond our present astronomers."

"Yes," I said; "and there are many other things which must also have a similar extension given to them, if our legislation is to be of any value. But can you tell me of any other suitable study?"

15 Plato is here proposing something not unlike our modern theoretical and mathematical astronomy. The stars, being physical bodies in an imperfect, physical universe, do not, he argues, in their movements follow with absolute precision the lines of ideal, mathematical figures. Astronomy, he insists, is more than looking at the sky.

"No," he said, "not without thinking."

"Motion," I said, "has many forms, and not one only; two of them are obvious enough even to wits no better than ours; and there are others, as I imagine, which may be left to wiser persons."

"But where are the two?"

"There is a second," I said, "which is the counterpart of the one already named."

"And what may that be?"

"The second," I said, "would seem relatively to the ears to be what the first is to the eyes; for I conceive that as the eyes are designed to look up at the stars, so are the ears to hear harmonious motions; and these are sister sciences—as the Pythagoreans [16] say, and we, Glaucon, agree with them?"

"Yes," he replied.

"But this," I said, "is a laborious study, and therefore we had better go and learn of them; and they will tell us whether there are any other applications of these sciences. At the same time, we must not lose sight of our own higher object."

"What is that?"

"There is a perfection which all knowledge ought to reach, and which our pupils ought also to attain, and not to fall short of, as I was saying that they did in astronomy. For in the science of harmony, as you probably know, the same thing happens. The teachers of harmony compare the sounds and consonances which are heard only, and their labor, like that of the astronomers, is in vain."

"Yes, by heaven!" he said; "and 'tis as good as a play to hear them talking about their condensed notes,[17] as they call them; they put their ears close alongside of the strings like persons catching a sound from their neighbor's wall—one set of them declaring that they distinguish an intermediate note and have found the least interval which should be the unit of measurement; the others insisting that

16 The school of Pythagoras (c. 500 B.C.) emphasized the study of a philosophical type of mathematics and musical harmony.
17 Or refined notes, a term for musical notes separated by the smallest possible interval.

the two sounds have passed into [18] the same—either party setting their ears before their understanding."

"You mean," I said, "those gentlemen who tease and torture the strings and rack them on the pegs of the instrument: I might carry on the metaphor and speak after their manner of the blows which the plectrum gives, and make accusations against the strings, both of backwardness and forwardness to sound; but this would be tedious, and therefore I will only say that these are not the men, and that I am referring to the Pythagoreans, of whom I was just now proposing to inquire about harmony. For they too are in error, like the astronomers; they investigate the numbers of the harmonies which are heard, but they never attain to problems—that is to say, they never reach the natural harmonies of number, or reflect why some numbers are harmonious and others not." [19]

"That," he said, "is a thing of more than mortal knowledge."

"A thing," I replied, "which I would rather call useful; that is, if sought after with a view to the beautiful and good; but if pursued in any other spirit, useless."

"Very true," he said.

"Now, when all these studies reach the point of intercommunion and connection with one another, and come to be considered in their mutual affinities, then, I think, but not till then, will the pursuit of them have a value for our objects; otherwise there is no profit in them."

"I suspect so; but you are speaking, Socrates, of a vast work."

"What do you mean?" I said; "the prelude or what? Do you not know that all this is but the prelude to the actual strain which we have to learn? For you surely would not regard the skilled mathematician as a dialectician?"

"Assuredly not," he said; "I have hardly ever known a mathematician who was capable of reasoning."

"But do you imagine that men who are unable to give and take a reason will have the knowledge which we require of them?"

18 Or merged into.
19 That is, never attempt a general theory of music.

"Neither can this be supposed."

"And so, Glaucon," I said, "we have at last arrived at the hymn of dialectic.[20] This is that strain which is of the intellect only, but which the faculty of sight will nevertheless be found to imitate; for sight, as you may remember, was imagined by us after a while to behold the real animals and stars, and last of all the sun himself. And so with dialectic; when a person starts on the discovery of the absolute by the light of reason only, and without any assistance of sense, and perseveres until by pure intelligence he arrives at the perception of the absolute good, he at last finds himself at the end of the intellectual world, as in the case of sight at the end of the visible."

"Exactly," he said.

"Then this is the progress which you call dialectic?"

"True."

"But the release of the prisoners from chains, and their translation from the shadows to the images and to the light, and the ascent from the underground den to the sun, while in his presence they are vainly trying to look on animals and plants and the light of the sun, but are able to perceive even with their weak eyes the images in the water (which are divine), and are the shadows of true existence (not shadows of images cast by a light of fire, which compared with the sun is only an image)—this power of elevating the highest principle in the soul to the contemplation of that which is best in existence, with which we may compare the raising of that faculty which is the very light of the body to the sight of that which is brightest in the material and visible world—this power is given, as I was saying, by all that study and pursuit of the arts which has been described."

"I agree in what you are saying," he replied, "which may be hard to believe, yet, from another point of view, is harder still to deny. This however is not a theme to be treated of in passing only, but will have to be discussed again and again."

20 The name Plato used for the practice of philosophic reasoning. The mind, trained by these various separate sciences to think exactly along abstract lines, now reaches the point where it can rise to consider the essential nature of the world as a whole and the absolute good above it.

Further praise of dialectic, which alone goes directly to first principles and does not depend, like the arts and sciences, on insecure hypotheses.

"And do you also agree," I said, "in describing the dialectician as one who attains a conception of the essence of each thing? And he who does not possess and is therefore unable to impart this conception, in whatever degree he fails, may in that degree also be said to fail in intelligence? Will you admit so much?"

"Yes," he said; "how can I deny it?"

"And you would say the same of the conception of the good? Until the person is able to abstract and define rationally the idea of good, and unless he can run the gauntlet of all objections, and is ready to disprove them, not by appeals to opinion, but to absolute truth, never faltering at any step of the argument—unless he can do all this, you would say that he knows neither the idea of good nor any other good; he apprehends only a shadow, if anything at all, which is given by opinion and not by science;—dreaming and slumbering in this life, before he is well awake here, he arrives at the world below, and has his final quietus."

"In all that I should most certainly agree with you."

"And surely you would not have the children of your ideal State, whom you are nurturing and educating—if the ideal ever becomes a reality—you would not allow the future rulers to be like posts, having no reason in them, and yet to be set in authority over the highest matters?"

"Certainly not."

"Then you will make a law that they shall have such an education as will enable them to attain the greatest skill in asking and answering questions?"

"Yes," he said, "you and I together will make it."

"Dialectic, then, as you will agree, is the coping stone of the sciences, and is set over them; no other science can be placed higher —the nature of knowledge can no further go?"

"I agree," he said.

"But to whom we are to assign these studies, and in what way they are to be assigned, are questions which remain to be considered."

"Yes, clearly."

"You remember," I said, "how the rulers were chosen before?"

"Certainly," he said.

"The same natures must still be chosen, and the preference again given to the surest and the bravest, and, if possible, to the fairest; and, having noble and generous tempers, they should also have the natural gifts which will facilitate their education."

"And what are these?"

"Such gifts as keenness and ready powers of acquisition; for the mind more often faints from the severity of study than from the severity of gymnastics: the toil is more entirely the mind's own, and is not shared with the body."

"Very true," he replied.

"Further, he of whom we are in search should have a good memory, and be an unwearied solid man who is a lover of labor in any line; or he will never be able to endure the great amount of bodily exercise and to go through all the intellectual discipline and study which we require of him."

"Certainly," he said; "he must have natural gifts."

"The mistake at present is that those who study philosophy have no vocation, and this, as I was before saying, is the reason why she has fallen into disrepute: her true sons should take her by the hand and not bastards."

"What do you mean?"

"In the first place, her votary should not have a lame or halting industry—I mean, that he should not be half industrious and half idle: as, for example, when a man is a lover of gymnastic and hunting, and all other bodily exercises, but a hater rather than a lover of the labor of learning or listening or inquiring. Or the occupation to which he devotes himself may be of an opposite kind, and he may have the other sort of lameness."

"Certainly," he said.

"And as to truth," I said, "is not a soul equally to be deemed halt and lame which hates voluntary falsehood and is extremely indignant at herself and others when they tell lies, but is patient of involuntary falsehood, and does not mind wallowing like a swinish beast in the mire of ignorance, and has no shame at being detected?"

"To be sure."

"And, again, in respect of temperance, courage, magnificence, and every other virtue, should we not carefully distinguish between the true son and the bastard? for where there is no discernment of such qualities, states and individuals unconsciously err; and the state makes a ruler, and the individual a friend, of one who, being defective in some part of virtue, is in a figure lame or a bastard."

"That is very true," he said.

"All these things, then, will have to be carefully considered by us; and if only those whom we introduce to this vast system of education and training are sound in body and mind, justice herself will have nothing to say against us, and we shall be the saviors of the constitution and of the State; but, if our pupils are men of another stamp, the reverse will happen, and we shall pour a still greater flood of ridicule on philosophy than she has to endure at present."

"That would not be creditable."

"Certainly not," I said; "and yet perhaps, in thus turning jest into earnest, I am equally ridiculous."

"In what respect?"

"I had forgotten," I said, "that we were not serious, and spoke with too much excitement. For when I saw philosophy so undeservedly trampled underfoot of men I could not help feeling a sort of indignation at the authors of her disgrace: and my anger made me too vehement."

"Indeed! I was listening, and did not think so."

"But I, who am the speaker, felt that I was. And now let me remind you that, although in our former selection we chose old men, we must not do so in this. Solon was under a delusion when he said that a man when he grows old may learn many things—for he can no more learn much than he can run much; youth is the time for any extraordinary toil."

"Of course."

"And, therefore, calculation and geometry and all the other elements of instruction, which are a preparation for dialectic, should be presented to the mind in childhood; [21] not, however, under any notion of forcing our system of education."

"Why not?"

"Because a freeman ought not to be a slave in the acquisition of knowledge of any kind. Bodily exercise, when compulsory, does no harm to the body; but knowledge which is acquired under compulsion obtains no hold on the mind."

"Very true."

"Then, my good friend," I said, "do not use compulsion, but let early education be a sort of amusement; you will then be better able to find out the natural bent."

"That is a very rational notion," he said.

"Do you remember that the children, too, were to be taken to see the battle on horseback; and that if there were no danger they were to be brought close up and, like young hounds, have a taste of blood given them?"

"Yes, I remember."

"The same practice may be followed," I said, "in all these things—labors, lessons, dangers—and he who is most at home in all of them ought to be enrolled in a select number."

"At what age?"

"At the age when the necessary gymnastics are over: the period whether of two or three years which passes in this sort of training is useless for any other purpose; for sleep and exercise are unpropitious to learning; and the trial of who is first in gymnastic exercises is one of the most important tests to which our youth are subjected."

"Certainly," he replied.

"After that time those who are selected from the class of twenty

21 Socrates sketches now a plan for the life of high training and service that will fall to the select and gifted group of rulers in his ideal state.

years old will be promoted to higher honor, and the sciences which
they learned without any order in their early education will now be
brought together, and they will be able to see the natural relationship
of them to one another and to true being."

"Yes," he said, "that is the only kind of knowledge which takes
lasting root."

"Yes," I said; "and the capacity for such knowledge is the great
criterion of dialectical talent: the comprehensive mind is always the
dialectical."

"I agree with you," he said.

"These," I said, "are the points which you must consider; and
those who have most of this comprehension, and who are most steadfast in their learning, and in their military and other appointed duties,
when they have arrived at the age of thirty will have to be chosen by
you out of the select class, and elevated to higher honor; and you will
have to prove them by the help of dialectic, in order to learn which of
them is able to give up the use of sight and the other senses, and in
company with truth to attain absolute being. And here, my friend,
great caution is required."

"Why great caution?"

"Do you not remark," I said, "how great is the evil which dialectic
has introduced?"

"What evil?" he said.

"The students of the art are filled with lawlessness." [22]

"Quite true," he said.

"Do you think that there is anything so very unnatural or inex-
cusable in their case? or will you make allowance for them?"

"In what way make allowance?"

"I want you," I said, "by way of parallel, to imagine a supposititious
son who is brought up in great wealth; he is one of a great and
numerous family, and has many flatterers. When he grows up to
manhood, he learns that his alleged are not his real parents; but who

---

22 A warning against the temporarily upsetting effect of much free thought and
criticism on the young and immature boys and girls, who then, like puppies, want
to pull every belief to pieces.

the real are he is unable to discover. Can you guess how he will be likely to behave towards his flatterers and his supposed parents, first of all during the period when he is ignorant of the false relation, and then again when he knows? Or shall I guess for you?"

"If you please."

"Then I should say that while he is ignorant of the truth he will be likely to honor his father and his mother and his supposed relations more than the flatterers; he will be less inclined to neglect them when in need, or to do or say anything against them; and he will be less willing to disobey them in any important matter."

"He will."

"But when he has made the discovery, I should imagine that he would diminish his honor and regard for them, and would become more devoted to the flatterers; their influence over him would greatly increase; he would now live after their ways, and openly associate with them, and, unless he were of an unusually good disposition, he would trouble himself no more about his supposed parents or other relations."

"Well, all that is very probable. But how is the image applicable to the disciples of philosophy?"

"In this way: you know that there are certain principles about justice and honor, which were taught us in childhood, and under their parental authority we have been brought up, obeying and honoring them."

"That is true."

"There are also opposite maxims and habits of pleasure which flatter and attract the soul, but do not influence those of us who have any sense of right, and they continue to obey and honor the maxims of their fathers."

"True."

"Now, when a man is in this state, and the questioning spirit asks what is fair or honorable, and he answers as the legislator has taught him, and then arguments many and diverse refute his words, until he is driven into believing that nothing is honorable any more than dishonorable, or just and good any more than the reverse, and so of all the notions which he most valued, do you think that he will still honor and obey them as before?"

"Impossible."

"And when he ceases to think them honorable and natural as heretofore, and he fails to discover the true, can he be expected to pursue any life other than that which flatters his desires?"

"He cannot."

"And from being a keeper of the law he is converted into a breaker of it?"

"Unquestionably."

"Now all this is very natural in students of philosophy such as I have described, and also, as I was just now saying, most excusable."

"Yes," he said; "and, I may add, pitiable."

"Therefore, that your feelings may not be moved to pity about our citizens who are now thirty years of age, every care must be taken in introducing them to dialectic."

"Certainly."

"There is a danger lest they should taste the dear delight too early; for youngsters, as you may have observed, when they first get the taste in their mouths, argue for amusement, and are always contra-dicting and refuting others in imitation of those who refute them; like puppy dogs, they rejoice in pulling and tearing at all who come near them."

"Yes," he said, "there is nothing which they like better."

"And when they have made many conquests and received defeats at the hands of many, they violently and speedily get into a way of not believing anything which they believed before, and hence, not only they, but philosophy and all that relates to it is apt to have a bad name with the rest of the world."

"Too true," he said.

"But when a man begins to get older, he will no longer be guilty of such insanity; he will imitate the dialectician who is seeking for truth, and not the eristic,[23] who is contradicting for the sake of amuse-

23 See *Phaedo*, note 22.

ment; and the greater moderation of his character will increase instead of diminishing the honor of the pursuit."

"Very true," he said.

"And did we not make special provision for this, when we said that the disciples of philosophy were to be orderly and steadfast, not, as now, any chance aspirant or intruder?"

"Very true."

"Suppose," I said, "the study of philosophy to take the place of gymnastics and to be continued diligently and earnestly and exclusively for twice the number of years which were passed in bodily exercise—will that be enough?"

"Would you say six or four years?" he asked.

"Say five years," I replied; "at the end of the time they must be sent down again into the den and compelled to hold any military or other office which young men are qualified to hold: in this way they will get their experience of life, and there will be an opportunity of trying whether, when they are drawn all manner of ways by temptation, they will stand firm or flinch."

"And how long is this stage of their lives to last?"

"Fifteen years," I answered; "and when they have reached fifty years of age, then let those who still survive and have distinguished themselves in every action of their lives and in every branch of knowledge come at last to their consummation. The time has now arrived at which they must raise the eye of the soul to the universal light which lightens all things, and behold the absolute good; for that is the pattern according to which they are to order the State and the lives of individuals, and the remainder of their own lives also; making philosophy their chief pursuit, but, when their turn comes, toiling also at politics and ruling for the public good, not as though they were performing some heroic action, but simply as a matter of duty; and when they have brought up in each generation others like themselves and left them in their place to be governors of the State, then they will depart to the Islands of the Blest and dwell there; and the city will give them public memorials and sacrifices and honor them, if the Pythian oracle consent, as demigods, but if not, as in any case blessed and divine."

"You are a sculptor, Socrates, and have made statues of our governors faultless in beauty."

"Yes," I said, "Glaucon, and of our governesses too; for you must not suppose that what I have been saying applies to men only and not to women as far as their natures can go."

"There you are right," he said, "since we have made them to share in all things like the men."

"Well," I said, "and you would agree (would you not?) that what has been said about the State and the government is not a mere dream, and although difficult not impossible, but only possible in the way which has been supposed; that is to say, when the true philosopher kings are born in a State, one or more of them, despising the honors of this present world which they deem mean and worthless, esteeming above all things right and the honor that springs from right, and regarding justice as the greatest and most necessary of all things, whose ministers they are, and whose principles will be exalted by them when they set in order their own city?"

"How will they proceed?"

"They will begin by sending out into the country all the inhabitants of the city who are more than ten years old, and will take possession of their children, who will be unaffected by the habits of their parents; these they will train in their own habits and laws, I mean in the laws which we have given them: and in this way the State and constitution of which we were speaking will soonest and most easily attain happiness, and the nation which has such a constitution will gain most."

"Yes, that will be the best way. And I think, Socrates, that you have very well described how, if ever, such a constitution might come into being."

"Enough then of the perfect State, and of the man who bears its image—there is no difficulty in seeing how we shall describe him."

"There is no difficulty," he replied; "and I agree with you in thinking that nothing more need be said."

BOOK VIII

Four inferior types of government—timocracy, oligarchy, democracy, and tyranny. Corresponding types of individuals. How from the better they degenerate to the worse.

"AND SO, Glaucon, we have arrived at the conclusion that in the perfect State wives and children are to be in common; and that all education and the pursuits of war and peace are also to be common, and the best philosophers and the bravest warriors are to be their kings?"

"That," replied Glaucon, "has been acknowledged."

"Yes," I said; "and we have further acknowledged that the governors, when appointed themselves, will take their soldiers and place them in houses such as we were describing, which are common to all, and contain nothing private, or individual; and about their property, you remember what we agreed?"

"Yes, I remember that no one was to have any of the ordinary possessions of mankind; they were to be warrior athletes and guardians, receiving from the other citizens, in lieu of annual payment, only their maintenance, and they were to take care of themselves and of the whole State."

"True," I said; "and now that this division of our task is concluded, let us find the point at which we digressed, that we may return into the old path."

"There is no difficulty in returning; you implied, then as now, that you had finished the description of the State: you said that such a State was good, and that the man was good who answered to it, although, as now appears, you had more' excellent things to relate both of State and man. And you said further, that if this was the true form, then the others were false; and of the false forms, you said, as I remember, that there were four principal ones, and that their defects, and the defects of the individuals corresponding to them, were worth examining. When we had seen all the individuals, and finally agreed as to who was the best and who was the worst of them, we were to consider whether the best was not also the happiest, and the worst the most miserable. I asked you what were the four forms of government of which you spoke, and then Polemarchus and Adeimantus put in their word; and you began again, and have found your way to the point at which we have now arrived."

"Your recollection," I said, "is most exact."

"Then, like a wrestler," he replied, "you must put yourself again in the same position; and let me ask the same questions, and do you give me the same answer which you were about to give me then."

"Yes, if I can, I will," I said.

"I shall particularly wish to hear what were the four constitutions of which you were speaking."

"That question," I said, "is easily answered: the four governments of which I spoke, so far as they have distinct names, are, first, those of Crete and Sparta,[1] which are generally applauded; what is termed oligarchy comes next; this is not equally approved, and is a form of government which teems with evils; thirdly, democracy, which naturally follows oligarchy, although very different; and lastly comes tyranny, great and famous, which differs from them all, and is the fourth and worst disorder of a State. I do not know, do you? of any other constitution which can be said to have a distinct character. There are lordships and principalities which are bought and sold, and some other intermediate forms of government. But these are nondescripts and may be found equally among Hellenes and among barbarians."

"Yes," he replied, "we certainly hear of many curious forms of government which exist among them."

"Do you know," I said, "that governments vary as the dispositions of men vary, and that there must be as many of the one as there are

1 The governments of Crete and Sparta, for which many Athenians professed great admiration, were what Socrates a little later calls timocracies or governments of honor. By this he means not an aristocracy or government of the wisest and best, as in the ideal state, but government by a soldier caste, ambitious for military glory and authority.

of the other? For we cannot suppose that States are made of 'oak and rock,' and not out of the human natures which are in them, and which in a figure turn the scale and draw other things after them?"

"Yes," he said, "the States are as the men are; they grow out of human characters."

"Then if the constitutions of States are five, the dispositions of individual minds will also be five?"

"Certainly."

"Him who answers to aristocracy, and whom we rightly call just and good, we have already described."

"We have."

"Then let us now proceed to describe the inferior sort of natures, being the contentious and ambitious, who answer to the Spartan polity; also the oligarchical, democratical, and tyrannical. Let us place the most just by the side of the most unjust, and when we see them we shall be able to compare the relative happiness or unhappiness of him who leads a life of pure justice or pure injustice. The inquiry will then be completed. And we shall know whether we ought to pursue injustice, as Thrasymachus advises, or in accordance with the conclusions of the argument to prefer justice."

"Certainly," he replied, "we must do as you say."

"Shall we follow our old plan, which we adopted with a view to clearness, of taking the State first and then proceeding to the individual, and begin with the government of honor?—I know of no name for such a government other than timocracy, or perhaps timarchy. We will compare with this the like character in the individual; and, after that, consider oligarchy and the oligarchical man; and then again we will turn our attention to democracy and the democratical man; and lastly, we will go and view the city of tyranny, and once more take a look into the tyrant's soul, and try to arrive at a satisfactory decision."

"That way of viewing and judging of the matter will be very suitable."

"First, then," I said, "let us inquire how timocracy (the government of honor) arises out of aristocracy (the government of the best).

Clearly, all political changes originate in divisions of the actual governing power; a government which is united, however small, cannot be moved."

"Very true," he said.

"In what way, then, will our city be moved, and in what manner will the two classes of auxiliaries [2] and rulers disagree among themselves or with one another? Shall we, after the manner of Homer, pray the Muses [3] to tell us 'how discord first arose'? Shall we imagine them in solemn mockery, to play and jest with us as if we were children, and to address us in a lofty tragic vein, making believe to be in earnest?"

"How would they address us?"

"After this manner: A city which is thus constituted can hardly be shaken; but, seeing that everything which has a beginning has also an end, even a constitution such as yours will not last forever, but will in time be dissolved. And this is the dissolution: In plants that grow in the earth, as well as in animals that move on the earth's surface, fertility and sterility of soul and body occur when the circumferences of the circles of each are completed, which in short-lived existences pass over a short space, and in long-lived ones over a long space. But to the knowledge of human fecundity and sterility all the wisdom and education of your rulers will not attain; the laws which regulate them will not be discovered by an intelligence which is alloyed with sense, but will escape them, and they will bring children into the world when they ought not.

In a very obscure passage Socrates explains mathematically the cycles of good and evil births.

When your guardians are ignorant of the law of births, and unite bride and bridegroom out of season, the children will not be goodly or fortunate. And though only the best of them will be appointed by their predecessors, still they will be unworthy to hold their fathers' places, and when they come into power as guardians, they will soon

2 That is, soldier guardians.
3 See the opening lines of the *Iliad*, I, 1-7.

be found to fail in taking care of us, the Muses, first by undervaluing music; which neglect will soon extend to gymnastic; and hence the young men of your State will be less cultivated. In the succeeding generation rulers will be appointed who have lost the guardian power of testing the metal of your different races, which, like Hesiod's, are of gold and silver and brass and iron.[4] And so iron will be mingled with silver, and brass with gold, and hence there will arise dissimilarity and inequality and irregularity, which always and in all places are causes of hatred and war. This the Muses affirm to be the stock from which discord has sprung, wherever arising; and this is their answer to us."

"Yes, and we may assume that they answer truly."

"Why, yes," I said, "of course they answer truly; how can the Muses speak falsely?"

"And what do the Muses say next?"

"When discord arose, then the two races were drawn different ways: the iron and brass fell to acquiring money and land and houses and gold and silver; but the gold and silver races, not wanting money but having the true riches in their own nature, inclined towards virtue and the ancient order of things. There was a battle between them, and at last they agreed to distribute their land and houses among individual owners; and they enslaved their friends and maintainers, whom they had formerly protected in the condition of freemen, and made of them subjects and servants; and they themselves were engaged in war and in keeping a watch against them."

"I believe that you have rightly conceived the origin of the change."

"And the new government which thus arises will be of a form intermediate between oligarchy [5] and aristocracy?"

"Very true."

"Such will be the change, and after the change has been made, how will they proceed? Clearly, the new State, being in a mean be-

4 See page 303.
5 Oligarchy, as we shall see later, means to Socrates government by the rich and by persons intent on making money.

tween oligarchy and the perfect State, will partly follow one and partly the other, and will also have some peculiarities."

"True," he said.

"In the honor given to rulers, in the abstinence of the warrior class from agriculture, handicrafts, and trade in general, in the institution of common meals, and in the attention paid to gymnastics and military training—in all these respects this State will resemble the former."

"True."

"But in the fear of admitting philosophers to power, because they are no longer to be had simple and earnest, but are made up of mixed elements; and in turning from them to passionate and less complex characters, who are by nature fitted for war rather than peace; and in the value set by them upon military stratagems and contrivances, and in the waging of everlasting wars—this State will be for the most part peculiar."

"Yes."

"Yes," I said; "and men of this stamp will be covetous of money, like those who live in oligarchies; they will have a fierce secret longing after gold and silver, which they will hoard in dark places, having magazines and treasuries of their own for the deposit and concealment of them; also castles which are just nests for their eggs, and in which they will spend large sums on their wives, or on any others whom they please."

"That is most true," he said.

"And they are miserly because they have no means of openly acquiring the money which they prize; they will spend that which is another man's on the gratification of their desires, stealing their pleasures and running away like children from the law, their father they have been schooled not by gentle influences but by force, for they have neglected her who is the true Muse, the companion of reason and philosophy, and have honored gymnastic more than music."

"Undoubtedly," he said, "the form of government which you describe is a mixture of good and evil."

"Why, there is a mixture," I said; "but one thing, and one thing only, is predominantly seen—the spirit of contention and ambition; and these are due to the prevalence of the passionate or spirited element."

"Assuredly," he said.

"Such is the origin and such the character of this State, which has been described in outline only; the more perfect execution was not required, for a sketch is enough to show the type of the most perfectly just and most perfectly unjust; and to go through all the States and all the characters of men, omitting none of them, would be an interminable labor."

"Very true," he replied.

"Now what man answers to this form of government—how did he come into being, and what is he like?"

"I think," said Adeimantus, "that in the spirit of contention which characterizes him, he is not unlike our friend Glaucon." 6

"Perhaps," I said, "he may be like him in that one point; but there are other respects in which he is very different."

"In what respects?"

"He should have more of self-assertion and be less cultivated, and yet a friend of culture; and he should be a good listener, but no speaker. Such a person is apt to be rough with slaves, unlike the educated man, who is too proud for that; and he will also be courteous to freemen, and remarkably obedient to authority; he is a lover of power and a lover of honor; claiming to be a ruler, not because he is eloquent, or on any ground of that sort, but because he is a soldier and has performed feats of arms; he is also a lover of gymnastic exercises and of the chase."

"Yes, that is the type of character which answers to timocracy."

"Such a one will despise riches only when he is young; but as he gets older he will be more and more attracted to them, because he has a piece of the avaricious nature in him, and is not single-minded towards virtue, having lost his best guardian."

6 Glaucon, it may be noticed, throughout the dialogue is the liveliest of the young arguers and the quickest wit.

"Who was that?" said Adeimantus.

"Philosophy," I said, "tempered with music, who comes and takes up her abode in a man, and is the only savior of his virtue throughout life."

"Good," he said.

"Such," I said, "is the timocratical youth, and he is like the timo-cratical State."

"Exactly."

"His origin is as follows: He is often the young son of a brave father, who dwells in an ill-governed city, of which he declines the honors and offices, and will not go to law, or exert himself in any way, but is ready to waive his rights in order that he may escape trouble."

"And how does the son come into being?"

"The character of the son begins to develop when he hears his mother complaining that her husband has no place in the government, of which the consequence is that she has no precedence among other women. Further, when she sees her husband not very eager about money, and instead of battling and railing in the law courts or assembly, taking whatever happens to him quietly; and when she observes that his thoughts always center in himself, while he treats her with very considerable indifference, she is annoyed, and says to her son that his father is only half a man and far too easy-going: adding all the other complaints about her own ill treatment which women are so fond of rehearsing."

"Yes," said Adeimantus, "they give us plenty of them, and their complaints are so like themselves."

"And you know," I said, "that the old servants also, who are supposed to be attached to the family, from time to time talk privately in the same strain to the son; and if they see anyone who owes money to his father, or is wronging him in any way, and he fails to prosecute them, they tell the youth that when he grows up he must retaliate upon people of this sort, and be more of a man than his father. He has only to walk abroad and he hears and sees the same sort of thing: those who do their own business in the city are called simpletons, and held in no esteem, while the busybodies are honored and applauded. The result is that the young man, hearing and seeing all these things—hearing, too, the words of his father, and having a nearer view of his way of life, and making comparisons of him and others—is drawn opposite ways: while his father is watering and nourishing the rational principle in his soul, the others are encouraging the passionate and appetitive; and he being not originally of a bad nature, but having kept bad company, is at last brought by their joint influence to a middle point, and gives up the kingdom which is within him to the middle principle of contentiousness and passion, and becomes arrogant and ambitious."

"You seem to me to have described his origin perfectly."

"Then we have now," I said, "the second form of government and the second type of character?"

"We have."

"Next, let us look at another man who, as Aeschylus says, 'is set over against another State'; [7] or rather, as our plan requires, begin with the State."

"By all means."

"I believe that oligarchy follows next in order."

"And what manner of government do you term oligarchy?"

"A government resting on a valuation of property, in which the rich have power and the poor man is deprived of it."

"I understand," he replied.

"Ought I not to begin by describing how the change from timocracy to oligarchy arises?"

"Yes."

"Well," I said, "no eyes are required in order to see how the one passes into the other."

"How?"

"The accumulation of gold in the treasury of private individuals is the ruin of timocracy; they invent illegal modes of expenditure; for what do they or their wives care about the law?"

7 Should be "gate." Aeschylus, *Seven Against Thebes*, 438.

"Yes, indeed."

"And then one, seeing another grow rich, seeks to rival him, and thus the great mass of the citizens become lovers of money."

"Likely enough."

"And so they grow richer and richer, and the more they think of making a fortune the less they think of virtue; for when riches and virtue are placed together in the scales of the balance, the one always rises as the other falls."

"True."

"And in proportion as riches and rich men are honored in the State, virtue and the virtuous are dishonored."

"Clearly."

"And what is honored is cultivated, and that which has no honor is neglected."

"That is obvious."

"And so at last, instead of loving contention and glory, men become lovers of trade and money; they honor and look up to the rich man, and make a ruler of him, and dishonor the poor man."

"They do so."

"They next proceed to make a law which fixes a sum of money as the qualification of citizenship; the sum is higher in one place and lower in another, as the oligarchy is more or less exclusive; and they allow no one whose property falls below the amount fixed to have any share in the government. These changes in the constitution they effect by force of arms, if intimidation has not already done their work."

"Very true."

"And this, speaking generally, is the way in which oligarchy is established."

"Yes," he said; "but what are the characteristics of this form of government, and what are the defects of which we were speaking?"

"First of all," I said, "consider the nature of the qualification. Just think what would happen if pilots were to be chosen according to their property, and a poor man were refused permission to steer, even though he were a better pilot?"

"You mean that they would shipwreck?"

"Yes; and is not this true of the government of anything?"

"I should imagine so."

"Except a city?—or would you include a city?"

"Nay," he said, "the case of a city is the strongest of all, inasmuch as the rule of a city is the greatest and most difficult of all."

"This, then, will be the first great defect of oligarchy?"

"Clearly."

"And here is another defect which is quite as bad."

"What defect?"

"The inevitable division: such a State is not one, but two States, the one of poor, the other of rich men; and they are living on the same spot and always conspiring against one another."

"That, surely, is at least as bad."

"Another discreditable feature is, that, for a like reason, they are incapable of carrying on any war. Either they arm the multitude, and then they are more afraid of them than of the enemy; or, if they do not call them out in the hour of battle, they are oligarchs indeed, few to fight as they are few to rule. And at the same time their fondness for money makes them unwilling to pay taxes."

"How discreditable!"

"And, as we said before, under such a constitution the same persons have too many callings—they are husbandmen, tradesmen, warriors, all in one. Does that look well?"

"Anything but well."

"There is another evil which is, perhaps, the greatest of all, and to which this State first begins to be liable."

"What evil?"

"A man may sell all that he has, and another may acquire his property; yet after the sale he may dwell in the city of which he is no longer a part, being neither trader, nor artisan, nor horseman, nor hoplite,[8] but only a poor, helpless creature."

"Yes, that is an evil which also first begins in this State."

8 A heavy-armed infantry soldier.

"The evil is certainly not prevented there; for oligarchies have both the extremes of great wealth and utter poverty."

"True."

"But think again: In his wealthy days, while he was spending his money, was a man of this sort a whit more good to the State for the purposes of citizenship? Or did he only seem to be a member of the ruling body, although in truth he was neither ruler nor subject, but just a spendthrift?"

"As you say, he seemed to be a ruler, but was only a spendthrift."

"May we not say that this is the drone in the house who is like the drone in the honeycomb, and that the one is the plague of the city as the other is of the hive?"

"Just so, Socrates."

"And God has made the flying drones, Adeimantus, all without stings, whereas of the walking drones he has made some without stings but others have dreadful stings; of the stingless class are those who in their old age end as paupers; of the stingers come all the criminal class, as they are termed."

"Most true," he said.

"Clearly then, whenever you see paupers in a State, somewhere in that neighborhood there are hidden away thieves and cut-purses and robbers of temples, and all sorts of malefactors."

"Clearly."

"Well," I said, "and in oligarchical States do you not find paupers?"

"Yes," he said; "nearly everybody is a pauper who is not a ruler."

"And may we be so bold as to affirm that there are also many criminals to be found in them, rogues who have stings, and whom the authorities are careful to restrain by force?"

"Certainly, we may be so bold."

"The existence of such persons is to be attributed to want of education, ill training, and an evil constitution of the State?"

"True."

"Such, then, is the form and such are the evils of oligarchy; and there may be many other evils."

"Very likely."

"Then oligarchy, or the form of government in which the rulers are elected for their wealth, may now be dismissed. Let us next proceed to consider the nature and origin of the individual who answers to this State."

"By all means."

"Does not the timocratical man change into the oligarchical on this wise?"

"How?"

"A time arrives when the representative of timocracy has a son: at first he begins by emulating his father and walking in his footsteps, but presently he sees him of a sudden foundering against the State as upon a sunken reef, and he and all that he has is lost; he may have been a general or some other high officer who is brought to trial under a prejudice raised by informers, and either put to death, or exiled, or deprived of the privileges of a citizen, and all his property taken from him."

"Nothing more likely."

"And the son has seen and known all this—he is a ruined man, and his fear has taught him to knock ambition and passion headforemost from his bosom's throne; humbled by poverty he takes to money-making and by mean and miserly savings and hard work gets a fortune together. Is not such a one likely to seat the concupiscent and covetous element on the vacant throne and to suffer it to play the great king within him, girt with tiara and chain and scimitar?"

"Most true," he replied.

"And when he has made reason and spirit sit down on the ground obediently on either side of their sovereign, and taught them to know their place, he compels the one [9] to think only of how lesser sums may be turned into larger ones, and will not allow the other [10] to worship and admire anything but riches and rich men, or to be

9 That is, his reason.
10 His spirit.

ambitious of anything so much as the acquisition of wealth and the means of acquiring it."

"Of all changes," he said, "there is none so speedy or so sure as the conversion of the ambitious youth into the avaricious one."

"And the avaricious," I said, "is the oligarchical youth?"

"Yes," he said; "at any rate the individual out of whom he came is like the State out of which oligarchy came."

"Let us then consider whether there is any likeness between them."

"Very good."

"First, then, they resemble one another in the value which they set upon wealth?"

"Certainly."

"Also in their penurious, laborious character; the individual only satisfies his necessary appetites, and confines his expenditure to them; his other desires he subdues, under the idea that they are unprofitable."

"True."

"He is a shabby fellow, who saves something out of everything and makes a purse for himself; and this is the sort of man whom the vulgar applaud. Is he not a true image of the State which he represents?"

"He appears to me to be so; at any rate money is highly valued by him as well as by the State."

*　*　*　*　*

"For these reasons such a one will be more respectable than most people; yet the true virtue of a unanimous and harmonious soul will flee far away and never come near him."

"I should expect so."

"And surely, the miser individually will be an ignoble competitor in a State for any prize of victory, or other object of honorable ambition; he will not spend his money in the contest for glory; so afraid is he of awakening his expensive appetites and inviting them to help and join in the struggle; in true oligarchical fashion he fights with a small part only of his resources, and the result commonly is that he loses the prize and saves his money."

"Very true."

"Can we any longer doubt, then, that the miser and money-maker answers to the oligarchical State?"

"There can be no doubt."

"Next comes democracy; [11] of this the origin and nature have still to be considered by us; and then we will inquire into the ways of the democratic man, and bring him up for judgment."

"That," he said, "is our method."

"Well," I said, "and how does the change from oligarchy into democracy arise? Is it not on this wise?—The good at which such a State aims is to become as rich as possible, a desire which is insatiable?"

"What then?"

"The rulers, being aware that their power rests upon their wealth, refuse to curtail by law the extravagance of the spendthrift youth because they gain by their ruin; they take interest from them and buy up their estates and thus increase their own wealth and importance?"

"To be sure."

"There can be no doubt that the love of wealth and the spirit of moderation cannot exist together in citizens of the same state to any considerable extent; one or the other will be disregarded."

"That is tolerably clear."

"And in oligarchical States, from the general spread of carelessness and extravagance, men of good family have often been reduced to beggary?"

"Yes, often."

"And still they remain in the city; there they are, ready to sting and fully armed, and some of them owe money, some have forfeited their citizenship; a third class are in both predicaments; and they hate and conspire against those who have got their property, and against everybody else, and are eager for revolution."

11 Democracy here takes the shape of the divided and demoralized citizens of Athens in the years after the Pelopennesian War.

"That is true."

"On the other hand, the men of business, stooping as they walk, and pretending not even to see those whom they have already ruined, insert their sting—that is, their money—into someone else who is not on his guard against them, and recover the parent sum many times over multiplied into a family of children: [12] and so they make drone and pauper to abound in the State."

"Yes," he said, "there are plenty of them—that is certain."

"The evil blazes up like a fire; and they will not extinguish it, either by restricting a man's use of his own property, or by another remedy."

"What other?"

"One which is the next best, and has the advantage of compelling the citizens to look to their characters: Let there be a general rule that everyone shall enter into voluntary contracts at his own risk,[13] and there will be less of this scandalous money-making, and the evils of which we were speaking will be greatly lessened in the State."

"Yes, they will be greatly lessened."

"At present the governors, induced by the motives which I have named, treat their subjects badly; while they and their adherents, especially the young men of the governing class, are habituated to lead a life of luxury and idleness both of body and mind; they do nothing, and are incapable of resisting either pleasure or pain."

"Very true."

"They themselves care only for making money, and are as indifferent as the pauper to the cultivation of virtue."

"Yes, quite as indifferent."

"Such is the state of affairs which prevails among them. And often rulers and their subjects may come in one another's way, whether on a journey or on some other occasion of meeting, on a pilgrimage or a march, as fellow-soldiers or fellow-sailors; aye and they may observe the behavior of each other in the very moment of danger—for where

12 Rich men lend money on ruinous terms and so increase the number of bankrupts and paupers.

13 That is, the state will cease to enforce money contracts.

danger is, there is no fear that the poor will be despised by the rich—
and very likely the wiry sunburnt poor man may be placed in battle
at the side of a wealthy one who has never spoilt his complexion and
has plenty of superfluous flesh—when he sees such a one puffing and
at his wits' end, how can he avoid drawing the conclusion that men
like him are only rich because no one has the courage to despoil
them? And when they meet in private will not people be saying to
one another: 'Our warriors are not good for much'?"

"Yes," he said, "I am quite aware that this is their way of talking."

"And, as in a body which is diseased the addition of a touch from
without may bring on illness, and sometimes even when there is no
external provocation a commotion may arise within—in the same way
wherever there is weakness in the State there is also likely to be illness, of which the occasion may be very slight, the one party introducing from without their oligarchical, the other their democratical
allies, and then the State falls sick, and is at war with herself; and
may be at times distracted, even when there is no external cause."

"Yes, surely."

"And then democracy comes into being after the poor have conquered their opponents, slaughtering some and banishing some,
while to the remainder they give an equal share of freedom and
power; and this is the form of government in which the magistrates
are commonly elected by lot."

"Yes," he said, "that is the nature of democracy, whether the revolution has been effected by arms, or whether fear has caused the opposite party to withdraw."

"And now what is their manner of life, and what sort of a government have they? for as the government is, such will be the man."

"Clearly," he said.

"In the first place, are they not free; and is not the city full of
freedom and frankness—a man may say and do what he likes?"

" 'Tis said so," he replied.

"And where freedom is, the individual is clearly able to order for
himself his own life as he pleases?"

"Clearly."

"Then in this kind of State there will be the greatest variety of human natures?"

"There will."

"This, then, seems likely to be the fairest of States, being like an embroidered robe which is spangled with every sort of flower. And just as women and children think a variety of colors to be of all things most charming, so there are many men to whom this State, which is spangled with the manners and characters of mankind, will appear to be the fairest of States."

"Yes."

"Yes, my good sir, and there will be no better in which to look for a government."

"Why?"

"Because of the liberty which reigns there—they have a complete assortment of constitutions; and he who has a mind to establish a State, as we have been doing, must go to a democracy as he would to a bazaar at which they sell them, and pick out the one that suits him; then, when he has made his choice, he may found his State."

"He will be sure to have patterns enough."

"And there being no necessity," I said, "for you to govern in this State, even if you have the capacity, or to be governed, unless you like, or to go to war when the rest go to war, or to be at peace when others are at peace, unless you are so disposed—there being no necessity also, because some law forbids you to hold office or be a dicast,[14] that you should not hold office or be a dicast, if you have a fancy—is not this a way of life which for the moment is supremely delightful?"

"For the moment, yes."

"And is not their humanity to the condemned in some cases quite charming? Have you not observed how, in a democracy, many persons, although they have been sentenced to death or exile, just stay where they are and walk about the world—the gentleman parades like a hero, and nobody sees or cares?"

14 Or "sit on juries."

"Yes," he replied, "many and many a one."

"See too," I said, "the forgiving spirit of democracy, and the 'don't care' about trifles, and the disregard which she shows of all the fine principles which we solemnly laid down at the foundation of the city —as when we said that, except in the case of some rarely gifted nature, there never will be a good man who has not from his childhood been used to play amid things of beauty and make of them a joy and a study—how grandly does she trample all these fine notions of ours under her feet, never giving a thought to the pursuits which make a statesman, and promoting to honor anyone who professes to be the people's friend."

"Yes, she is of a noble spirit."

"These and other kindred characteristics are proper to democracy, which is a charming form of government, full of variety and disorder, and dispensing a sort of equality to equals and unequals alike."

"We know her well."

"Consider now," I said, "what manner of man the individual is, or rather consider, as in the case of the State, how he comes into being."

"Very good," he said.

"Is not this the way—he is the son of the miserly and oligarchical father who has trained him in his own habits?"

"Exactly."

"And, like his father, he keeps under by force the pleasures which are of the spending and not of the getting sort, being those which are called unnecessary?"

"Obviously."

Necessary pleasures are those that come from satisfying natural and essential needs, such as need of eating. Unnecessary are those that a man can as well or better do without, such as the eating of luxurious food. The first are not costly and keep a man in health and strength. The second are wasteful of money and may be hurtful.

"When a young man who has been brought up as we were just now describing, in a vulgar and miserly way, has tasted drones' honey and has come to associate with fierce and crafty natures who are able to provide for him all sorts of refinements and varieties of pleasure—then, as you may imagine, the change will begin of the oligarchical principle within him into the democratical?"

"Inevitably."

"And as in the city like was helping like, and the change was effected by an alliance from without assisting one division of the citizens, so too the young man is changed by a class of desires coming from without to assist the desires within him, that which is akin and alike again helping that which is akin and alike?"

"Certainly."

"And if there be any ally which aids the oligarchical principle within him, whether the influence of a father or of kindred, advising or rebuking him, then there arises in his soul a faction and an opposite faction, and he goes to war with himself."

"It must be so."

"And there are times when the democratical principle gives way to the oligarchical, and some of his desires die, and others are banished; a spirit of reverence enters into the young man's soul and order is restored."

"Yes," he said, "that sometimes happens."

"And then, again, after the old desires have been driven out, fresh ones spring up, which are akin to them, and because he their father does not know how to educate them, wax fierce and numerous."

"Yes," he said, "that is apt to be the way."

"They draw him to his old associates, and holding secret intercourse with them, breed and multiply in him."

"Very true."

"At length they seize upon the citadel of the young man's soul, which they perceive to be void of all accomplishments and fair pursuits and true words, which make their abode in the minds of men who are dear to the gods, and are their best guardians and sentinels."

"None better."

"False and boastful conceits and phrases mount upwards and take their place."

"They are certain to do so."

"And so the young man returns into the country of the lotus-eaters, and takes up his dwelling there in the face of all men; and if any help be sent by his friends to the oligarchical part of him, the aforesaid vain conceits shut the gate of the king's fastness; and they will neither allow the embassy itself to enter, nor if private advisers offer the fatherly counsel of the aged will they listen to them or receive them. There is a battle and they gain the day, and then modesty, which they call silliness, is ignominiously thrust into exile by them, and temperance, which they nickname unmanliness, is trampled in the mire and cast forth; they persuade men that moderation and orderly expenditure are vulgarity and meanness, and so, by the help of a rabble of evil appetites, they drive them beyond the border."

"Yes, with a will."

"And when they have emptied and swept clean the soul of him who is now in their power and who is being initiated by them in great mysteries, the next thing is to bring back to their house insolence and anarchy and waste and impudence in bright array having garlands on their heads, and a great company with them, hymning their praises and calling them by sweet names; insolence they term breeding, and anarchy liberty, and waste magnificence, and impudence courage. And so the young man passes out of his original nature, which was trained in the school of necessity, into the freedom and libertinism of useless and unnecessary pleasures."

"Yes," he said, "the change in him is visible enough."

"After this he lives on, spending his money and labor and time on unnecessary pleasures quite as much as on necessary ones; but if he be fortunate, and is not too much disordered in his wits, when years have elapsed, and the heyday of passion is over—supposing that he then re-admits into the city some part of the exiled virtues, and does not wholly give himself up to their successors—in that case he balances his pleasures and lives in a sort of equilibrium, putting the government of himself into the hands of the one which comes first and wins the turn; and when he has had enough of that, then into the hands of another; he despises none of them but encourages them all equally."

"Very true," he said.

"Neither does he receive or let pass into the fortress any true word of advice; if anyone says to him that some pleasures are the satisfactions of good and noble desires, and others of evil desires, and that he ought to use and honor some and chastise and master the others—whenever this is repeated to him he shakes his head and says that they are all alike, and that one is as good as another."

"Yes," he said; "that is the way with him."

"Yes," I said, "he lives from day to day indulging the appetite of the hour; and sometimes he is lapped in drink and strains of the flute; then he becomes a water-drinker, and tries to get thin; then he takes a turn at gymnastics; sometimes idling and neglecting everything, then once more living the life of a philosopher; often he is busy with politics, and starts to his feet and says and does whatever comes into his head; and, if he is emulous of anyone who is a warrior, off he is in that direction, or of men of business, once more in that. His life has neither law nor order; and this distracted existence he terms joy and bliss and freedom; and so he goes on."

"Yes," he replied, "he is all liberty and equality."

"Yes," I said; "his life is motley and manifold and an epitome of the lives of many; he answers to the State which we described as fair and spangled. And many a man and many a woman will take him for their pattern, and many a constitution and many an example of manners is contained in him."

"Just so."

"Let him then be set over against democracy; he may truly be called the democratic man."

"Let that be his place," he said.

"Last of all comes the most beautiful of all, man and State alike, tyranny and the tyrant; these we have now to consider."

"Quite true," he said.

"Say then, my friend, in what manner does tyranny arise?—that it has a democratic origin is evident."

"Clearly."

"And does not tyranny spring from democracy in the same manner as democracy from oligarchy—I mean, after a sort?"

"How?"

"The good which oligarchy proposed to itself and the means by which it was maintained was excess of wealth—am I not right?"

"Yes."

"And the insatiable desire of wealth and the neglect of all other things for the sake of money-getting was also the ruin of oligarchy?"

"True."

"And democracy has her own good, of which the insatiable desire brings her to dissolution?"

"What good?"

"Freedom," I replied; "which, as they tell you in a democracy, is the glory of the State—and that therefore in a democracy alone will the freeman of nature deign to dwell."

"Yes; the saying is in everybody's mouth."

"I was going to observe that the insatiable desire of this and the neglect of other things introduces the change in democracy, which occasions a demand for tyranny."

"How so?"

"When a democracy which is thirsting for freedom has evil cup-bearers presiding over the feast, and has drunk too deeply of the strong wine of freedom, then, unless her rulers are very amenable and give a plentiful draught,[15] she calls them to account and punishes them, and says that they are cursed oligarchs."

"Yes," he replied, "a very common occurrence."

"Yes," I said; "and loyal citizens are insultingly termed by her slaves who hug their chains and men of naught; she would have subjects who are like rulers, and rulers who are like subjects: these are men after her own heart, whom she praises and honors both in

15 Or "give her freedom without limit."

private and public. Now, in such a State, can liberty have any limit?"

"Certainly not."

"By degrees the anarchy finds a way into private houses, and ends by getting among the animals and infecting them."

"How do you mean?"

"I mean that the father grows accustomed to descend to the level of his sons and to fear them, and the son is on a level with his father, he having no respect or reverence for either of his parents; and this is his freedom, and the metic is equal with the citizen and the citizen with the metic, and the stranger is quite as good as either."

"Yes," he said, "that is the way."

"And these are not the only evils," I said—"there are several lesser ones: In such a state of society the master fears and flatters his scholars, and the scholars despise their masters and tutors; young and old are all alike; and the young man is on a level with the old, and is ready to compete with him in word or deed; and old men condescend to the young and are full of pleasantry and gaiety; they are loth to be thought morose and authoritative, and therefore they adopt the manners of the young."

"Quite true," he said.

"The last extreme of popular liberty is when the slave bought with money, whether male or female, is just as free as his or her purchaser; nor must I forget to tell of the liberty and equality of the two sexes in relation to each other."

"Why not, as Aeschylus says,[16] utter the word which rises to our lips?"

"That is what I am doing," I replied; "and I must add that no one who does not know would believe, how much greater is the liberty which the animals who are under the dominion of man have in a democracy than in any other State: for truly, the she-dogs, as the proverb says, are as good as their she-mistresses, and the horses and asses have a way of marching along with all the rights and dignities

16 Aeschylus, Fragment 351.

of freemen; and they will run at anybody who comes in their way if he does not leave the road clear for them: and all things are just ready to burst with liberty."

"When I take a country walk," he said, "I often experience what you describe. You and I have dreamed the same thing."

"And above all," I said, "and as the result of all, see how sensitive the citizens become; they chafe impatiently at the least touch of authority, and at length, as you know, they cease to care even for the laws, written or unwritten; they will have no one over them."

"Yes," he said, "I know it too well."

"Such, my friend," I said, "is the fair and glorious beginning out of which springs tyranny."

"Glorious indeed," he said. "But what is the next step?"

"The ruin of oligarchy is the ruin of democracy; the same disease magnified and intensified by liberty overmasters democracy—the truth being that the excessive increase of anything often causes a reaction in the opposite direction; and this is the case not only in the seasons and in vegetable and animal life, but above all in forms of government."

"True."

"The excess of liberty, whether in States or individuals, seems only to pass into excess of slavery."

"Yes, the natural order."

"And so tyranny naturally arises out of democracy, and the most aggravated form of tyranny and slavery out of the most extreme form of liberty?"

"As we might expect."

"That, however, was not, as I believe, your question—you rather desired to know what is that disorder which is generated alike in oligarchy and democracy, and is the ruin of both?"

"Just so," he replied.

"Well," I said, "I meant to refer to the class of idle spendthrifts, of whom the more courageous are the leaders and the more timid the followers, the same whom we were comparing to drones, some stingless, and others having stings."

"A very just comparison."

"These two classes are the plagues of every city in which they are generated, being what phlegm and bile are to the body. And the good physician and lawgiver of the State ought, like the wise bee-master, to keep them at a distance and prevent, if possible, their ever coming in; and if they have anyhow found a way in, then he should have them and their cells cut out as speedily as possible."

"Yes, by all means," he said.

"Then, in order that we may see clearly what we are doing, let us imagine democracy to be divided, as indeed it is, into three classes; for in the first place freedom creates rather more drones in the democratic than there were in the oligarchical State."

"That is true."

"And in the democracy they are certainly more intensified."

"How so?"

"Because in the oligarchical State they are disqualified and driven from office, and therefore they cannot train or gather strength; whereas in a democracy they are almost the entire ruling power, and while the keener sort speak and act, the rest keep buzzing about the bema [17] and do not suffer a word to be said on the other side; hence in democracies almost everything is managed by the drones."

"Very true," he said.

"Then there is another class which is always being severed from the mass."

"What is that?"

"They are the orderly class, which in a nation of traders is sure to be the richest."

"Naturally so."

"They are the most squeezable persons and yield the largest amount of honey to the drones."

"Why," he said, "there is little to be squeezed out of people who have little."

"And this is called the wealthy class, and the drones feed upon them."

17 The speaker's stand in an assembly.

"That is pretty much the case," he said.

"The people are a third class, consisting of those who work with their own hands; they are not politicians, and have not much to live upon. This, when assembled, is the largest and most powerful class in a democracy."

"True," he said; "but then the multitude is seldom willing to congregate unless they get a little honey."

"And do they not share?" I said. "Do not their leaders deprive the rich of their estates and distribute them among the people; at the same time taking care to reserve the larger part for themselves?"

"Why, yes," he said, "to that extent the people do share."

"And the persons whose property is taken from them are compelled to defend themselves before the people as they best can?"

"What else can they do?"

"And then, although they may have no desire of change, the others charge them with plotting against the people and being friends of oligarchy?"

"True."

"And the end is that when they see the people, not of their own accord, but through ignorance, and because they are deceived by informers, seeking to do them wrong, then at last they are forced to become oligarchs in reality; they do not wish to be, but the sting of the drones torments them and breeds revolution in them."

"That is exactly the truth."

"Then come impeachments and judgments and trials of one another."

"True."

"The people have always some champion [18] whom they set over them and nurse into greatness."

"Yes, that is their way."

"This and no other is the root from which a tyrant springs; when he first appears above ground he is a protector."

"Yes, that is quite clear."

---

18 The following description of the rise of a tyrant in a weakened and disordered state sounds as true for the twentieth century as for the fourth B.C.

"How then does a protector begin to change into a tyrant? Clearly when he does what the man is said to do in the tale of the Arcadian temple of Lycaean Zeus."

"What tale?"

"The tale is that he who has tasted the entrails of a single human victim minced up with the entrails of other victims is destined to become a wolf. Did you never hear it?"

"Oh, yes."

"And the protector of the people is like him; having a mob entirely at his disposal, he is not restrained from shedding the blood of kinsmen; by the favorite method of false accusation he brings them into court and murders them, making the life of man to disappear, and with unholy tongue and lips tasting the blood of his fellow-citizens; some he kills and others he banishes, at the same time hinting at the abolition of debts and partition of lands: and after this, what will be his destiny? Must he not either perish at the hands of his enemies, or from being a man become a wolf—that is, a tyrant?"

"Inevitably."

"This," I said, "is he who begins to make a party against the rich?"

"The same."

"After a while he is driven out, but comes back, in spite of his enemies, a tyrant full grown."

"That is clear."

"And if they are unable to expel him, or to get him condemned to death by a public accusation, they conspire to assassinate him."

"Yes," he said, "that is their usual way."

"Then comes the famous request for a bodyguard, which is the device of all those who have got thus far in their tyrannical career—'Let not the people's friend,' as they say, 'be lost to them.' "

"Exactly."

"The people readily assent; all their fears are for him—they have none for themselves."

"Very true."

"And when a man who is wealthy and is also accused of being an enemy of the people sees this, then, my friend, as the oracle said to Croesus,

> By pebbly Hermus' shore he flees and rests not, and is not ashamed to be a coward." [19]

"And quite right too," said he, "for if he were, he would never be ashamed again."

"But if he is caught he dies."

"Of course."

"And he, the protector of whom we spoke, is to be seen, not larding the plain' with his bulk, but himself the overthrower of many, standing up in the chariot of State with the reins in his hand, no longer protector, but tyrant absolute."

"No doubt," he said.

"And now let us consider the happiness of the man, and also of the State in which a creature like him is generated."

"Yes," he said, "let us consider that."

"At first, in the early days of his power, he is full of smiles, and he salutes everyone whom he meets; he to be called a tyrant, who is making promises in public and also in private! liberating debtors, and distributing land to the people and his followers, and wanting to be so kind and good to everyone!"

"Of course," he said.

"But when he has disposed of foreign enemies by conquest or treaty, and there is nothing to fear from them, then he is always stirring up some war or other, in order that the people may require a leader."

"To be sure."

"Has he not also another object, which is that they may be impoverished by payment of taxes, and thus compelled to devote themselves to their daily wants and therefore less likely to conspire against him?"

"Clearly."

19 Herodotus, I, 55.

"And if any of them are suspected by him of having notions of freedom, and of resistance to his authority, he will have a good pretext for destroying them by placing them at the mercy of the enemy; and for all these reasons the tyrant must be always getting up a war."

"He must."

"Now he begins to grow unpopular."

"A necessary result."

"Then some of those who joined in setting him up, and who are in power, speak their minds to him and to one another, and the more courageous of them cast in his teeth what is being done."

"Yes, that may be expected."

"And the tyrant, if he means to rule, must get rid of them; he cannot stop while he has a friend or an enemy who is good for anything."

"He cannot."

"And therefore he must look about him and see who is valiant, who is high-minded, who is wise, who is wealthy; happy man, he is the enemy of them all, and must seek occasion against them whether he will or no, until he has made a purgation of the State."

"Yes," he said, "and a rare purgation."

"Yes," I said, "not the sort of purgation which the physicians make of the body; for they take away the worse and leave the better part, but he does the reverse."

"If he is to rule, I suppose that he cannot help himself."

"What a blessed alternative," I said, "to be compelled to dwell only with the many bad, and to be by them hated, or not to live at all!"

"Yes, that is the alternative."

"And the more detestable his actions are to the citizens the more satellites and the greater devotion in them will he require?"

"Certainly."

"And who are the devoted band, and where will he procure them?"

"They will flock to him," he said, "of their own accord, if he pays them."

"By the dog!" I said, "here are more drones, of every sort and from every land."

"Yes," he said, "there are."

"But will he not desire to get them on the spot?"

"How do you mean?"

"He will rob the citizens of their slaves; he will then set them free and enroll them in his bodyguard."

"To be sure," he said; "and he will be able to trust them best of all."

"What a blessed creature," I said, "must this tyrant be; he has put to death the others and has these for his trusted friends."

"Yes," he said; "they are quite of his sort."

"Yes," I said, "and these are the new citizens whom he has called into existence, who admire him and are his companions, while the good hate and avoid him."

"Of course."

Eventually, when the people find how cruelly the tyrant oppresses them, they will try to drive him out. But by then he will be too strong for them. They will learn what the tyranny of slaves is.

"Thus liberty, getting out of all order and reason, passes into the harshest and bitterest form of slavery."

"True," he said.

"Very well; and may we not rightly say that we have sufficiently discussed the nature of tyranny, and the manner of the transition from democracy to tyranny?"

"Yes, quite enough," he said.

BOOK IX

The tyrant as the most unjust and most miserable of men. The just and wise man as ruler over himself and therefore the happiest.

"Last of all comes the tyrannical man, about whom we have once more to ask, how is he formed out of the democratical? and how does he live, in happiness or in misery?"

"Yes," he said, "he is the only one remaining."

"There is, however," I said, "a previous question which remains unanswered."

"What question?"

"I do not think that we have adequately determined the nature and number of the appetites, and until this is accomplished the inquiry will always be confused."

"Well," he said, "it is not too late to supply the omission."

"Very true," I said; "and observe the point which I want to understand: Certain of the unnecessary pleasures and appetites I conceive to be unlawful; everyone appears to have them, but in some persons they are controlled by the laws and by reason, and the better desires prevail over them—either they are wholly banished or they become few and weak; while in the case of others they are stronger, and there are more of them."

"Which appetites do you mean?"

"I mean those which are awake when the reasoning and human and ruling power is asleep; then the wild beast within us, gorged with meat or drink, starts up and having shaken off sleep, goes forth to satisfy his desires; and there is no conceivable folly or crime—not excepting incest or any other unnatural union, or parricide, or the eating of forbidden food—which at such a time, when he has parted company with all shame and sense, a man may not be ready to commit."

"Most true," he said.

"But when a man's pulse is healthy and temperate, and when before going to sleep he has awakened his rational powers, and fed them on noble thoughts and inquiries, collecting himself in meditation; after having first indulged his appetites neither too much nor too little, but just enough to lay them to sleep, and prevent them and their enjoyments and pains from interfering with the higher principle —which he leaves in the solitude of pure abstraction, free to contemplate and aspire to the knowledge of the unknown, whether in past, present, or future: when again he has allayed the passionate element, if he has a quarrel against anyone—I say, when, after pacifying the two irrational principles, he rouses up the third,[1] which is reason, before he takes his rest, then, as you know, he attains truth most nearly, and is least likely to be the sport of fantastic and lawless visions."

"I quite agree."

"In saying this I have been running into a digression; but the point which I desire to note is that in all of us, even in good men, there is a lawless wild-beast nature, which peers out in sleep.[2] Pray, consider whether I am right, and you agree with me."

"Yes, I agree."

"And now remember the character which we attributed to the democratic man.[3] He was supposed from his youth upwards to have been trained under a miserly parent, who encouraged the saving appetites in him, but discountenanced the unnecessary, which aim only at amusement and ornament?"

"True."

"And then he got into the company of a more refined, licentious sort of people, and taking to all their wanton ways rushed into the opposite extreme from an abhorrence of his father's meanness. At last, being a better man than his corruptors, he was drawn in both

1 The three principles or elements that together make up human nature, the animal appetites, the passionate and spirited will, and the reasoning intellect, have already been briefly described in Book IV, page 325.
2 The idea here seems almost an anticipation of Freud.
3 See page 447 ff.

directions until he halted midway and led a life, not of vulgar and slavish passion, but of what he deemed moderate indulgence in various pleasures. After this manner the democrat was generated out of the oligarch?"

"Yes," he said; "that was our view of him, and is so still."

"And now," I said, "years will have passed away, and you must conceive this man, such as he is, to have a son, who is brought up in his father's principles."

"I can imagine him."

"Then you must further imagine the same thing to happen to the son which has already happened to the father: he is drawn into a perfectly lawless life, which by his seducers is termed perfect liberty; and his father and friends take part with his moderate desires, and the opposite party assist the opposite ones. As soon as these dire magicians and tyrant-makers find that they are losing their hold on him, they contrive to implant in him a master passion, to be lord over his idle and spendthrift lusts—a sort of monstrous winged drone —that is the only image which will adequately describe him."

"Yes," he said, "that is the only adequate image of him."

"And when his other lusts, amid clouds of incense and perfumes and garlands and wines, and all the pleasures of a dissolute life, now let loose, come buzzing around him, nourishing to the utmost the sting of desire which they implant in his drone-like nature, then at last this lord of the soul, having Madness for the captain of his guard, breaks out into a frenzy; and if he finds in himself [4] any good opinions or appetites in process of formation, and there is in him any sense of shame remaining, to these better principles he puts an end, and casts them forth until he has purged away temperance and brought in madness to the full."

"Yes," he said, "that is the way in which the tyrannical man is generated."

Socrates describes the further steps in the development of the tyrannical man, his reckless pursuit of amusement, money, and

[4] Or "in the man."

love, his maltreatment of his father, his treachery to his friends,
the evil he and his gang do to the city.

"Let me ask you not to forget the parallel of the individual and the State; bearing this in mind, and glancing in turn from one to the other of them, will you tell me their respective conditions?"

"What do you mean?" he asked.

"Beginning with the State," I replied, "would you say that a city which is governed by a tyrant is free or enslaved?"

"No city," he said, "can be more completely enslaved."

"And yet, as you see, there are freemen as well as masters in such a State?"

"Yes," he said, "I see that there are—a few; but the people, speaking generally, and the best of them are miserably degraded and enslaved."

"Then if the man is like the State," I said, "must not the same rule prevail? his soul is full of meanness and vulgarity—the best elements in him are enslaved; and there is a small ruling part, which is also the worst and maddest."

"Inevitably."

"And would you say that the soul of such a one is the soul of a freeman, or of a slave?"

"He has the soul of a slave, in my opinion."

"And the State which is enslaved under a tyrant is utterly incapable of acting voluntarily?"

"Utterly incapable."

"And also the soul which is under a tyrant (I am speaking of the soul taken as a whole) is least capable of doing what she desires; there is a gadfly which goads her, and she is full of trouble and remorse?"

"Certainly."

"And is the city which is under a tyrant rich or poor?"

"Poor."

"And the tyrannical soul must be always poor and insatiable?" [5]

"True."

5 Or "unsatisfied."

"And must not such a State and such a man be always full of fear?"

"Yes, indeed."

"Is there any State in which you will find more of lamentation and sorrow and groaning and pain?"

"Certainly not."

"And is there any man in whom you will find more of this sort of misery than in the tyrannical man, who is in a fury of passions and desires?"

"Impossible."

"Reflecting upon these and similar evils, you held the tyrannical State to be the most miserable of States?"

"And I was right," he said.

"Certainly," I said. "And when you see the same evils in the tyran-nical man, what do you say of him?"

"I say that he is by far the most miserable of all men."

"There," I said, "I think that you are beginning to go wrong."

"What do you mean?"

"I do not think that he has as yet reached the utmost extreme of misery."

"Then who is more miserable?"

"One of whom I am about to speak."

"Who is that?"

"He who is of a tyrannical nature, but instead of leading a pri-vate life has been cursed with the further misfortune of being a public tyrant."

"From what has been said, I gather that you are right."

"Yes," I replied, "but in this high argument you should be a little more certain, and should not conjecture only; for of all questions, this respecting good and evil is the greatest."

"Very true," he said.

"Let me then offer you an illustration, which may, I think, throw a light upon this subject."

"What is your illustration?"

"The case of rich individuals [6] in cities who possess many slaves:

6 Or "private citizens."

from them you may form an idea of the tyrant's condition, for they both have slaves; the only difference is that he has more slaves."

"Yes, that is the difference."

"You know that they live securely and have nothing to apprehend from their servants?"

"What should they fear?"

"Nothing. But do you observe the reason of this?"

"Yes; the reason is, that the whole city is leagued together for the protection of each individual."

"Very true," I said. "But imagine one of these owners, the master say of some fifty slaves, together with his family and property and slaves, carried off by a god into the wilderness, where there are no freemen to help him—will he not be in an agony of fear lest he and his wife and children should be put to death by his slaves?"

"Yes," he said, "he will be in the utmost fear."

"The time has arrived when he will be compelled to flatter divers of his slaves, and make many promises to them of freedom and other things, much against his will—he will have to cajole his own servants."

"Yes," he said, "that will be the only way of saving himself."

"And suppose the same god, who carried him away, to surround him with neighbors who will not suffer one man to be the master of another, and who, if they could catch the offender, would take his life?"

"His case will be still worse, if you suppose him to be everywhere surrounded and watched by enemies."

"And is not this the sort of prison in which the tyrant will be bound —he who being by nature such as we have described, is full of all sorts of fears and lusts? His soul is dainty and greedy, and yet alone, of all men in the city, he is never allowed to go on a journey, or to see the things which other freemen desire to see, but he lives in his hole like a woman hidden in the house, and is jealous of any other citizen who goes into foreign parts and sees anything of interest."

"Very true," he said.

"And amid evils such as these will not he who is ill-governed in his own person—the tyrannical man, I mean—whom you just now decided to be the most miserable of all—will not he be yet more miserable when, instead of leading a private life, he is constrained by fortune to be a public tyrant? He has to be master of others when he is not master of himself: he is like a diseased or paralytic man who is compelled to pass his life, not in retirement, but fighting and combating with other men."

"Yes," he said, "the similitude is most exact."

"Is not his case utterly miserable? and does not the actual tyrant lead a worse life than he whose life you determined to be the worst?"

"Certainly."

"He who is the real tyrant, whatever men may think, is the real slave, and is obliged to practice the greatest adulation and servility, and to be the flatterer of the vilest of mankind. He has desires which he is utterly unable to satisfy, and has more wants than anyone, and is truly poor, if you know how to inspect the whole soul of him: all his life long he is beset with fear and is full of convulsions and distractions, even as the State which he resembles: and surely the resemblance holds?"

"Very true," he said.

"Moreover, as we were saying before, he grows worse from having power: he becomes and is of necessity more jealous, more faithless, more unjust, more friendless, more impious, than he was at first; he is the purveyor and cherisher of every sort of vice, and the consequence is that he is supremely miserable, and that he makes everybody else as miserable as himself."

"No man of any sense will dispute your words."

"Come, then," I said, "and as the general umpire in theatrical contests proclaims the result, do you also decide who in your opinion is first in the scale of happiness, and who second, and in what order the others follow: there are five of them in all—they are the royal,[7] timocratical, oligarchical, democratical, tyrannical."

[7] The word "royal" here stands for the best type of man, he, who, like the ideal state, is ruled by the noblest element in him, or who, as Socrates says, is "king over himself."

"The decision will be easily given," he replied; "they shall be choruses coming on the stage, and I must judge them in the order in which they enter, by the criterion of virtue and vice, happiness and misery."

"Need we hire a herald, or shall I announce that the son of Ariston (the best) [8] has decided that the best and justest is also the happiest, and that this is he who is the most royal man and king over himself; and that the worst and most unjust man is also the most miserable, and that this is he who being the greatest tyrant of himself is also the greatest tyrant of his State?"

"Make the proclamation yourself," he said.

"And shall I add, whether seen or unseen by gods and men?"

"Let the words be added."

"Then this," I said, "will be our first proof; and there is another, which may also have some weight."

"What is that?"

Socrates repeats with slight change his division of the human soul into three principles, the intellect that loves knowledge and wisdom, the passionate spirit that loves power and fame, and the sensual appetites that desire wealth as means to their satisfaction.

"We may begin by assuming that there are three classes of men— lovers of wisdom, lovers of honor, lovers of gain?"

"Exactly."

"And there are three kinds of pleasure, which are their several objects?"

"Very true."

"Now, if you examine the three classes of men, and ask of them in turn which of their lives is pleasantest, each will be found praising his own and depreciating that of others: the money-maker will contrast the vanity of honor or of learning if they bring no money with the solid advantages of gold and silver?"

8 The adjective "aristos" in Greek means "best."

"True," he said.

"And the lover of honor—what will be his opinion? Will he not think that the pleasure of riches is vulgar, while the pleasure of learning, if it brings no distinction, is all smoke and nonsense to him?"

"Very true."

"And are we to suppose," I said, "that the philosopher sets any value on other pleasures in comparison with the pleasure of knowing the truth, and in that pursuit abiding, ever learning, not so far indeed from the heaven of pleasure? Does he not call the other pleasures necessary, under the idea that if there were no necessity for them, he would rather not have them?"

"There can be no doubt of that," he replied.

"Since, then, the pleasures of each class and the life of each are in dispute, and the question is not which life is more or less honorable, or better or worse, but which is the more pleasant or painless—how shall we know who speaks truly?"

"I cannot myself tell," he said.

"Well, but what ought to be the criterion? Is any better than experience and wisdom and reason?"

"There cannot be a better," he said.

"Then," I said, "reflect. Of the three individuals, which has the greatest experience of all the pleasures which we enumerated? Has the lover of gain, in learning the nature of essential truth, greater experience of the pleasure of knowledge than the philosopher has of the pleasure of gain?"

"The philosopher," he replied, "has greatly the advantage; for he has of necessity always known the taste of the other pleasures from his childhood upwards: but the lover of gain in all his experience has not of necessity tasted—or, I should rather say, even had he desired, could hardly have tasted—the sweetness of learning and knowing truth."

"Then the lover of wisdom has a great advantage over the lover of gain, for he has a double experience?"

"Yes, very great."

"Again, has he greater experience of the pleasures of honor, or the lover of honor of the pleasures of wisdom?" [9]

"Nay," he said, "all three are honored in proportion as they attain their object; for the rich man and the brave man and the wise man alike have their crowd of admirers, and as they all receive honor they all have experience of the pleasures of honor; but the delight which is to be found in the knowledge of true being is known to the philosopher only."

"His experience, then, will enable him to judge better than anyone?"

"Far better."

"And he is the only one who has wisdom as well as experience?"

"Certainly."

"Further, the very faculty which is the instrument of judgment is not possessed by the covetous or ambitious man, but only by the philosopher?"

"What faculty?"

"Reason, with whom, as we were saying, the decision ought to rest."

"Yes."

"And reasoning is peculiarly his instrument?"

"Certainly."

"If wealth and gain were the criterion, then the praise or blame of the lover of gain would surely be the most trustworthy?"

"Assuredly."

"Or if honor or victory or courage, in that case the judgment of the ambitious or pugnacious would be the truest?"

"Clearly."

"But since experience and wisdom and reason are the judges—"

"The only inference possible," he replied, "is that pleasures which are approved by the lover of wisdom and reason are the truest."

"And so we arrive at the result, that the pleasure of the intelligent

9 Better translated, "Has he had less experience of the pleasure of honor than the lover of honor has had of the pleasure of wisdom?"

part of the soul is the pleasantest of the three, and that he of us in whom this is the ruling principle has the pleasantest life."

"Unquestionably," he said, "the wise man speaks with authority when he approves of his own life."

"And what does the judge affirm to be the life which is next, and the pleasure which is next?"

"Clearly that of the soldier and lover of honor; who is nearer to himself than the money-maker."

"Last comes the lover of gain?"

"Very true," he said.

"Twice in succession, then, has the just man overthrown the unjust in this conflict; and now comes the third trial, which is dedicated to Olympian Zeus the savior: a sage whispers in my ear that no pleasure except that of the wise is quite true and pure—all others are a shadow only; and surely this will prove the greatest and most decisive of falls?"

"Yes, the greatest; but will you explain yourself?"

Many things which men count pleasures belong in fact to the neutral ground of physical release from bodily hungers, desires, and pain. Pure pleasures, that have no antecedent in pain, the soul finds best in the high regions of true and immortal being.

"In general, those kinds of things which are in the service of the body have less of truth and essence than those which are in the service of the soul?"

"Far less."

"And has not the body itself less of truth and essence than the soul?"

"Yes."

"What is filled with more real existence, and actually has a more real existence, is more really filled than that which is filled with less real existence and is less real?"

"Of course."

"And if there be a pleasure in being filled with that which is according to nature,[10] that which is more really filled with more real being will more really and truly enjoy true pleasure; whereas that which participates in less real being will be less truly and surely satisfied, and will participate in an illusory and less real pleasure?"

"Unquestionably."

"Those then who know not wisdom and virtue, and are always busy with gluttony and sensuality, go down and up again as far as the mean; and in this region they move at random throughout life, but they never pass into the true upper world; thither they neither look, nor do they ever find their way, neither are they truly filled with true being, nor do they taste of pure and abiding pleasure. Like cattle, with their eyes always looking down and their heads stooping to the earth, that is, to the dining table, they fatten and feed and breed, and, in their excessive love of these delights, they kick and butt at one another with horns and hoofs which are made of iron; and they kill one another by reason of their insatiable lust. For they fill themselves with that which is not substantial, and the part of themselves which they fill is also unsubstantial and incontinent."

"Verily, Socrates," said Glaucon, "you describe the life of the many like an oracle."

"Their pleasures are mixed with pains—how can they be otherwise? For they are mere shadows and pictures of the true, and are colored by contrast, which exaggerates both light and shade, and so they implant in the minds of fools insane desires of themselves; and they are fought about as Stesichorus [11] says that the Greeks fought about the shadow of Helen at Troy in ignorance of the truth."

"Something of that sort must inevitably happen."

The farther away a man's pleasures are from reason and philosophy, the more of a mockery and a shadow they become. The tyrant is at the farthest extreme from the philosopher king. By

10 Or "is in harmony with nature."

11 According to one strange legend, attributed to the poet Stesichorus (590 B.C.), the real Helen was all the time in Egypt and only her wraith went with Paris to Troy. The tragedy writer Euripides, a contemporary of Socrates, based his play *Helena* on this legend.

mathematical calculation the latter lives 729 times more happily than he.

"Well," I said, "and now having arrived at this stage of the argument, we may revert to the words which brought us hither: Was not someone saying that injustice was a gain to the perfectly unjust who was reputed to be just?"

"Yes, that was said."

"Now then, having determined the power and quality of justice and injustice, let us have a little conversation with him."

"What shall we say to him?"

"Let us make an image of the soul, that he may have his own words presented before his eyes."

"Of what sort?"

"An ideal image of the soul, like the composite creations of ancient mythology, such as the Chimera or Scylla or Cerberus,[12] and there are many others in which two or more different natures are said to grow into one."

"There are said to have been such unions."

"Then do you now model the form of a multitudinous, many-headed monster, having a ring of heads of all manner of beasts, tame and wild, which he is able to generate and metamorphose at will."

"You suppose marvelous powers in the artist; but, as language is more pliable than wax or any similar substance, let there be such a model as you propose."

"Suppose now that you make a second form as of a lion, and a third of a man,[13] the second smaller than the first, and the third smaller than the second."

"That," he said, "is an easier task; and I have made them as you say."

12 All three were monstrous, many-headed beasts. For a description of the Chimera, see *Iliad*, VI, 179-182; of Scylla, *Odyssey*, XII, 85-100; of Cerberus, Heriod, *Theogony*, 311-312.

13 Note that as Socrates describes this complex creature, containing in itself a many-headed monster, a lion's heart and a reasoning man, he is simply repeating his idea already expressed of the three natures shut up in each human soul.

"And now join them, and let the three grow into one."

"That has been accomplished."

"Next fashion the outside of them into a single image, as of a man, so that he who is not able to look within, and sees only the outer hull, may believe the beast to be a single human creature."

"I have done so," he said.

"And now, to him who maintains that it is profitable for the human creature to be unjust, and unprofitable to be just, let us reply that, if he be right, it is profitable for this creature to feast the multitudinous monster and strengthen the lion and the lion-like qualities, but to starve and weaken the man, who is consequently liable to be dragged about at the mercy of either of the other two; and he is not to attempt to familiarize or harmonize them with one another—he ought rather to suffer them to fight and bite and devour one another."

"Certainly," he said; "that is what the approver of injustice says."

"To him the supporter of justice makes answer that he should ever so speak and act as to give the man within him in some way or other the most complete mastery over the entire human creature. He should watch over the many-headed monster like a good husbandman, fostering and cultivating the gentle qualities, and preventing the wild ones from growing; he should be making the lion-heart his ally, and in common care of them all should be uniting the several parts with one another and with himself."

"Yes," he said, "that is quite what the maintainer of justice will say."

"And so from every point of view, whether of pleasure, honor, or advantage, the approver of justice is right and speaks the truth, and the disapprover is wrong and false and ignorant?"

"Yes, from every point of view."

"Come, now, and let us gently reason with the unjust, who is not intentionally in error. 'Sweet sir,' we will say to him, 'what think you of things esteemed noble and ignoble? Is not the noble that which subjects the beast to the man, or rather to the god in man; and the ignoble that which subjects the man to the beast?' He can hardly avoid saying Yes, can he now?"

"Not if he has any regard for my opinion."

"But, if he agree so far, we may ask him to answer another question: Then how would a man profit if he received gold and silver on the condition that he was to enslave the noblest part of him to the worst? Who can imagine that a man who sold his son or daughter into slavery for money, especially if he sold them into the hands of fierce and evil men, would be the gainer, however large might be the sum which he received? And will anyone say that he is not a miserable caitiff who remorselessly sells his own divine being to that which is most godless and detestable? Eriphyle [14] took the necklace as the price of her husband's life, but he is taking a bribe in order to compass a worse ruin."

"Yes," said Glaucon, "far worse—I will answer for him."

"Has not the intemperate been censured of old, because in him the huge multiform monster is allowed to be too much at large?"

"Clearly."

"And men are blamed for pride and bad temper when the lion and serpent element in them disproportionately grows and gains strength?"

"Yes."

"And luxury and softness are blamed, because they relax and weaken this same creature, and make a coward of him?"

"Very true."

"And is not a man reproached for flattery and meanness who subordinates the spirited animal to the unruly monster, and, for the sake of money, of which he can never have enough, habituates him in the days of his youth to be trampled in the mire, and from being a lion to become a monkey?"

"True," he said.

"And why are mean employments and manual arts a reproach? Only because they imply a natural weakness of the higher principle; the individual is unable to control the creatures within him, but has to court them, and his great study is how to flatter them."

14 *Odyssey*, XI, 326, 327.

"Such appears to be the reason."

"And therefore, being desirous of placing him under a rule like that of the best, we say that he ought to be the servant of the best, in whom the Divine rules; not, as Thrasymachus supposed,[15] to the injury of the servant, but because everyone had better be ruled by divine wisdom dwelling within him; or, if this be impossible, then by an external authority, in order that we may be all, as far as possible, under the same government, friends and equals."

"True," he said.

"And this is clearly seen to be the intention of the law, which is the ally of the whole city; and is seen also in the authority which we exercise over children, and the refusal to let them be free until we have established in them a principle analogous to the constitution of a state, and by cultivation of this higher element have set up in their hearts a guardian and ruler like our own, and when this is done they may go their ways."

"Yes," he said, "the purpose of the law is manifest."

"From what point of view, then, and on what ground can we say that a man is profited by injustice or intemperance or other baseness, which will make him a worse man, even though he acquire money or power by his wickedness?"

"From no point of view at all."

"What shall he profit, if his injustice be undetected and unpunished? He who is undetected only gets worse, whereas he who is detected and punished has the brutal part of his nature silenced and humanized; the gentler element in him is liberated, and his whole soul is perfected and ennobled by the acquirement of justice and temperance and wisdom, more than the body ever is by receiving gifts of beauty, strength and health, in proportion as the soul is more honorable than the body."

"Certainly," he said.

"To this nobler purpose the man of understanding will devote the energies of his life. And in the first place, he will honor studies

---

15 For Thrasymachus' assertion that the just man was always the loser in any situation, turn back to page 236.

which impress these qualities on his soul, and will disregard others?"

"Clearly," he said.

"In the next place, he will regulate his bodily habit and training, and so far will he be from yielding to brutal and irrational pleasures, that he will regard even health as quite a secondary matter; his first object will be not that he may be fair or strong or well, unless he is likely thereby to gain temperance, but he will always desire so to attemper the body as to preserve the harmony of the soul?"

"Certainly he will, if he has true music in him."

"And in the acquisition of wealth there is a principle of order and harmony which he will also observe; he will not allow himself to be dazzled by the foolish applause of the world, and heap up riches to his own infinite harm?"

"Certainly not," he said.

"He will look at the city which is within him, and take heed that no disorder occur in it, such as might arise either from superfluity or from want; and upon this principle he will regulate his property and gain or spend according to his means."

"Very true."

"And, for the same reason, he will gladly accept and enjoy such honors as he deems likely to make him a better man; but those, whether private or public, which are likely to disorder his life, he will avoid?"

"Then, if that is his motive, he will not be a statesman."

"By the dog of Egypt, he will! in the city which is his own he certainly will, though in the land of his birth perhaps not, unless he have a divine call."

"I understand! you mean that he will be a ruler in the city of which we are the founders, and which exists in idea only; [16] for I do not believe that there is such a one anywhere on earth?"

"In heaven," I replied, "there is laid up a pattern of it, methinks, which he who desires may behold, and beholding, may set his own

16 The final justification for building a city of the ideal, in which the soul, if not the body, may take up its abode. From this passage the Stoics and other men after Plato built up their idea of a heavenly city of God.

house in order. But whether such a one exists, or ever will exist in fact, is no matter; for he will live after the manner of that city, having nothing to do with any other."

"I think so," he said.

BOOK X

Further reasons for excluding poetry from the state. The rewards of justice and wisdom in this life and the next.

"OF THE many excellences which I perceive in the order of our State, there is none which upon reflection pleases me better than the rule about poetry.

> *Socrates adds new arguments to those he earlier made use of, in Book III, in support of his "rule about poetry." The great Homer, whom he admits he has always loved, and the tragic poets must be banished from the ideal state, for they are but imitators of the life of visible nature and so paint an inferior view of truth. They "feed and water" the emotions and passions of men instead of restraining them by reason.*

Therefore, Glaucon," I said, "whenever you meet with any of the eulogists of Homer declaring that he has been the educator of Hellas, and that he is profitable for education and for the ordering of human things, and that you should take him up again and again and get to know him and regulate your whole life according to him, we may love and honor those who say these things—they are excellent people, as far as their lights extend; and we are ready to acknowledge that Homer is the greatest of poets and first of tragedy writers; but we must remain firm in our conviction that hymns to the gods and praises of famous men are the only poetry which ought to be admitted into our State. For if you go beyond this and allow the honeyed muse to enter, either in epic or lyric verse, not law and the reason of mankind, which by common consent have ever been deemed best, but pleasure and pain will be the rulers in our State."

"That is most true," he said.

"And now since we have reverted to the subject of poetry, let this our defense serve to show the reasonableness of our former judgment in sending away out of our State an art having the tendencies which we have described; for reason constrained us. But that she may not impute to us any harshness or want of politeness, let us tell her that there is an ancient quarrel between philosophy and poetry; of which there are many proofs, such as the saying of 'the yelping hound howling at her lord,' [1] or of one 'mighty in the vain talk of fools,' and 'the mob of sages circumventing Zeus,' and the 'subtle thinkers who are beggars after all'; and there are innumerable other signs of ancient enmity between them. Notwithstanding this, let us assure our sweet friend and the sister arts of imitation, that if she will only prove her title to exist in a well-ordered State we shall be delighted to receive her—we are very conscious of her charms; but we may not on that account betray the truth. I dare say, Glaucon, that you are as much charmed by her as I am, especially when she appears in Homer?"

"Yes, indeed, I am greatly charmed."

"Shall I propose, then, that she be allowed to return from exile, but upon this condition only—that she make a defense of herself in lyrical or some other meter?"

"Certainly."

"And we may further grant to those of her defenders who are lovers of poetry and yet not poets the permission to speak in prose on her behalf: [2] let them show not only that she is pleasant but also useful to States and to human life, and we will listen in a kindly spirit; for if this can be proved we shall surely be the gainers—I mean, if there is a use in poetry as well as a delight?"

"Certainly," he said, "we shall be the gainers."

"If her defense fails, then, my dear friend, like other persons who

---

1 The source of this and the following quotations is unknown.

2 The challenge was taken up by Plato's pupil Aristotle in his *Poetics* and by many who have written defenses of poetry in the centuries since.

are enamoured of something, but put a restraint upon themselves when they think their desires are opposed to their interests, so too must we after the manner of lovers give her up, though not without a struggle. We too are inspired by that love of poetry which the education of noble States has implanted in us, and therefore we would have her appear at her best and truest; but so long as she is unable to make good her defense, this argument of ours shall be a charm to us, which we will repeat to ourselves while we listen to her strains; that we may not fall away into the childish love of her which captivates the many. At all events we are well aware that poetry being such as we have described is not to be regarded seriously as attaining to the truth; and he who listens to her, fearing for the safety of the city which is within him, should be on his guard against her seductions and make our words his law."

"Yes," he said, "I quite agree with you."

"Yes," I said, "my dear Glaucon, for great is the issue at stake, greater than appears, whether a man is to be good or bad. And what will anyone be profited if under the influence of honor or money or power, aye, or under the excitement of poetry, he neglect justice and virtue?"

"Yes," he said; "I have been convinced by the argument, as I believe that anyone else would have been."

"And yet no mention has been made of the greatest prizes [3] and rewards which await virtue."

"What, are there any greater still? If there are, they must be of an inconceivable greatness."

"Why," I said, "what was ever great in a short time? The whole period of three score years and ten is surely but a little thing in comparison with eternity?"

"Say rather 'nothing,' " he replied.

---

3 Having now satisfactorily proved, as he set out to do, that the righteous life, regardless of outside circumstances, is itself its one reward, Plato closes the dialogue with a picture of the good man, as he actually lives, beloved of God in this world and the next. Already in the *Phaedo* he had argued at length for the immortality of the human soul. Now he presents one more argument and crowns it with an imaginative and awe-inspiring vision.

"And should an immortal being seriously think of this little space rather than of the whole?"

"Of the whole, certainly. But why do you ask?"

"Are you not aware," I said, "that the soul of man is immortal and imperishable?"

He looked at me in astonishment, and said: "No, by heaven! And are you really prepared to maintain this?"

"Yes," I said, "I ought to be, and you too—there is no difficulty in proving it."

"I see a great difficulty; but I should like to hear you state this argument of which you make so light."

"Listen, then."

"I am attending."

"There is a thing which you call good and another which you call evil?"

"Yes," he replied.

"Would you agree with me in thinking that the corrupting and destroying element is the evil, and the saving and improving element the good?"

"Yes."

"And you admit that everything has a good and also an evil; as ophthalmia is the evil of the eyes and disease of the whole body; as mildew is of corn, and rot of timber, or rust of copper and iron: in everything, or in almost everything, there is an inherent evil and disease?"

"Yes," he said.

"And anything which is infected by any of these evils is made evil, and at last wholly dissolves and dies?"

"True."

"The vice and evil which is inherent in each is the destruction of each; and if this does not destroy them there is nothing else that will; for good certainly will not destroy them, nor again, that which is neither good nor evil."

"Certainly not."

"If, then, we find any nature which having this inherent corruption cannot be dissolved or destroyed,[4] we may be certain that of such a nature there is no destruction?"

"That may be assumed."

"Well," I said, "and is there no evil which corrupts the soul?"

"Yes," he said, "there are all the evils which we were just now passing in review: unrighteousness, intemperance, cowardice, ignorance."

"But does any of these dissolve or destroy her? And here do not let us fall into the error of supposing that the unjust and foolish man, when he is detected, perishes through his own injustice, which is an evil of the soul. Take the analogy of the body: The evil of the body is a disease which wastes and reduces and annihilates the body; and all the things of which we were just now speaking come to annihilation through their own corruption attaching to them and inhering in them and so destroying them. Is not this true?"

"Yes."

"Consider the soul in like manner. Does the injustice or other evil which exists in the soul waste and consume her? do they by attaching to the soul and inhering in her at last bring her to death, and so separate her from the body?"

"Certainly not."

"And yet," I said, "it is unreasonable to suppose that anything can perish from without through affection of external evil which could not be destroyed from within by a corruption of its own?"

"It is," he replied.

"Consider," I said, "Glaucon, that even the badness of food, whether staleness, decomposition, or any other bad quality, when confined to the actual food, is not supposed to destroy the body; although, if the badness of food communicates corruption to the body, then we should say that the body has been destroyed by a corruption of itself, which is disease, brought on by this;[5] but that the body, being one thing, can be destroyed by the badness of food, which is

4 Or better, "which has an evil that corrupts but is not able to dissolve or destroy it."
5 Or "by the food."

another, and which does not engender any natural infection—this we shall absolutely deny?"

"Very true."

"And, on the same principle, unless some bodily evil can produce an evil of the soul, we must not suppose that the soul, which is one thing, can be dissolved by any merely external evil which belongs to another?"

"Yes," he said, "there is reason in that."

"Either, then, let us refute this conclusion, or, while it remains unrefuted, let us never say that fever, or any other disease, or the knife put to the throat, or even the cutting up of the whole body into the minutest pieces, can destroy the soul, until she herself is proved to become more unholy or unrighteous in consequence of these things being done to the body; but that the soul, or anything else if not destroyed by an internal evil, can be destroyed by an external one, is not to be affirmed by any man."

"And surely," he replied, "no one will ever prove that the souls of men become more unjust in consequence of death."

"But if someone who would rather not admit the immortality of the soul boldly denies this, and says that the dying do really become more evil and unrighteous, then, if the speaker is right, I suppose that injustice, like disease, must be assumed to be fatal to the unjust, and that those who take this disorder die by the natural inherent power of destruction which evil has, and which kills them sooner or later, but in quite another way from that in which, at present, the wicked receive death at the hands of others as the penalty of their deeds?"

"Nay," he said, "in that case injustice, if fatal to the unjust, will not be so very terrible to him, for he will be delivered from evil. But I rather suspect the opposite to be the truth, and that injustice which, if it have the power, will murder others, keeps the murderer alive— aye, and well awake too; so far removed is her dwelling-place from being a house of death."

"True," I said; "if the inherent natural vice or evil of the soul is unable to kill or destroy her, hardly will that which is appointed to be

the destruction of some other body, destroy a soul or anything else
except that of which it was appointed to be the destruction."

"Yes, that can hardly be."

"But the soul which cannot be destroyed by an evil, whether inherent or external, must exist forever, and if existing forever, must be
immortal?"

"Certainly."

"That is the conclusion," I said; "and, if a true conclusion, then
the souls must always be the same, for if none be destroyed they will
not diminish in number. Neither will they increase, for the increase
of the immortal natures must come from something mortal, and all
things would thus end in immortality."

"Very true."

"But this we cannot believe—reason will not allow us—any more
than we can believe the soul, in her truest nature, to be full of variety
and difference [6] and dissimilarity."

"What do you mean?" he said.

"The soul," I said, "being, as is now proven, immortal, must be the
fairest of compositions and cannot be compounded of many elements?"

"Certainly not."

"Her immortality is demonstrated by the previous argument, and
there are many other proofs; but to see her as she really is, not as we
now behold her, marred by communion with the body and other
miseries, you must contemplate her with the eye of reason, in her
original purity; and then her beauty will be revealed, and justice and
injustice and all the things which we have described will be manifested more clearly. Thus far, we have spoken the truth concerning
her as she appears at present, but we must remember also that we
have seen her only in a condition which may be compared to that of
the sea-god Glaucus,[7] whose original image can hardly be discerned
because his natural members are broken off and crushed and dam-

6 Or "diversity and contradiction in itself."
7 A sea god, depicted in art as a bearded old man with a body ending in a fish's tail
and covered with seaweed and shells.

aged by the waves in all sorts of ways, and incrustations have grown over them of seaweed and shells and stones, so that he is more like some monster than he is to his own natural form. And the soul which we behold is in a similar condition, disfigured by ten thousand ills. But not there, Glaucon, not there must we look."

"Where then?"

"At her love of wisdom. Let us see whom she affects, and what society and converse she seeks in virtue of her near kindred with the immortal and eternal and divine; also how different she would become if wholly following this superior principle, and borne by a divine impulse out of the ocean in which she now is, and disengaged from the stones and shells and things of earth and rock which in wild variety spring up around her because she feeds upon earth, and is overgrown by the good things of this life as they are termed: then you would see her as she is, and know whether she have one shape only or many, or what her nature is. Of her affections and of the forms which she takes in this present life I think that we have now said enough."

"True," he replied.

"And thus," I said, "we have fulfilled the conditions of the argument; we have not introduced the rewards and glories of justice, which, as you were saying, are to be found in Homer and Hesiod; but justice in her own nature has been shown to be best for the soul in her own nature. Let a man do what is just, whether he have the ring of Gyges [8] or not, and even if in addition to the ring of Gyges he put on the helmet of Hades." [9]

"Very true."

"And now, Glaucon, there will be no harm in further enumerating how many and how great are the rewards which justice and the other virtues procure to the soul from gods and men, both in life and after death."

"Certainly not," he said.

"Will you repay me, then, what you borrowed in the argument?"

8 See page 256.
9 The helmet which made the wearer invisible. *Iliad*, V, 844, 845.

"What did I borrow?"

"The assumption that the just man should appear unjust and the unjust just: [10] for you were of opinion that even if the true state of the case could not possibly escape the eyes of gods and men, still this admission ought to be made for the sake of the argument, in order that pure justice might be weighed against pure injustice. Do you remember?"

"I should be much to blame if I had forgotten."

"Then, as the cause is decided, I demand on behalf of justice that the estimation in which she is held by gods and men and which we acknowledge to be her due should now be restored to her by us; since she has been shown to confer reality, and not to deceive those who truly possess her, let what has been taken from her be given back, that so she may win that palm of appearance which is hers also, and which she gives to her own."

"The demand," he said, "is just."

"In the first place," I said, "and this is the first thing which you will have to give back—the nature both of the just and unjust is truly known to the gods."

"Granted."

"And if they are both known to them, one must be the friend and the other the enemy of the gods, as we admitted from the beginning?"

"True."

"And the friend of the gods may be supposed to receive from them all things at their best, excepting only such evil as is the necessary consequence of former sins?"

"Certainly."

"Then this must be our notion of the just man, that even when he is in poverty or sickness, or any other seeming misfortune, all things will in the end work together for good to him in life and death: for

10 When Socrates in Book II began his serious argument, he agreed as one condition of it that his just man should go unrecognized and despised by gods and men. See page 259. Now he declares the condition unreal. As a matter of fact, he says, the just receive here and now the special care of the gods and the esteem and honor of men.

the gods have a care of anyone whose desire is to become just and to be like God, as far as man can attain the divine likeness, by the pursuit of virtue?"

"Yes," he said; "if he is like God he will surely not be neglected by him."

"And of the unjust may not the opposite be supposed?"

"Certainly."

"Such, then, are the palms of victory which the gods give the just?"

"That is my conviction."

"And what do they receive of men? Look at things as they really are, and you will see that the clever unjust are in the case of runners, who run well from the starting place to the goal but not back again from the goal: they go off at a great pace, but in the end only look foolish, slinking away with their ears draggling on their shoulders, and without a crown; but the true runner comes to the finish and receives the prize and is crowned. And this is the way with the just; he who endures to the end of every action and occasion of his entire life has a good report and carries off the prize which men have to bestow."

"True."

"And now you must allow me to repeat of the just the blessings which you were attributing to the fortunate unjust. I shall say of them, what you were saying of the others, that as they grow older, they become rulers in their own city if they care to be; they marry whom they like and give in marriage to whom they will; all that you said of the others I now say of these. And, on the other hand, of the unjust I say that the greater number, even though they escape in their youth, are found out at last and look foolish at the end of their course, and when they come to be old and miserable are flouted alike by stranger and citizen; they are beaten and then come those things unfit for ears polite, as you truly term them; they will be racked and have their eyes burned out, as you were saying. And you may suppose that I have repeated the remainder of your tale of horrors. But will you let me assume, without reciting them, that these things are true?"

"Certainly," he said, "what you say is true."

"These, then, are the prizes and rewards and gifts which are bestowed upon the just by gods and men in this present life, in addition to the other good things which justice of herself provides."

"Yes," he said; "and they are fair and lasting."

"And yet," I said, "all these are as nothing either in number or greatness in comparison with those other recompenses which await both just and unjust after death. And you ought to hear them, and then both just and unjust will have received from us a full payment of the debt which the argument owes to them."

"Speak," he said; "there are few things which I would more gladly hear."

"Well," I said, "I will tell you a tale; not one of the tales which Odysseus tells to the hero Alcinous,[11] yet this too is a tale of a hero, Er [12] the son of Armenius, a Pamphylian by birth. He was slain in battle, and ten days afterwards, when the bodies of the dead were taken up already in a state of corruption, his body was found unaffected by decay, and carried away home to be buried. And on the twelfth day, as he was lying on the funeral pile, he returned to life and told them what he had seen in the other world. He said that when his soul left the body he went on a journey with a great company, and that they came to a mysterious place at which there were two openings in the earth; they were near together, and over against them were two other openings in the heaven above. In the intermediate space there were judges seated, who commanded the just, after they had given judgment on them and had bound their sentences in front of them, to ascend by the heavenly way on the right hand; and in like manner the unjust were bidden by them to descend by the lower way on the left hand; these also bore the symbols of their deeds, but

11 *Odyssey*, XVII, 415-444.

12 As to whether this Er was an actual person, or he and his tale pure inventions of Plato himself there has been much discussion. The name of his country, Pamphylia, might be translated Everyman.

fastened on their backs. He drew near, and they told him that he was to be the messenger who would carry the report of the other world to men, and they bade him hear and see all that was to be heard and seen in that place. Then he beheld and saw on one side the souls departing at either opening of heaven and earth when sentence had been given on them; and at the two other openings other souls, some ascending out of the earth dusty and worn with travel, some descending out of heaven clean and bright. And arriving ever and anon they seemed to have come from a long journey, and they went forth with gladness into the meadow, where they encamped as at a festival; and those who knew one another embraced and conversed, the souls which came from earth curiously inquiring about the things above, and the souls which came from heaven about the things beneath. And they told one another of what had happened by the way, those from below weeping and sorrowing at the remembrance of the things which they had endured and seen in their journey beneath the earth (now the journey lasted a thousand years), while those from above were describing heavenly delights and visions of inconceivable beauty. The story, Glaucon, would take too long to tell; but the sum was this: He said that for every wrong which they had done to anyone they suffered tenfold; or once in a hundred years—such being reckoned to be the length of man's life, and the penalty being thus paid ten times in a thousand years. If, for example, there were any who had been the cause of many deaths, or had betrayed or enslaved cities or armies, or been guilty of any other evil behavior, for each and all of their offenses they received punishment ten times over, and the rewards of beneficence and justice and holiness were in the same proportion. I need hardly repeat what he said concerning young children dying almost as soon as they were born. Of piety and impiety to gods and parents, and of murderers, there were retributions other and greater far which he described. He mentioned that he was present when one of the spirits asked another, 'Where is Ardiaeus the Great?' (Now this Ardiaeus lived a thousand years before the time of Er: he had been the tyrant of some city of Pamphylia, and had murdered his aged father and his elder brother, and was said to have committed many other abominable crimes.) The answer of the other spirit was: 'He comes not hither and will never come. And this,' said he, 'was one of the dreadful sights which we ourselves witnessed. We were at the mouth of the cavern, and, having completed all our experiences, were about to reascend, when of a sudden Ardiaeus appeared and several others, most of whom were tyrants; and there were also besides the tyrants private individuals who had been great criminals: they were just, as they fancied, about to return into the upper world, but the mouth, instead of admitting them, gave a roar, whenever any of these incurable sinners or someone who had not been sufficiently punished tried to ascend; and then wild men of fiery aspect, who were standing by and heard the sound, seized and carried them off; and Ardiaeus and others they bound head and foot and hand, and threw them down and flayed them with scourges, and dragged them along the road at the side, carding them on thorns like wool, and declaring to the passers-by what were their crimes, and that they were being taken away to be cast into hell.' And of all the many terrors which they had endured, he said that there was none like the terror which each of them felt at that moment, lest they should hear the voice; and when there was silence, one by one they ascended with exceeding joy. These, said Er, were the penalties and retributions, and there were blessings as great.

"Now when the spirits which were in the meadow had tarried seven days, on the eighth they were obliged to proceed on their journey, and, on the fourth day after, he said that they came to a place where they could see from above a line of light, straight as a column, extending right through the whole heaven and through the earth, in color resembling the rainbow, only brighter and purer; another day's journey brought them to the place,[13] and there, in the midst of the light, they saw the ends of the chains of heaven let down from above: for this light is the belt of heaven, and holds together the circle of the universe, like the undergirders of a trireme.[14] From these ends is ex-

---

13 Or "to it."
14 A large, three-banked ship, propelled by oars and sail.

tended the spindle of Necessity, on which all the revolutions [15] turn. The shaft and hook of this spindle are made of steel, and the whorl is made partly of steel and also partly of other materials. Now the whorl is in form like the whorl used on earth; and the description of it implied that there is one large hollow whorl which is quite scooped out, and into this is fitted another lesser one, and another, and another, and four others, making eight in all, like vessels which fit into one another; the whorls show their edges on the upper side, and on their lower side all together form one continuous whorl. This is pierced by the spindle, which is driven home through the center of the eighth. The first and outermost whorl has the rim broadest, and the seven inner whorls are narrower, in the following proportions— the sixth is next to the first in size, the fourth next to the sixth; then comes the eighth; the seventh is fifth, the fifth is sixth, the third is seventh, last and eighth comes the second. The largest (or fixed stars) is spangled, and the seventh (or sun) is brightest; the eighth (or moon) colored by the reflected light of the seventh; the second and fifth (Saturn and Mercury) are in color like one another, and yellower than the preceding; the third (Venus) has the whitest light; the fourth (Mars) is reddish; the sixth (Jupiter) is in whiteness second. Now the whole spindle has the same motion; but, as the whole revolves in one direction, the seven inner circles move slowly in the other, and of these the swiftest is the eighth; next in swiftness are the seventh, sixth, and fifth, which move together; third in swiftness appeared to move according to the law of this reversed motion the fourth; the third appeared fourth and the second fifth. The spindle turns on the knees of Necessity; and on the upper surface of each circle is a siren, who goes round with them, hymning a single tone or note. The eight together form one harmony; and round about, at equal intervals, there is another band, three in number, each sitting upon her throne: these are the Fates, daughters of Necessity, who are

15 Or "orbits." The spindle of Necessity is the axis on which revolves first the outermost sphere of the fixed stars, then within it the progressively smaller orbits of what were known as the seven planets. Their names are given below. In the center, of course, is our earth.

clothed in white robes and have chaplets upon their heads, Lachesis
and Clotho and Atropos, who accompany with their voices the harmony of the sirens—Lachesis singing of the past, Clotho of the
present, Atropos of the future; Clotho from time to time assisting with
a touch of her right hand the revolution of the outer circle of the
whorl or spindle, and Atropos with her left hand touching and guid-
ing the inner ones, and Lachesis laying hold of either in turn, first
with one hand and then with the other.

"When Er and the spirits arrived, their duty was to go at once to
Lachesis; but first of all there came a prophet who arranged them in
order; then he took from the knees of Lachesis lots and samples of
lives, and having mounted a high pulpit, spoke as follows: 'Hear the
word of Lachesis, the daughter of Necessity. Mortal souls, behold a
new cycle of life and mortality. Your genius will not be allotted to
you, but you will choose your genius;[16] and let him who draws the
first lot have the first choice, and the life which he chooses shall be
his destiny. Virtue is free, and as a man honors or dishonors her he
will have more or less of her; the responsibility is with the chooser—
God is justified.' When the Interpreter had thus spoken he scattered
lots indifferently among them all, and each of them took up the lot
which fell near him, all but Er himself (he was not allowed), and
each as he took his lot perceived the number which he had obtained.
Then the Interpreter placed on the ground before them the samples
of lives; and there were many more lives than the souls present, and
they were of all sorts. There were lives of every animal and of man
in every condition. And there were tyrannies among them, some
lasting out the tyrant's life, others which broke off in the middle and
came to an end in poverty and exile and beggary; and there were
lives of famous men, some who were famous for their form and beauty
as well as for their strength and success in games, or, again, for their
birth and the qualities of their ancestors; and some who were the reverse of famous for the opposite qualities. And of women likewise;
there was not, however, any definite character in them, because the

16 Or better, "No divinity shall cast lots for you but you shall choose your own
divinity."

soul, when choosing a new life, must of necessity become different.[17]
But there was every other quality, and they all mingled with one another, and also with elements of wealth and poverty, and disease and
health; and there were mean states also. And here, my dear Glaucon,
is the supreme peril of our human state; and therefore the utmost
care should be taken. Let each one of us leave every other kind of
knowledge and seek and follow one thing only, if peradventure he
may be able to learn and may find someone who will make him able
to learn and discern between good and evil, and so to choose always
and everywhere the better life as he has opportunity. He should consider the bearing of all these things which have been mentioned
severally and collectively upon virtue; he should know what the effect of beauty is when combined with poverty or wealth in a particular soul, and what are the good and evil consequences of noble and
humble birth, of private and public station, of strength and weakness, of cleverness and dullness, and of all the natural and acquired
gifts of the soul, and the operation of them when conjoined; he will
then look at the nature of the soul, and from the consideration of all
these qualities he will be able to determine which is the better and
which is the worse; and so he will choose, giving the name of evil
to the life which will make his soul more unjust, and good to the
life which will make his soul more just; all else he will disregard. For
we have seen and know that this is the best choice both in life and
after death. A man must take with him into the world below an ada-
mantine faith in truth and right, that there too he may be undazzled
by the desire of wealth or the other allurements of evil, lest, coming
upon tyrannies and similar villainies, he do irremediable wrongs to
others and suffer yet worse himself; but let him know how to choose
the mean and avoid the extremes on either side, as far as possible, not
only in this life but in all that which is to come. For this is the way
of happiness.

"And according to the report of the messenger from the other world

---

17 "And of women likewise. But there was no assignment of kinds of souls, for
the soul as it chooses a new life must inevitably itself become new."

this was what the prophet said at the time: 'Even for the last comer, if he chooses wisely and will live diligently, there is appointed a happy and not undesirable existence. Let not him who chooses first be careless, and let not the last despair.' And when he had spoken, he who had the first choice came forward and in a moment chose the greatest tyranny; his mind having been darkened by folly and sensuality, he had not thought out the whole matter before he chose, and did not at first sight perceive that he was fated, among other evils, to devour his own children. But when he had time to reflect, and saw what was in the lot, he began to beat his breast and lament over his choice, forgetting the proclamation of the prophet; for, instead of throwing the blame of his misfortune on himself, he accused chance and the gods, and everything rather than himself. Now he was one of those who came from heaven, and in a former life had dwelt in a well-ordered State, but his virtue was a matter of habit only, and he had no philosophy. And it was true of others who were similarly overtaken that the greater number of them came from heaven and therefore they had never been schooled by trial, whereas the pilgrims who came from earth having themselves suffered and seen others suffer were not in a hurry to choose. And owing to this inexperience of theirs, and also because the lot was a chance, many of the souls exchanged a good destiny for an evil or an evil for a good. For if a man had always on his arrival in this world dedicated himself from the first to sound philosophy, and had been moderately fortunate in the number of the lot, he might,[18] as the messenger reported, be happy here, and also his journey to another life and return to this, instead of being rough and underground, would be smooth and heavenly. Most curious, he said, was the spectacle—sad and laughable and strange; for the choice of the souls was in most cases based on their experience of a previous life. There he saw the soul which had once been Orpheus choosing the life of a swan out of enmity to the race of women, hating to be born of a woman because they had been his

18 Better translated, "Yet if at each return to the life of this earth, a man loved wisdom and health and the number of his lot fell not among the last, he might."

murderers; he beheld also the soul of Thamyras [19] choosing the life of a nightingale; birds, on the other hand, like the swan and other musicians, wanting to be men. The soul which obtained the twentieth lot chose the life of a lion, and this was the soul of Ajax the son of Telamon, who would not be a man, remembering the injustice which was done him in the judgment about the arms.[20] The next was Agamemnon, who took the life of an eagle, because, like Ajax, he hated human nature by reason of his sufferings. About the middle came the lot of Atalanta; [21] she, seeing the great fame of an athlete, was unable to resist the temptation: and after her there followed the soul of Epeus [22] the son of Panopeus passing into the nature of a woman cunning in the arts; and far away among the last who chose, the soul of the jester Thersites [23] was putting on the form of a monkey. There came also the soul of Odysseus having yet to make a choice, and his lot happened to be the last of them all. Now the recollection of former toils had disenchanted him of ambition, and he went about for a considerable time in search of the life of a private man who had no cares; he had some difficulty in finding this, which was lying about and had been neglected by everybody else; and when he saw it, he said that he would have done the same had his lot been first instead of last, and that he was delighted to have it. And not only did men pass into animals, but I must also mention that there were animals tame and wild who changed into one another and into corresponding human natures—the good into the gentle and the evil into the savage, in all sorts of combinations.

All the souls had now chosen their lives, and they went in the order of their choice to Lachesis, who sent with them the genius [24] whom

19 An ancient singer who challenged the Muses to a contest of song and was by them deprived of both sight and the gift of singing.

20 Ajax, as the bravest of the surviving Greeks, claimed the arms of the dead Achilles, which were, however, as he thought unjustly, awarded to Odysseus. *Odyssey*, XI, 543-564.

21 Queen of the Amazons, swift especially in the foot-race.

22 The builder of the Trojan horse, in the body of which the Greeks entered Troy. *Odyssey*, XI, 523.

23 The uncouth clown whom Homer describes in the *Iliad*, II, 212-222.

24 Or "divinity."

they had severally chosen, to be the guardian of their lives and the fulfiller of the choice: this genius led the souls first to Clotho, and drew them within the revolution of the spindle impelled by her hand, thus ratifying the destiny of each; and then, when they were fastened to this, carried them to Atropos, who spun the threads and made them irreversible, whence without turning round they passed beneath the throne of Necessity; and when they had all passed, they marched on in a scorching heat to the plain of Forgetfulness, which was a barren waste destitute of trees and verdure; and then towards evening they encamped by the river of Unmindfulness,[25] whose water no vessel can hold; of this they were all obliged to drink a certain quantity, and those who were not saved by wisdom drank more than was necessary; and each one as he drank forgot all things. Now after they had gone to rest, about the middle of the night there was a thunderstorm and earthquake, and then in an instant they were driven upwards in all manner of ways to their birth, like stars shooting. He himself was hindered from drinking the water. But in what manner or by what means he returned to the body he could not say; only, in the morning, awaking suddenly, he found himself lying on the pyre.

"And thus, Glaucon, the tale has been saved and has not perished, and will save us if we are obedient to the word spoken; and we shall pass safely over the river of Forgetfulness and our soul will not be defiled. Wherefore my counsel is, that we hold fast ever to the heavenly way and follow after justice and virtue always, considering that the soul is immortal and able to endure every sort of good and every sort of evil. Thus shall we live dear to one another and to the gods, both while remaining here and when, like conquerors in the games who go round to gather gifts, we receive our reward. And it shall be well with us both in this life and in the pilgrimage of a thousand years which we have been describing."

25 Or "Forgetfulness."

PRONOUNCING GLOSSARY OF NAMES

ACHAEANS (A kee' anz), one of the chief races of ancient Greece.

ACHERON (Ak' er on), the River of Woe in the lower world, crossed by the dead in Charon's boat.

ACHERUSIAN LAKE (Ak e roo' zi an), a lake in the lower world.

ACHILLES (A kil' eez), son of Peleus and Thetis; great Greek hero of the Trojan War and Homer's *Iliad.*

ACROPOLIS (A krop' o lis), the "City Height" or citadel of a Greek town.

ACUSILAUS (A koo si lay' us), a poet mentioned by Plato, otherwise unknown.

ADEIMANTUS (Ad i man' tus), son of Ariston; brother of Plato.

ADMETUS (Ad mee' tus), king of Thessaly whose wife, Alcestis, died in his place but was restored by Heracles.

AEACUS (Ee' a kus), son of Zeus and Aegina; lived on the island of Aegina; renowned for his justice; later a judge of the dead in the lower world.

AEGEAN (Ee jee' an), the part of the Mediterranean Sea between Greece and Asia Minor.

AEANTODORUS (Ee an to do' rus), brother of Socrates' follower Apollodorus, present at Socrates' trial.

AEGINA (Ee jy' na), a rocky island in the Saronic Gulf between Attica and Argolis; the legendary home of Aeacus.

AESCHINES (Es' ki neez), son of Lysanias; a devoted follower of Socrates.

AESCHYLUS (Es' ki lus or Ees' ki lus), one of the three great tragic poets and dramatists of Greece (525-456 B.C.).

AESOP (Ee' sop), a slave who lived in the 6th century B.C.; wrote fables about animals.

AGAMEMNON (Ag a mem' non), son of Atreus and brother of Menelaus; king of Argos and Mycenae; led the Greek forces to Troy; murdered by his wife, Clytemnestra.

AGATHON (Ag' a thon), an Athenian tragic poet; won the first prize for tragedy in 416 B.C.

AGORA (Ag' o ra), the market place or business center of a Greek city, where citizens commonly assembled.

AJAX (Ay' jaks), son of Telamon; next to Achilles the bravest and strongest of the Greeks who fought against the Trojans; committed suicide when he failed to receive Achilles' armor.

ALCESTIS (Al ses' tis), daughter of Pelias; died in place of her husband, Admetus; rescued and brought back from death by Heracles.

ALCIBIADES (Al si by' a deez), an Athenian politician of noble birth; friend of Socrates; talented, but dissolute (450-404 B.C.); responsible for much of the Athenian disaster at the close of the Peloponnesian War.

ALCINOUS (Al sin' o us), wealthy king of the Phaeacians to whom the shipwrecked Odysseus told the story of his wanderings; provided the ship which conveyed Odysseus to his home.

AMPHIPOLIS (Am fip' o lis), an Athenian colony on the river Strymon in Thrace, where the Spartans defeated the Athenians in 422 B.C.

ANAXAGORAS (An aks ag' or us), a Greek philosopher of Clazomenae in Asia Minor; flourished c. 455 B.C.

ANTENOR (An tee' nor), a wise elder of Troy, who advised that Helen be restored to the Greeks.

ANTIPHON (An' ti fon) of Cephisia, father of Socrates' pupil Epigenes; present at Socrates' trial.

ANTISTHENES (An tis' then eez), an Athenian; one of Socrates' pupils; later founded the school of the Cynic philosophers.

ANYTUS (An' i tus), a wealthy and influential tanner of Athens; one of the accusers of Socrates.

APHRODITE (Af ro dy' tee), the Greek goddess of love and beauty; wife of Ares, god of war; identified by the Romans with Venus.

APOLLO (A pol' o), one of the greatest of the Greek divinities: god of medicine, music, archery, prophecy, light and youth, often identified with the sun; son of Zeus and Leto (or Latona) and the twin brother of the moon goddess Artemis.

APOLLODORUS (A pol o do' rus), devoted follower of Socrates.

ARCADIA (Ar kay' di a), a mountainous region in the center of the Peloponnesus.

ARCHILOCHUS (Ar kil' o kus), a celebrated Greek poet of the 7th century B.C., famous for his biting satires.

ARDIAEUS (Ar di ee' us), a cruel tyrant of Pamphylia condemned to eternal punishment after death.

ARES (Ay' reez), the Greek god of war; son of Zeus and Hera and lover of Aphrodite; identified with Mars by the Romans.

ARGINUSAE (Ar ji noo' see), small islands south of Lesbos, near which the Athenians defeated the Spartans in a sea battle in 406 B.C.

ARGIVES (Ar' jyvz), inhabitants of the Achaean city of Argos or the surrounding plain of Argolis, in the eastern part of the Peloponnesus.

ARION (A ry' on), a Greek poet of the 7th century B.C. celebrated for his hymns to Dionysus; the hero of several legendary exploits.

ARISTIPPUS (Ar is tip' us), a Greek philosopher of Cyrene; a student of Socrates; founder of the Cyrenaic school of philosophy.

ARISTODEMUS (Ar is to dee' mus), a devoted follower of Socrates.

ARISTOGEITON (Ar is to jy' ton), leader, with his friend Harmodius, in an attempt to overthrow the tyrants of Athens in 514 B.C.

ARISTON (A ris' ton), father of Plato, Adeimantus, and Glaucon.

ARISTONYMUS (Ar is ton' i mus), father of Cleitophon.

ARISTOPHANES (Ar is tof' a neez), the greatest comic playwright of Greece (c. 448-380 B.C.).

ARISTOTLE (Ar' is totl), one of the greatest of the Greek philosophers (384-322 B.C.); studied under Plato.

ARMENIUS (Ar men' i us), father of Er the Pamphylian.

ASCLEPIUS (As klee' pi us), son of Apollo; god of healing and medicine; called by the Romans Aesculapius.

ATALANTA (At a lan' ta), an attractive maiden famed as a runner; wife of Hippomenes.

ATE (A' tee), the personification of blind folly or infatuation, who led both gods and men into rash and inconsiderate actions.

ATHENE (A thee' nee), favorite daughter of Zeus; Greek goddess of wisdom and defensive warfare; patroness of arts and handicrafts; identified with Minerva by the Romans.

ATREUS (Ay' troos or Ay' tree us), son of Pelops; king of Argos and Mycenae; father of Agamemnon and Menelaus.

ATROPOS (At' ro pos), one of the three fates. The others were Clotho and Lachesis.

AUTOLYCUS (Aw tol' i kus), grandfather of Odysseus; notorious for trickery and thieving.

BIAS (By' us), of Priene in Ionia; one of the famous Seven Wise Men of Greece (flourished 6th century B.C.).

BOEOTIA (Bee o' shi a), the district in Greece northwest of Attica. Its chief city was Thebes.

BRASIDAS (Brass' i dus), brave Spartan general, killed at Amphipolis in 422 B.C., when his troops were defeated by the Athenians.

CADMUS (Kad' mus), the son of Agenor of Phoenicia; brother of Europa; legendary founder of the Greek city of Thebes; married Harmonia, daughter of Ares and Aphrodite.

CALLIAS (Kall' i·us), a wealthy Athenian; patron of the Sophists; brother-in-law of Alcibiades.

CEBES (Se' beez), a disciple of Socrates from Thebes; offered to provide money for Socrates' escape from prison.

CEOS (Se' os), an island in the Aegean Sea.

CEPHALUS (Sef' a lus), a wealthy Syracusan; lived in Athens as a resident alien; father of Polemarchus and Lysias, the orator.

CEPHISIA (See fis' i a), a township of Attica.

CERBERUS (Sur' bur us), the three-(or fifty-)headed watchdog of Hades.

CHAEREPHON (Kee' re fon), a devoted follower of Socrates, who consulted the oracle at Delphi about him.

CHARMANTIDES (Kar man' ti deez), an acquaintance of Polemarchus; otherwise unknown.

CHARMIDES (Kar' mi deez), a beautiful youth of noble family; friend of Socrates.

CHARONDAS (Kar on' dus), a great lawgiver of the Greek communities in Italy and Sicily.

CHIMAERA (Ki mee' ra or Ky mee' ra), a fire-breathing monster, with the head of a lion, body of a goat, and tail of a dragon.

CLAZOMENAE (Kla zom' e nee), one of the twelve Ionian cities of Asia Minor; home of Anaxagoras.

CLEITOPHON (Kly' to fon), son of Aristonymus, an acquaintance of Polemarchus.

CLEOMBROTUS (Kle om' bro tus), a friend of Socrates.

CLOTHO (Klo' tho), one of the three Fates.

COCYTUS (Ko sy' tus), the River of Wailing in the lower world.

CODRUS (Kod' rus), last king of Athens; died to save his kingdom from the Dorians.

CORYBANTES (Kor i ban' teez), frenzied attendants of the goddess Cybele.

CRETE (Kreet), one of the largest islands of the Mediterranean, southeast of Greece.

CRITO (Kry' to), friend of Socrates who urged him to escape from prison.

CRITOBULUS (Kri to' bu lus), son of Crito; pupil of Socrates.

CROESUS (Kree' sus), a king of Lydia in the 6th century B.C., famed for his great wealth.

CRONOS (Kro' nus), a brutal Titan divinity; dethroned his father Uranus and was dethroned by his son, the greater god, Zeus.

CTESIPPUS (Te sip' us), a follower of Socrates, present at his death.

CYDATHENAEUM (Sid ath en ee' um), a township of Attica.

DAEDALUS (Ded' a lus or Dee' da lus), a famous sculptor of antiquity; ancestor of Socrates.

DELIUM (Dee' li um), a town on the coast of Boeotia, where the Athenians were defeated by the Boeotians in 424 B.C.

DELOS (Dee' los), a small island in the Aegean Sea, legendary birthplace of Apollo and sacred to him.

DELPHI (Del' fy), a town in Phocis, Greece, near which Apollo's famous oracle was located.

DEMETER (Dee mee' tur), Greek goddess of agriculture and the fruits of the earth; identified by the Romans with Ceres.

DEMODOCUS (Dee mod' o kus), father of Paralus and of Socrates' follower Theages.

DIALECTIC (Dy a lek' tik), according to Plato, the logical process, by which we learn to use the facts and theories of science, not as final results, but as points from which to gain an understanding of the higher abstractions, such as Truth, Justice, and Goodness.

DIOCLES (Dy' o kleez), father of Socrates' friend Euthydemus.

DIOMED (Dy' o meed), son of Tydeus; bold Greek captain among the fighters against Troy.

DIONE (Dy o' nee), mother of Aphrodite by Zeus.

DIONYSUS (Dy o ny' sus), Greek god of the vine; worshiped with hymns and orgiastic rites; also called Bacchus.

DIOTIMA (Dy o tee' ma), a wise woman of Mantinea, who Socrates said had been his teacher.

ECHECRATES (E kek' ra teez), a citizen of Phlius, to whom Phaedo gave an account of Socrates' death.

ELEUSIS (E lue' sis), a village of Attica northwest of Athens, near the sea; seat of the great shrine of Demeter.

ELIS (Ee' lis), a state in the northwestern part of the Peloponnesus, including the plain of Olympia.

ENDYMION (En dim' i on), a youth loved by the moon-goddess Selene; chose eternal sleep instead of death.

EPEIUS (Ep ee' us), inventor of tricks; maker of the wooden horse by which the Greek warriors entered Troy.

EPHIALTES (Ef i al' teez), a giant who tried with Otus to climb to heaven, but was killed by Apollo.

EPIGENES (E pi' jen eez), a pupil of Socrates; son of Antiphon.

ER (Ur), son of Arminius of Pamphylia, whose soul returned to his body after a brief visit to the lower world.

ERIPHYLE (Er i fy' lee), for a bribe persuaded her husband to join a perilous expedition against Thebes.

EROS (Er' os), the Greek god of love; by the Romans identified with Cupid.

ERYXIMACHUS (Er ix im' a kus), a physician; one of Agathon's guests at the Symposium.

EUCLID (You' klid), a pupil of Socrates, who later taught at Megara; not the great mathematician.

EURIPIDES (You rip' i deez), one of the three great tragic poets of Greece (480-406 B.C.).

EURIPUS (You ry' pus), the strait separating the island of Euboea from Boeotia.

EURYPYLUS (You rip' i lus), a Greek chieftain in the Trojan War.

EUTHYDEMUS (You thi dee' mus), son of Diocles, a friend of Socrates.

EVENUS (E vee' nus), a poet and rhetorician of some note; a contemporary of Socrates.

GLAUCON (Glaw' kon), son of Ariston and brother of Plato and Adeimantus.

GLAUCUS (Glaw' kus), a minor Greek god of the sea.

GORGIAS (Gor' ji us), a celebrated sophist of Sicily; in Athens in 427 B.C.

GYGES (Gy' jeez), usurper of the throne of Lydia in Asia Minor about 685 B.C.

HADES (Hay' deez), the dark realm of the dead; or the god presiding over it, whose helmet made the wearer invisible.

HARMODIUS (Har mo' di us), friend of Aristogeiton; attempted with him to overthrow the tyrants of Athens in 514 B.C.

HARMONIA (Har mo' ni a), daughter of the gods Ares and Aphrodite, and wife of Cadmus, who founded Thebes.

HECTOR (Hek' tor), son of Priam, King of Troy, and chief defender of the city; killed by Achilles.

HELLAS (Hel' ass), Greece.

HELLENES (Hel' eenz or Hel' en eez), the Greeks.

HELLESPONT (Hel' es pont), now called the Dardanelles, a narrow strait between Europe and Asia.

HEPHAESTUS (Hee fes' tus or Hee fees' tus), Greek god of fire and metallurgy, son of Zeus and Hera; by the Romans identified with Vulcan.

HERACLITUS (Her a cly' tus), one of the greatest early Greek philosophers, flourished *c.* 500 B.C.

HERACLES (Her' a kleez), Greek hero, son of Zeus, famed for his labors; also called Hercules.

HERA (Hee' ra), sister and wife of Zeus; queen of the gods; also called Here; by the Romans identified with Juno.

HERODICUS (Her od' i kus), a Thracian physician of the 5th century B.C.

HESIOD (Hee' si od), a didactic poet of the 8th century B.C., whom the Greeks often coupled with Homer.

HIPPIAS (Hip' i us), a sophist from Elis; a contemporary of Socrates.

HIPPOCRATES (Hip ok' ra teez), a Greek of the 5th century B.C.; the father of scientific medicine.

HIPPONICUS (Hip o ny' kus), father of Callias; a contemporary of Socrates.

HOMER (Ho' mur), the supreme epic poet of Greece, author of the *Iliad* and the *Odyssey.*

IAPETUS (Eye a' pe tus), a Titan of Greek mythology; brother of Cronus and father of Atlas and Prometheus.

ILIAD (Il' i ad), a Greek epic poem narrating certain events of the last year of the Trojan War; ascribed to Homer.

ILION (Il' i on), the ancient city of Troy; also called Ilium.

INACHUS (In' a kus), a river god of Greece, son of Oceanus.

IOLAUS (Eye o lay' us), nephew and trusty attendant of Heracles.

ISMENIAS (Is mee' ni as), a wealthy Theban of private station but great influence.

LACEDAEMON (Las e dee' mon), Sparta.

LACHES (Lak' eez), an Athenian general, friend of Socrates; killed in the Peloponnesian War.

LACHESIS (Lak' e sis), one of the three Fates.

LEONTIUM (Le on' ti um), a town of Sicily, near Syracuse; also called Leontini.

LYCEAN ZEUS (Ly see' an Zoos), Zeus as worshiped in his forest temple on Mt. Lycaeus in Arcadia.

LYCEUM (Ly see' um), a gymnasium and temple in Athens, sacred to Apollo.

LYCON (Ly' kon), one of Socrates' accusers.

LYCURGUS (Ly kur' gus), legendary Spartan lawgiver of uncertain date.

LYDIAN (Li' di an), of Lydia, a rich country in western Asia Minor.

LYSANIAS (Ly say' ni us), father of Socrates' follower Aeschines.

LYSIAS (Lis' i us), son of Cephalus; Athenian orator of the 5th and 4th centuries B.C.

MACHAON (Ma kay' on), son of Asclepius; surgeon to the Greeks during the Trojan War.

MANTINEA (Man ti nee' a), a town in Arcadia, in the Peloponnesus.

MARSYAS (Mar' si us), a satyr of Phrygia; a skilled player on the flute; he was flayed by Apollo after a musical contest.

MEDEA (Mee dee' a), barbarian princess of Colchis; aided Jason in securing the Golden Fleece, then was deserted by him; heroine of a tragedy by Euripides.

MEGARA (Meg' a ra), a city near the base of the Isthmus of Corinth.

MELETUS (Me lee' tus), one of Socrates' accusers.

MENELAUS (Men e lay' us), son of Atreus, younger brother of Agamemnon, king of Sparta; husband of Helen.

MENEXENUS (Men ex' en us), friend of Socrates; present at his death.

METIS (Mee' tis), first wife of Zeus; her name means Discretion; Socrates calls her mother of Poros (Plenty).

MINOS (My' nos), ancient king and lawgiver of Crete; later a judge among the dead.

MUSAEUS (Mu see' us), a legendary poet of Greece; said to have been a son of Orpheus.

MYRRHINUSIAN (Mur i nu' zi an), an inhabitant of the township Myrrhinus, in Attica.

NEMESIS (Nem' e sis), Greek goddess who brings retribution for sin.

NESTOR (Nes' tor), the aged, wise counselor of the Greeks in the Trojan War.

NICERATUS (Nis er' a tus), son of Nicias, present at the talk on the Republic; put to death later by the Thirty Tyrants of Athens.

NICIAS (Nish' i as), an Athenian general and friend of Socrates; killed in Sicily in 413 B.C.

NICOSTRATUS (Ni kos' tra tus), son of Theosdotides; brother of Socrates' pupil, Theodotus; present at Socrates' trial.

NIOBE (Ny' o bee), daughter of Tantalus; her children were all slain by Apollo in punishment for her pride.

OCEANUS (O see' a nus), the ancient Greek god of the sea.

ODYSSEUS (O dis' oos), a Greek hero famed for crafty wisdom and for his adventures on his return from Troy; also called Ulysses.

ODYSSEY (Od' i see), the superb epic poem describing Odysseus' return home from Troy; ascribed to Homer.

OEAGRUS (Ee ag' rus), father of Orpheus.

OLYMPIA (O lim' pi a), a small plain of Elis, in western Peloponnesus, where the Olympic Games were held.

OLYMPUS (O lim' pus), the mountain in northeastern Greece famed as the home of the gods.

OLYMPUS (O lim' pus), the earliest semi-mythical master of the flute.

ORPHEUS (Or' fee us or Or' foos), the most famous of the legendary bards and musicians of Greece.

OTYS or OTUS (O' tis or O' tus), a giant who, with Ephialtes, tried vainly to climb to heaven.

PAEANIAN (Pee ay' ni an), an inhabitant of the township of Paeania, in Attica.

PALAESTRA (Pa les' tra), a wrestling school or gymnasium.

PALAMEDES (Pal a mee' deez), a Greek hero of the Trojan War, falsely accused of treachery and put to death.

PAMPHYLIA (Pam fil' i a), a narrow district on the southern coast of Asia Minor.

PANCRATIUM (Pan kray' shi um), an all-out contest of strength, involving boxing and wrestling.

PANDARUS (Pan' da rus), an ally of the Trojans; a great archer, who wantonly broke the sworn truce with the Greeks.

PANOPEUS (Pan' o peus), father of the contriver of the wooden horse, Epeius.

PARALUS (Par' a lus), son of Demodocus; brother of Socrates' follower, Theages.

PARMENIDES (Par men' i deez), Greek philosopher of the 5th century B.C., from Elea in Italy; admired by Socrates.

PAROS (Pay' ros or Par' os), an island of the Aegean, famed for its marble.

PATROCLUS (Pa tro' klus), intimate comrade of Achilles; killed by Hector at Troy; Achilles avenged his death by killing Hector.

PAUSANIAS (Pau san' i us or Pau say' ni us), a disciple of the sophist Prodicus; an admirer of Agathon and one of the speakers at his Symposium.

PEIRAEUS (Py ree' us), the port-town of Athens, about four miles distant.

PELEUS (Pee' loos), king of Phthia; son of Aeacus; father of Achilles by the sea nymph Thetis.

PELIAS (Pel' i us or Pee' li us), father of Admetus' wife, Alcestis.

PELOPONNESUS (Pel o po nee' sus), the peninsula which forms the whole southern part of Greece.

PELOPS (Pee' lops), son of Tantalus, father of Atreus, founder of the kingdom of Argos in South Greece, from whom the Peloponnesus or Island of Pelops received its name.

PENELOPE (Pe nel' o pee), faithful wife of Odysseus who for twenty years awaited his return from Troy.

PERDICCAS (Per dik' us), able king of Macedonia; died in 414 B.C.

PERIANDER (Per i an' der), ruler of Corinth from 625-585 B.C.; one of the Seven Wise Men of Greece.

PERICLES (Per' i kleez), brilliant aristocratic leader of Athens during her supremacy (460-429 B.C.).

PHAEDO (Fee' do), devoted follower of Socrates; present at his death.

PHAEDONIDES (Fee don' i deez), one of those present at Socrates' death.

PHAEDRUS (Fee' drus), a disciple of Hippias and a friend of Socrates and Agathon; one of the speakers at the *Symposium*.

PHALERUM (Fal ee' rum), one of the harbors of Athens; the other was Piraeus.

PHILOLAUS (Fil o lay' us), an elder contemporary of Socrates; taught Pythagorean philosophy.

PHLIUS (Fly' us), an independent city in the northeastern part of the Peloponnesus.

PHOCYLIDES (Fo sil' i deez), a Greek poet and author of maxims in verse of the 6th century B.C.

PHOENICIAN (Fee nish' an), of Phóenicia, a narrow mountainous strip of Syria along the Mediterranean coast.

PHOENIX (Fee' niks), a son of Philip; nothing is known of either man but his name is mentioned in the *Symposium*.

PHTHIA (Thy' a), a district in southeastern Thessaly; Achilles' home.

PINDAR (Pin' der), the greatest and loftiest Greek lyric poet (522-448 B.C.).

PITTACUS (Pit' a kus), of Mitylene, one of the Seven Wise Men; died in 569 B.C.

POLEMARCHUS (Pol e mar' kus), son of Cephalus, at whose house Socrates discoursed on the *Republic*; later murdered by the Thirty Tyrants.

POLYDAMAS (Po li' da mass), an athlete famed for victories in the pancratium.

POLYHYMNIA (Pol i him' ni a), the Muse of religious poetry.

POROS (Por' os), "Plenty," called the son of Metis (Discretion).

POSEIDON (Po sy' don), the Greek god of the sea; brother of Zeus; by the Romans identified with Neptune.

POTIDAEA (Pot i dee' a), a town in Macedonia; revolted from

Athens in 432 B.C., scene of an important battle in the Peloponnesian War.

PRAMNIAN (Pram' ni an), from Mt. Pramne on the island of Icaria, famous for its wine.

PRODICUS (Prod' i kus), a celebrated sophist from Ceos; a contemporary of Socrates.

PROTEUS (Pro' te us or Pro' toos), a minor Greek sea god, famous for his ability to change his form at will.

PRYTANEUM (Pri ta nee' um), the town-hall of a Greek city, consecrated to the hearth-goddess Hestia, where important citizens and foreign ambassadors dined.

PYRIPHLEGETHON (Pir i fleg' e thon), the River of Fire in the lower world.

PYTHAGOREANS (Pith ag o ree' anz), followers of the Greek philosopher, Pythagoras, who lived in the 6th century B.C.; they specialized in the study of mathematics and music.

PYTHIAN (Pith' i an), of Delphi, Apollo's great prophetic shrine.

RHADAMANTHUS (Rad a man' thus), son of Zeus; brother of Minos; one of the judges of the dead.

SALAMIS (Sal' a mis), a small island off Athens in the Saronic Gulf.

SATYR (Say' ter), a mischievous Greek sylvan deity with pointed ears, small horns, and the tail of a goat or a horse.

SCYLLA (Sil' a), a six-headed monster, described in the *Odyssey,* who seized any sailors who sailed near her cave.

SCYTHIA (Si' thi a), the country north of the Black Sea, inhabited by warlike nomads.

SERIPHIAN (Ser if' i an), of Seriphus, a small island in the Aegean Sea.

SILENUS (Sy lee' nus), a Greek woodland deity resembling a satyr.

SIMMIAS (Sim' i us), a Theban; first a Pythagorean; later a follower of Socrates and present at his death.

SIMONIDES (Sy mon' i deez), a serious Greek lyric poet from Ceos (556-468 B.C.).

SIREN (Sy' ren), one of a group of Greek sea-nymphs noted for their singing, whose songs lured men to shipwreck and death.

SISYPHUS (Sis' i fus), a legendary king of Corinth, condemned to spend eternity pushing a huge stone up a hill.

SOCRATES (Sok' ra teez), Plato's teacher and the principal figure in his *Dialogues* (469-399 B.C.).

SOLON (Sol' un), an Athenian poet and lawgiver; one of the Seven Wise Men (c. 638-555 B.C.).

SOPHIST (Sof' ist), a teacher of rhetoric, philosophy, politics and the art of successful living.

SOPHOCLES (Sof' o kleez), one of the three great Greek tragic poets (496-406 B.C.).

SPHETTUS (Sfet' us), a township of Attica.

STESICHORUS (Stes ik' o rus), a celebrated lyric poet from Sicily (632-552 B.C.), who sang of the tale of Helen and Troy; his work are all lost.

STYX (Sticks), the River of Hate in the lower world.

SUNIUM (Soo' ni um), the southern promontory of Attica.

SYRACUSAN (Sear a kue' zan), from Syracuse, the most important city of Sicily.

TARTARUS (Tar' ta rus), a chasm in the depths of the world, as far below Hades as the earth is below the heavens.

TELAMON (Tel' a mon), son of Aeacus; king of Salamis; father of Ajax.

TELEPHUS (Tel' e fus), son of Heracles, wounded and later cured by Achilles at Troy.

TERPSION (Terp sy' on), present at Socrates' death; otherwise unknown.

THAMYRAS (Tham' i rus), a mythical bard of Thrace, blinded by the Muses because of his boastfulness.

THEAGES (The' a jeez), a follower of Socrates; son of Demodocus; brother of Paralus.

THEBES (Theebz), the chief city of Boeotia.

THEMIS (Them' is), the personification of Law and Order; sometimes called Zeus' second wife.

THEMISTOCLES (The mis' to kleez), hero of the second Persian War; created the Athenian Navy (519-449 B.C.).

THEODOTUS (The od' o tus), pupil of Socrates; son of Theosdotides; brother of Nicostratus.

THEOSDOTIDES (The os do' ti deez or The o zo' ti deez), father of the brothers, Theodotus and Nicostratus.

THERSITES (Ther sy' teez), the ugliest, loose-mouthed private in the Greek army at Troy; flogged for insolence by Odysseus.

THESEUS (Thee' soos or Thee' se us), the chief legendary hero of Attica; son of Aegeus, king of Athens; slew the Minotaur and delivered Athens from the tyranny of Crete.

THESSALY (Thes' a li), the largest division of Greece, lying to the north and next to Macedonia.

THETIS (Thee' tis), a daughter of the sea-god Nereus; mother of Achilles by Peleus.

THRASYMACHUS (Thra sim' a kus), a sophist, who starts the argument with Socrates in the *Republic*.

TRIPTOLEMUS (Trip tol' e mus), legendary favorite of the grain-goddess Demeter; taught the arts of agriculture; later a judge of the dead.

URANIA (You ray' ni a), the Muse of Astronomy; according to Plato, the Heavenly Muse.

URANUS (You' ray nus), the personification of Heaven; son and husband of Earth (Gaea); father of the Titans and Cyclopes; dethroned by his son Cronus.

XANTIPPE (Zan tip' e or Zan thip' e), Socrates' wife; her peevish scolding has become proverbial.

XERXES (Zurk' seez), king of Persia, 485-465 B.C.; son of Darius; tried unsuccessfully to conquer Greece.

ZEUS (Zoos), the king of the Greek gods; son of Cronus; identified by the Romans with Jupiter.